Instream Flows

for Riverine Resource Stewardship

Revised Edition

Instream Flows for Riverine Resource Stewardship

Revised Edition

Authors:

Tom Annear - *Wyoming Game and Fish Department*

Ian Chisholm - *Minnesota Department of Natural Resources*

Hal Beecher - *Washington Department of Fish and Wildlife*

Allan Locke - *Alberta Sustainable Resource Development*

Peter Aarrestad - *Connecticut Department of Environmental Protection*

Chuck Coomer - *Georgia Department of Natural Resources*

Christopher Estes - *Alaska Department of Fish and Game*

Joel Hunt - *Manitoba Water Stewardship*

Rick Jacobson - *Connecticut Department of Environmental Protection*

Gerrit Jöbsis - *South Carolina Department Natural Resources*

John Kauffman - *Virginia Department of Game and Inland Fisheries*

John Marshall - *Ohio Department of Natural Resources*

Kevin Mayes - *Texas Parks and Wildlife Department*

Gary Smith - *California Department of Fish and Game*

Rod Wentworth - *Vermont Department of Fish and Wildlife*

Clair Stalnaker

Cheyenne, Wyoming

ISBN 0-9716743-1-0

Printed in the United States of America by BookMasters, Inc., Ashland, Ohio

The paper used in this publication meets the minimum requirements of the American National Standard for Information Sciences—Permanence of Paper for Printed Library Materials. ANSI Z39.48-1984.

Cover: Bow River in south central Alberta, Canada (Photo by Lorne Fitch, Alberta Sustainable Resource Development, Fish and Wildlife Division)

Reference as:
Annear, T., I. Chisholm, H. Beecher, A. Locke, and 12 other authors. 2004. Instream flows for riverine resource stewardship, revised edition. Instream Flow Council, Cheyenne, WY.

The Instream Flow Council
5400 Bishop Bouldvard
Cheyenne, Wyoming 82006

Contents

Figures

Tables

Foreword

In the first half of the twentieth century there was little consideration or direction for recommending instream flows for fisheries or related riverine resources. Early in the second half of the period, significant interest and efforts emerged in some American states and Canadian provinces, as well as territories, in response to growing concern by the public for the health of their streams and rivers. Each state and province has sovereign responsibility over the natural resources within its respective jurisdiction and each has sought to address the needs of its citizens as it thought best. However, because this was a completely new field of interest, there was no template for how best to meet this need; therefore, each state and province developed different approaches. Many of those approaches fell more than a little short of the mark.

Post-World War II construction and development of reservoirs, highways, bridges, subdivisions, farms, and forests contributed to a dire need for better streamflow recommendations and management. Many early recommendations were based on either professional judgment or simplistic and highly subjective rule-of-thumb estimates. As such, most of those recommendations were inconsistent, impractical, and imprecise and often failed to address real resource needs for managing fishery resources. Biologists began to include more practical, equitable, and scientifically based considerations in their endeavors. In the past 50 years, they have produced more than three-dozen various methods—34 of which are presented in this text.

Instream Flows for Riverine Resource Stewardship is by far the best and most comprehensive treatise on the subject of instream flows to date. The material represents an exhaustive treatment of a very complex and highly technical subject. It frequently, and appropriately, stresses the importance of addressing five riverine components (i.e., hydrology, geomorphology, biology, water quality, and connectivity) when developing, commenting on, or designing instream flow programs and recommending instream flow prescriptions. There is adequate warning and justification against the use of single-flow recommendations, like $7Q_{10}$, for fishery and riverine management. Because the science of instream flow is necessarily multidisciplinary, the authors emphasize the need to incorporate legal, institutional, and public involvement components in addition to the five riverine components in efforts to preserve fishery and wildlife resources. When all eight components are integrated, riverine management is most effective.

Ample consideration is given to water law in general (including the eastern riparian doctrine versus the western prior appropriation doctrine) as well as to agency rights and responsibilities; public trust and public interest philosophies; the importance of public participation and effective communication; streamflow measurements and U.S. Geological Survey data records, which are the basis of many methodologies; and macro- meso- and micro-habitat. Also emphasized is the need to mimic and preserve natural flow regimes and understand the effects of channelization, stream straightening, riprap, bank armoring, and in-channel and riparian mining. The authors underscore the vital key of protecting all aquatic habitats, including the riparian-floodplain zones, and argue for a drought policy by which water shortages would be shared equitably by all. The many Instream Flow Council position statements and critical opinions highlighted throughout will be of considerable help to agencies and others who have long sought such statements. There is truly something here to address almost every instream flow issue or opportunity.

Special thanks are due the 16 authors who compiled this in-depth work. The fact that so many instream flow specialists from across the United States and Canada have been willing to share their practical management experiences by contributing to the book speaks volumes about the significance of the material. That they found the time to contribute to this collective effort while also meeting the demands of their normally heavy work schedules speaks to their dedication as well. The commitment made by the authors' state and provincial fishery and wildlife agencies to allow their employees time to work on this project is also a clear indication of the critical need for such information and guidance—both of which are needed every bit as much today as in 1950.

Instream Flows for Riverine Resource Stewardship is a most valuable resource that is sure to be used for years to come by all vested interests of instream flows.

Donald L. Tennant

Preface

The first edition of *Instream Flows for Riverine Resource Stewardship* was published in March 2002. Absent any promotion, demand for the book was greater than anticipated—including interest by a broad international audience. Thus, a second book printing was required just four months after initial publication.

Agency managers, consultants, academicians, legal experts, and libraries have all expressed a strong interest in the book. Comments received have also identified ways in which the book could be improved. Consequently, the Instream Flow Council sought and received funding to add new text, reorganize, illustrate, and publish a revised edition.

Over the course of working on this project, the authors have developed a greater appreciation for the seemingly slow and sometimes painful process of protecting and restoring our riverine heritage. In fact, it would be difficult to come away from this book without realizing that the best science by itself, while crucial, is often insufficient. As scientists, we tend to think that science can provide a guiding light for all to follow. But, as Mollie Matteson (Wuerthner and Matteson 2002) noted, there is a flaw in that thinking. "Science cannot give us all the answers. In fact, the most difficult questions, the most persistent problems are not matters of science, but of values. Science can tell us what is happening, but it cannot make us do anything about it."

Nor can mere demands from an impassioned public always sway a decision. Whatever positives result from the efforts of river managers and the public must occur within the constraints of established laws, regulations, and institutions. It is the combination of good science, laws, policies, and public involvement that enable effective instream flow management.

Water controversies will continue well into the future—perhaps less a result of scientific uncertainties or planning deficiencies than the public's divergent interests and competing values regarding the best use of water. There indeed lies the dilemma because there is not one voice or one choice for water management but a chorus of ever-increasing perspectives. The ongoing challenge is to respect the legitimacy of differing values while seeking cooperative solutions to the complex and often troublesome issues of improving integrated management of river systems.

Ultimately, it will of course be the laws of nature that have the final say in how our world looks and functions. But to the extent that we can modify our world by the decisions we make, it is important to act as responsible stewards of the resources entrusted to us and to leave the world at least no worse for wear and maybe better than we found it. To that end, we hope this revised edition of *Instream Flows for Riverine Resource Stewardship* can play some small role.

Thomas C. Annear

Preface to First Edition

Beginning with the last century and earlier, the science of managing the many environmental elements that affect the character of riverine resources has been understood conceptually by some naturalists. Intuitively, it is not difficult to appreciate that the natural forces and processes that formed streams and rivers, as we know them today, are essential for maintaining those natural features into the future. As North American society developed, the value of maintaining those processes was outweighed by the social value of those resources for developing and maintaining a high standard of living. It was only when society realized that the trade-off for such a standard of living was the quality of its environment—and that a healthy and diverse environment was as important as any other aspect of human existence—that scientists were sufficiently motivated to find quantifiable answers to the question of how much water development could occur before the natural character of rivers was irreparably diminished.

Something like the race to put a man on the moon, river managers in many disciplines tried to answer that question. From 1950 onward, the science of managing water to maintain or restore natural hydrographs developed rapidly but, like many such endeavors, not all treatments ended successfully. However, the experience led to a growing realization that the more that was learned about managing riverine resources, the less that was really understood. Despite the useful advancements in riverine science, the knowledge was not applied equally in all regions of North America. And, where it was applied, political and institutional limitations complicated and frustrated the efforts of state and provincial fishery and wildlife agency managers in fulfilling their legitimate responsibilities to effectively manage riverine resources.

It was within this environment that a first step was taken to find common ground and identify those elements of riverine resource management that were most appropriate and useful. Christopher Estes and Keith Bayha (who were among the earliest proponents of instream flow protection) secured a grant from the U.S. Fish and Wildlife Service (USFWS) Office of Federal Aid to conduct a National Instream Flow Program Assessment (NIFPA) project. In 1995 they brought together the instream flow coordinators, or their equivalents, from each of the 50 states and the federal instream flow coordinator from each of the seven regions of the USFWS. In the process of developing a protocol for evaluating state and USFWS instream flow programs, an amazing thing happened; the participants discovered a common bond. Quite simply, these individuals who had not known their counterparts in neighboring states before NIFPA found that they all shared similar challenges and difficulties in dealing with instream flow issues. And, they quickly realized that they no longer needed to solve those problems in a vacuum.

When the group met again in 1996 in Denver, Colorado, they finished the NIFPA project by evaluating their respective programs according to the protocol they had developed. Through this process participants realized that establishing an instream flow program and conducting instream flow studies extended far beyond the technical aspects of the science. They acknowledged what many of them intuitively knew—that they must also address legal and institutional challenges and make public involvement a conscious and continuous part of any successful program.

They also concluded that there was a dire need to continue the networking they had begun and to standardize the science. Further, they recognized considerable commonalities in resource management and institutional characteristics between the United States and Canada and that managers in each country could expand their effectiveness by incorporating lessons learned in the other. In the two years that followed, a nine-member steering committee met to draft a charter and bylaws for their new organization. That effort culminated in the formation of the Instream Flow Council (IFC) at its first meeting in March 1998. Comprised of state and provincial fishery and wildlife agencies, the IFC was established as a nonprofit organization whose mission is to improve the effectiveness of instream flow programs for conserving aquatic resources.

From the outset, state and provincial agency members expressed a strong desire for guidance in developing instream flow programs and designing study plans. To that end, the IFC took up the challenge to provide such guidance—a project that resulted in the publication of *Instream Flows for Riverine Resource Stewardship*. The book was initially intended as a "bluebook" of sorts that could readily be used primarily by state and provincial fishery and wildlife managers as an industry standard for designing agency programs and developing comprehensive studies for riverine resource management. However, the project wound up exceeding the modest expectations of even its early proponents and now leaves the IFC well positioned to more fully meet its mission as an organization of state and provincial fishery and wildlife agencies helping each other solve the complex challenges of managing the continent's riverine resources for present and future generations.

Thomas C. Annear

Acknowledgments

Instream Flows for Riverine Resource Stewardship came to fruition through the collective efforts of many. In particular, the work reflects the countless hours and dedication of its 16 authors whose involvement was encouraged and supported by their employers—Alaska Department of Fish and Game; Alberta Sustainable Resource Development; California Department of Fish and Game; Connecticut Department of Environmental Protection; Georgia Department of Natural Resources; Manitoba Conservation; Minnesota Department of Natural Resources; Ohio Department of Natural Resources; South Carolina Department of Natural Resources; Texas Department of Parks and Wildlife; Vermont Department of Fish and Wildlife; Virginia Department of Game and Inland Fisheries; Washington Department of Fish and Wildlife; and the Wyoming Department of Game and Fish. We gratefully acknowledge these progressive agencies for their assistance in advancing the science, policy, and practice of instream flows.

Nina Burkardt wrote the majority of Chapter 3, Public Involvement. Ms. Burkardt is a research social scientist with the U. S. Geological Survey in Fort Collins, Colorado and we are especially appreciative of her very significant contributions to this chapter. We lament that her agency's internal policies prevented her from being listed as an author of this book.

An early draft was reviewed by governing Council representatives and their co-workers from 22 additional state and provincial fishery and wildlife management agencies. Special thanks are due Del Lobb, Missouri Department of Conservation; Jay Skinner, Colorado Division of Wildlife; Larry Hutchinson, Nebraska Game and Parks Commission; Chuck Newcombe and staff, British Columbia Ministry of Environment, Lands and Parks; Kasey Clipperton, Alberta Sustainable Resource Development; Cindy Robertson, Idaho Department of Fish and Game; Paul Dey, Wyoming Department of Game and Fish. These individuals contributed valuable input and encouragement for the project.

Additionally, experts outside the ranks of the IFC reviewed the work. Richard Roos-Collins, senior counsel at the Natural Heritage Institute in San Francisco, provided useful insights regarding the Public Trust Doctrine and helped shape much of the material in Chapter 4. His suggestions improved the accuracy and credibility of these portions of the text. Don Orth, Virginia Tech University, and Tom Wesche, University of Wyoming (retired), provided thoughtful comments on technical portions of the book while David Percy, University of Alberta Law School, Arlene Kwasniak, Executive Director, Alberta Environmental Law Centre, and Larry MacDonnell, Of Counsel to Porzak, Browning and Bushong in Boulder, Colorado, and former director of the Natural Resources Law Center at the University of Colorado School of Law, offered valuable comments on legal portions of the text. Jennifer McKay, University of South Australia, clarified instream flow opportunities in Australia.

Susan Lamb provided valuable editorial review resulting in a better organized, more focused, and readable work. Sandy Cochran Graphic Design did a superb job of laying out the book. Vanita Fowden of Fullspectrum Graphics provided original art or touched up existing IFC illustrations for the revised edition, contributing greatly to its aesthetic properties and overall usefulness.

Funding for the work was made possible, in part, by a generous contribution from the Minnesota Department of Natural Resources and through two grants from the U.S. Fish and Wildlife Service, Office of Federal Aid; grant numbers 14-48-98210-9-G330 and WY M-1-T. We gratefully appreciate the commitment and support of these agencies.

To all, we extend our thanks.

Executive Summary

Federal, state, provincial, tribal, and local governments are charged with stewardship responsibilities to wisely manage the quantity and quality of waters within their jurisdictions for current and future generations. Fundamental to that charge is ensuring that sufficient water is retained in rivers and lake systems at all times of year to sustain fishery and aquatic wildlife resources and ecological processes.

In the United States, the authority of state fishery and wildlife agency stewardship is derived, in part, from the Public Trust Doctrine. The basic tenets of the doctrine, as described in this book, intertwine principles of common and statutory law, including property law. When combined with other laws, the doctrine can be a very powerful tool for protecting and restoring instream flows in some situations. At present, the Public Trust Doctrine forms no recognized basis of law in Canada. Instead, Canadian stewardship responsibilities are broadly based on the provinces' need to act in the public interest. Although the Public Trust Doctrine is not formally incorporated in statute, we argue that the principles of the doctrine may be included in current Canadian law.

Instream Flows for Riverine Resource Stewardship presents the collective views and recommendations of the Instream Flow Council's (IFC) state and provincial fishery and wildlife agency members regarding appropriate instream flow strategies for managing, maintaining, or restoring riverine fishery and aquatic wildlife resources and processes. We also identify eight components that should serve as guidelines in establishing or improving existing agency instream flow programs and in developing prescriptions to be addressed in each instream flow assessment. These components include hydrology, geomorphology, biology, water quality, and connectivity as well as legal, institutional, and public involvement.

Although our work is similar to that of other works published on instream flow methods, it

extends beyond a mere listing of methods and a description of their strengths and weaknesses; it incorporates ideas, policies, and recommendations that the IFC believes should, at a minimum, be addressed in all instream flow assessments.

In overseeing the management of game, fishery, and wildlife programs, resource managers routinely set goals and objectives, monitor progress, and evaluate performance. The IFC recommends that this approach be expanded to include the management of instream flow programs and that program development and evaluation encompass the concepts recommended herein. When developing goals and objectives for riverine management, it is important that resource managers seek strategies that explicitly address public demands and help them fulfill their legal responsibilities to maintain and restore healthy aquatic ecosystems.

The IFC promotes the goal of maintaining the ecological integrity of unregulated rivers and restoring regulated rivers to the ecological conditions that more nearly approximate their natural form and function. To move toward this goal in any increment, instream flow practitioners should address the eight ecosystem components in developing an instream flow program and incorporate them as appropriate.

Prior to the 1980s, many of the instream flows that were provided for water projects were limited to a flat-line "minimum" flow because water developers and managers had little or no appreciation for the importance of natural flow variability. In most of these cases, water managers ignored the recommendations of the early instream flow practitioners who noted the potential shortcomings and negative riverine effects that could result from a flat-line minimum instream flow versus maintaining or restoring variable flows that more nearly resemble the seasonal flow patterns and processes that sustain natural ecological functions.

Since the 1980s, laws and regulations have been developed in many states and some provinces to begin addressing these water management needs. These statutory and regulatory changes, combined with better understanding of riverine processes and enlightened attitudes, have improved the opportunity for instream flow practitioners to quantify and establish variable flow regimes for sustaining viable fisheries and riverine processes. Although opportunities now exist for protecting instream flows in most jurisdictions, the legal and institutional opportunities for reserving water for riverine purposes in most states and provinces are still more restrictive than those that exist for out-of-channel users and uses.

We provide guidelines for quantifying flow regimes and developing recommendations for replacing formerly assigned minimum flows and insufficient flow caps with more appropriate variable flows. Before initiating plans that will modify the flow of streams and rivers, water developers and managers should ask what the maximum amount of water is that can be removed at any given time without adversely altering the river system and its natural functions and processes rather than the minimum flow needed to sustain the resource.

The natural flow paradigm (preservation of the natural flow variability and ecological function of river systems) is axiomatic to ecological integrity of river systems. Managers establishing instream flows must recognize the importance of inter- and intra-annual flow variability in riverine systems because different flow levels enable critical ecological processes that cannot occur otherwise. For example, it was formerly accepted, and in some cases is still believed, that higher flows represent "excess" water in rivers and that flood water can be removed without harm and, perhaps, even benefit the ecological function of the river. However, as initially recognized by instream flow practitioners as early as the 1970s, seasonal high flows are critical components of river ecology. This is especially true at the terrestrial/aquatic interface where high flows deposit sediment, shape channels, rejuvenate and maintain riparian vegetation and habitats, improve water quality, expand and enrich food webs, maintain the valley, and provide access to spawning and rearing sites in the floodplain. The same can be said about the importance of natural periods of low flow (drought). Likewise, there is a growing body of evidence that supports the maintenance of natural processes of ice formation and breakup.

Most traditional state and provincial fishery and wildlife instream flow programs have limited, if any, staff primarily trained as fishery biologists. Although many agencies provide some training in instream flow assessment methods, trained staff often spends limited time on instream flow issues. Effective instream flow programs entail more than an occasional instream flow study or periodic mitigation negotiation with water development interests or consultants for a planned water project. Such programs require well-trained specialists who are capable of integrating the five riverine components into complex legal and institutional procedures while also ensuring effective public involvement. This is a daunting challenge for state and provincial fishery managers and one that makes their responsibilities uniquely different from those of instream flow practitioners whose assignment is less broad.

In developing an instream flow prescription to enhance or restore a degraded stream, it is prudent to involve all stakeholders, formally identify the problems to be addressed, solicit technical expertise, and devote attention to study design. Perhaps the most critical aspect of developing an instream flow prescription is to routinely and formally document the rationale used to decide a particular course of action. The strategy should address the riverine components individually and collectively, whether or not inclusion of a particular component in the study design is warranted. This approach drives the practitioner to consider all factors in developing prescriptions, documents the considerations for the record, and provides the basis for adjusting recommendations as new information or opportunities become available.

There is no universally accepted method, or combination of methods, that is appropriate for establishing instream flows on all rivers or streams. Selection of a method or adaptation of methods is dependent on the water body and potential modification under consideration. Moreover, selected methods should only be applied in accordance with the guidelines recommended in this document to ensure a solid scientific basis for establishing an instream flow prescription. Only when used in conjunction with other techniques can a specific tool afford adequate instream flow protection for all of a river's needs.

In some situations, scientifically sound demonstrations of tangible harm and benefit resulting from a range of experimentally controlled instream flow levels over extended periods of time may be required. Adaptive management may be a useful tool in some, but not all, of these situations. It is most appropriate when financial investment is significant, values for riverine resources are high, risk to all parties is considerable, and the time frame for the project allows prolonged monitoring.

Further, binding commitments among stakeholders must be established at the start of studies to ensure that adequate resources (water and money) are available to fulfill testing needs for the full range of potential mitigation strategies, and that safeguards are provided to avoid irrecoverable impacts to riverine resources. As we emphasize throughout this work, studies that focus on only a limited number of components, such as the response of fish populations, should be avoided because they are often confounded by interrelations with riverine components other than streamflow. Consequently, managers must be critical of efforts to ascribe perceived short-term changes, or lack thereof, to a single factor such as streamflow alone. Measurable targets or conditions and defined decision points are essential.

Of the many instream flow quantification methods and variations developed over the last 30 years, we assess 34 of those most commonly used. In some cases, a broad class of methods is addressed collectively within a single review (e.g., flushing flow methods and biological response correlations). Although not exhaustive, tool evaluation is sufficiently broad to allow practitioners to identify an appropriate methodology for most study designs that may be encountered. Evaluation addresses 14 categories, ranging from the method's purpose to the IFC's critical opinion.

Understanding the underlying mechanism(s) responsible for the biological, physical, and chemical outcomes evident in river systems must underpin the instream flow prescriptions if they are to succeed. However, much remains to be learned about the role and interrelations of factors governing riverine resources and processes. We do not presume to imply that this document is the definitive resource for all instream flow study needs. The science of instream flow management is a relatively young and evolving discipline and much additional research is needed. Although we do not provide a summary of additional research needs, we note that research is being conducted in many settings throughout the United States, Canada, and elsewhere. Clearly, there is a need for research that better identifies how to build a flow prescription that addresses the eight ecosystem components in concert. We urge instream flow practitioners and water managers to remain open to the application of new assessment tools as they continue to be developed and accepted by the instream flow community.

You cannot escape the responsibility of tomorrow by evading it today.
— President Abraham Lincoln

CHAPTER ONE

Introduction

The concept of instream flow is simple. At its most basic level, the term means water flowing in a stream. Most streams have some level of flow, but flow is no guarantee that all is well for the organisms (including humans) that depend on the river's resources. At the dawn of civilization, instream flows were adequate enough to sustain the full range of river-dependent organisms and processes. But as civilization advanced, competing uses by humans altered, diminished, and contaminated original riverine uses. Today, natural resource managers are faced with the complicated task of protecting and restoring public values to rivers while honoring existing uses. To meet this responsibility, managers are challenged to identify appropriate methods to quantify instream flow needs and defend the methods they use and the results they obtain. In the absence of a consensus on acceptable protocols and policies, this task has proven difficult for some state and provincial fishery and wildlife management agencies.

Indeed, it is water as much as any single factor that helps define society and culture. It is one of the primary elements that affects where, how, and how well we live. As the human species evolved, our use of water progressed from first ensuring adequate supplies for our basic needs to finding ways to use water more efficiently to now determining how water can provide more value to society—monetarily and esthetically.

This book is a collective effort by state and provincial fishery and wildlife managers to illustrate the complexity and difficulty of maximizing the use and value of water for society as well as to present recommendations for developing instream flow programs and strategies that will create or maintain healthy streams and river ecosystems. The principles and concepts presented should help to resolve much of the contention associated with the preservation and rehabilitation of instream flows to rivers throughout the United States and Canada for the enjoyment and use of present and future generations. Although we broadly address various considerations involved in administering water resources, none of the discussions are intended as a complete treatise on a specific topic. We further acknowledge the need to similarly address water management tools and strategies that relate to water volume modifications in lentic (lake), estuarine, and wetland environments. Literature citations referenced throughout the work should guide those readers in search of more detailed information.

HISTORICAL PERSPECTIVE

People value streams and rivers for different reasons: drinking water, navigation, municipal and industrial use, irrigation, hydroelectric power, sewage treatment (and dilution), recreation, aesthetics, and fish and wildlife. Streams are particularly important on private land. Properties with good fishing streams running through them typically have greater economic worth than comparable properties with impaired or degraded streams, poor water quality, and no fish. Flowing water attracts people who subsequently build cities, factories, and homes on riverbanks, thus modifying stream channels and altering stream functions in ways that negatively affect natural processes. These changes reduce the value of streams.

Competing uses have resulted in degraded river ecosystems in every region of the United States and Canada. Although much progress has been made over the past 25 years to reduce water pollution, attempts to rehabilitate degraded habitat resulting from stream modification have met with far less success. Despite efforts to "clean up" and rehabilitate rivers, many ecosystems still do not support healthy aquatic communities (Figure 1-1).

Stewardship of rivers in most parts of the world today faces a distinct but universal challenge: meeting the needs of increasing human use while accounting for and preserving the natural variability and ecosystem function to the greatest extent possible. Historically, the full range of values associated with healthy rivers was not understood or appreciated until fishing opportunities were lost or the river was impaired to the point of affecting other characteristics or functions, such as water quality, erosion, or flooding. There was a tendency to view the many components of riverine systems as individual rather than interconnected parts of a complex cycle. This perspective led to unrestrained development of groundwater and surface waters even though these are two of the smallest components of water on Earth (Figure 1-2).

To be successful today, river managers need a level of ecosystem understanding that is unprecedented; we are no longer afforded the luxury of focusing solely on fish. Today's issues require knowledge of habitat, the processes that form habitat, the nature and effect of alterations on the land in the watershed and their effects on the hydrology, and the interdependence of organisms in the system. It is within this framework that state and provincial fishery and wildlife management agencies strive to fulfill their stewardship responsibilities to conserve these resources in perpetuity.

Historically, rivers have been manipulated for human use. Dating from 1 A.D., the Native Americans of the southwestern United States constructed irrigation canals and water control structures to aid agricultural production (Gumerman 1988). Examples of these water management structures exist to this day. Canals built by the Anasazi Pueblo Indians (1000-1100 A.D.) of New Mexico were restored by early European settlers to the area and remain in current use. Irrigation canals in the Santa Fe area date to the earliest Spanish colonization of the region, many of which were probably either rehabilitated prehistoric irrigation channels or appropriated active Pueblo irrigation systems. Similarly, prehistoric irrigation systems constructed by the Hohokam people are still visible today in the vicinity of Tucson, Arizona.

By the 1750s, North American rivers began to change dramatically when beaver (*Castor canadensis*) were hunted and trapped, thus altering hydrologic processes, sediment transport characteristics, and riparian conditions (Grasse and Putnam 1950; Novak 1972; Hill 1982). Soon thereafter, milldams were constructed to provide hydromechanical power for such things as grain processing, saw mills, and factories (Figure 1-3).

For centuries, rivers have served as main thoroughfares for transportation and commerce and, as a consequence, many river channels have

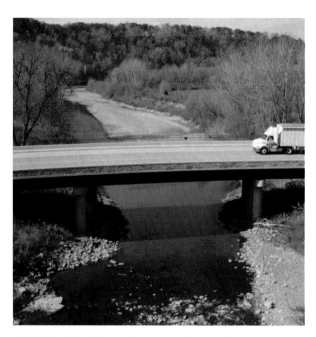

FIGURE 1-1. Preserving or restoring the ecosystem function of rivers, like the Le Sueur River near Mankato, Minnesota, while meeting the developmental needs of society is a significant challenge to state and provincial natural resource management agencies.

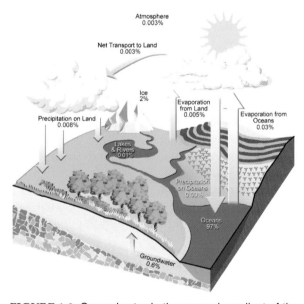

FIGURE 1-2. Groundwater is the second smallest of the four main pools of water on Earth and river flow to the oceans is one of the smallest fluxes. Yet groundwater and surface water are the components of the hydrologic system that humans use most (Adapted from Schelesinger 1991).

been greatly modified to enhance navigation—often with adverse consequences for fish and wildlife habitat. By the 1800s, relatively large-scale ditching and draining was occurring to convert wetlands into farmland. The first use of moving water to produce electricity was a waterwheel on the Fox River in Wisconsin in 1882, two years after Thomas Edison unveiled the incandescent light bulb (McCann 1998). When flooding occurred in the southern United States in the 1920s, projects were undertaken to provide flood control. From the 1940s through the 1960s, many large storage reservoirs were built in the United States and Canada in an effort to "reclaim" desert lands, control floods, and produce hydroelectricity. The 1970s and 1980s witnessed a surge in small hydropower development, particularly in the Pacific Northwest and New England region of the United States and parts of eastern Canada. The National Inventory of Dams 1995-1996 (U.S. Army Corps of Engineers 1996) listed 76,953 dams in the United States and its territories (Figure 1-4).

Other riverine habitat losses occurred when dams flooded fishery and wildlife resources and replaced them with flat-water reservoir fisheries, particularly in western states and provinces. The trend toward habitat loss ultimately led to increased public concern for the health of entire ecosystems and caused natural resource managers to evaluate changes in flow regime on fish habitat. The need to evaluate habitat change led to the development of tools to quantify instream flow needs (Stalnaker 1994; Bovee et al. 1998). In describing the movement toward concern for habitat loss, Poff et al. (1997) noted, "It is now recognized that harnessing of streams and rivers comes at great cost. Many rivers no longer support socially valued native species or sustain healthy ecosystems that provide important goods and services." Karr and Chu (1997) observed, "Devastation is obvious, even to the untrained eye. River channels have been destroyed by dams; straightening and dredging; and water withdrawal for irrigation, industrial, and domestic uses. Degradation of living systems inevitably follows." (Figure 1-5)

In the United States, concerns for environmental change led to passage of the National Environmental Policy Act (NEPA) in 1969. Under NEPA, agencies that are planning activities that affect streams must consider the effects of their actions on natural resources.

Prior to NEPA, water developers seldom considered, nor were they required, to address ways to mitigate the loss of river segments flooded

FIGURE 1-3. Bradford Mill Dam and Bradford Paper Mill, Bradford, Vermont (Circa 1880). First settled in the 1760s, Bradford Village is located around the falls of the Waits River—a short distance to the west of the Waits River's confluence with the Connecticut River. Beginning in the late eighteenth century, a succession of dams was constructed across the falls to provide waterpower to the village's developing industries and, later, nineteenth century mills. The timber crib dams, which supplied early hydromechanical power, are now gone and the paper mill long closed. However, in the early 1900s the uppermost dam was replaced by a concrete dam, which currently provides water to a small hydroelectric project (Source: Vermont Historical Society).

FIGURE 1-4. Dam construction in the United States is a relatively recent phenomenon. Of the approximately 77,000 dams accounted for by the National Inventory of Dams 1995-1996, most were built in the 1960s and 1970s (Source: U.S. Army Corps of Engineers 1996).

by dams. Although most natural resource managers were aware that minimum flows were needed to sustain the natural functions of streams, they lacked defensible methods to quantify those needs (Tennant 1975). Therefore, the perspective of single minimum flow or flat-line instream flow became established as a way of thinking for many project developers and this perspective persists today.

During the late 1960s and 1970s, the science of instream flow began to develop as reflected by a proliferation of methods to assess instream flow needs (Orsborn and Allman 1976). Some of these attempts to develop "better" methods resulted from hydrologic statistics or "rules-of-thumb." We now know that the resulting minimum flows for one life stage of one species, such as summer spawning, do not ensure that ecosystem functions, sustained aquatic communities, or adequate habitat protection will continue even for the species for which the minimum flow was established (Calow and Petts 1992, 1994). Increased access to computers in the 1970s and 1980s coupled with increased

This logo was used as a theme for the American Fisheries Society California-Nevada Chapter conference titled "River System Symposium," held in Redding, California, 1999. Such graphics reflect a growing recognition of the importance of hydrologic variability to the vitality of river stems (Prepared by Mike Meinz, Maria Bozionelos, and Jim Canaday, American Fisheries Society, Cal-Neva Chapter).

FIGURE 1-5. Concrete, which characterizes the Los Angeles River channel in Los Angeles, California (*upper left photo*), is becoming more commonplace in large metropolitan areas throughout North America—as further evidenced by the Chaska River in Chaska, Minnesota (*middle photo*) and at the confluence of Sixteen Mile Creek and Mill Creek in Milton, Ontario (*lower right photo*). Aside from the initial expense and maintenance costs, concrete channels degrade the river's water quality, resulting in loss of habitat and fish. The upper photo was taken from the Rosecrans Avenue Bridge, Paramount, California, in a location that supported runs of anadromous salmonids 100 years ago (Source: *Upper left photo*, Dwayne Maxwell, California Department of Fish and Game; *Middle photo*, Ian Chisholm, Ecological Services Division, Minnesota Department of Natural Resources; *Lower right photo*, Lorne Fitch, Alberta Sustainable Resource Development, Fish and Wildlife Division).

knowledge of aquatic systems and organisms resulted in more sophisticated methods. However, even when approaches such as the Instream Flow Incremental Methodology (IFIM) were employed, the tendency was to focus on only one or a few river-dwelling species (usually sport fish), life stages, or habitat needs (Stalnaker 1993). A single-species orientation remains the hallmark of instream flow analysis. Even methods such as the much used Physical Habitat Simulation (PHAB-SIM) system have often focused on assessing one species or setting one minimum flow (Stalnaker et al. 1995). Whereas most of the new methods provided better justification of flow requirements than previous professional estimates—and provided natural resource managers with a basis for negotiation—the results still often consisted of only a single minimum flow value for all years and times of year (Stalnaker 1994; Poff et al. 1997; Bovee et al. 1998). Reviews of many of these techniques were reported in Morhardt (1986) and Reiser et al. (1989). Many of the methods developed in the mid-1970s remain in use today, and, while they are not appropriate for identifying all the requirements for effective stewardship, some may be useful in situations such as project screening or feasibility assessment (Stalnaker 1990).

More sophisticated assessment methods did not overcome the legal and institutional barriers to instream flow protection. The pressures on state and provincial natural resource management agencies to establish minimum flows arise, in part, from the framework of water allocation law. Prior to 1973, and to some extent today, instream flow protection activities undertaken by state fishery and wildlife agencies in the United States fell within the context of a legal system that mainly recognized out-of-stream uses (National Instream Flow Program Assessment Steering Committee [NIFPA], unpublished report). Moreover, state protection activities occurred essentially independent of any exchange or interaction among the various agencies charged with environmental protection. Traditionally, water quality programs have not been coordinated with water allocation programs; fishery and wildlife managers have not collaboratively managed with health agencies; and these programs have not acted in concert with land use agencies. Also, professionals in state and provincial fishery and wildlife agencies have not shared their experiences and procedures among themselves, resulting in little uniformity in the design of studies, use of techniques, or application of results. These combined actions within the legal and insti-

tutional environment have reduced the effectiveness of river management (NIFPA Steering Committee, unpublished report).

To better understand how state and provincial fishery and wildlife agencies could more effectively achieve instream flow protection within this legal and institutional environment, NIFPA conducted a project in 1995 and 1996 to evaluate the history and operation of instream flow programs in the United States. Participants of the project developed an assessment protocol by drawing on the experiences and expertise of instream flow specialists and aquatic biologists from each of the fifty states; seven U.S. Fish and Wildlife Service regions; and the U.S. Geological Survey, Biological Resources Division. The participants identified six elements as crucial to successful instream flow programs: hydrologic, biologic, physical, legal, institutional, and public involvement (NIFPA Steering Committee, unpublished report).

The Instream Flow Council (IFC) has expanded upon NIFPA's identification scheme by adding the elements of water quality and connectivity to the hydrologic, biologic, and physical (redefined as geomorphology) components and labeling them "riverine components." The legal, institutional, and public involvement components are presented as "policy components." Combined together, we refer to these eight elements as "ecosystem components" to emphasize that ecosystems include the complex of community and its environment functioning together as an ecological unit in nature. We believe that our model reflects a holistic approach to the evaluation of instream flows and provides important guidelines to state and provincial fishery and wildlife managers for effective riverine stewardship.

The main principle of this model is that flow regime is the dominant variable in determining the form and function of a river. Factors such as the shape of its channel, abundance and diversity of its fish and other organisms, and sustainability are directly determined by flow patterns (Hynes 1970; Poff et al. 1997). Consequently, to maintain or rehabilitate the integrity of flowing water ecosystems, instream flow practitioners must recognize the importance of both inter- and intraannual streamflow patterns for maintaining natural processes in streams. Where possible, managers should base decisions on the concept of natural flow variability and the need to balance sediment input with transport capability. Thus, a true minimum flow to maintain riverine processes is a *quantity* of water rather than a single, continuous *rate* of flow distributed over time in varying amounts to maintain natural stream processes. The IFC promotes an integrated, holistic approach to instream flow management—integrated in terms of the breadth of scientific inquiry and holistic in terms of ecosystem goals.

The main principle…is that flow regime is the dominant variable in determining the form and function of a river.

OBSTACLES TO INSTREAM FLOW PROTECTION

Regulated streams are a fact of life in most regions of the United States and Canada and tend to degrade riverine ecosystems. Fortunately, opportunities to prevent degradation of healthy unregulated stream systems still exist in sparsely populated areas (Tyus 1990; Estes 1998). Even where rivers have been degraded, the opportunity exists to reverse the trend because rivers are dynamic ecosystems. However, instream flow protection and river corridor management are inherently complex, and that complexity is tied to judgments based on societal values that are sometimes at odds with scientific findings (Edwards 1988).

As key resource managers for some of the state and provincial fishery and wildlife management agencies in the United States and Canada, we are sensitive to the fact that in too many situations our agencies have not assumed a proactive enough trustee role in conserving and sustaining the public's fishery and wildlife resources. The standard operating procedures of water-use administrators and natural resource agencies often perpetuate inconsistencies between water management objectives and legally mandated levels of aquatic resource protection. Moreover, the public is often ill informed about management of riverine ecosystems. As ecological processes are becoming better understood by resource professionals, assessment methods are becoming more sophisticated. The resulting spiral of complexity is a challenge for managers and citizens who must face the difficult decisions (Garcia 1994; Kay and Schneider 1994; Nabhan 1995).

The solution is a balanced approach to river corridor management that is consistent with public stewardship responsibilities and legal mandates. Ideally, rivers and streams should have instream flow regimes that provide sustainable, healthy, and diverse aquatic ecosystems. Where possible, high quality ecosystems should be protected and degraded systems rehabilitated. Such a balanced approach is based on establishing measurable goals and objectives.

The IFC believes that measurable goals and objectives can be based on the natural flow paradigm as a key principle in rehabilitating and conserving river ecosystems. This does not, however, imply that existing scientific knowledge and understanding can provide all the answers to every river management question. In many settings, some level of uncertainty must be accepted in order for ecosystem-level management and understanding to advance.

Although uncertainty is inevitable, more research is needed. As stewards of our states' and provinces' fishery and aquatic wildlife resources, we know full well the difficulties of addressing complex river management questions and the hard realities of implementing policy. We believe that the recommendations, suggestions, and principles

---

A balanced approach to river corridor management is consistent with public stewardship responsibilities and legal mandates.

---

presented in this manual should provide the basis for sound water management decisions. We contend that restoring the natural flow patterns that drive riverine processes of regulated systems is the most effective and least expensive way to rehabilitate significantly altered rivers and provide sustainable flows.

PURPOSE

Many publications have described the various instream flow methods developed over the years (Stalnaker and Arnette 1976; Wesche and Rechard 1980; Camp, Dresser and McKee 1986; Morhardt 1986; Dunbar et al. 1998).

Instream Flows for Riverine Resource Stewardship builds upon these earlier works but extends beyond a mere listing and description of the strengths and weaknesses of methods. It recommends tools and approaches that are most appropriate—within various geophysical and legal settings—for developing effective instream flow protection programs. It also highlights useful examples, in text and graphics, and sets out guiding principles and policies (Appendix A) that the IFC believes should, at a minimum, be addressed in all instream flow assessments. The authors' collective efforts reflect their experience and expertise as fishery and wildlife managers accumulated over the past 25 years. It is this collegial, agency-based approach that further sets this book apart from previous instream flow management and methodology evaluation reports.

To help fishery and wildlife agencies improve their ability to protect and manage riverine resources, we discuss legal principles under which most state and provincial fishery and wildlife agencies function; the natural flow paradigm and the need for an ecosystem approach; the

importance of flow in shaping the physical, chemical, and biological processes of a riverine environment; goals for managing instream flows; steps for designing instream flow studies and assessing instream flow needs; and the need for public involvement in the instream flow determination process.

Establishing instream flow programs, designing instream flow studies, and implementing instream flow prescriptions is a complex and technical business. In recognizing these challenges, we emphasize the need to base approaches and solutions on five riverine components (i.e., hydrology, geomorphology, biology, water quality, and connectivity) (Figure 1-6). Although address-

FIGURE 1-6. Riverine resource stewardship is achieved by integrating scientific studies (e.g., riverine components) with effective public involvement within a system of legal and institutional opportunity (Photo by: *Lorne Fitch, Alberta Sustainable Resource Development, Fish and Wildlife Division*).

ing appropriate elements of these components is essential to facilitating a good understanding of riverine processes, fishery managers must also include public involvement, legal, and institutional components in their efforts to preserve fishery and wildlife resources. Informing and involving the public is important because it is public values that must ultimately be reflected in water management decisions. Also, involving the public at the outset helps to build trust in terms of the process and outcomes and may enhance the public's ability to achieve outcomes via political means. But, perhaps the greatest challenge to implementing successful solutions involves understanding, incorporating, and improving legal and institutional components. All eight components are interrelated in unique and complex ways for each instream flow setting and each must be incorporated to achieve effective instream flow programs and prescriptions. No one component is more important than the other. Each situation is unique and the role of each component in helping achieve a desired outcome will most certainly change from one situation to the next.

We also evaluate 34 methods currently used for assessing instream flows. Each evaluation addresses 14 criteria, ranging from the method's purpose to the IFC's critical opinion.

In addition, we present a series of policies for instream flow program elements and protocols based on our efforts to manage fisheries in the streams, rivers, and lakes of our respective states and provinces. These policies are not a mandate for IFC members or others; rather, they are intended to provide fishery and wildlife managers with the means to develop effective programs. They may also be useful in designing instream flow studies and working with stakeholders to explain strategies and solicit support for management decisions. We do not provide a single strategy for all situations because no single approach fits all circumstances. The approach chosen must be based on the unique riverine and policy needs and opportunities of a particular issue.

Our suggestions have been developed in the context of regulatory proceedings for approval of the storage, diversion, and allocation of water through permits or licenses. Western states typically have regulatory systems that require such approval in the form of an appropriative water right. The developing trend in eastern states is also toward the issuance of permits and licenses, which has been referred to as a system of regulated riparianism (Dellapenna 1998). Even in the absence of such regulatory systems, our recommendations should be helpful for quantifying the needs of riverine resources and helping secure or protect favorable instream flows.

When one tugs at a single thing in nature, he finds it attached to the rest of the world.

— John Muir

Instream Flows in the Context of Riverine Ecology

DEVELOPING THE RATIONALE FOR INSTREAM FLOW MANAGEMENT PRESCRIPTIONS

Riverine values can only be maintained by preserving the processes and functions of the river ecosystem. The structure and function of riverine systems are based on five riverine components: hydrology, geomorphology, biology, water quality, and connectivity (Figure 2-1). Explicit documentation of these elements is necessary when developing recommendations for or reviewing instream flow alternatives. Documentation should include the rationale for evaluating or excluding each element. Management of one element, such as the biology or status of a single species, is usually not effective because each element of a riverine ecosystem continuously interacts with the others (Winter et al. 1998). Even statutory language (e.g., CALIFORNIA FISH AND GAME CODE § 5937) calling for sufficient flows to maintain fish in good condition, addresses all riverine components.

Inter- and intraannual instream flow prescriptions are needed to preserve the ecological health of a river.

The objective of an instream flow prescription should be to sustain, rehabilitate, or restore ecosystem processes through inter- and intraannual variable flow regimes to the greatest extent possible. Flow regimes must also address instream and out-of-stream needs and integrate biotic and abiotic processes. For these reasons, inter- and intraannual instream flow prescriptions are needed to preserve the ecological health of a river. It is only by using those time frames that it is possible to adequately represent the five riverine components (Hill et al. 1991; Bovee et al. 1998). The ideal instream flow prescription will employ this spatio-

temporal framework and include the institutional flexibility to allow adoption of new techniques as the science and understanding of rivers progresses.

Hydrology

Various authors (Amoros 1987; Ward 1989) have advanced the notion that there are four dimensions of hydrology: longitudinal (headwater to mouth), lateral (channel to floodplain), vertical (channel bed with groundwater), and chronological (Figure 2-2). The River Continuum Concept (RCC; Vannote et al. 1980) described the entire fluvial system as a continuously integrating series of physical gradients and associated biotic adjust-

FIGURE 2-1. The central character of rivers is typically defined by hydrology, but rivers are in fact described more completely when all five riverine components are addressed. These components, and their interactions with each other, ultimately determine the character of rivers and all must be considered in the management of riverine ecosystems.

ments as the river flows from headwater to mouth (Figure 2-3). The flood pulse concept (Figure 2-4) applied the RCC to the lateral dimension as a "batch process," operating distinctly from upstream inputs and accounting for the existence, productivity, and interactions of major biota in river-floodplain systems (Junk et al. 1989). Streams interact with groundwater in two basic ways: streams gain water from inflow of groundwater through the streambed; they lose water to ground-water by outflow through the streambed, or they do both—gaining in some reaches and losing in others (Winters et al. 1998). These processes are directly related to the five riverine components.

Because they interrupt the longitudinal, ver-tical, and chronological processes, human activi-ties—such as land use, wetland drainage, channel-ization, and water withdrawal—alter flow regimes. Land use practices such as removal of permanent cover, grazing, row crop agriculture, and urbanization can accentuate high and low flows and reduce habitat diversity and length of the lateral edge between the terrestrial and aquatic environments (Schlosser 1991). Wetland drainage can increase peak flows and decrease base flows by reducing bank storage (Moore and Larson 1979). Channelizing and diking can increase peak flows

(Campbell et al. 1872; Gordon et al. 1992) and accentuate low flows (Karr and Schlosser 1978). Miller and Frink (1984) estimated that 5% of the total variability in peak flows of the Red River at Grand Forks, North Dakota, was associated with changes in land use (including drainage). Direct withdrawals for industry, irrigation, municipal water supplies, and other uses reduce streamflow. In cases where water is withdrawn, stored, and later released, flow regimes can be dramatically shifted in time (Figure 2-5). For example, heavy withdrawals for wild rice production from the Clearwater River in northwestern Minnesota have resulted in low spring flows when rice paddies are filled and high summer flows when rice paddies are drained (U.S. Geological Survey 1991, 1992).

FIGURE 2-2. Rivers are connected in four dimensions—from headwaters to their mouth, from channel to flood-plain and valley, vertically from their bed to the ground-water, and through time. Rivers are shaped and charac-terized by movements of water through the longitudinal, lateral, and vertical dimensions, which transfer materi-als, energy, and organisms. The time dimension (dura-tion and rate of change) is also a critically important con-sideration in establishing instream flow prescriptions because of the dynamic nature of the riverine compo-nents (From Ward 1989).

FIGURE 2-3. The River Continuum Concept (RCC) emphasizes the longitudinal dimension of stream ecosystems. The RCC proposes a progressive shift, from headwaters to mouth, of physical gradients and energy inputs and accompanying shift in trophic organi-zation and biological communities (From Vannote et al. 1980).

Historic streamflow data are required to develop hydrologic time series and, if needed, water budgets. Streamflow records for gaged streams are available from the U.S. Geological Survey (USGS) and Environment Canada. If streamflow data have not been gathered or if a sufficient period of record is not available, several methods can be used to estimate hydrology (Bovee et al. 1998; Wurbs and Sisson 1999). Hydrologic simulation models (e.g., HEC-HMS, WMS) use information on watershed characteristics, precipitation, and runoff patterns to synthesize or extend a streamflow record (Figure 2-6). Furthermore, if streamflow data are available from gages within a region, runoff patterns for the watershed of interest can be synthesized by establishing

statistical relations with similar watersheds. The underlying foundation for accurate synthesis of streamflow records from another river is the similarity of watershed characteristics (e.g., soil, area, topography) and precipitation patterns.

Hydrologic records are critical for understanding and investigating stream components other than flow. A hydrologic record is needed to assess habitat changes, hydraulic functions, water quality factors, channel maintenance, and riparian and valley forming processes. For example, an instream flow prescription will most likely include flows with some recurrence interval to maintain alluvial channels. Some geomorphologists have suggested that flows with a 1.5-year recurrence interval are needed—roughly corresponding to bankfull discharge—and others have recommended that bankfull flow should be evaluated for each stream or river (Hill et al. 1991; Rosgen 1996). Either approach requires a hydrologic record.

Riparian Zone. Riparian ecosystems are the complex assemblage of organisms and their environment that exist adjacent to or near flowing water and are directly influenced by it (Figure 2-7). These systems are connected to other ecosystems and are maintained by groundwater and flood pulses (Ewing 1978).

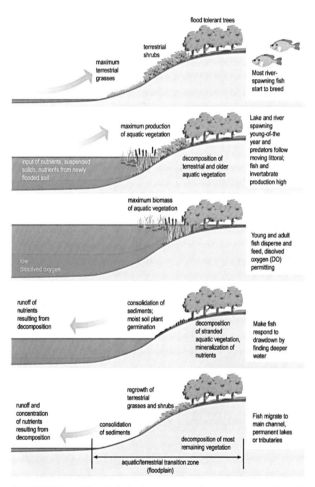

FIGURE 2-4. Floodplain rivers experience seasonal variation in water levels, which sustain riverine processes. Natural patterns of inter- and intraannual hydrologic variability are needed to match biological requirements (e. g., plant phenology, the life histories of aquatic organisms) and environmental context (e. g., nutrient cycling, temperature regimes, sediment transfer and deposition) (Copyright, American Institute of Biological Sciences 1989).

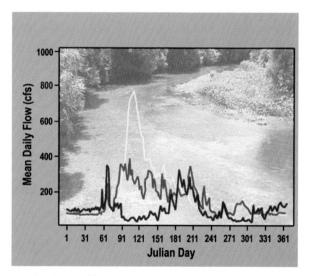

FIGURE 2-5. Human activities can and do affect the hydrographs of rivers—at times dramatically. On the Clearwater River in northwestern Minnesota the spring peak flows have been virtually eliminated due to off-stream withdrawals for wild rice production (Source: Luther Aadland, Minnesota Department of Natural Resources).

FIGURE 2-6. This USGS stream gage on Seneca Creek, near Rockville, Maryland, was one of three used by Luna Leopold to develop the theory of bankfull flow as the primary discharge, which, over time, carries the largest sediment load and therefore forms and maintains the channel. Development of such significant relations underscores the importance of basic streamflow data and the USGS gaging network. Recent pressure to reduce the number of stream gages is particularly alarming, in light of the increasing need for fundamental understanding of stream ecosystems (Source: Sandy Verry, U.S. Forest Service, North Central Research Station, Grand Rapids, Minnesota).

Stream bank form depends on a balance between the erosive forces of flowing water and resistance of the bed, bank, and streamside vegetation (Platts 1979). Vegetation buffers the stream bank from flowing water and flowing water, in turn, keeps the vegetation from encroaching into the channel (Rosgen 1996). Riparian zones can modify, incorporate, dilute, or concentrate substances before they enter the stream (Chauvet and Décamps 1989; Johnson and Ryba 1992). In small to mid-size streams, forested riparian zones can moderate temperatures, reduce sediment inputs, provide important sources of organic matter, and stabilize stream banks (Osborne and Kovacic 1993). The riparian corridor provides critical physical and biological linkages between terrestrial and aquatic environments (Gregory et al. 1991) including fish habitat and wildlife migration corridors (Johnson and Ryba 1992).

In recent years, riparian zones have come to be viewed as distinct habitats in the planning and management of state, federal, and provincial lands (Haugen 1985). Such recognition should continue and increase. Research indicates that the quantity and quality of riparian areas in the United States

FIGURE 2-7. Healthy riparian zones—such as along the Battle River in Alberta—help maintain channel shape, store water, and buffer the effects of floods, provide habitat for aquatic organisms during spawning, contribute nutrients and organic matter, and provide habitat and corridors for movement of mammals and birds (Source: Lorne Fitch, Alberta Sustainable Resource Development, Fish and Wildlife Division).

have declined dramatically throughout the 1900s (Brinson et al. 1981; Swift 1984; Ohmart and Anderson 1986; Noss et al. 1995; Mac et al. 1998). However, there is no broadly based program for monitoring the condition of riparian areas or identifying the linkages between hydrological or land management changes and riparian response (National Research Council 2002). Not surprisingly, there are no universally accepted methods for determining flow quantity and duration needed to maintain riparian habitats and their surrounding floodplains (Hill et al. 1991; Scott et al. 1996). The methods that are emerging include review of stage-discharge relations for a given stream reach. One approach is to use a hydraulic model, such as the U.S. Army Corps of Engineers' (USACE) HEC-2 model, to identify discharges at a given set of elevations and related upper and lower elevations of riparian habitat (see National Research Council 2002 for a more complete discussion of riparian function, monitoring, measurement, and management).

Not all valley types support riparian vegetation. For example, steep-sided, V-shaped valleys that lack floodplains, or even terraces, may not require riparian maintenance flows. In these situations, high flows may be more appropriate for other stream management purposes such as nutrient cycling, recharging water tables, gravel recruitment and downstream flow needs (Figure 2-8).

The most productive work to delineate riparian maintenance flows is typically local or specific in scope and fairly intensive. Auble et al. (1994) presented a method for relating riparian vegetation to magnitude and duration of inundation and predicting changes in vegetation as expressed in area occupied by each cover type. They suggested that substantial changes in riparian vegetation can occur without changing the mean annual flow because riparian vegetation is especially sensitive to changes in minimum and maximum flows (Figure 2-9). Bovee and Scott (2002) also confirmed this phenomenon and noted that changes in peak flows can reduce seedling recruitment and lead to gradual decline of riparian stands. Mahoney and Rood (1998) described how recruitment of cottonwood seedlings is limited to a narrow elevation zone—the "recruitment zone" defined at the top by a combination of late summer flow and at the bottom by the potential for subsequent scouring and deposition. They noted that river stage must decline gradually in order to permit the seedling root growth to keep pace with the capillary fringe above the water table. Stromberg

and Patten (1990) found a strong relation between flow and riparian tree growth in Rush Creek, California, and recommended flows for protecting the most flow-sensitive species as a way to maintain complex riparian systems.

There is an urgent need for more holistic methods of identifying flow needs to sustain riparian ecosystems that can be applied at the local, landscape, and basin levels.

FIGURE 2-8. Flows that form the floodplains and valleys of rivers can be very large. Instream flow recommendations must consider the geologic setting and account for the presence of human settlement and other encroachment on the floodplain. In situations where floodplains do not exist—as this photo indicates—bed-load transport may be the primary consideration driving the need for recommendations for higher flows.

FIGURE 2-9. Existing riparian vegetation may die off and recruitment of new plants can be eliminated along regulated rivers where the mean annual flow remains the same but the magnitude and timing of peak flows is changed, as illustrated by this decadent riparian community along the St. Mary's River, Alberta (Source: John M. Mahoney, Water Management Operations Division, Alberta Environment).

Although never plentiful, riparian poplars graced the banks of the lower St. Mary River, Alberta, Canada, until the latter half of the twentieth century. Instream flow patterns have been altered considerably since the damming of the lower St. Mary River in the 1950s. Diversion of water from the river now exceeds 80% of natural flow much of the year, reducing the floodplain water table that these trees depend on in an otherwise semi-arid landscape. Chronic rapid rates of flow decline impose stress on existing trees and prohibit the establishment of new seedlings. (Rood and Heinze-Milne 1989; Rood et al. 2000).

The relation between river flow and riparian poplar growth is illustrated by a remnant poplar grove along the highly regulated lower St. Mary River (Figure 2-9). The tree stand succumbed to chronic drought stress due to operation of the St. Mary River Dam (*upper left photo*). Occasional trees survive close to the river channel but even these exhibit substantial crown die back, a sign of severe chronic drought stress (*upper right photo*). Beaver herbivory is evident, which also contributes to the demise of riparian poplars along this reach.

Loss of poplars along this entire river reach has been abrupt and is nearly complete due to inadequate provision of flows to meet poplar life cycle needs. Flows are inadequate to even support trees found very close to the river channel (*lower left and lower right photos*). Significant poplar seedling recruitment along the lower St. Mary River, which had been initiated following a large flood event (>1:50 year return interval) in 1995, was not sustained due to subsequent water management practices (Rood et al. 1998; Rood and Mahoney 2000). All the photos in Figure 2-9 show how the recent water management operations prevented new seedlings from establishing closer to the river channel.

Such a holistic approach must include consideration of the magnitude, frequency, and timing of flow. The development and maintenance of riparian vegetation in the floodplain is dictated by the magnitude and frequency of a range of flows (Figure 2-10) because those variables affect reproduction, growth, and resilience of riparian species. In addition, riparian viability is dependent on the intraannual timing of flows (Figure 2-11). Although the timing of peak flows may be approximately the same from year-to-year, the magnitude of peak flows and low flows will vary. Consequently, the range of peak flows reflected in Figure 2-11 (stage 1) may, for example, constitute stages A, B, or even C in Figure 2-10 depending on the runoff level experienced in any given year. Riparian communities are adapted to variability in flow between years as well as within years and it is not necessary that all of the flow levels noted in Figure 2-10 be provided each year (Rood et al. 1995, 1998).

Valley Form and Floodplain Maintenance. Changes within a river corridor occur when fluvial processes are altered to reduce natural flooding. When this happens (1) associated wetlands are no longer maintained; (2) local water tables are not recharged; (3) stream bar and channel areas no longer become inundated and scoured; (4) sediment collects on bars and channel edges and forms lower, narrower stream banks; (5) side channels and backwater areas become disconnected from the main channel or abandoned by the mainstream as they fill in; (6) tributary channel confluences with main stems aggrade locally and push out into the main channel; and (7) the ratio of pools to riffles is significantly altered (Morisawa 1968; Platts 1979; Leopold and Emmett 1983; Hill et al. 1991). Hill et al. (1991) identified valley floodplain forming flows as those peak discharges that approximate Q_{25} but cautioned practitioners about establishing this flow. Flow recommendations at this magnitude must consider the impact resulting from human encroachment onto the valley floodplain (Figure 2-12). Roads, homes, businesses, and schools may now occupy valleys. In addition, there is the uncertainty associated with accurately determining a Q_{25} flow. Consequently, recommendations for providing flows of this magnitude may be most feasible for protecting or restoring healthy streams in areas where water development and human settlement are minimal.

FIGURE 2-10. This diagram provides a cross section of a river floodplain showing the relation between river stages (A-D), riparian water table levels, and the river flow levels needed to meet poplar life cycle requirements. Stage A: Bankfull flows, and higher, offer the chance for general seedling recruitment over large areas of the floodplain. These flows can alter riverbanks substantially and generate new nursery sites for seedling establishment. Stage B: Flows that are typically 0.6-2.0 m above late summer flow permit seedling recruitment along the riverbank. Seedling survival occurs only if flows recede slowly following seed release, so seedlings can adapt to the declining water table. Stage C: Moderate flows provide good growing conditions for existing plants but do not permit seedling recruitment at riverbank elevations that are secure from subsequent scouring and deposition. Stage D: Late summer flows provide a minimum water level to ensure survival of all poplar life stages (From Mahoney and Rood 1998).

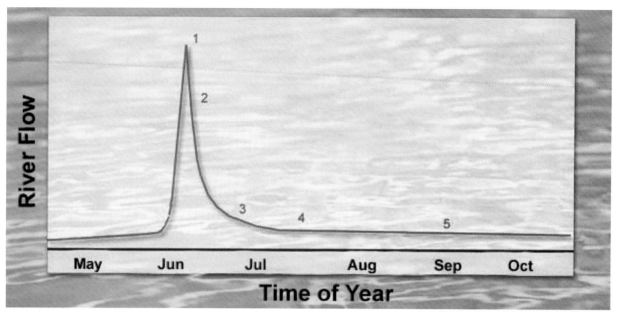

FIGURE 2-11. Generalized discharge hydrograph of long-term average flows for a typical foothills river in southern Alberta, which shows the five hydrologic stages that are important for establishment and long-term survival of the riparian poplar forest. Stage 1: High springtime flows to prepare seedling nursery sites. Stage 2: Declining river levels in late spring that coincide with seed release to expose seedling nursery sites at a range of stream bank elevations. Stage 3: Flows following seed germination in early summer, which gradually recede at a rate that permits seedling root growth to maintain contact with the water supply. Stage 4: Summer water levels necessary to support seedlings and trees throughout the hot, dry growing season. Stage 5: Base flow water supply for trees to ensure a favorable water balance through the fall and winter (From Mahoney and Rood 1998).

FIGURE 2-12. Development in river floodplains such as those near Edmonton, Alberta, poses difficult problems for society. Initial watershed and riparian conditions, which drew settlement close to the river for transportation, access to clean water, and convenient sewage disposal, gradually erode. Over time, development becomes more permanent and society demands a level of protection against the high waters that formed and maintained the floodplain and provided the river's ecological function. Continued river channel "training" encourages further encroachment, which requires additional energy and resources for protection from high waters. At the same time, hydrologic conditions in the watershed are changing due to increased runoff from urbanization and agriculture and the potential for high water increases (Source: Lorne Fitch, Alberta Sustainable Resource Development, Fish and Wildlife Division).

Geomorphology

Hydraulic habitat for riverine organisms is provided by the shape of the channel and the water that flows through and sometimes over it. Instream flow studies that focus on habitat-discharge relations must also address the dynamic nature of alluvial and colluvial channels. It is important to recognize that the physical habitat essential to maintaining the aquatic community is formed by periodic disturbance, which—in the short-term—may be detrimental to the growth and survival of individual fish or entire year classes of fish. On the other hand, high flows reset the system by forming new channels in some instances, scouring vegetation and fine sediments, abandoning side channels, and creating habitat beneficial for some species over the long-term. Periodic resetting of the system is an essential process. For example, a transbasin diversion project will add water to the receiving stream. The result may be a new, more consistent discharge pattern that is beneficial to a specific species. But the new flow pattern will change the disturbance regime of the receiving system, perhaps resulting in higher channel-forming flows or altered sediment transport processes. If channel form is altered by the increased magnitude or duration of flows, previously estimated habitat-discharge relations will be rendered meaningless. Any comprehensive instream flow analysis must account for these kinds of changes by prescribing flows necessary to maintain the dynamic nature of an alluvial channel (Figure 2-13).

Channel Form. Channel form is a direct result of interactions among eight variables: discharge, sediment supply, sediment size, channel width, depth, velocity, slope, and roughness of channel materials (Leopold et al. 1964; Heede 1992; Leopold 1994). For many alluvial streams in their natural state, the channel exists in a state of dynamic equilibrium in which the sediment load is balanced with the stream's transport capacity over time (Bovee et al. 1998). When sediment load exceeds transport capacity, aggradation or other alteration of channel form will occur. When transport capacity exceeds sediment load, as is often the case below a reservoir, the channel may adjust through enlarging the channel or degrading the bed (Figure 2-14). Clearly, alteration of flow regimes (Schumm 1969), sediment loads (Komura and Simmons 1967), and riparian vegetation will cause changes in the morphology of stream channels.

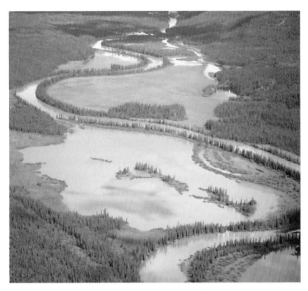

FIGURE 2-13. High water is a regular occurrence in unimpounded rivers, such as the Stikine River in northwestern British Columbia. Over bank flow serves to rejuvenate the floodplain and riparian vegetation, form channels, scour in-channel habitat, and attenuate the severity of flooding downstream. Such resetting of the system is an essential process (Source: Lorne Fitch Alberta Sustainable Resource Development, Fish and Wildlife Division).

FIGURE 2-14. The Missouri River downstream of Fort Peck Dam in northeastern Montana, erodes its stream banks, a result of the characteristically sediment-hungry water below impoundments and regulation of flows for hydropower that increase flows relative to the natural hydrograph during the winter. Colder water has an increased capacity to carry sediment (Source: Lorne Fitch, Alberta Sustainable Resource Development, Fish and Wildlife Division).

Bankfull flows are important for maintaining and forming stream channels and habitat in alluvial streams (Leopold et al. 1964). Bankfull stage (Figure 2-15) is generally defined as the height of the floodplain surface or the flow that "just fills the stream to its banks" (Gordon et al. 1992; U.S. Forest Service 2003) or the stage at which water starts to flow over the floodplain (Dunne and Leopold 1978). The floodplain is the relatively flat depositional area adjacent to the river that is formed by the river as a result of existing and long-term climatic and hydrologic conditions (U.S. Forest Service 1995). Bankfull flow is subject to minimum flow resistance (Petts and Foster 1985) and produces the most sediment transport over time (Inglis 1949; Richards 1982). Bankfull events have a recurrence interval of approximately 1.5-3.0 years (Leopold et al. 1964; Mosley 1981), but in streams with sharp peak flows and accentuated low flows the channel capacity may be more influenced by less frequent, higher events (Gregory and Walling 1973). Creating or maintaining high quality habitat is also a function of bankfull flows because scour of fines from pools and deposition of bedload in riffles is most predominant at bankfull flow (Leopold et al. 1964). Determining the bankfull flow condition through field observation is difficult and subjective (Johnson and Heil 1996). Floodplains may not exist along all stream channels; they are most noticeable along low-gradient streams. In steep-gradient channels, floodplains may be intermittent, on alternate sides of meander bends, or completely absent. It is also important not to confuse the level of the low terrace—located approximately 2-4 feet above the present stream—with that of the floodplain and to be able to recognize disturbed and incised channels (U.S. Forest Service 1995). The use of regional relations between bankfull discharge and channel characteristics, such as those found in Dunne and Leopold (1978), can be helpful for determining where to look for the floodplain and bankfull stage in specific geographic regions of the country. In severely altered systems the bankfull discharge concept may be too simplistic. In these cases, site-specific studies of bedload relations and transport capacity may be needed.

Water managers should look at the whole picture and not rule out providing important flows simply because they do not occur within a frequency defined by a "rule-of-thumb" standard of availability or are not mentioned in a policy. That whole picture includes efforts to maintain or return the stream to a condition of dynamic equilibrium. Because channel-forming, channel-maintaining, and flushing flows may not be included in some rule-of-thumb instream flow methods, it is

FIGURE 2-15. Bankfull flow is traditionally used as a surrogate for the range of flows that move sediment and shape natural channels. It is an important component of an effective instream flow prescription on alluvial streams.

easy to overlook the very significant effect of these higher flows on stream ecology (Wesche et al. 1987; Reiser et al. 1989; Kondolf 1998; Whiting 1998).

Geomorphologic considerations include more than providing bankfull flows. It is also important to include channel migration, sediment transport, scour and deposition, bank erosion, and vegetation encroachment. Changes in bed profile, substrate distribution, instream cover, overhead cover, velocity patterns, island/bar formation and removal, among others, should be considered during study design. Streambeds that are in disequilibrium may confound stage-discharge relations over time because instream features may change, leading to misrepresentation of physical habitat and calibration problems for hydraulic modeling. Bovee et al. (1998) provided guidance on dealing with channel disequilibrium. Expertise in fluvial geomorphology is often essential when addressing instream flow issues in alluvial streams.

Ice and ice formation and breakup processes can be important channel-forming variables in temperate regions prone to ice formation (Prowse 2001a, 2001b). The presence of an ice cover (Figure 2-16) adds an additional flow boundary and roughness component that modifies the velocity distribution, shear stress, and mixing parameters within the channel (Larsen 1973; Shen and Harden 1978; Lau 1982). During the period of ice formation, frazil ice is a dominant form in rivers and is known to naturally scavenge sediment once it is mobilized from the bed (Arden and Wigle 1972). Anchor ice, which often forms on the bottom of streams when turbulence drives frazil ice to the bed (Figure 2-17), can accumulate in such quantities that it actually buoys large sections of stream bottoms or large boulders and transports them considerable distances (Larsen and Billfalk 1978; Beltaos 1995). A stable ice cap typically reduces flow velocity and shear stress, which reduce sediment and bed load transport rates (Milburn and Prowse 1996). The general result of this phenomenon is an accumulation of fine materials in slower moving sections of the stream.

The ice-out or breakup stage of ice can have significant effects on geomorphic characteristics as well, by the process of scour and the formation of ice jams and associated hydraulic effects. Erosional

FIGURE 2-16. Pancake ice formation in the Green River near Pinedale, Wyoming. In northern rivers, ice formation and breakup can significantly affect sediment transport and aquatic habitat and alter hydrologic and geomorphologic processes. Native aquatic and riparian communities have adapted to ice processes in cold region streams. To avoid potential impacts in regulated streams to the extent possible, instream flow managers should consider strategies that favor maintenance of historic ice formation and breakup processes.

processes associated with ice-out are usually observed along banks (Smith 1980) in the form of such features as undercut banks. However, scouring forces are also thought to encourage scour of riverbeds (Collinson 1971). Ice jams typically form at major constrictions and meander bends of rivers, and, in some cases, cause flow to seek other overland passageways that can cut off meanders and temporarily reduce sinuosity until the channel readjusts again to its natural form and function (Mackay et al. 1974). Ice breakup may be the major hydrologic event of the year for high-latitude rivers and often is the period of greatest sediment transport (Prowse 1994). In a study of the Colville River in Alaska, one-half of the discharge and three-fourths of the annual sediment load were carried within a 4-week period associated with ice breakup (Walker 1969). In some situations, the peak sediment concentrations during these events can be several times larger than comparable flow events under open water conditions (Prowse 1993).

Sediment Transport. Part of any comprehensive stream management plan should address sediment movement processes through riparian corridors and stream channels. At least 30 variables are tied to sedimentation processes. However, the degree of interdependence among these variables is not fully understood (Heede 1992). It is known that the condition of the watershed and stream form can have a significant effect on the sediment component of water quality (Hynes 1975). The relation between discharge and sediment transport is important because the complex interactions between these elements determines whether the stream channel is stable, aggrading or degrading (Lane 1955; Figure 2-18). Whatever the trend, the resulting balance or imbalance has potentially significant effects on the form and function of the stream channel and the organisms that are found therein.

Because discharge is the key variable connecting the stream to its riparian corridor and

FIGURE 2-17. Frazil ice forms in super-cooled open water in turbulent habitat (riffles) and can coat rocks and the streambed as anchor ice. Both forms are physical factors in the transport of sediment and bed materials and affect available aquatic habitat (Source: Steven Daly, U.S. Army Corps of Engineers, Cold Regions Research Laboratory, Hanover, New Hampshire).

floodplain, it follows that specific attention must be paid to sediment in terms of maintaining the transport process, riparian corridor, and channel integrity. Livestock grazing standards (including fencing), conservation tillage practices, and sediment retention standards for urban runoff may be appropriate considerations. Whenever a stream is in sediment disequilibrium, and rehabilitation of channel form and function is the goal, specialists trained in river mechanics, sediment yield from all sources, and sediment transport can be an essential part of the interdisciplinary instream flow team. Maintaining a condition of sediment equilibrium or managing inputs to restore sediment equilibrium are important management objectives.

Biology

To adequately address natural resource issues, many biological questions need to be addressed such as: What is the composition of biological communities? What species, aquatic and terrestrial, are likely to be impacted? Should particular species be targeted for protection (e.g., game species, forage species, threatened/endangered species)? Are resources available to target ecosystem level protection or will efforts focus on vertebrates (e.g., fish, turtles, snakes), macroinvertebrates, or aquatic macrophytes? Are there out-of-channel, hydrologic connection considerations that need to be addressed (e.g., oxbows, bottomland hardwoods, wetlands)? The published literature provides valuable information. These resources include fish and game agency inventories of fishes found within their jurisdictions, state and federal fish and game agency surveys, and other water-oriented agency publications. Other sources of data include natural history collections at local universities, environmental assessments, land use surveys, and the like. After these resources have been examined, it may be necessary to undertake field studies to supply missing data. The result should be a thorough assessment of flora and fauna sufficient enough to build an understanding of community composition, connectivity, and function.

Many scientists now understand that ice formation and break-up can significantly affect a variety of biological processes (Beltaos 1995; Prowse

(Sediment LOAD) x (Sediment SIZE)   ∝   (Stream SLOPE) x (Stream DISCHARGE)

FIGURE 2-18. Lane's Balance Equation has been used to show the concept of stable channel balance and relate sediment load and sediment size to slope and discharge. A change in any one of the parameters will set up a series of adjustments in companion variables and, ultimately, result in changing the river channel. For example, an increase in discharge in a river (e.g., through upstream watershed drainage or urbanization) will adjust channel dimensions and profile, increase the river's capacity for work, and degrade the stream banks and streambed (From Lane 1955).

2001b). The manner of formation and type of ice present can affect (1) migration of fish under ice, (2) variation of velocity during ice formation and break-up, (3) physiological condition of local fish populations and types of fish, (4) available physical winter habitat, and (5) bedload scour and sediment transport. Consequently, instream flow recommendations should be based on habitat needs and processes from all times of year where significant changes in habitat and life stage requirements are known or suspected to occur (Maki-Petays et al. 1999; Whalen et al. 1999).

Life History Cues. Information on the life history of a species should be obtained to address questions concerning spawning and feeding habits, habitat use, migration patterns, and other needs. This information will allow study participants to identify obligate and facultative riverine species, generalists and specialists, and assess species-specific spatial and temporal issues such as critical habitats, critical life stages, and habitat bottlenecks. Bovee et al. (1998) provided some perspective on the nature of habitat bottlenecks, critical habitats, and their relation to population limitations.

The life history of all aquatic organisms has adapted to naturally occurring seasonal flow regimes. For instance, fish that spawn in riffles—most trout, most darters, and many suckers—do so during the spring when high flows provide the most riffle habitat (Becker 1983; Aadland 1993). The fry of many late-breeding fishes—minnows and sunfish—are intolerant of high water velocity (Simonson and Swenson 1990). Eggs of these species generally hatch in late spring to mid-summer when flows and velocities are usually lower. For those species, high-summer flows have been associated with reduced year classes (Schlosser 1985). Human-caused changes that affect hydrol-

---

Providing hydraulic habitat is a necessary part of any instream flow prescription, but it is not sufficient by itself.

---

ogy can reset the controlling variables for fish communities, eventually resulting in vastly different species assemblages if flow regimes are permanently changed (Figure 2-19). The resulting decline in biodiversity can alter the performance or function of ecosystems (Naeem et al. 1994; Figure 2-20).

Preimpoundment

Postimpoundment

FIGURE 2-19. River basin development projects, such as the construction of dams and irrigation diversions, by state and federal government partnerships during the 1950s and 1960s pose pervasive threats to riverine ecosystems. These projects—as depicted here in a stylized view of the Missouri River—have significantly altered the physical characteristics of most of the region's major river systems resulting in many adverse effects including the decline or loss of many native plant and animal species, especially fishes or their replacement with nonnative organisms (Adapted from Mac et al. 1998).

Preimpoundment Fish Community Composition   **Postimpoundment Fish Community Composition**

MG 37%
FS 56%
FR 7%

MG 53%
FS 29%
FR 18%

MG-Macrohabitat Generalist Species
FS-Fluvial Specialist Species
FR-Fluvial Restricted Species

FIGURE 2-20. Pie charts showing preimpoundment fish community composition (1962-1963) and postimpoundment fish community composition (1995-1997) in the White River, northeastern Arkansas, immediately below the Beaver Dam, which is a hydropeaking facility. A distinct shift from fluvial specialist to macrohabitat generalist species occurred after the dam was constructed as a result of flow and water temperature changes and a loss of longitudinal connectivity (From Quinn and Kwak 2003).

One cause of decline in biodiversity is rapidly varying flow regimes, such as hydroelectric peaking. Such a regime may favor generalized fish species that quickly recolonize. On the one hand, human induced flow patterns that are rapid and varied may be unfavorable to young, small individuals and result in unstable communities characterized by low species richness. On the other hand, systems with high natural temporal variability may have evolved unique native biota. Examples of natural high flow variability can be found in the southwestern United States. While rapidly varying flows favor one type of fish community, stable flow regimes often favor piscivorous fish species, including old, large individuals and high species richness (Horowitz 1978; Schlosser 1982a, 1982b, 1990).

Hydraulic Habitat. Providing suitable hydraulic habitat for aquatic organisms is a necessary part of any instream flow prescription, but it is not sufficient by itself. Habitat defined through hydraulic characteristics (such as water depth and velocity) and channel characteristics (such as substrate, cover, stream width) is sometimes referred to as hydraulic habitat. Aquatic organisms select habitat based, in part, on the physical characteristics of their surroundings. For some monitoring studies, hydraulic habitat is chosen as a surrogate for biological response because it is fundamental to an organism's existence and is directly related to flow (Figure 2-21). This approach is powerful because it ties the organism(s) of interest to the variable (discharge) that water managers can control. To

FIGURE 2-21. Suitability of predicted habitat versus observed juvenile locations for Chinook salmon (*Oncorhynchus tshawytscha*) within the Trees of Heaven study site on the Klamath River in southern Oregon. Fish collections were made at approximately 6,000 cfs. Simulated flows are approximately 6,500 cfs. Simulation of a flow rate closer to the fish observations would shift the distribution of high quality habitat toward the center of the stream and improve the already good agreement between observed fish and predicted habitat quality and location (From Hardy and Addley 2001).

evaluate existing hydraulic conditions as they relate to aquatic organisms, the relation of streamflow to habitat must be quantified over time. Existing or proposed projects may affect streamflow and habitat in different ways depending on location, design, and operation.

The variables usually associated with hydraulic habitat include depth, velocity, substrate, and cover. Many researchers have observed these flow-dependent microhabitat characteristics for fish (Hynes 1970; Giger 1973; Hooper 1973; Bovee 1974; Wesche 1976; Gorman and Karr 1978; Paragamian 1978; Platts 1979; Schlosser 1982a; Ross 1986), and invertebrates (Cushman 1985; Gislason 1985; Jowett and Richardson 1990; Gore et al. 2001). Each species and life stage has specific microhabitat preferences that may vary with temperature or other factors (Peters 1982; Peters et al. 1989; Aadland et al. 1991). The quantity of suitable microhabitat can be correlated with population size in some set-

tings (Orth and Maughan 1982; Orth 1987; Nehring 1988; Schlosser and Angermeier 1990). The microhabitat associated with a given streamflow can be assessed with models such as the Physical Habitat Simulation System (PHABSIM), which is a component of the Instream Flow Incremental Methodology (IFIM) developed by the U.S. Fish and Wildlife Service (Bovee 1982). This group of models incorporates site-specific hydraulic data with habitat suitability criteria to determine an index of habitat (Weighted Useable Area [WUA]) available for a given species and life stage over a range of streamflows (Bovee 1982; Figure 2-22). The concept of total usable habitat is derived from PHABSIM analysis and consists of integrating microhabitat with macrohabitat integrated over the entire distance of affected stream. Estimating the timing and duration of total usable habitat can be expressed as a habitat time series (Bovee et al. 1998), which allows the identification of habitat bottlenecks and the estimation of the

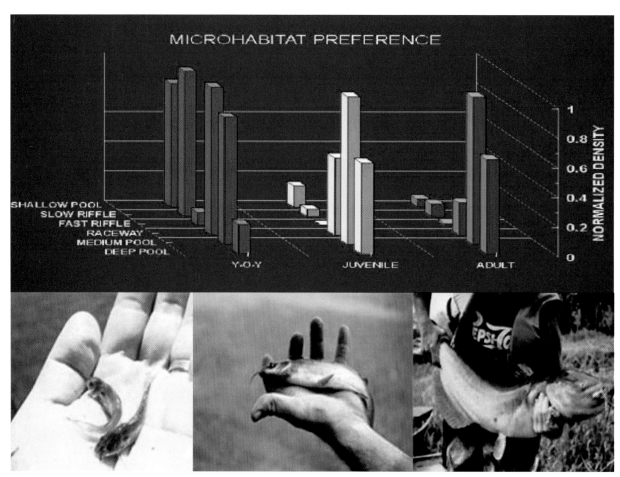

FIGURE 2-22. Mathematical representations of fish habitat preferences for each life stage and species are an integral component of some instream flow methods, as illustrated by this data set for channel catfish. These kinds of analyses ultimately depend on basic, sound fish sampling design and representative habitat measurements.

recurrence interval of habitat events.

The hydraulic habitat needs of species will be different in warm- and coolwater streams. There is a significant correlation between habitat diversity and fish species diversity (Schlosser 1982a). Warm- and coolwater streams differ from coldwater streams because of the diversity of habitat and fish and invertebrate assemblages (Schlosser 1982a; Leonard and Orth 1988, Aadland et al. 1991; Lobb and Orth 1991; Aadland 1993). The extent of species diversity and the resulting ecological integrity are increasingly recognized as important attributes of stream ecosystems (Karr 1991).

Because the prescribed flow regime directly affects ecological integrity, it is important to remember several basic relations for warm- and coolwater streams (Figure 2-23). First, base flow conditions generally favor shallow pool habitat, which is important for spawning smallmouth bass (*Micropterus dolomieui*), minnows, and young-of-year fishes, but provides little riffle and run habitat (Schlosser 1985; Leonard and Orth 1988; Aadland 1993). Second, high flow conditions generally

favor riffle and raceway habitat that is important for food production (Schlosser 1982a; Vadas 1992), mussels (Neves and Widlak 1987), and other invertebrates (Schlosser 1989). High flows also provide spawning for species such as walleye (*Stizostedion vitreum*), suckers, darters, dace, and stonerollers (Leonard and Orth 1988; Aadland et al. 1991; Aadland 1993). Third, moderate flows generally provide diverse habitat with moderate to high amounts of riffle, pool, and raceway habitat (Leonard and Orth 1988; Aadland 1993).

Natural droughts are an important contributor to interannual hydraulic habitat variability. Droughts are needed to sustain biotic and abiotic resources and processes and can have both negative and positive effects on individual species. Low flows can result in downstream fish migration (Ross et al. 1985) as well as direct destruction of fishes by high water temperatures, low dissolved oxygen (DO) levels, and physiological stress (Becker et al. 1981; Schlosser 1991). Other site-specific factors associated with droughts include disruption of fish migration (Neel 1963; Fraser 1972),

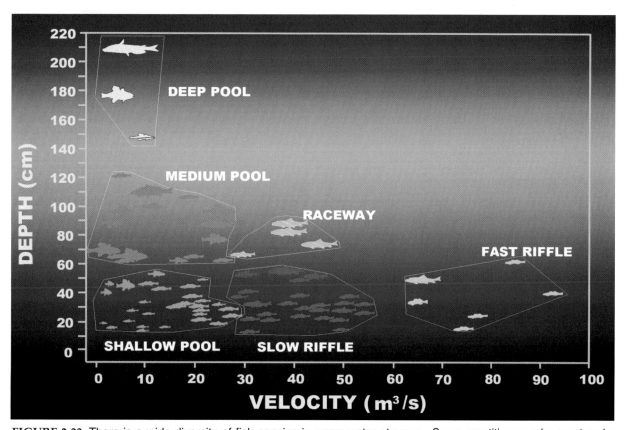

FIGURE 2-23. There is a wide diversity of fish species in warm water streams. Some practitioners who must make flow recommendations to protect these communities have developed the habitat guild approach as a way to address this diversity. The approach allows practitioners to define representative habitat types and select representative fish species' life stages to model the requirements for a larger group of species using the same type(s) of habitat.

FIGURE 2-24. The Little Snake River in northwestern Colorado provides an example of how periodic, naturally occurring low flows can sometimes favor native, drought-tolerant species in arid areas and limit establishment of nonnative fishes. Mimicking the natural flow benefits native species because they are adapted to this flow regime. The timing, magnitude, and duration of the low flows are critical; artificially induced periods of low flows that do not match these natural flow patterns may not generate this effect (Source: John Hawkins, Larval Fish Laboratory, Colorado State University, Fort Collins, Colorado).

FIGURE 2-25. These photos of Dead Man's Rapids on the Little Fork River in northern Minnesota, taken during spring 1990, provide an example of the importance and ephemeral nature of high flows and habitat for sturgeon spawning. Upper left photo: Flows at 4,110 cfs provide only marginally suitable habitat for sturgeon spawning because velocities are too high. *Upper right photo:* Flows at 2,700 cfs provide near optimum suitability. *Lower left photo:* Flows at 2,230 cfs show marginal spawning habitat due to low velocities. *Lower right photo:* Flows at 1,820 cfs result in unsuitable habitat for spawning due to zero velocity and suffocation of eggs (Source: Ian Chisholm and Luther Aadland, Ecological Services Division, Minnesota Department of Natural Resources).

increased predation by birds and mammals (Lowe-McConnell 1987; L.P. Aadland, personal observation) and reduced invertebrate production. In some instances, periods of extremely low flow can select against introduced or nonadapted fish in arid area streams where native fishes are drought-tolerant (Figure 2-24) (Hawkins et al. 1997). Drought can also favor encroachment of woody vegetation, which can produce organic inputs, complex habitats, and sediment deposition. Although natural droughts can benefit the aquatic community, permanently induced droughts or low flows do not provide sustained ecological benefits; instead, they may lead to extreme habitat alteration and negative biological consequences.

Flooding is just as important as drought for maintaining ecological processes (Figure 2-25). Although flooding can limit reproductive success of some fish species by displacing eggs and fry (Harvey 1987), covering eggs with sediment (Everest et al. 1987), and reducing food availability (Stock and Schlosser 1991) it may provide favorable habitat and functions for other species (Crance 1988; Tyus and Haines 1991). Flooding can increase fish reproduction in floodplains by (1) providing spawning habitat for species, such as northern pike that spawn on submerged terrestrial vegetation (Becker 1983); (2) enhancing food availability; (3) increasing the area of habitat available to juvenile fish; and (4) increasing the amount of time juvenile fish can use the floodplain before returning to the main channel. Because of these benefits, flooding can be a major determinant of overall river productivity (Junk et al. 1989; Schlosser 1991).

However, frequent or unusually rapid changes in flow, like the flow regimes often found downstream of "hardened watersheds," or below some kinds of dams, can have a negative effect on the productivity of habitat. For instance, eggs spawned in habitat that is suitable at one flow can be destroyed due to changes in flow, which make that habitat unsuitable. Many invertebrates also lack the mobility to adapt to rapidly changing habitat conditions and perish when flows change radically (Figure 2-26). Fish, mussels, and other invertebrates can be adversely affected by predation from terrestrial predators, stranding, and desiccation due to rapid flow decreases (Powell 1958; Neel 1963; Pearson and Franklin 1968; Corning 1970; Fisher and LaVoy 1972; Kroger 1973; Bayha and Koski 1974; Bauersfeld 1978a, 1978b; Becker et al. 1981; Extence 1981). Flow fluctuations below hydropower facilities can cause reductions in fish

population density and invertebrate diversity (Reed 1989), fishery productivity (Powell 1958; Fraser 1972; Trotzky and Gregory 1974; Becker et al. 1981), aquatic plant and benthic invertebrate productivity (Powell 1958; Fisher and Lavoy 1972; Bayha and Koski 1974; Trotzky and Gregory 1974; Covich et al. 1978; Gislason 1985) and wildlife (Bayha and Koski 1974).

The process of ice formation and breakup has typically been overlooked in many instream flow assessments. However, a growing body of research indicates that the physical forces associated with these processes can significantly affect hydraulic habitat and a variety of biological processes in regions prone to ice formation (Swales et al. 1986; Brown et al. 1994; Brown and MacKay 1995; Annear et al. 2002; Barrineau 2003; Lindstrom 2003). Prowse (2001a, 2001b) provided a thorough discussion regarding the range of biological effects associated with winter and ice processes as a function of the hydrologic, geomorphic, and water quality characteristics of ice. At a minimum, the manner of formation and type of ice present can affect the availability and suitability of hydraulic habitat for all aquatic organisms.

FIGURE 2-26. Invertebrates, such as this mussel shown in the Otter Tail River in northwestern Minnesota, can be stranded by rapid fluctuations in discharge that commonly occur below dams. Organisms that cannot move with the receding water, and are left exposed, will often desiccate and die or fall prey to mammals or birds (Source: Shawn Johnson, Minnesota Department of Natural Resources).

Under certain conditions small, shallow streams may completely freeze, or channels only partly freeze, blocking flow and redirecting flow to other channels or onto floodplains (Anderson and MacKay 1973; Figure 2-27). The formation of an ice cap adds another roughness layer to the stream, altering velocity distribution patterns from open water conditions and changing the hydraulic characteristics of areas of the stream that may have been suitable for aquatic organisms during other seasons (Larsen 1973; Lau 1982; Simpkins et al. 2000).

Depending on the manner and extent of ice formation, the physiological condition of fish may also be affected (Annear et al. 2002), thus possibly resulting in fish mortality (Post and Parkinson 2001). Studies by Brown and MacKay (1995), Simpkins et al. (2000), and others have documented specific movement patterns of some fish species in response to the formation of ice. Prowse (2001a) noted that the increase in river stage associated with ice formation and the additional roughness layer provided by ice cover increases river stage, which can be important for supplying water to riparian and floodplain habitats (Figure 27). Vegetation communities in perched basins adjacent to rivers have also been found to be dependent on overbank flows associated with ice formation and breakup (Prowse and Conly 1996). In some situations, side channels, off-channel ponds, and wetlands can provide important winter habitat for some species (Komadina-Douthwright et al. 1997). Prowse (2001b) noted that the upper limit of ice formation is often associated with the lower limit of tree growth along stream banks.

As with many, if not all, natural processes the effects of ice that benefit one ecological function, such as an ice jam that floods riparian vegetation and wetlands, may have negative consequences for other organisms such as fish or aquatic insects downstream from the ice jam where the stream becomes dewatered or frozen solid. Tesaker (2000) aptly observed that, "the modification of geometry of flow may change the winter habitat for the better or worse depending on the organism or process of interest." Consequently, instream flow studies and recommendations that are based solely on summer observations and consider only physical habitat for a single organism, such as a particular species of fish, will often yield only a partial understanding of important ecological processes (Maki-Petays et al. 1999, Whalen et al. 1999).

Analysis of hydraulic habitat should employ methods suitable for examining drought, flooding, rapid flow fluctuation, and ice formation. Available

FIGURE 2-27. *Upper photo:* Extreme cold combined with acute low flows discharged from Fremont Lake Dam resulted in formation of an ice jam on a wide, shallow riffle in Pine Creek, Pinedale, Wyoming, as observed on 12 February 2002. Water had begun seeping through the blockage when this picture was taken. *Middle photo:* During the preceding summer (July 2001) the water level of 60 cfs—about 1,000 feet upstream from the ice jam—was several feet below the top of the streambank. Note the pine tree leaning over the stream on the right hand side of the picture. *Lower photo:* After formation of the ice jam, a layer of ice about 5-feet thick formed in the same section of stream causing the stream to overflow onto the floodplain. Events like this can have negative consequences to organisms living in the stream channel by dewatering some habitats and may diminish bank habitat by accelerating bank erosion. However, such conditions can benefit riparian vegetation by hydrating the floodplain. Managers should be aware that manipulating flow levels in cold region streams during ice-prone periods can have a variety of consequences.

approaches include representative reaches (Bovee et al. 1998), mesohabitat mapping (Morhardt et al. 1983; Bovee et al. 1998), and spatially explicit indices (see Leclerc et al. 1995; Hardy 1998). The tools necessary to characterize, quantify, and map physical habitat were summarized by Frissell et al. (1986) and Hawkins et al. (1993). The difficulties in building a biologically relevant characterization of habitat stem from several factors, including the complexity of interactions between biotic and abiotic factors, the high degree of environmental heterogeneity at various scales, and the tendency of people to describe dynamic processes in terms of static numbers. Compounding these difficulties is the influence of temporal flow variation on the hydraulic habitat. Hildebrand et al. (1999) discussed this problem in regard to habitat models, habitat availability, and fisheries management.

Water Quality

The amount of flow is one of several factors that affects maintenance of water quality, including the physical, chemical, and biological attributes of water. Chemical characteristics of a river, such as DO and levels of alkalinity, nitrogen, and pH reflect local geography, land use, climate, and sources of organic matter. These factors ultimately determine the river's biological productivity. Managers seldom look at additive measures to enhance chemical characteristics of river water because the effects are generally short-lived and often unpredictable. However, regulation of point source (e.g., chemical, temperature) and nonpoint source (e.g., sediment) pollutants is an important, on-going effort. Of these, sediment and temperature are the primary physical constituents of water quality assessments.

In 1977, the Federal Water Pollution Control Act of 1972 was amended and renamed the Clean Water Act (CWA)(33 U.S.C. § 1251 et seq.). This new statute set the basic structure for regulating discharges of pollutants in waters of the United States. The 1977 amendments focused on toxic pollutants. In 1987, the CWA was reauthorized and again focused on toxic substances, authorized citizen lawsuits, and funded sewage treatment plants under the Construction Grants Program. Although the U.S. Environmental Protection Agency (EPA) retained oversight, the CWA allowed the EPA to delegate many permitting, administrative, and enforcement responsibilities to state governments.

The EPA was authorized to set effluent standards on an industry basis (i.e., technology-based

standards) and continued the requirement that water quality standards be set for all contaminants in surface waters. As a result of the CWA, low flow statistics provided some of the design criterion for wastewater treatment plants. The now infamous $7Q_{10}$ low (the lowest flow present for 7 consecutive days in a 10-year period) was developed for setting a water volume to establish point discharge pollution thresholds and it remains the statistic typically used today. Although the $7Q_{10}$ flow represents a "worst case" situation for waters receiving wastewater discharges, it has been inappropriately promoted in several states (i.e., New Jersey, Pennsylvania, and Georgia) as a minimum instream flow for fisheries (Reiser et al. 1989; Figure 2-28). The $7Q_{10}$—and other statistics for similar, infrequent low discharges, such as $3Q_{20}$ and $7Q_2$— are relevant only for designating the lowest streamflow into which a pollutant discharge can be allowed. This group of methods and the flow levels derived from them should not be approved as the instream flow for any other stream management purpose. In recent years, concerns about lower DO and changes in temperature resulting from alteration of a natural hydrologic regime, decreased discharges and slower average veloci-

FIGURE 2-28. Swallows ply the air for insects above the Assiniboine River near Portage La Prairie, Manitoba, on 6 June 2002. Discharge was 13.0 m³/s (460 cfs). This flow has been met or exceeded 99.9% of the time over the last 87 years. By comparison, mean annual flow at this site is 52.4 m³/s (1850 cfs), and the $7Q_{10}$ flow for June is 11.3 m³/s (399 cfs). Assigning minimum values, such as the $7Q_{10}$, as a protected flow level is not a valid standard for protecting riverine resources; if demand increases to the point of the minimum flow, the river is relegated to that condition for inordinate periods of time.

ties, and the higher waste loads from such minimum flow approaches have set the stage for implementing analytical water quality assessment tools.

...changes in water quality can affect...fish growth...and have a more profound impact...by enhancing the competitive advantage of more tolerant species.

In the United States, the Environmental Protection Agency (EPA) uses the Index of Biotic Integrity (IBI) to assess fish and invertebrate community structure because it serves as an indicator of the history and current health of a stream system (Karr and Chu 1997). Reduction of DO significantly impacts fish populations through its effects on physiological, biochemical, and behavioral processes (Davis 1975). Organisms in riverine communities respond to environmental and biological interactions, resulting in the species assemblage of fish and invertebrates. For example, changes in water quality can affect game fish growth by 10% per month and have a more profound impact on the numbers of game fish present—not through direct die-offs of fish, but by enhancing the competitive advantage of more tolerant species. As human populations rapidly increase in metropolitan areas, the need to address water quality issues through wastewater treatment plant upgrades or regulation modifications (water quality and quantity) will become even more important than it is today.

In Canada, the federal government has limited regulatory authority over water quality through its constitutional power over fisheries pursuant to section 92 (10) (c) of the Constitution Act, 1867 ([U. K.] 30 and 31 Vict., c. 3). Under this authority, Parliament passed the Fisheries Act (R.S.C. 1980, C. F-14.), which prohibits water pollution in waters frequented by fish, as well as the destruction of fish habitat, except as allowed by permit or regulation. This Act applies throughout Canada.

The authority of the Canadian federal government to regulate water quality is derived from its constitutional authority over federal lands and property. The federal government also may regulate some aspects of water quality throughout Canada under other constitutional powers. For example, under its power over criminal matters, the federal government may regulate toxic releases into the environment, including water. It does this through the Canadian Environmental Protection Act (S. C. 1988, c. 22).

However, provinces are the main regulators of water quality. Provinces may regulate water quality within their boundaries, except on federal lands; the federal government may agree to allow provincial regulation on federal lands. Water quality regulation is typically accomplished through environmental laws such as the Alberta Environmental Protection and Enhancement Act (S. A. 1992, C. E. 13-3).

Temperature. Water temperature is one of the most important environmental factors in flowing water, affecting all forms of aquatic life (Figure 2-29). Temperature influences fish migration, spawning, timing and success of incubation, maturation and growth, inter- and intraspecific competition, proliferation of disease and parasites, other lethal factors and synergisms (Fry 1947; Armour 1991). Stream temperatures are directly affected by any alteration of flow, shade, and channel morphology.

Water temperature is one of the most important environmental factors in flowing water, affecting all forms of aquatic life.

Augmentation, impoundment, or release of flow can change light, temperature, and flow timing as well as distribution of nutrient and organic inputs, sediment, and biota in downstream reaches (Ward and Stanford 1979; Cummins 1980; Crisp 1987; Newbold 1987; Gilvear 1987)(Figure 2-30). Stratification of reservoirs makes level of flow release at all seasons a significant tool for controlling temperature, nutrient content, and biota downstream (Hudson and Lorenson, unpublished paper; Ploskey 1986).

Alteration of temperature and temperature regimes can have simple and complex effects on river systems. Impoundment behind dams, even small ones, increases surface area and thereby raises thermal input and increases water temperature. Downstream influences, which are affected by temperature change, vary depending on the season, depths, and rates of withdrawal or reservoir release. Downstream waters are generally cooler in the summer and warmer in the winter (Baxter 1977). Such changes in temperature can affect fish at the genotypic level—favoring fish that are more tolerant of an unpredictable discharge schedule.

Richmond and Zimmerman (1978) isolated a "cool-water" isozyme in populations of red shiners (*Cyprinella lutrensis*) in tailwater areas significantly influenced by hypolimnial discharges (i.e., within 60 km of the dam). Lower temperatures decrease the viscosity of water and may cause faster settling of some solid particles. Temperature increase causes a decrease in oxygen solubility; at the same time the oxidation rate increases, further depleting the oxygen content. The combination of higher temperature and lower DO can have significant ecological effects. Artificially higher water temperature typically leads to less desirable types of algae in water. With the same nutrient levels, green alga

tends to become dominant at higher temperatures and diatoms decline, whereas at the highest temperatures blue-green algae thrive and often develop into heavy blooms (Dunne and Leopold 1978). In extreme cases, fish can be killed by wide temperature fluctuations, lethally high temperatures below power plants, or in dewatered reaches. At high temperatures, fish metabolism accelerates and their efficiency of oxygen use decreases. Coldwater species, like trout, may suffer direct mortality whereas other fish species may not be killed outright but suffer increased mortality because some other aspect of their existence becomes unfavorable.

Super-cooled water (<0°C), of which frazil ice is an indicator, can also cause physiological stress in fish. At temperatures less than 7°C, fish gradually lose the ability for ion exchange and the efficiency of normal metabolic processes decreases (Evans 1997). At water temperatures near 0°C, most fish have very limited ability to assimilate oxygen or rid cells of carbon dioxide and other waste products. If fish are forced into an active mode under these thermal conditions (such as to avoid the negative physical effects of frazil ice or if changing hydraulic conditions force them to find areas of more suitable depth or velocity), mortality can occur (Post and Parkinson 2001). The extent of impact is dependent on the magnitude, frequency, and duration of frazil events and the availability (proximity) of alternate escape habitats (Jakober et al. 1998).

FIGURE 2-29. Water temperature is one of the most important environmental factors in flowing water, affecting all forms of life. Streams naturally vary in temperature and exhibit natural fluctuations and extremes. However, flow regulation can alter temperature regimes and cause changes in downstream aquatic communities. In some situations, where large dams are constructed on rivers with endemic populations of cold water-dependent organisms, operations that increase temperatures more frequently than natural conditions may result in sublethal and lethal effects. In other cases involving dams placed on rivers with organisms adapted to warm water environments, releases of water from lower portions of the reservoir can lower the temperature regime and also change the fish and invertebrate communities.

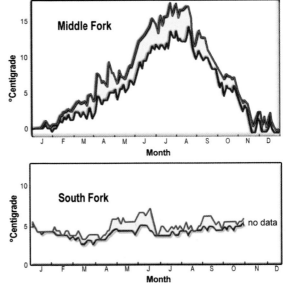

FIGURE 2-30. Thermal regimes on the unregulated Middle Fork and regulated South Fork of the Flathead River, northwestern Montana, 1977 (Adapted from Ward and Stanford 1983).

The temperature of most North American rivers generally increases toward the mouth, such that in larger river systems the main channel is at or very near mean monthly air temperature (Hynes 1975), although a few exceptions exist. Temperature varies diurnally in streams, depending on water depth, proximity to source, shading, and surface area. Temperature can also be significantly altered by dams because they disrupt longitudinal linkages in the stream (Ward and Stanford 1983).

Fine Sediment. The amount of fine sediments produced by human activities is significant; sediment is the major pollutant of U.S. waters (Waters 1995; Figure 2-31). The U.S. Fish and Wildlife Service (USFWS) concluded that excessive siltation was the most important factor adversely affecting stream habitat (Judy et al. 1984).

Erosion is a natural watershed and stream-channel process (Figure 2-32). A variety of natural disturbances can account for temporarily increased levels of soil erosion, such as periods following vegetation removal by fire. Natural high flow events can likewise mobilize sediment from the bed and banks of streams. The period of ice-out in temperate regions is also one where sediment mobilization and transport as a function of both hydraulic and physical forces of ice can constitute

a significant seasonal pulse in the water quality of some rivers loads (Milburn and Prowse 1996). Water flow, channel morphology, and watershed characteristics—including type of underlying bedrock, soil profile, and vegetation—all affect erosion rate (Leopold et al. 1964). Human activities that increase erosion and sediment production include agriculture, forestry, mining, and urban development (U.S. Environmental Protection Agency 1990). Agriculture is by far the most important cause of sediment pollution—providing over three times the amount of sediment contributed by the next leading source (U.S. Environmental Protection Agency 1990).

The fact that erosion is a natural phenomenon does not justify initiating or tolerating higher rates of soil loss than what might occur naturally. Sediment arising from the actions of humans can be controlled by prevention, interdiction (e.g., capturing sediment somewhere between source and stream), and restoration (Waters 1995). Prevention is the more preferable option because the cost of intervention—to both the environment and society—increases the farther away from the source (Figure 2-33).

Connectivity

Connectivity of a river system refers to the flow, exchange, and pathways that move organisms, energy, and matter through these systems. These pathways are not always linear. The interre-

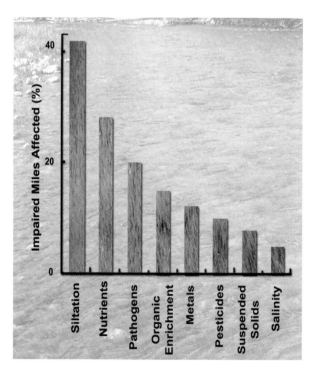

FIGURE 2-31. Relative importance of pollutants affecting streams in the United States (Source: U.S. Environmental Protection Agency 1990).

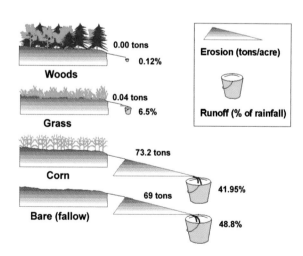

FIGURE 2-32. Watershed land use impacts the amount of runoff and erosion in streams. Results from plot studies of runoff and erosion under various types of land use in the midwestern United States show the greatest erosion from row crop agriculture (From Dunne and Leopold 1978).

lated components of watershed, hydrology, geo-morphology, biology, and water quality, together with climate, determine the flow and distribution of energy and material in river ecosystems. Complexity and interdependence is the hallmark of connectivity. The interaction of primary factors (i.e., water, energy and matter) creates an extensive physical environment that varies over time. The resulting habitat may be modified by the activities of animals that selectively eat vegetation; burrow, trample and wallow in soils; and build dams (Naiman and Rogers 1997).

As with hydrology, river system connectivity is manifested along four dimensions: longitudi-nal, lateral, vertical, and time (Ward 1989; Figure 2-34). Lateral connectivity is critical to the func-tioning of large floodplain river ecosystems. Nutrients and organic matter transported from the floodplain to the river encourage the development of aquatic plants, plankton, and benthic inverte-brates, and, in turn, provide a rich food source for fish (Junk et al. 1989). Seasonal flooding also brings nutrients and organic matter from terrestri-al areas to the river, enriching the river and bene-

FIGURE 2-33. Exclusion fencing, shown here on the Little Saskatchewan River in Manitoba, Canada, is an effective means of controlling vegetation loss and sub-sequent erosion and is especially critical to apply along stream banks or otherwise highly erodible land. Protection of riparian areas, through fencing, rotational grazing, and expansion of land easement programs is a key means for integrating stream and land management (Source: Martin Erickson, Manitoba Water Stewardship, Fisheries Branch).

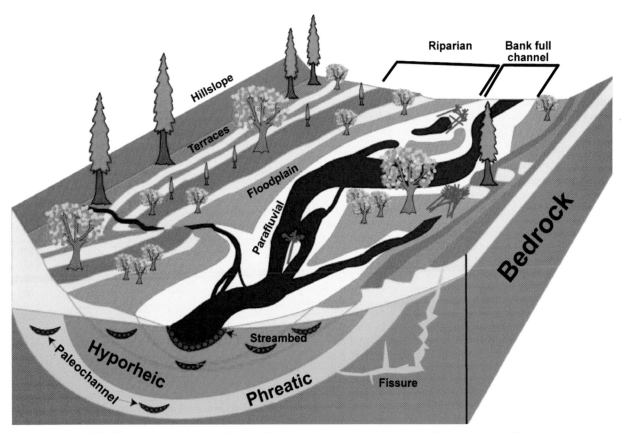

FIGURE 2-34. This illustration shows the longitudinal, lateral, and vertical connectivity of rivers. Natural connectivity patterns of these dimensions over time are an essential character of healthy rivers (From Stanford and Gonser 1998).

33

fiting the aquatic communities. Bankside vegetation provides habitat and acts as a regulator of water temperature, light, seepage, erosion, and nutrient transfer. Isolation of the main river from its alluvial plain, eliminating access to backwaters, floodplain, lakes, and wetlands, has had a major effect on both the ecological diversity of the highly productive alluvial corridor and riverine fish populations (Petts 1989). The river corridor is especially important for birds and mammals in high latitude watersheds (Nilsson and Dynesius 1994) and in arid lands (Brown et al. 1977). The seasonal flooding of an unregulated river maintains a variety of successional vegetation stages, thus creating excellent conditions for an abundant and diverse wildlife community (Nilsson and Dynesius 1994). Flooding also creates and maintains diverse species of vegetation (Nilsson et al. 1989), which, in turn, favors animal diversity.

When developing instream flow prescriptions, practitioners must account for the presence of physical, chemical, and even biological barriers to connectivity. Examples include an assessment of dams, including their position in the watershed; dam operation (hydrology); effects on water quality (e.g., DO, mercury methylization); sediment and thermal regimes; natural history of fishes in the area; and effect on aquatic communities (i.e., lacustrine or exotic species, predator concentrations). Even without dams, flow reduction through water withdrawal can affect connectivity by rendering riffles too shallow for passage of migratory fish. Fragmentation of an ecosystem in any of its dimensions disrupts the individual components and natural processes of the river system as a whole. Examples of disruption include physical (e.g., dams), biological (e.g., exotic species introductions or extinction of native biota), hydrological (e.g., dewatering of aquifers), and water quality (e.g., endocrine disruption, thermal, chemical, or sediment pollution). Vaughan (2002) suggested that culverts and other barriers in stream channels can have negative effects on the upstream movement of some invertebrates.

Although not as well studied as longitudinal connectivity, examinations of vertical connectivity have led to remarkable observations documenting the extensive biomass of riverine invertebrates living within the hyporheic zone. Stanford and Ward (1988) found stoneflies in 10-m deep wells in the floodplain of the Flathead River, Montana, as far as 2 km from the river channel and concluded that the biomass in the hyporheic zone may exceed the benthic biomass of the river.

Nutrient Cycling and Energy Pathways. River corridors are linear systems, at least in part, in which a gradient of physical, chemical, and biological change occurs from source to mouth. The RCC described biotic adjustments and organic matter processing along a river's length in response to the downstream gradient of physical conditions. Food relations usually play a large role in determining the structure and function of stream communities. Disruption of the physical and hydrologic connectivity will change the biological structure (Vannote et al. 1980; Figure 2-35).

Continuity of upstream and downstream reaches is a critical aspect of the river system. Nutrient spiraling (i.e., the downstream transport of organic matter and its coincident cycling—uptake, use, and release—by the instream biota) is the mechanism of energy transfer in headwater streams (Elwood et al. 1983). A stream and its watershed are critically linked (Hynes 1975; Likens et al. 1977); stream invertebrates are key components in the energy cycling dynamics of stream systems, directly breaking down terrestrial plant inputs or linking the processing of primary producers to higher trophic levels. Invertebrate consumers are important in regulating energy flow and nutrient cycling in stream ecosystems (see Brock 1967;

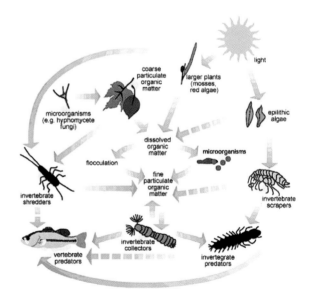

FIGURE 2-35. Energy transfer in river systems can be very complex. Interactions between one level can affect the energy amount and type available for subsequent levels, thereby influencing trophic level competition and, ultimately, the species composition of aquatic communities (Source: Federal Interagency Stream Restoration Working Group 1998).

Wallace et al. 1977; Elwood et al. 1983). The rate of spiraling and cycling nutrients and organic matter is influenced by the interaction of flow and channel form. Thus, physical retention of terrestrial inputs and macroinvertebrate processing are important mechanisms, along with microbial action, for closing or tightening the recycling process in streams and preventing the rapid through-put of materials (Minshall et al. 1985). In essence, the diversity and productivity of lower trophic levels (i.e., microbial and invertebrate populations and productivity) determine the diversity and productivity of higher trophic levels along the stream gradient. Fish species are particularly sensitive to discontinuity in bio-energetic processes associated with changes in the thermal regime below dams.

The concept of serial discontinuity explains the effect of dams, which displace aquatic communities along the river continuum (Ward and Stanford 1983; Figure 2-36). Modifying thermal

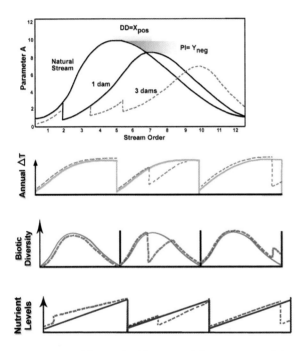

FIGURE 2-36. Theoretical framework for conceptualizing the impact of dams on selected ecological parameters. The relative influence of one and three dams is shown in the upper graph. Discontinuity distance (DD) is the positive downstream or negative upstream shift of a parameter a given distance (X) due to stream regulation. The change in parameter intensity (PI) is also defined. The relative changes in three of many potentially affected parameters as a function of stream order and postulated effects of locating a dam at different points on the continuum are shown in the lower three graphs (From Ward and Stanford 1983).

and flow regimes by impoundment were considered to be "major disruptions of continuum processes." Changes in flow regime, water temperature, oxygen, turbidity, and the quality and quantity of food particles in the river downstream of impoundments shift the upstream-downstream patterns of biotic structure and function predicted by the RCC. The serial discontinuity concept predicts the way dams shift the expected continuum. The reach immediately downstream of the dam may be reset as measured by 16 variables, including the ratio of coarse particulate to fine particulate organic matter, relation of substrate size to biodiversity, and environmental heterogeneity. A dam may result in some conditions being more like those of the headwaters (an upstream shift), while other conditions become more like those of downstream segments (a downstream shift) (Ward and Stanford 1983). Other characteristics may not fit either paradigm (Annear and Neuhold 1983). Moreover, dams and reservoirs create lentic environments where production is based on plankton rather than the benthic algae and allochthonous material on which lotic production is usually based. When reservoir water is released to a stream, it carries with it the plankton that would otherwise be scarce in streams. The instream flow practitioner must consider these potential changes and document the rationale used to arrive at decisions pertaining to quantification of instream flow needs.

Riverine connectivity is inextricably linked to hydrology and operates on several scales. For example, each watershed has a drainage network that is related to its shape, geology, geographic position, and climate. Drainage density and pattern are used to describe the drainage network and have been related to flood flows. According to laboratory studies on watershed models, drainage pattern (e.g., dendritic, trellis, radial, palmate) is more important than drainage density in influencing peak flows and lag times (Black 1972). Intensifying the drainage network, through tiling, channelization, and wetland draining, modifies the natural hydrograph and results in several potential costs, including channel instability, increased bank erosion, bed degradation or aggradation, simplification or modification of riparian or instream biota (Dunne and Leopold 1978). Urbanization and creation of impervious surfaces (watershed hardening) have similar effects (Figure 2-37).

Although riverine food webs are highly sensitive to the natural history attributes of the biota, discharge is the "master variable" that limits and resets river populations through entire drainage

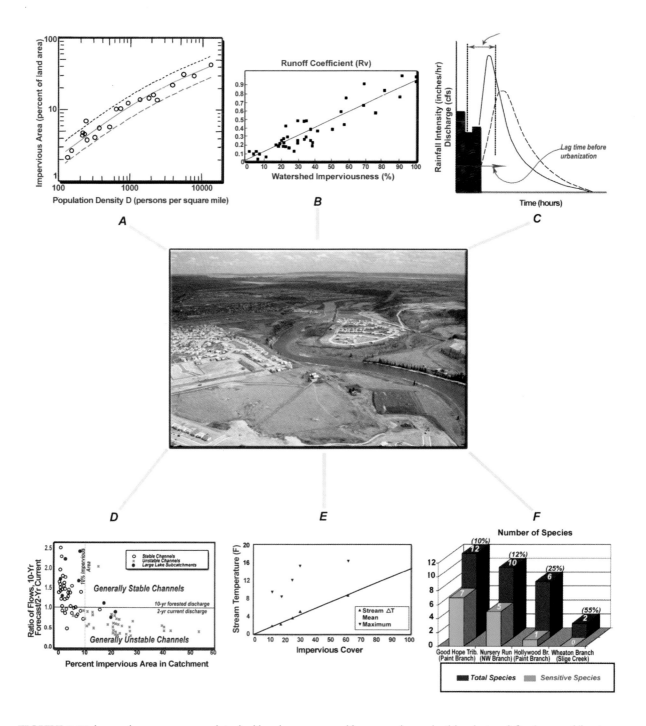

FIGURE 2-37. Impervious areas associated with urban communities—as shown in this photo of Cochrane, Alberta—are powerful influences on stream ecosystems. Increases in human population are likely to result in increases in the impervious area (a). As the percent of impervious area in a watershed increases, the amount of runoff increases (b), and changes in runoff amount and pattern will often change the shape of the hydrograph (c). Channel stability is also inversely related to the percent of impervious area in the watershed (d). The physical effect of an increase in impervious area can also affect water quality and biological processes. Percent of impervious area has been shown to increase stream temperatures (e), and was found to be inversely related to fish diversity (f), presumably as a result of the changes in the hydrograph (e.g., increased runoff and disassociation of peak flows with temperature cues), alteration of channel stability (and increases in channel sediment), and increases in stream temperature (Source: Figures A and B from Stankowski 1972; Figure C from Leopold 1968; figure D from Booth et al. 2003; figure E from Galli 1990; figure F from Schueler and Galli 1992. Photograph courtesy of Lorne Fitch, Alberta Sustainable Resource Development, Fish and Wildlife Division).

Although riverine food webs are highly sensitive to the natural history attributes of the biota, discharge is the "master variable" that limits and resets river populations through entire drainage networks...

networks (Power et al. 1995; Figure 2-38). Trophic pathways on floodplains of southeastern rivers consist of dry and wet systems (Wharton et al. 1982). Flows can affect migration of fish from lake or ocean into streams; these migratory fishes redistribute nutrients and energy in the course of their migrations. Ponding (i.e., the creation of natural or artificial pools) can change the aquatic ecosystem from an allochthonous-based food chain to an autochthonous-based food chain; the relation between flow and pond volume can influence where on the allochthonous-autochthonous continuum the system will be. Flows can affect the transport of terrestrial nutrients into a channel or stream nutrients into the floodplain. Fishes of floodplain rivers, particularly in the southeastern

FIGURE 2-38. Instream flow protection should address the entire range of flows that the watershed provides to the river. The Yellow Medicine River, southwestern Minnesota, is shown at four flow levels: 5,390 cfs (*upper left*) constitutes a flood flow for this river and forms the channel and floodplain, providing floodplain habitat (visible in the foreground of the picture); 292 cfs (*upper right*) is a typical spring flow and provides good spawning habitat for walleye (*Stizostedion vitreum*) and other riffle spawners; 112 cfs (*lower left*) provides sufficient flow for all types of fish habitat (fast and slow riffles, runs, and deep, medium, and shallow pools) as measured through Physical Habitat Simulation study; and 2 cfs (*lower right*) characterizes severe drought conditions in a channel dominated by shallow pool habitat, which provides diminished habitat area and low habitat diversity. Under high water demand, setting "minimum flow" protection levels at 2 cfs would fail to address the functions and processes that accompany the higher flow levels and would lead to degradation of the river system (Source: Luther Aadland, Stream Habitat Program, Ecological Services Division, Minnesota Department of Natural Resources).

United States and drainages to the Gulf of Mexico, depend heavily on annual excursions into the floodplain to feed and these excursions require floodplain inundation (Wharton et al. 1982).

The highest productivity of southeastern streams occurs during seasonal flooding (Conner and Day 1976; Odum 1978; Wharton et al. 1982; Gregory et al. 1991). Winter is the season when annual flooding produces the greatest benefit for floodplain forest productivity (Gosselink et al. 1981; Figure 2-39). Fish movement onto inundated floodplains during high flow season is extensive, particularly at night in southeastern floodplain rivers (Wharton et al. 1982). Crayfish also heavily use these habitats during periods of over-bank flow (Wharton et al. 1982). Ross and Baker (1983) described the importance of seasonal flooding of southeastern floodplains for the spawning, survival, and growth of some fish species. In examining a stream in eastern Canada, Halyk and Balon (1983) concluded that the growth rate of some species of young fish that were spawned in the stream is controlled by the duration of the stream's connection to the floodplain. Oxbow lakes can be very productive fish habitats, supporting high densities of species that are highly sought after by humans (Lambou 1959; Beecher et al. 1973). On the Danube River floodplain, fish yield per-unit-area increased substantially from short inundation to long (half-year) inundation (Stankovic and Jankovic 1971). Fish were also shown to move onto the floodplain in a North Carolina stream (Walker 1980).

Fragmentation and its Effects on Fish Movement. Fragmentation of river systems by dams is pervasive and affects 77% of the total water discharge in the northern third of the world (Dynesius and Nilsson 1994). Introduction of barriers, especially to migrant spawning fish, has had a widespread impact that is not solely confined to the large dams of the mid-1900s. The most visible effects are those occurring to salmon production as a result of the damming of the river systems in the Pacific Northwest (Goldman and Horne 1983; Figure 2-40). Atlantic salmon (*Salmo salar*) disappeared from the

FIGURE 2-40. Multiple dams in the Columbia River system, Oregon, have fragmented the river and led to declines of salmon runs. Migration disruption is one of the causes that is responsible for the decline. A number of approaches have been developed to move fish past the barriers. Strategies such as moving fish around barriers by trucks (*upper photo*) and barges (*lower photo*) have been used but are expensive and marginally successful (Source: U.S. Army Corps of Engineers; http://images.usace.army.mil/main.html).

FIGURE 2-39. Winter high flows in the Apalachicola River, which coincide with the high rainfall season in north and central Georgia, inundate floodplain forests near Sumatra, Florida. Inundation increases water surface area many-fold. Flooding enables higher primary productivity as water velocities are decreased in the forested floodplain and water retention and nutrient uptake are increased. Subsequently, productivity at higher trophic levels is increased and inundation allows access to diverse habitats for spawning fish and invertebrates—ultimately increasing survival and growth for a wide range of aquatic organisms.

Dordogne River, France, soon after the first dams were built on the lower reaches between 1842 and 1904 (Decamps et al. 1979). Delayed up- and down-stream migrations related to fish movement through reservoirs can adversely affect the survival and reproduction of migratory species. This observation seems valid irrespective of dam height (Raymond 1979). Adams and Street (1969) found that blueback herring (*Alosa aestivalis*) spawn in floodplains of Georgia rivers that are only accessible when annual high water coincides with spawning season. In an Illinois stream, flow was an important factor that limited immigration of fish in fall (Schlosser 1982a).

Disconnections Caused by Changes in Water Quality. There is increasing concern about the effects of chemicals in our environment and on the endocrine systems of fish, wildlife, and humans (Folmar et al. 1996; Harries et al. 1996; Jobling et al. 1998; Colborn and Thayer 2000). At least 45 chemicals have been identified as potential endocrine-disrupting contaminants (Colborn et al. 1993). The chemicals in question—including pesticides, PCB's, plasticizers, and petrochemicals—have been known to cause sex changes in fish. Decreased fertility (fewer gametes), hatchability, viability (less robust gametes), altered sex ratios in gametes, and altered sexual development and behavior are among the reproductive injuries reported to date (Colborn and Clement 1992). The endocrine disruptors enter rivers concentrated in point-source discharges or more diffusely in nonpoint source runoff (Harries et al. 1996).

Temporal discontinuity may also be occurring between generations of fish. For example, fish affected by endocrine disruption from organic contaminants may be unable to interact with older fish that are not affected. Downstream of large cities, sewage treatment effluent containing detergent metabolites (i.e., nonyphenols and surfactants), alkylphenols ethoxylates APE's, and human estrogen and birth control pills (17a-ethynylestradiol) has been implicated in endrocrine disruption in fishes (Purdom et al. 1994; Jobling et al. 1998; Barber et al. 2000). Biomarkers, like egg protein in males (vitellogenin), are being used to determine if fish are affected by water quality changes traceable to endocrine disruptors such as steroid hormones, 17B-estradiol-female, and 11-ketotesterone. The use of these and other biomarkers of potential endocrine disruption will be important for detecting and monitoring adverse effects of environmental contaminants on aquatic organisms (Goodbred et al. 1997).

The tie between contaminant levels, the occurrence of endocrine disruption, and water discharge has important implications for instream flow practitioners, particularly those who work on river systems with large municipal wastewater treatment facilities. Organic contaminants released from treated municipal wastewater systems may effectively disconnect different seg-

---

Practitioners must realize that flow recommendations for water quality that traditionally focused on assimilation of sewage, now must also account for the presence of estrogenic chemicals.

---

ments of the river system spatially by segregating populations according to water quality and the physiological health of the aquatic community. Dilution of treated sewage effluent through increases in discharge has been offered as an explanation for a reduced effect of exogenous estrogens on trout held in cages at increasing distances below the plant outflow (Harries et al. 1996). Still the problem is likely to be widespread: reconnaissance assessment of carp from U.S. streams indicates that fish in some streams within all regions studied may be experiencing some degree of endocrine disruption (Goodbred et al. 1997).

The degree of dilution and disconnectivity is a function of flow. Increasing flows to provide dilution can transport pollutants downstream and ultimately lead to deposition and impacts elsewhere. Practitioners must realize that flow recommendations for water quality that traditionally focused on assimilation of sewage, now must also account for the presence of estrogenic chemicals. Because these chemicals are very persistent, their removal is not accomplished solely by increased flow and is unlikely to occur for some time. Prescriptions must be made in the context of what is currently possible. Because national standards for endocrine-disrupting chemicals are not currently in place, the practitioner is relegated to considering dilution as the only available solution. Still, walking away from a problem after prescribing a flow regime does not ensure successful natural resource management; in fact, it may lead to failure to fulfill public stewardship responsibilities if the other elements are ignored.

Estuarine Production. Estuaries, where lotic systems terminate in marine systems, are highly productive for fish and wildlife (Benson 1981; Cross and Williams 1981). Productivity and the form of estuarine habitats are affected by the rate of flow entering estuaries (Nixon 1981; Figure 2-41). Flow rate, sediment transport, and deposition are major factors that control the form of the estuary and the distribution of salinities. The level of salinity controls trophic interactions and community composition by selectively limiting species distribution according to salinity tolerance. For example, certain bivalve mollusks can tolerate lower salinities than their primary gastropod predators, thereby optimizing oyster growth in a predator-free zone (Livingston et al. 1997; Rodriguez et al. 2001). Various species of plants and animals differ in their tolerances of salinity as well as other conditions. Consequently, the distribution of salinity with respect to physical features affects the distribution and production of estuarine flora and fauna. The Texas Water Code 11.147(a) states, "...'beneficial inflows' means a salinity, nutrient,

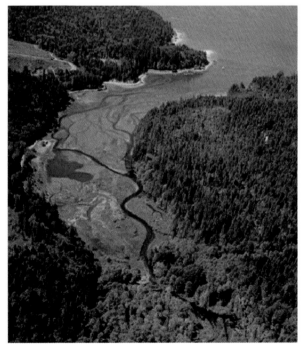

FIGURE 2-41. Oyster productivity at the mouth of the Dewatto River, in the southwestern portion of Kitsap Peninsula, Washington, is affected by the amount of sediment and nutrients transported from its upstream watershed and may be influenced by continuing changes in watershed land use. Future instream flow prescriptions on the Dewatto, as well as other rivers that feed estuaries, should consider estuarine needs (Source: Washington State Department of Ecology).

and sediment loading regime adequate to maintain an ecologically sound environment in the receiving bay and estuary system that is necessary for the maintenance of productivity of economically important and ecologically characteristic sport or commercial fish and shellfish species and estuarine life upon which such fish and shellfish are dependent."

Estuarine habitat includes main channel, distributary channels, and flats, which are dominated by seagrasses, marsh grasses (including sedges and rushes), or sediment. Flats are locations of high primary and secondary productivity, but they are inundated only during higher tides or streamflows. As tides recede, some of the nutrients and material produced on the flats is flushed through steep-banked tidal channels. Fish feed in these channels and use the channels as routes to feeding excursions onto the flats during high water periods. Low inflows can leave tidal channels dewatered.

The amount of estuarine aquatic habitat varies with flow and tide, which interact to control water surface elevation, thus determining how much habitat is inundated. In most coastal areas there are two high tides and two low tides each

---

Fish production and migration in estuaries and adjacent marine waters are correlated to pulses of fresh water and associated nutrients.

---

day, although along parts of the Gulf of Mexico there is only a single high and a single low tide each day. As tide rises, it pushes saltwater upstream into the river channel, raising the overlying freshwater surface. Fish and crustaceans follow the tides onto inundated areas to feed, then retreat to deeper water as water recedes. Water depth is a result of tide height plus stream height in estuarine zones between lowest and highest tide, with the contribution to water depth or stage being greatest from streamflow at the upstream limit of high tide and greatest from tide at the low tide line.

Fish production and migration in estuaries and adjacent marine waters are correlated to pulses of fresh water and associated nutrients (Copeland 1966; Day et al. 1977; Meeter et al. 1979; Sheridan and Livingston 1979; White et al. 1979; Yin et al. 1997). Wharton et al. (1982) reviewed literature relating river pulse delivery of different nutrients to estuaries and concluded that specific methods to evaluate riverine connectivity must entail data collection and review of empirical relations rather than the use of formulas for recommending flows.

More recently, monitoring and modeling of salinity distribution as a function of freshwater inflow has been used in a number of estuaries, including along the Gulf of Mexico (Doering et al. 2002; Flannery et al. 2002; Mattson 2002; Powell et al. 2002), in San Francisco Bay (Kimmerer 2002), and South Africa (Adams et al. 2002); these approaches complement the vertical stage effect of river inflow modeling that was used in the Skagit estuary of Puget Sound (see Tidal Distributary/Estuary Method described in Chapter 6).

ECOLOGICAL CONSIDERATIONS FOR HABITAT AND SCALE

Physical habitat conditions must be tied to a broad understanding of ecosystem processes. The five riverine components help practitioners address the whole ecosystem when making instream flow prescriptions. It is necessary to keep these factors in mind when using integrative assessment methods such as the IFIM. Models in the IFIM are based on an analysis of habitat and do not directly predict animal populations. The primary advantages of the IFIM models are that historical patterns of physical habitat structure and the effects of project operating schemes can be quantified in terms of time and space. These scales are extremely important parts of any flow recommendation or watershed management plan.

Spatial Scales

A management or study reach is that part of a stream system where instream flow analysis or management occurs. It is the point of reference for geographic scale discussion. Spatial scales range from global to micro. River scale is a nested hierarchy; the smaller spatial scales, including micro-, meso-, and macrohabitats, are nested within larger landscape features, such as reach, stream segment, and watershed (Naiman et al. 1992). The relative importance of controlling factors changes with the spatial scale, as does a manager's ability to influence those factors uniquely; however, to be effective, managers must be aware of regional and global trends (Figure 2-42).

FIGURE 2-42. River scale is a nested hierarchy; the smaller spatial scales are nested within larger landscape features, such as reach, stream segment, watershed, region and, ultimately, the globe (Adapted from Frissell et al. 1986).

The Global Scale. For migratory fish—whether white sturgeon (*Acipenser transmontana*), American eel (*Anguilla rostrata*), American shad (*Alosa sapidissima*), chinook salmon (*Oncorhynchus tshawytscha*), and many others, including those with less extensive migration areas—a spatial scale larger than the watershed should be considered. Even fish that spend their entire lives in a single pool are in some way affected by global changes such as temperature and precipitation patterns because these factors influence all ecosystems and populations (e.g., see Jager et al. 1999 for a discussion of climate change effects on fish, particularly salmonids). For these reasons, even resource agencies that have little ability to influence global scale phenomena should consider global trends when making management decisions. Important questions to ask are whether instream flow prescriptions will be adequate to meet objectives if climate changes the timing or magnitude of flows in the system, and if water will maintain an acceptable temperature if the air temperature increases.

The Watershed Scale. Watershed, catchment, or river basin refers to a scale at which state and provincial agencies have more management control. Often management at this scale is achieved by subdivision of major basins, such as the St. Lawrence, Mississippi, Rio Grande, Colorado, Sacramento-San Joaquin, Columbia, Fraser, Yukon, Mackenzie, or Saskatchewan-Nelson. In these large systems, looking at subdivisions is more practical because instream flow management decisions generally influence a subbasin scale watershed more directly and information at the subbasin scale is more easily understood (Figure 2-43).

Conditions of a watershed directly affect the channel form and the timing and magnitude of flow in the management reach (Hill et al. 1991). Watershed interacts with climate, topography, and geology to influence vegetation, stream channel, groundwater, and streamflow. Vegetation influences the channel through erosion and deposition patterns and rates. The effects of fire illustrate the connection of watershed, stream, and fish populations (Gresswell 1999). That connection is evident in the way that land use activities—such as urban or suburban development, road building, agriculture, and forestry—modify vegetation, erosion, and sedimentation, as well as the temporal relation between precipitation and streamflow. Watershed conditions such as migration barriers may limit movement of fish into or out of a management reach. Types of downstream habitat might allow

or preclude a species' use of a management reach; for example, sockeye salmon (*Oncorhynchus nerka*) are unlikely to use a stream reach that is not accessible from a lake. Watersheds that contain lakes and wetlands modify hydrology and store and release water somewhat more gradually than in watersheds without lakes (Leopold 1994).

The Stream Segment Scale. Many instream flow analyses are based on stream segments in which flow, gradient, and channel form a consistent mosaic throughout the study area. In defining a stream segment, tributaries that change flow by ≥10%, geological boundaries, gradient changes, or other features that modify channel form and valley form provide typical segment boundaries (Bovee and Milhous 1978). Instream flow analyses often entail sampling a series of adjacent stream reaches and riparian and floodplain zones within each segment.

Many stream fishes were long believed to reside throughout their lives in a single stream segment or perhaps even a smaller habitat unit (Gerking 1950, 1959). However, recent evidence of the variety of movement patterns has emerged (Gowan et al. 1994). Because fish are now known to move in and out of stream reaches, it is essential, as part of the stream segment scale, that the spatial and temporal distribution for all life stages of each species of interest be understood and stream sampling stratified accordingly. This requires some description of the stream network (subbasin) occupied throughout the life history of the species of concern. Often stream segments are sampled throughout the subbasin followed by extrapolation to describe the total habitat available (see Bartholow and Waddle [1986] for a discussion of stream network habitat analysis and associated computer models included under the IFIM suite of models).

The Macrohabitat Scale. Geomorphologists have coined the term "hydraulic biotope" to describe the flow-dependent abiotic environment of a community or species assemblage (Wadeson and Rowntree 1998). These occur at different levels such as macro- meso-, and microhabitat. Macrohabitat includes many reach and larger scale phenomena, primarily dealing with abiotic habitat conditions (such as channel morphology and chemical or physical properties of water) that control the longitudinal distribution of aquatic organisms. The mix of mesohabitats (see below), such as the ratio of pools to riffles, is determined by macro-

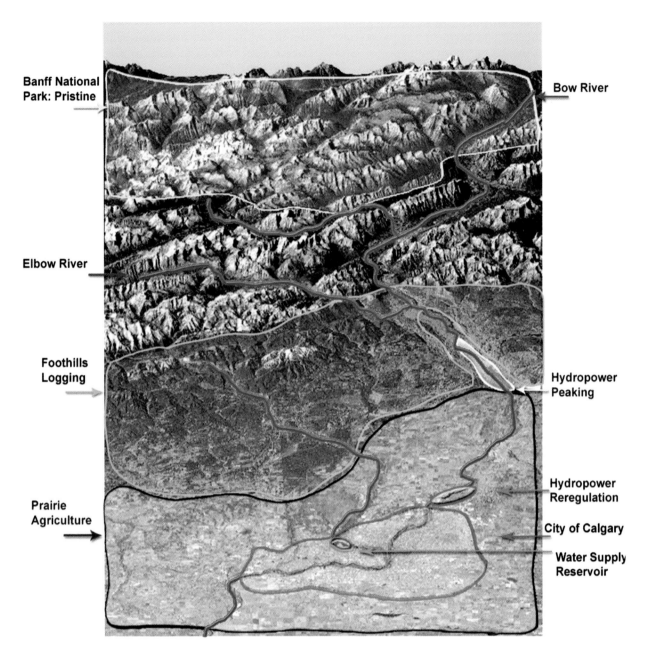

Banff National Park: Pristine

Elbow River

Foothills Logging

Prairie Agriculture

Bow River

Hydropower Peaking

Hydropower Reregulation

City of Calgary

Water Supply Reservoir

FIGURE 2-43. Watershed management is often more effective by partitioning the entire watershed into smaller units, such as subbasins—shown here on the Bow River, a subbasin of the South Saskatchewan River basin in southwestern Alberta, Canada. In the most upper reaches of the watershed, there is relatively little development because most of the watershed lies within Banff National Park. In this region, the watershed and river are relatively pristine. Just outside the Park, in the foothills region, there has been and continues to be logging and some oil and gas activity. Forestry activities such as tree harvesting and road building influence watershed conditions by altering rates of sedimentation and the timing and duration of runoff. From the foothills down to the City of Calgary, there are 11 hydropower dams on the main stem of the Bow River and its major tributaries. These structures significantly alter the hydrology of the river at an instantaneous, hourly, daily, weekly, monthly and annual time step. As well, these dams act as barriers to fish movement, effectively segregating the fish populations. The City of Calgary, as with all urban areas, acts to "harden" the watershed and, therefore, alters the hydrology in addition to contributing to the usual water quality issues. Lower in the watershed, agriculture also influences the hydrology. All land use activities in the upper Bow River basin—urban development, road building, agriculture, forestry, hydropower—modify the native plant community and erosion and sedimentation rates as well as the temporal relation between precipitation and streamflow (Source: PhotoSat Information Ltd., Vancouver, B.C., Canada).

habitat. Macrohabitat is determined by long-term geological setting, climate interaction with geology, vegetation, and the shorter term influence of land use superimposed on the preceding processes. It includes such factors as net rate of sediment transport and type of sediments transported, as well as abundance and distribution of sediment, large woody debris, and boulders. Infrequent high flows are also a major influence on macrohabitat. Flows that form channels, floodplains, and valleys were discussed by Hill et al. (1991) and Whiting (1998).

The Mesohabitat Scale. Mesohabitat refers to a combination of pools, riffles, runs, cascades, waterfalls, and off-channel habitats within a reach (Bisson et al. 1988; Kershner and Snider 1992; Hawkins et al. 1993; Vadas and Orth 1998). At least at low flows, certain combinations and ranges of depth and velocity are associated with different mesohabitats (Vadas and Orth 1998). Relative proportions of different mesohabitats appear to vary with flow as depth and velocity distributions change (Vadas and Orth 1998; Hildebrand et al. 1999). However, work by others (Rowntree and Wadeson 1998; Wadeson and Rowntree 1998) suggested that geomorphic-defined units do not change with discharge (when the stream and its watershed are in "dynamic equilibrium"). Certain life stages of certain fish species are associated with particular mesohabitats (Bisson et al. 1988).

The connectivity among mesohabitats is often flow-dependent. A connection among habitats at certain times is critical to the life history of some fishes. Passage through or around migration barriers—such as shallow riffles, cascades, waterfalls—and access to the floodplain depends on flow (Smith 1973; Powers and Orsborn 1985).

The Microhabitat Scale. Microhabitat refers to the hydraulic features determined by the unique combination of depth, velocity, substrate, and cover at specific points in a stream (Bovee 1982). Many commonly used instream flow methods focus on the hydraulics of microhabitat. One commonly used tool is the PHABSIM component of the IFIM, which allows analysis of the distribution of hydraulic habitat at different flows (Bovee and Milhous 1978; Bovee 1982; Bovee et al. 1998). The microhabitat variables provide a reasonable within-reach description of hydraulic features selected and avoided by fish at different flows within a reach (Orth and Maughan 1982; Beecher et al. 1993, 1995; Shuler and Nehring 1993; Thomas and Bovee 1993; Shuler et al. 1994; Gallagher and Gard 1999).

Although PHABSIM results are useful for identifying how the hydraulic features of microhabitat vary with flow, units of microhabitat must be sufficiently large or contiguous to support the species and life stages of interest (Gallagher and Gard 1999).

The Temporal Scales. Streams are dynamic systems, changing over time. Yet a fundamental problem in the development of a general model of system response to river alteration is the failure to consider changes within an appropriate time-scale (Petts 1984). For example, hydraulic simulation models such as PHABSIM must be used with the assumption that the channel is stable during data collection and analysis. When data collection and analysis take several months or even years, the channel form must be described anew if and when its geometric characteristics change significantly.

The present status of a watershed reflects its history, as expressed in the volume, stratification, and slope of deposits—all of which affect the present dynamics of the channel. Moreover, as climate, discharge, and sediment change, the geomorphic characteristic of a river also changes (Amoros et al. 1987) and different components of the system respond at different rates (Petts 1987). In watersheds undisturbed by human activity, all these factors usually operate in a dynamic equilibrium. Human actions can change process rates by several orders of magnitude, disrupting the equilibrium. The minimum time required for system adjustment to a new set of conditions is dependent on those variables that require the longest time to achieve a stable structure. The relative importance of these factors changes with the spatial scale, which is inversely related to the time scale of

---

Hydrologic events are stochastic, with shorter and extreme events less predictable than averages and some trends, but extreme events can have great significance on stream functions, processes, and channel forms.

---

potential persistence. Microhabitats may change daily; mesohabitats may change annually; stream reaches may change with the occurrence of landslides, log inputs or washouts, dam building, and the like; and the watershed may change through tectonic uplift, subsidence, glaciation, or climate shifts (Frissell et al. 1986; Figure 2-44).

Petts (1987) demonstrated the length of time required for channel morphology to adjust to impoundment and regulation of flow by dams in the United Kingdom. For instream flow analysis and water management, relevant time scales range from geological effects (106 to 109 years) to single floods (minutes or hours). Patterns of variation over time range over similar scales. Hydrologic events are stochastic, with shorter and extreme events less predictable than averages and some trends, but extreme events can have great significance to stream functions, processes, and channel forms. In recent years, increased attention has focused on extreme events such as channel forming, channel-maintenance, and flushing flows (Wesche et al. 1987; Reiser et al. 1989; Kondolf 1998; Whiting 1998). These flows may have low frequencies of occurrence—with recurrence intervals measured in years, decades, or longer—but their effect on maintaining long-term ecological processes is critical.

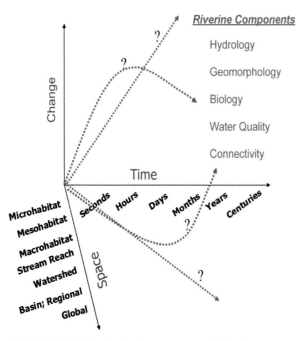

FIGURE 2-44. Each riverine component functions over the full range of spatial and temporal scales (e.g., microhabitat to global and seconds to centuries and beyond). The riverine components respond to natural and human induced perturbations at different rates. Those system variables that require the longest time to reach equilibrium determine the time of adjustment (Adapted from Frissell et al. 1986).

LESSONS FROM STREAM ECOLOGY

The Importance of Flow Variability

The importance of the natural hydrograph to stream resource stewardship has been demonstrated by the outcomes from earlier water developments (Karr 1991; Hughes and Noss 1992; Stalnaker 1994; Castleberry et al. 1996; Frissell and Bayles 1996; Rasmussen 1996; Poff et al. 1997; Richter et al. 1997; Bovee et al. 1998; Hardy 1998; Ward 1998; Goldstein 1999; Potyondy and Andrews 1999; Ward et al. 1999). The lesson is that those developments somehow altered the variability of the system to the detriment of the ecological system. Poff et al. (1997) pointed out that "the natural flow regime of virtually all rivers is inherently variable and that this variability is critical to ecosystem function and native biodiversity." Year-to-year variation in flow drives processes that periodically reset physical, chemical, and biological functions essential to the ecosystem. Some species do well in wet years and other species do well in dry years. For this reason, providing a single flow value (minimum, optimal, or otherwise) cannot simultaneously meet the requirements for all species or maintain a fishery. Instream flow recommendations may include high flows to maintain, improve, or restore stream habitat. Channel maintenance flows are high flows necessary to drive these ecological processes and maintain productivity and sustainability of stream habitat. High flows may be described as instantaneous maximum discharge, flow duration, and flow frequency, or by hydraulic criteria of velocity, depth, or competence.

To ensure sustained biological diversity and dynamic ecosystem functions, both inter- and intraannual flow regimes that attain critical threshold levels necessary to drive important ecological functions must be maintained or provided.

Flows that vary over time create and maintain dynamic channel and floodplain conditions, create essential habitats for aquatic and riparian species (Figure 2-45), and directly regulate numerous ecological processes. High flows as a result of snowmelt or rain sort and transport sediments, create discrete distributions of different-sized particles, move bed material, provide a sediment balance, control submerged, emergent, and streamside vegetation, influence the structural stability of stream banks, and prevent vegetation encroachment into the active channel. Floods import particulate organic matter and woody debris into the channel thereby creating habitat and providing food sources for some species. Ice formation and breakup processes have similar functions (Prowse 2001a, b). All of these benefits may be disrupted by flow and temperature regimes that do not maintain the natural patterns and seasonality of unregulated streams.

Life cycles of many aquatic and riparian species are timed to either avoid or exploit flows of variable magnitudes. Predictable high and low streamflows provide cues for certain life cycle events (e.g., spawning movements, egg hatching, rearing, movement into and out of floodplain areas and upstream and downstream movement). Seasonal access to floodplain wetlands for spawning and rearing is essential for certain riverine fishes to spawn and rear young fish to larger size. When access to floodplains is reduced due to the alteration of high flow events (or other land management activities), such species may become reduced or eliminated (Robinson et al. 1998; Wydoski and Wick 1998; Muth et al. 2000). Many riparian plants also have life cycles that are adapted to the seasonal timing of natural flow regimes (Figure 2-46). Seasonal sequences of flowering, seed dispersal, germination, and seedling growth are timed to natural flow events. The scouring of the floodplain by these high flows rejuvenates habitat for some types of plant species. Seasonal variation in flow, including drought, can prevent

the successful establishment of nonnative species with specific moisture requirements or inundation tolerances.

The rate of change, or flashiness, in flow conditions can influence species persistence and coexistence. In some areas, natural flow can change abruptly. Nonnative species generally are not adapted to such situations and lack the behavioral and physiological adaptations to survive. However, if the flow regime is altered to become more stable, they may out-compete native species (Hawkins et al. 1997; Tyus et al. 2000). On the other hand, rapid flow increases often serve as spawning cues for native species whose rapidly developing eggs are either broadcast into the water column (e.g., Taylor and Miller 1990) or attached to submerged structures as floodwaters recede. More gradual, seasonal rates of change in flow conditions also regulate the persistence of many aquatic and riparian species. In the case of cottonwoods, the rate of floodwater recession is critical to seedling germination because seedling roots, as they grow downward, must remain connected to a receding water table (Rood and Mahoney 1990).

The Need for Ecosystem-Level Management
All watersheds are complex webs of interrelated physical, chemical, and biological components (Calow and Petts 1992, 1994) that have been

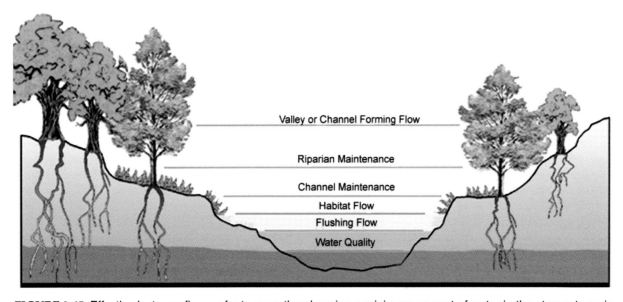

FIGURE 2-45. Effective instream flows refer to more than keeping a minimum amount of water in the stream to maintain fish survival. A range of river flows provides specific, important ecological functions that can be related generally to the five riverine components. Preservation of river flow variability—properly timed—is essential to sustaining river structure and function and ecosystem health. The types and relative levels of flow shown above are examples of the various flows that might be needed for any individual river and are not intended as a standard to be applied to every stream and situation (Source: Karim Aziz, Texas Parks and Wildlife Department).

FIGURE 2-46. Representative cross-sectional profiles from the Sprague (*upper graph*) and Upper Williamson (*lower graph*) rivers in the Klamath River basin of south central Oregon, show distribution of community type and elevation of the riparian flood flow (middle line), the 2-year peak flow (lower line) and the 10-year peak flow (upper line). Distribution and abundance of riparian vegetation are dependent on the hydrologic regime; alterations of the hydrologic regime will alter the riparian community (From Chapin et al. 2002).

affected by human activities at some scale—whether micro, macro, regional, or global. These activities have altered and, in many cases, degraded stream ecosystems by affecting food (energy) source, water quality, habitat structure, flow regime, and biotic interactions (Karr 1991). In fact, human activities affect all five of the riverine components—hydrology, geomorphology, biology, water quality, and connectivity (Figure 2-47). In the ongoing debate about the impacts of human activities on the ecosystem(s), biodiversity has emerged as a key concept for identifying impacts, developing solutions, and defining success. For

example, ecosystem degradation is manifested as lost biological diversity when humans disturb watersheds by removing permanent vegetation (for agricultural purposes or urban development), building dams that store and/or divert water, or by otherwise physically modifying stream channels. Noss and Cooperrider (1994) noted that "all land management is biodiversity management—whether intended or not."

There has been much discussion about the precise definition and usefulness of the term biodiversity. Noss (1990) proposed focusing, instead, on the characteristics that together determine and

FIGURE 2-47. Human activity is pervasive and affects all five riverine components, which interact with each other in complex ways. Activities in one area (space), or that affect one component directly, may eventually affect other areas (e.g., downstream watersheds) and the other components (Adapted from Karr 1991).

constitute the biodiversity of an area (Figure 2-48). Biological diversity and ecological integrity essentially refer to the variety of life at the genetic, taxonomic, and ecosystem levels and include function, structure, and naturalness (Hocutt 1981; Karr and Dudley 1981; Pimm 1984; Hughes and Noss 1992; Goldstein 1999). The major components of biodiversity—composition, structure, and function— were first recognized by Franklin et al. (1981). Composition refers to the identity and variety of elements in a collection and includes species lists and measures of species diversity and genetic diversity. Structure is the physical organization or pattern of a system, from habitat complexity—as measured within communities—to the pattern of

patches and other elements at a landscape scale. Function involves ecological and evolutionary processes, including gene flow, disturbances, and nutrient cycling. Noss (1990) noted that the growing concern over compositional diversity has not been accompanied by an awareness of structural and functional diversity, which we have also observed. Noss (1990) expanded the three attributes of biodiversity to include a nested hierarchy— depicting them as a series of circles (Figure 2-48) because they are interdependent and the spheres are interconnected and bounded by a larger sphere of concern (i.e., Earth). The decisions made concerning rivers and land use will impact biodiversity. Degradation of biodiversity often leads to at

FIGURE 2-48. An example of how ecosystem structure, composition, and function affect biological diversity and ecological integrity (From Noss 1990).

least localized shifts in species community or even the loss of some species.

> …complex issues must be addressed through interdisciplinary studies that involve hydrologists, geomorphologists, water quality specialists, aquatic biologists, and riparian ecology experts.

Historically, most land use decisions have been made with little understanding or regard for their effect on the interconnectedness of river and landscape (Schlosser 1991). Long-term solutions in natural resource management depend on a holistic view of the river system, including the geology, hydrology, fluvial dynamics, biological interactions with habitat, and water quality. To achieve this perspective for rivers, it is necessary to identify major interactive pathways, hierarchical structure, and temporal dynamics by making full use of our knowledge while recognizing its limitations.

This requires that water management decisions extend beyond the needs of a single species or recreational use. Such complex issues must be addressed through interdisciplinary studies that involve hydrologists, geomorphologists, water quality specialists, aquatic biologists, and riparian ecology experts.

This philosophy reflects the emerging consensus endorsed by the IFC that river managers should assess riverine flow management needs over the entire range of natural flows (Stalnaker 1994; Rasmussen 1996; Poff et al. 1997; Bovee et al. 1998; Potyondy and Andrews 1999) and make flow recommendations that are related in some fashion to the physical, biological, and chemical processes embodied in the natural flow regime. The first step for state and provincial natural resource managers working on instream flow issues is to define goals based on ecosystem objectives.

If you are thinking one year ahead, sow seed. If you are thinking 10 years ahead, plant a tree. If you are thinking 100 years ahead, educate the people.

— Chinese proverb

CHAPTER THREE

Public Involvement

Public involvement and support are critical elements of instream flow protection programs. The public has a vested interest in natural resources management because they are the ones for whom natural resources are held in trust (Slade et al. 1997). As a result, the public has a legitimate right and responsibility to be involved in the decision-making process. Public involvement in instream flow quantification processes may increase support for protection of instream resources and inform people about what they can do to help protect fishery and wildlife resources and habitats (Figure 3-1). Opportunities for seeking and including public input in water management decisions may be defined by statute in some jurisdictions or created by institutional mechanisms and agency policies. Although public involvement is very important, it is also important for public interests and agencies to understand that governmental agencies—as trustee over fishery and wildlife resources—cannot give up their authority or responsibility to act on behalf of the general public.

FIGURE 3-1. Recreational use of rivers, such as on the James River in Virginia, is not confined to average flow conditions. Low flows provide an opportunity to enjoy river activities under more relaxed conditions.

Public involvement, as defined by the National Instream Flow Program Assessment Project (NIFPA), pertains to elements of an instream flow program that inform the public; raise public awareness of instream values, uses, and water rights; solicit input on instream flow issues; and motivate public support for instream flow programs, including budgetary needs or other concerns. Society values flowing water for multiple uses (e.g., recreation, fishing, municipal uses, power generation, and irrigation), as well as nonuse (i.e., scenic beauty, environmental protection, and preservation of the resource for future generations). Benefits accrue to the public whether or not the natural resource is put to use. The challenge for natural resource managers is how best to determine and include these values and preferences in water management decisions, primarily because nonuse values are frequently among the most difficult to quantify (Mitchell and Carson 1989; Harpman et al. 1993).

In public involvement programs, the public communicates to the resource agencies what they value in instream flow resources and agencies communicate to the public how flowing water affects the ecological health of a stream system and the level of protection that is possible under various management plans. Public involvement is not a "one-size-fits-all" proposition. The purpose and type of involvement is based on the magnitude of instream flow problems, as well as the level of conflict within a state or province. Agency strategies for public involvement should include short- and long-term goals and ongoing evaluation to adjust the program as needed. As a general principle, public involvement plans should include nonregulatory approaches, such as mediation and education, to explore commonalities among stakeholders regarding projects and activities that affect instream flows.

Public participation is important to instream flow management programs at various stages.

Some states and provinces have found that public participation has made a difference in the content of authorizing legislation because the public demanded specific assurances about the protection offered by a program. Once an instream flow program is in place, the public may have opportunities to comment on proposed instream flow designations or nominate stream segments for protection. State and provincial fishery and wildlife agencies should recognize that the cost of public involvement is outweighed by the benefits of public support for instream flow protection.

PUBLIC INVOLVEMENT OPPORTUNITIES

Public involvement can be represented on a continuum in terms of the type of method used to solicit input and the nature of feedback (Thomas 1993; Steelman and Ascher 1997). As Table 3-1 illustrates, public involvement can also be thought of in terms of the level of input or influence over the decision-making process that is afforded to involved parties (Chase et al. 2002). Although agencies use a variety of methods for public involvement, they should include, when feasible, those opportunities that provide ongoing feedback.

Level I public involvement allows agencies to build a base of support by educating the public about the value of public resources and the agency's resource protection efforts. All states and provinces should, at a minimum, be involved in outreach and educational efforts. Although there is no guarantee that an informed public will support the programs favored by managers (Moore 1996; Koontz 1999), the more aware the public is about instream flow issues, the better prepared it is to effectively participate in decisions (Figure 3-2). The weakness of this type of public involvement is that it does not provide opportunity for feedback. Information tends to travel one way—from the agency to the public. Nevertheless, it is an essential base without which other forms of public involvement may be ineffective. People may not care about things they do not understand (Tarrant et al. 1997; Wondolleck and Yaffee 2000).

Level II public involvement is motivated by a need to fulfill legal and statutory requirements. Such a meeting is held when resource managers conduct a public hearing for a regulatory action or other proposed activity. In such a case, the public may have some interest in the action but may be overwhelmed by the amount of technical information presented. The meeting may be structured to discourage dialogue; for example, the experts may

TABLE 3-1. Public involvement opportunities reflecting type of involvement and level of feedback.

Level	Type of Involvement	Level of Feedback
I.	Outreach and education—information is provided that explains management decisions, agency goals, and programs.	Little or no opportunity to shape programs. These settings are typically designed to share information with citizens to enhance their understanding of agency programs.
II.	Public hearings and comments to comply with legal requirements	Public feedback may be considerable on controversial issues. The effect of input may or may not be significant depending on biological, legal, or political constraints.
III.	Public meeting, either informal or formal, to exchange information and solicit public input.	Opportunity for meaningful feedback may be greater than for Level II. Feedback functions as a two-way process between citizens and agencies.
IV.	Working groupsthat include the management agency.	Ongoing and open process for feedback among all parties. Citizens might help craft plans and play a role in long-term implementation and monitoring of projects.

take questions from the audience but may or may not respond to them on the spot. However, the meeting fulfills the agency's legal requirement to involve the public. This form of involvement is often frustrating to all participants and leaves citizens disillusioned about the effectiveness of the public's role. To solicit broader public support, managers should provide information that is jargon free and understandable by nonprofessionals. (Level I educational programs may be useful in this regard.) Managers should also fully explain the implications of their decisions. Otherwise, citizen mistrust of government officials and programs is likely to increase and public support for instream flow protection is likely to erode.

Level III public involvement attempts to build positive relationships between agencies and stakeholders (e.g., other natural resource managers, water developers, planning or permitting agencies, news media, and interest groups). This level of public involvement can take one of two forms: open houses or facilitated meetings. The distinguishing characteristic that sets this approach apart from other public involvement meetings is two-way communication. In this setting, agency personnel share information but also listen and respond to citizen concerns.

Open houses are informal meetings in which managers can discuss specific plans or actions in greater depth. Agency personnel may also staff "information stations" in an effort to better address citizen concerns one-on-one. This approach can be viewed as a more sophisticated form of Level I

FIGURE 3-2. Public involvement can take many forms and cover a variety of activities. Success of some river projects is often the result of inviting citizens to participate at early stages, such as this group helping with data collection.

involvement or as a chance to enter into more meaningful conversations with participants. Open houses are most effective when (1) the level of conflict about the proposed plan or program is low; (2) the public need for information and discussion is genuine; and (3) the decision-making process will be lengthy, thus allowing the agency time to develop a working relationship with supporters.

The facilitated meeting is a formal meeting conducted by a third party who is perceived as neutral by all participants. In such meetings, objectives are well defined and participants are presented with a specific issue to discuss and resolve; for example, one meeting might address the geographic boundaries of a study area. When multidimensional, complex issues are considered, it is very likely that a series of meetings will be necessary before solutions can be reached. The facilitated meeting is most effective when the level of conflict is high, or a strong show of public support for a particular issue is necessary in order for a resource agency to meet strategic goals.

Whereas Level III public involvement is beneficial in encouraging two-way communication, it is not appropriate for all types of decisions, primarily because it is time consuming. However, when the problem and the benefits of participation are compelling, the public and resource agencies will be motivated to invest the necessary time and resources to the process.

Level IV public involvement focuses on changing the nature of the decision-making process. Rather than agency personnel resolving instream flow problems exclusively, individuals and groups outside of state and provincial agencies are involved in decisions (Figure 3-3). An example of this kind of involvement is a comprehensive management plan for a river basin. Frequently, river basin planning crosses state and provincial geographic lines and nongovernmental groups may wish to be involved in the planning. Because planning is complex, it requires input from a variety of stakeholders and one-on-one meetings with key stakeholders, such as private landowners, may be very effective.

The most effective way to implement Level IV involvement is to find creative ways in which to address the diverse interests of stakeholders and, thereby, build support for instream flow management. One way to approach a large-scale planning process, such as river basin planning, is to form various working groups under a central coordinating authority, which could include state agencies, a group of state governors, or other entities that are authorized to fulfill this role. Each group, which is bound to a set of rules defining the process and expected outcomes, is directed to address a specific part of the problem, generate options for resolution, and report back to the central authority. Although this integrated approach is more difficult to implement—partially because it requires a departure from more traditional top-down approaches to problem solving—it provides a more level playing field and introduces a broader array of values for consideration in the decision-making process. For example, one group would define hydrological and biological components of the plan and other groups would examine economic, social, and institutional aspects. All components would be included in the final plan.

On a large scale, Level IV public involvement is only appropriate in certain circumstances because

of the high level of effort required by all participants. On a smaller scale, resource agencies might determine that ongoing public involvement benefits instream flow management discussions. In these cases, soliciting public input may involve little effort yet produce desirable outcomes in determining which riverine values are important to a community and to what extent citizens are willing to protect those values. Agencies should strive to solicit public involvement at this level because a more knowledgeable and involved public lends credibility to the outcome. In a related effort, agencies may also wish to consider creation of a statewide organization of watershed groups that advocate instream flow protection policy and legislation.

Although all four levels of public involvement are useful, it is important to determine the appropriate approach for each situation in order to be most effective. However, if an agency has not built a cadre of knowledgeable citizens through Level I activities (outreach and education), moving to Level IV involvement, which is the most sophisticated, may be difficult or impossible. As agencies move from Level I to Level IV activities, the time commitment and effort for resource managers intensifies. Managers need to be realistic about time and resource constraints and candid with the public in terms of how public preferences will be considered in the decision-making process.

Another way of looking at public involvement includes the extent to which stakeholders outside of government agencies influence decisions. Chase et al. (2002) described the process of public involvement as a continuum that includes five key approaches: authoritative, passive-receptive, inquisitive, transactional, and co-managerial.

FIGURE 3-3. In some situations, the decision-making process may involve the public in addition to scientists and agency personnel. Getting to informed consent for a particular project or viewpoint among all interested parties effectively and consistently requires objectives-based communication.

Washington State formally recognized the importance of broad public involvement in some watershed management and instream flow quantification issues by statutorily providing a process for engaging local interests. That statute reads, in part:

The legislature finds that the local development of watershed plans for managing water resources and for protecting existing water rights is vital to both state and local interests. The local development of these plans serves vital local interests by placing it in the hands of people: Who have the greatest knowledge of both the resources and the aspirations of those who live and work in the watershed; and who have the greatest stake in the proper, long-term management of the resources. The development of such plans serves the state's vital interests by ensuring that the state's water resources are used wisely, by protecting existing water rights, by protecting instream flows for fish, and by providing for the economic well-being of the state's citizenry and communities. Therefore, the legislature believes it necessary for units of local government throughout the state to engage in the orderly development of these watershed plans (RCW 90.82.010).

At one end of the continuum, the agency makes a decision based on its own authority—with little or no input from the public. At the other end, a co-management approach allows citizens to participate in all phases of the decision-making process, including long-term implementation and monitoring of the agreement. Between these two extremes there exists (1) a passive-receptive approach, in which an agency considers but does not actively seek public input; (2) an inquisitive approach, in which an agency seeks public input and attempts to incorporate that information into a policy decision; and (3) a transactional approach, in which citizens are included as active participants in the planning and decision-making process but are not included in the implementation phase. Whereas the authoritative, passive-receptive, and inquisitive approaches maintain the locus of control within the management agency, the transactional and co-managerial approaches allow agencies and stakeholders alike to share control at some level. If not specified by statute or policy, the balance between agency authority and stakeholder influence must be determined on a case-by-case basis, sometimes with the assistance of legal counsel.

Because instream flow policy decisions sometimes involve conflicts among competing values, public input in the form of environmental activism is not uncommon. This form of public input, however, differs from other forms of public involvement in several important ways. First, environmental activism is neither controlled nor requested by state or provincial fishery and wildlife agencies. Rather, individual citizens or groups of citizens, who perceive formal channels for public input to be ineffective, undertake environmental activism through informal meetings to promote specific objectives. Second, nongovernmental organizations (NGOs), which represent a more formal entity, often meet frequently to promote environmental activism around a specific interest or issue. Their level of involvement includes the collective efforts of a larger, well-organized group—as opposed to the limited efforts of a smaller, less organized group, or lone citizen. Third, environmental activism, which is perceived to challenge the status quo, often implies a demand for change in the decision-making process—not only regarding how decisions are made but the outcomes of the process as well. Fourth, environmental activists may use strategies beyond those typically associated with public involvement techniques to accomplish their objectives. For example, such strategies may include

protests or demonstrations, pleas to political officials, civil disobedience, promotion of ballot initiatives, the use of courts, and other methods. For these reasons, agency officials often view environmental activism as unpredictable and disruptive.

Nevertheless, environmental activism has resulted in many positive benefits at all levels of government. For example, environmental activism is much easier to accept when it supports an organization's particular point of view. Sometimes an agency discovers that its own positions seem rather mild compared to the stronger demands of environmental advocacy groups. However, advocacy positions can be beneficial in a water negotiation because they illuminate a fuller range of options. Instead of perceiving environmental activism as a detriment, it may be possible in some instances to incorporate these movements proactively into the decision-making process through public involvement.

This proactive measure can be accomplished in several ways by (1) reviewing proposed agency actions to identify as many potential stakeholders as possible, (2) using various forms of media to invite potential stakeholders and others to public meetings, (3) making educational materials and meeting minutes available to the public and sending these items directly to identified stakeholders, and (4) continuing to provide project information to stakeholders and others. Although these steps may not eliminate activism, a proactive approach keeps all parties informed so that areas of disagreement are more clearly identified and dissenting activism can be more readily anticipated.

It is also important to develop realistic expectations for potential outcomes knowing that public opinion will differ on how water should be used. Although managers may not share the perspectives of some public groups, it is important to keep in mind that all opinions are legitimate. In any public involvement process, part of the agency's goal should be to help competing interests understand and respect conflicting opinions and values rather than try to convince them to change their opinions. Such a position may not generate support for an instream flow project, but it may help remove opposition.

OTHER USEFUL COMMUNICATION TOOLS

In addition to the public involvement opportunities described above, other tools are available to help build public awareness and support for riverine ecology and instream flow protection. In particular, it is essential to help citizens make a connection to the river based on the resources they value. For example, some residents may benefit from knowing the cultural and social history of local streams and rivers as well as the biological and physical characteristics (Figure 3-4). In developing a public awareness campaign (Appendix B), fishery and wildlife agencies should include a mix of educational tools and outreach activities that are broad-based and far-reaching. Such tools include, but are not limited to:

- Agency publications
- News media releases
- Paid advertising
- Public service radio announcements
- Public service television announcements
- Guest presentations on radio programs
- University programs
- Participation in community education programs or river festivals
- Participation in school-based educational programs

- Participation in administrative hearing testimony
- Participation in litigation and legislative testimony
- Presentations to advocacy and adversarial groups
- Videos
- Web pages
- Exhibits at state facilities (such as state hatcheries)
- Exhibits at state fairs

Once a base of public support for instream flow protection is identified, proponents might benefit from additional information regarding protection mechanisms and constraints. Some of these mechanisms are the result of state or national legislation; some are related to administrative processes. Citizens also want to know how their efforts can make a difference. For example, should they practice water conservation, write their state legislator, or join a special interest group. Natural

FIGURE 3-4. Informing citizens about an agency's departmental programs and approaches to river management is an important, long-term commitment. In north central Michigan, the conversion of the Oden hatchery to a public education center is a prime example of innovative approaches to reach the public and revitalize state resources (Source: Gary Whelan, Michigan Department of Natural Resources).

resource managers can help direct citizen participation to the appropriate channel by discussing such topics as:

- Purchase or lease of water or water rights that benefit or reserve instream flows (if allowed)
- Beneficial instream flow legislation, regulations, and policies
- Arbitration and mediation approaches
- Water conservation practices
- Compliance monitoring and enforcement
- Formation of private sector volunteer programs to support instream flow activities

Whereas these educational and outreach activities are geared toward the general public, it is also important—and often more productive—to target user groups, professional organizations, legislative and political entities, and government agencies. More specifically, these include (1) municipal, agricultural, recreational, navigational, and industrial water users; (2) academic institutions; (3) environmental groups; (4) federal, state, and local legislators and officials; (5) state and federal agencies; and (6) governments of adjacent states and countries.

More technical information is appreciated by these groups and should include such topics as streamflow data collection and analysis methods, methods for quantifying and recommending instream flows, methods for negotiating and defending an instream flow regime, instream flow management strategies, and instream flow related case histories. However, a key issue in providing this type of information is to target the appropriate audience at the appropriate level.

INCORPORATING PUBLIC INPUT

Public participation in natural resources decision-making is increasingly common, yet the public is often disappointed with the process as well as the results. In some cases, this is inevitable because decisions may not reflect the interests of all participants. For example, a fishery consists of aquatic organisms, their habitat, and the people who use them. However, an instream flow recommendation must be based on the physical characteristics of a river as well as the public's notion of how the stream should look and function. Lackey (1998) defined ecosystem management as, "...the application of ecological and social information, options, and constraints to achieve desired social benefits within a defined geographic area and over a specified period."

One way to overcome some of the disappointment is to be clear about the boundaries of the decision-making process and the expected outcomes. In explaining the nature of the process, resource managers should also explain the agency's public trust responsibilities to ensure that public resources are managed for the use and enjoyment of future generations.

An example of public participation in the decision-making process might require a series of public meetings to determine which stream segments to recommend for inclusion in a state or provincial instream flow protection program. If the public is involved in an effort of this type, it is important to explain at the beginning of the process:

- Why the agency is addressing this issue
- The responsibilities of the agency to the public
- The laws that authorize instream flow protection
- How instream flow protection is defined
- How instream uses coordinate with out-of-stream uses
- Who has the authority to make the final decision
- The legal authority for public involvement
- What role is legally defined for public involvement
- The extent of public involvement
- How long the process will take
- The intermediate decision points
- The role that is legally defined for other state or provincial agencies
- How the public can assist the process
- Public recourse if they are unhappy with the final decision

Additional information can be included that addresses specific circumstances of a state or province. Citizens tend to be more satisfied with the outcome of a public involvement process if they are told the limits of their involvement at the beginning of the meeting and can then, accordingly, determine how to most effectively address the issues at hand (Lawrence et al. 1997; Koontz 1999; McCool and Guthrie 2001).

IFC Public Input Policy Statement: Effective instream flow programs should incorporate public input in the decision-making process.

Encouraging Public Involvement

Although many individuals and groups may express support for the concept of instream flow protection and restoration, such expressions typically offer little benefit when fishery and wildlife managers are defending programs or instream flow prescriptions in the face of opposition. Indeed, there is an important distinction between public support and public involvement that many managers and members of the public often overlook. The reality is that opportunities abound at various levels for the public to get involved with the complex business of managing instream flows—whether at the level of setting instream flow prescriptions, helping agencies develop effective programs, developing new or better laws, or encouraging water administrators to adopt policies that afford instream flow the same privilege and opportunity as other uses of water.

Whenever possible, citizen groups can and should be involved in establishing mitigation, rehabilitation, and restoration efforts and postproject monitoring and evaluation of instream flow projects. Carrying out the many activities of an instream flow protection program is time consuming and costly. Whereas agency budgets may support the most basic functions of a program, agencies may need to pursue private sector funding and the assistance of volunteers to oversee some activities and functions, including:

- Purchases, donation, and leases of water or water rights that will be used to benefit instream flow uses or reserve instream flows
- Support for instream flow protection arbitration/mediation
- Support for water conservation practices
- Support for public relation activities involving instream flow protection
- Formation of volunteer programs to support instream flow protection

IFC Public Education Policy Statement: State and provincial instream flow programs should include specific actions to inform the public about instream flow concepts, how instream flows are administered, what benefits the programs provide, and what opportunities exist for public involvement.

Making Information Understandable

Public support, as emphasized throughout this chapter, is dependent on an informed and involved citizenry, which means resource managers should conduct some kind of needs assessment to determine the level of knowledge the public has about instream flows. Technical information that explains the issues must then be presented in basic, jargon- free language suitable for a nontechnical audience. A glossary of technical terms and an explanation of official documents can be helpful and should also be made available to the public. In a study of technical terms used in U.S. Forest Service planning documents, Lamb and Ponds (1999) found that the general public had little understanding of many of the terms commonly used to describe management practices. In situations like this—when the public is asked to comment on draft plans—citizens may be unable to assess many of the plans' basic features.

To determine the knowledge and preferences of citizens who do not attend meetings, or comment on proposals, state or provincial fishery and wildlife agencies may be able to contract with universities or other entities to conduct focus groups or surveys that measure public understanding of instream flow terms. Feedback from these efforts can be helpful to agencies in determining how best to communicate with the public. If a large-scale data-gathering effort is not feasible, agencies may be able to rely on in-house information officers to develop educational materials that would be made available to the general population or develop interactive web pages to test people's knowledge.

IFC Effective Communication Policy Statement: Information intended for public consideration in instream flow decision-making processes should be straightforward, free of jargon, and provide a basic understanding of technical and legal concepts, biological processes, and trade-offs.

Just the Facts, Ma'am

Agency biologists are often asked to explain the issues associated with riverine management to a public that may not readily understand the complexities of those issues. One of the most effective ways to relay information to people quickly and inexpensively is through simple fact sheets, which can be highly effective for several reasons.

First, although some assistance from the agency's information officer can be helpful, biologists can assemble fact sheets by themselves in a relatively short amount of time (days not weeks).

Second, fact sheets reduce complex issues to their most basic elements. The unfortunate fact is that most people don't want to read much more than the 500 words or so that fit on a fact sheet—a little more than twice the length of this text box.

Third, fact-sheets are less expensive to print or duplicate than fancy or professional brochures. Although there is a time and place for brochures, CD's, and popular articles, fact sheets help convey the agency's concern for timeliness and budget management.

There are a variety of ways to communicate messages to the public, each chosen for its effectiveness in a certain situation. But one of the best ways to reach the public quickly and effectively is with nothing more than a simple fact sheet (Adapted from a fact sheet on fact sheets by Tom Dickson, Minnesota Department of Natural Resources).

We have been quick to assume rights to use water but slow to recognize obligations to preserve and protect it. In short, we need a water ethic—a guide to right conduct in the face of complex decisions about natural systems we do not and cannot fully understand.

—Sandra Postel, *Last Oasis: Facing The Limits*

CHAPTER FOUR

Legal and Institutional Elements

The preceding chapters established the importance of technical elements and public involvement in the process of managing instream flows for riverine resource stewardship. These components represent the bases for quantifying and protecting instream flows. In essence, the technical elements tell biologists what they *should* do from a management perspective to protect, rehabilitate, or restore riverine resources. Public involvement conveys what the public *wants* agencies to do. But, it is the legal and institutional components that define and authorize what *can* be done.

Statutes can empower state and provincial fishery and wildlife management agencies in their efforts to protect instream flows. However, preexisting water rights (or permits) for using water can and do limit those efforts. Successful riverine stewardship is not possible without a clear and supportive legal and institutional framework. To have permanence and full legal protection, instream flows must usually be administered under state, provincial, or federal laws or regulations. Agreements reached among private interests to provide a negotiated flow may provide additional flow in some settings, but typically offer neither permanence nor legal protection from other users if the agreement is not incorporated into a permit or water right.

In general, most existing state and provincial laws are inadequate to enable meaningful riverine stewardship. Historically, the majority of laws relating to streamflow reflected the preoccupation with economic uses of water, such as hydro and mechanical power, navigation, or out-of-stream diversion for consumptive use. Little or no legal recognition was given to instream fishery and aquatic needs. Today, efforts to protect instream riverine values run headlong into these often archaic legal mechanisms for managing water. It is this outmoded legal structure—more than any other single factor—that handicaps efforts to protect, rehabilitate, and restore riverine resources and their essential functions for the enjoyment and benefit of present and future generations.

Although statutes constrain as well as guide instream flow management efforts, other legal principles, such as the Public Trust Doctrine (doctrine) provide guidance in terms of how natural resource laws can be written, changed, or interpreted to benefit riverine resources. In some situations, state and provincial fishery and wildlife agencies can and should provide assistance to lawmakers to ensure that they effectively incorporate those principles into law. Likewise, agencies can provide information to help the public understand how existing laws affect fish, wildlife, and their habitats.

A well-informed and supportive public is the foundation of good laws and favorable institutional processes, which are manifested in the bureaucratic will to protect instream flows. Even the best laws and highest quality science will yield little meaningful protection unless bureaucratic will is based on a political environment in which an aware and involved public supports objective application of the laws. Instream flow proponents should not assume that seemingly good laws would be administered in a manner that addresses their full potential to protect or restore riverine resources without the presence of a supportive public.

We provide legal guidelines and principles that each state or province may consider during water allocation proceedings and in developing new, or improving upon existing, comprehensive water resource management programs. Our suggestions can be used to design legal mechanisms, provide agency administrators with the tools to build and maintain a fishery and wildlife management safety net, and inform the public about instream flow protection.

Notes On Terminology And Scope Of Legal Policies

Our treatment of the Public Trust Doctrine refers primarily to the protection of instream flows. Although the doctrine also provides authority for public access to navigable waters, the management of fishery and wildlife populations (including hunting), and public ownership of submerged lands, we do not directly address those applications.

Use of the term "regulatory law" refers to codified statutes for managing natural resources and the rules and policies of state and provincial fishery and wildlife agencies that administer these statutes. We also use the term to distinguish codified law from the Public Trust Doctrine, which is uncodified common law interpreted by courts in individual cases.

The Public Trust Doctrine

The nation behaves well if it treats the natural resources as assets, which it must turn over to the next generation increased, and not impaired, in value.
—President Theodore Roosevelt

The Public Trust Doctrine is one of the most unusual and potentially useful doctrines for natural resource management in the United States' legal system (Sax 1999) and one that has a long history of development and application. To date, the doctrine forms no recognized basis of law in Canada, but arguments can be made that it may have application in the Canadian legal system (Maguire 1996).

"By the law of nature these things are common to mankind—the air, running water, the sea, and consequently the shore of the sea."

In the United States, the Public Trust Doctrine forms the basis of each state's fishery and wildlife resource and habitat management responsibilities. Pursuant to the doctrine, each state holds fishery and wildlife resources and habitats in trust for its citizens. As trustee, it is the responsibility of the states to manage waters, submerged lands, and living resources for the benefit of present and future generations (Slade et al. 1997).

In this chapter, we examine some of the basic characteristics of the Public Trust Doctrine to illustrate how its principles can and should be used by instream flow practitioners to advocate responsible aquatic resource management in the face of contrary political and economic forces. A brief summary of the doctrine's characteristics and ways the doctrine has been used in the United States is presented in Appendix C. (see Slade et al. 1997 for a more complete treatment of the Public Trust Doctrine.)

Scope Of The Public Trust Doctrine

Where it is formally recognized, the Public Trust Doctrine is considered a mix of common law, state law, property law, and a public right (Dawson 1999; Sax 1999). This broad basis makes the doctrine flexible and reflective of current thinking, a fundamental right of all citizens, and a right that cannot be taken away (Blease 1999). The Public Trust Doctrine is of central importance to state instream flow programs because it forms the cornerstone of fishery and wildlife management agencies' resource management responsibilities, obligations, and opportunities.

In its traditional form, the Public Trust Doctrine requires that waters remain usable for the purposes of navigation (including small boats), related commerce, and fishing; that is, those water-based benefits held in trust for the enjoyment of each state's citizens. In some jurisdictions, the doctrine has recently been interpreted to encompass aesthetic beauty, recreation, and preservation of natural conditions of submerged and riparian lands. As common law, the Public Trust Doctrine has developed differently in each state, but it generally requires that subject waters, lands, and dependent fishery and wildlife resources be managed for the benefit of each state's citizens to ensure long-term sustainability for trust purposes. In this sense, the doctrine can be considered a type of fiduciary responsibility of the government to manage specific resources for the general, sustained benefit of its citizens. However, state and provincial fishery and wildlife management agencies seldom have regulatory authority to manage the habitat of fish and wildlife; rather their role is to serve as the environmental conscience for the state or province. Because the doctrine has evolved in each state out of its unique interpretation of common law, the argument by some that this legal principle poses a national or global threat to private property ownership is unfounded.

Too often the concept of "public interest" is considered the same as "public trust." As a rule, governments are typically charged with acting in the public interest and rightfully strive to base most decisions and actions on the public interest. In fact, the two concepts are considerably different. Public interest relates primarily to economic or value considerations. Almost any action that has public value or generates economic gain is in the

---

Although the concept of public interest can and does complement public trust, it is quite possible (and common) that actions can be taken in the public interest that harm the public trust.

---

public interest. Public trust, conversely, refers to matters of common property (like water, fish, or wildlife) that is held in trust by a sovereign (state or province) for the use and benefit of the beneficiaries (present and future generations). Although the concept of public interest can and does complement public trust, it is quite possible (and common) that decisions made in the public interest may harm the public trust (Richard Roos-Collins, senior counsel for the Natural Heritage Institute, personal communication).

DEVELOPMENT OF THE PUBLIC TRUST DOCTRINE IN THE UNITED STATES

In the United States, the Public Trust Doctrine is common law that has been developed and articulated by courts in individual cases. Because it is common law, many of its characteristics are the same in each state; however, the exact nature of the doctrine is determined by each state on a case-by-case basis. Therefore, no universally recognized application exists.

The Public Trust Doctrine, which originated as Roman Civil Code in the sixth century A.D., stated that, "By the law of nature these things are common to mankind—the air, running water, the sea, and, consequently, the shore of the sea." England adopted the Public Trust Doctrine as common law, and the French Civil Code and Spanish Civil Law, likewise, acknowledged the concept of common property. In turn, the Public Trust Doctrine was imported into the 13 original U.S. colonies. Following independence of the colonies,

the Public Trust Doctrine potentially became part of the basic law in each state. It remains valid today as common law in jurisdictions where its principles have been enacted in statute (including the implementation of rules and policies) to manage subject waters and lands.

Pursuant to the Public Trust Doctrine, states hold the waters of navigable streams and their nonnavigable tributaries, submerged lands, and fishery and wildlife resources in trust for the benefit of all people (Sax 1999; *Illinois Central Railroad v. State of Illinois*, 146 U.S. 387 [1892]). These public resources must be used in a manner consistent with the enjoyment of public trust benefits as provided by the Public Trust Doctrine. Principally, the doctrine forms the "bedrock of modern (fish and) wildlife regulation" (Veiluva 1981). It is under the principles of the Public Trust Doctrine that courts and state legislatures have recognized their basic sovereign obligation to act in the best interests of their citizens and developed legal authorities for the states to control the management and use of fishery, wildlife, and water resources that are held in trust for the public.

The simplest expression of the Public Trust Doctrine is that government owes its citizens a special duty of stewardship regarding common property resources, which the state holds in trust for the public. The doctrine holds that government must act as a fiduciary in its management of the resources that constitute the corpus of the trust. The beneficiaries of the trust are the citizens of the state, including future generations. Common property resources—including water, fish, wildlife, and land—are held by the states in their sovereign capacity and are subject to the public trust. (Cook 1993)

State governments may also have trust responsibility and obligations for other natural resources (*United Plainsmen Association v. North Dakota State Water Conservation Commission*, 247 NW 2d 457 [1976]). In some jurisdictions, the trust has been interpreted to include the protection of fish and wildlife habitat, coastal access, and aesthetic characteristics, as well as traditional trust resources. Another application of the public trust may include the protection of public health and prevention of flooding, erosion, and water pollution (Dawson 1984).

Acknowledgment of the trust responsibility for water resources is growing slowly. The principal case establishing the role of the Public Trust Doctrine for water resources came in *National Audubon Society v. Superior Court of Alpine County* (189 Cal. Rptr. 346 [1983]) in which the California Supreme Court held that consumptive water rights are subject to the Public Trust Doctrine. This case is more widely known as the Mono Lake case. The doctrine requires the government to exercise its trust responsibilities when making decisions about allocating resources to private uses. The government's failure to consider the public trust in allocating public water to individual use may result in the reversal of a decision, even years after the decision was made (Bingham and Gould 1992).

Another California case offers an example of courts applying the Public Trust Doctrine to streamflow. In *Environmental Defense Fund, Inc. et al. v. East Bay Municipal Utility District* (Superior Court for Alameda County, No. 425955, Statement of Decision [1989]), the court found that the Public Trust Doctrine applied to decisions allocating water in the American River. The judge also found that the Public Trust Doctrine must be integrated with the reasonable use doctrine (Cal. Const. art. X, § 2; Somach 1990). This section of the constitution declares that the state's water resources must be put to beneficial use to the fullest extent of which they are capable, that the waste or unreasonable use or unreasonable method of use of water be prevented, and that the conservation of such waters is to be exercised with a view to the reasonable and beneficial use thereof in the interest of the people and for the public welfare. The judge found that, whenever possible, he was required to integrate the two doctrines rather than decide between them. Therefore, the judge mandated a plan by which water could be diverted and instream values protected.

Public Trust Doctrine Opportunities in Canada

Although the Public Trust Doctrine is relatively well established in the legal system of the United States, it has not yet been formally incorporated in Canadian law. To date, the doctrine has not formed the basis of a judicial decision in Canada although there have been unsuccessful attempts to test its existence (*Green v. R.*, 34 D. L. R. [3d] 20 [Ont. H. C.] [1972]). More recent arguments have described the Public Trust Doctrine in light of the long recognized right of Canadian subjects to access and use Crown resources for certain specified purposes (Maguire 1996).

Given the English and French roots of the legal system in Canada and the United States, where the Public Trust Doctrine exists in various forms, it is curious that the doctrine has not developed along similar lines in each country. However, because the doctrine has not yet been formally recognized in Canada is not necessarily proof that it does not exist. In the United States, the Public Trust Doctrine was first recognized by the United States Supreme court in the case of *Martin v. Waddell*, 41 U.S. (16 Pet.) 367(1842), and the concept of state trusteeship over public resources was formally recognized in 1892 (*Illinois Central Railway v. Illinois*, 146 U.S. 387 [1892]). Certainly there seem to be several factors suggesting existence of the Public Trust Doctrine in Canada whether or not it is formally recognized.

The French roots of the Public Trust Doctrine can be traced to the French Civil Code, which endorsed the concept of common property in "navigable rivers and streams, beaches, ports and harbors." The feudal system was exported to New France in the seventeenth century when all French colonies in North America (including Louisiana) were declared subject to the legal system then in force in Paris (Reed 1986). Even after the conquest of Quebec by the British, the Quebec Act of 1774 preserved French Civil Law in Canada as well as, arguably, its philosophical feudal notions of common property. Section 109 of the Constitution Act, 1867, seems to affirm the Crown's underlying proprietary interest in all public land when it granted the beneficial use of all public lands to the provinces "subject to any trusts existing in respect thereof, and to any interest other than that of the province in the same."

Despite some Canadian courts' assertions to the contrary, recent actions seem to suggest an implied responsibility to act in a trust-like manner to protect public benefits in some settings. Specifically in a 1990 decision (*R. v. Sparrow*, 1 S.C.R. 1075 at 1108, [1990]) the court ruled that Aboriginal rights to fish could be curtailed in an apparent move to recognize the government's responsibility to protect environmental resources for the public interest.

Other examples of the Public Trust Doctrine's existence in Canada are found in some of its territories. In 1990, the Northwest Territories enacted its Environmental Rights Act, which provided in

Section 6 the need "to protect the integrity, biological diversity, and productivity of the ecosystems in the Northwest Territories" and the right to protect the environment and the public trust. In 1991, the Yukon Territory enacted its Environment Act in which it recognized that government is "trustee of the public trust to protect the natural environment from actual or likely impairment." Neither of these statutes has yet been tested to affirm their effectiveness in protecting public natural resources. Until there is broader acceptance of a doctrinal concept in Canada similar to the Public Trust Doctrine applied in the United States, the actions of natural resource managers will continue to be based primarily on that country's broad, flexible responsibility for natural resource stewardship and the desire to implement "wise policy" to protect the public interest rather than by a legal obligation imposed by a public trust.

DUTIES OF TRUSTEES

Where it applies, the Public Trust Doctrine creates a duty of supervisory control, or stewardship, over the waters of navigable streams, their nonnavigable tributaries, and fishery and wildlife resources. In addition, trust purposes and obligations are being extended to land resources (Sax 1999). Although navigable and nonnavigable waters are widely appropriated for drinking, industrial, agricultural supplies, or other off-stream uses, the Public Trust Doctrine requires that harm to trust purposes be prevented or minimized whenever feasible. Water rights or other regulatory approvals for private uses may not, and do not, vest in a manner harmful to these purposes. Further, such water rights must remain subject to review and amendment on the basis of current knowledge and needs. Put differently, no private uses are grandfathered against continuing supervision to achieve the trust purposes. Regulations that authorize such private uses should be administered in a manner consistent with trust purposes.

The leading precedent, *National Audubon Society v. Superior Court of Alpine County* (33 Cal.3d 419 [1983]), confirmed that the Public Trust Doctrine, as common law, implicitly conditions water rights granted under regulation. The Mono Lake cases concerned the City of Los Angeles Department of Water and Power (LADWP) appropriation of all flows of the nonnavigable tributaries to Mono Lake—a terminal lake on the eastern slope of the Sierra Nevada (Figure 4-1). The California State Water Resources Control Board (SWRCB) had unconditionally granted these appropriation rights

in 1941. The Board based its granting of these rights on its interpretation that the California Water Code did not authorize any mitigation of foreseeable harm to environmental quality. Forty-two years later, the level and water quality of the lake had declined to such an extent that great harm was occurring to habitat for migratory waterfowl, two species of invertebrates, and fish habitat in tributary streams. These streams once supported vibrant trout fisheries, but, after 42 years of exploitation, had essentially become dry washes (Figure 4-2). The California Supreme Court held that LADWP's rights remain subject to review and amendment under authority of the Public Trust Doctrine. The court mandated that the lower courts and the SWRCB undertake an objective review to determine whether the trust purposes of the lake and tributaries could be restored and protected, and if such restoration would be consistent with LADWP's legitimate need to provide water supply. In subsequent proceedings, the SWRCB determined that it was necessary to reduce LADWP's water diversions from Mono Lake tributaries by three-quarters in order to raise and maintain the lake to a level sufficient to protect waterfowl and other avian and invertebrate species and to meet fish, habitat, and channel dynamic needs in the affected tributaries. The SWRCB also mandated that LADWP develop and implement a plan to restore the degraded stream channels.

FIGURE 4-1. Demand for water by the City of Los Angeles from Rush Creek and other tributaries to Mono Lake, in the Sierra Nevada, resulted in lake level declines of more than 40 feet. Subsequent degradation of trout populations in Rush Creek prompted a landmark lawsuit based, in part, on the Public Trust Doctrine.

FIGURE 4-2. Rush Creek, the principle tributary to Mono Lake in the Sierra Nevada, California, was historically subject to periodic dewatering by the City of Los Angeles (*upper photo*). Restoration of flows (*lower two photos*) was an important aspect of the court's ruling in the Mono Lake case. Note the recovery of riparian vegetation following flow restoration.

Navigable waters throughout the United States and Canada have been developed for water supply and other necessary off-stream uses. Although the Public Trust Doctrine does not prohibit such development, it does direct that such uses should be consistent with trust purposes whenever feasible. The doctrine has not been implemented consistently in water allocation decisions, and, in fact, was seldom implemented until the late 1990s (Slade et al. 1997). This is evidenced by the widespread and substantial degradation or loss of fish and wildlife populations and habitats, even in circumstances where such degradation was avoidable.

In jurisdictions where it exists, the doctrine can vary considerably in its form and application, as shaped by individual cases. Such variation can be viewed as both a strength and limitation. But, whether currently expressed in law or not, the tenets of the Public Trust Doctrine provide the legal basis and responsibility for states and provinces to actively advocate for aquatic natural resource management even in the face of strong political and economic forces to the contrary.

Although the Public Trust Doctrine is a potentially powerful tool when used in the right circumstances, it is not a self-enforcing doctrine. Rather, it is only effective when used in tandem with other statutes, regulations, or policies—and then only applies to federally defined navigable waters. In situations where it can be shown that water allocation is causing significant harm to trust resources, the doctrine can strengthen other environmental laws.

Society faces increasingly difficult choices in deciding river management approaches for such things as navigation, wastewater treatment, and industrial cooling, which were traditionally thought to be beneficial or, at worst, benign. Navigation (Figure 4-3) is a widely recognized beneficial use of large river systems. However, impacts to river ecosystems from barge traffic, the operation of locks and dams, and maintenance of the associated dredging channel are now recognized as potentially significant. Consequently, ongoing public support for this management approach is becoming more controversial as competing visions for river management raise questions about the long-term costs and benefits.

Federal laws developed in the United States in the 1970's are intended to protect clean water. However, as populations increase in large cities, additional strain is placed on sewage systems and the expense to treat the water rises along with pressure to relax water quality standards (Figure 4-4).

Nuclear energy is a source of power in the United States that requires large amounts of water for cooling (Figure 4-5). Such water withdrawals represent potential impacts to a variety of riverine organisms—including diverse mussel and fisheries populations. Impacts to aquatic life need to be addressed in energy development plans.

The effectiveness of all these legal remedies increases when supported by sound, multidisciplinary scientific investigations. Such investigations should reflect the importance, dynamics, and interconnectivity of biological, physical, and hydrological processes. Because the doctrine forms the basis for resource decisions, the IFC encourages an awareness of its principles in whatever capacity the doctrine may exist in a particular jurisdiction. Perhaps more than any other legal instrument, the

principles of the Public Trust Doctrine support state and provincial instream flow practitioners who are confronted with activities that may harm public natural resources.

Where it is recognized, the doctrine may be incorporated directly into regulatory laws that codify and implement the doctrine. When recognized in statute, the doctrine expressly conditions administrative processes and approvals for water allocation or reservation. For example, the Connecticut Environmental Protection Act (CONN. GEN. STAT. §§ 22a-14 through 22a-20) requires a prudent balance of development and conservation of the state's waters, where impairment of environmental quality is prevented or mitigated to the extent feasible. It states, "That there is a public trust in the air, water, and other natural resources of the state of Connecticut, and that each person is entitled to the protection, preservation, and enhancement of the same."

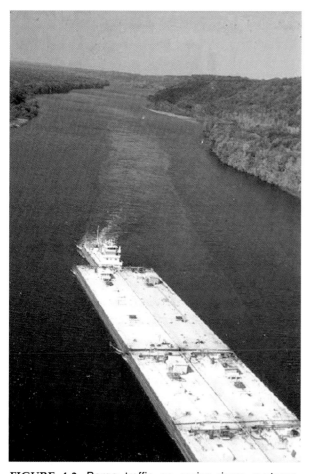

FIGURE 4-3. Barge traffic on major rivers systems, shown here on the upper Mississippi River, can have a wide range of negative effects on trust resources—effects that were often overlooked when river navigation facilities were put in place.

FIGURE 4-4. The importance of wastewater treatment plants—such as the Red Wing, Minnesota, sewage treatment plant on the Mississippi River—continues to grow in proportion to population.

FIGURE 4-5. Xcel Energy's Prairie Island Nuclear Power Plant on the Mississippi River, southeastern Minnesota.

Regulatory laws may also incorporate the doctrine's concepts and obligations by providing recognition and consideration of specific natural values. For example, California prohibits development of certain waters whose highest and best use is preservation in their wild and natural condition (CAL. PUB. RES. CODE § 5093.50; Figure 4-6):

It is the policy of the state of California that certain rivers which possess extraordinary scenic, recreational, fishery, or wildlife values shall be preserved in their free-flowing state, together with the immediate environments, for the benefit and enjoyment of the people of the state. The Legislature declares that such use of these rivers is the highest and most beneficial use and is a reasonable and beneficial use of water within the meaning of Section 2 of Article X of the California Constitution. It is the purpose of this chapter to create a California Wild and Scenic Rivers System to be administered in accordance with the provisions of this chapter.

In addition to being specifically referenced in statute, duties under the doctrine have been incorporated into the constitutions of some states. The Pennsylvania Constitution (art. I, § 27) states that:

The people have a right to clean air, pure water, and preservation of the natural, scenic, and esthetic values of the environment. Pennsylvania public natural re-

sources are the common property of all of the people, including generations yet to come. As trustee for these resources, the Commonwealth shall conserve and maintain them for the benefit of all the people.

In Hawaii, some rivers are afforded protection under the constitution to preserve their natural beauty for present and future generations (Figure 4-7). The Waiahole, Waianu, Waikane, and Kahana streams were affected by the Waiahole Ditch Contested Case Hearing (Hawaii Commission on Water Resource Management, Contested Case Hearing number CCH-OA95-1), which was appealed to the Hawaii Supreme Court and remanded back to the State Commission on Water Resource Management (Commission) for additional findings and conclusions. In its final decision on remand, the Commission set interim instream flow standards for the four streams "far in excess of the flow in these streams during the 1960s, when witnesses for the windward parties have testified that the vitality of these streams was still in evidence." The state supreme court's decision "acknowledged

FIGURE 4-7. Under Hawaii's Constitution, the Waikane River on Oahu Island has been protected, in part, for its natural beauty to benefit present and future generations (Source: Dean Uyeno, Commission on Water Resource Management, Hawaii Department of Land and Natural Resources).

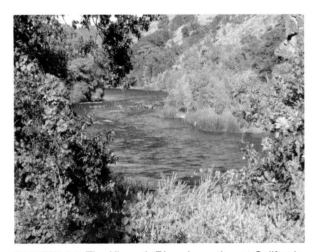

FIGURE 4-6. The Klamath River, in northwest California, is an example of a river that has been protected from development by California law on the basis of its wild and natural condition.

resource protection, with its numerous derivative public uses, benefits, and values, as an important underlying purpose of the reserved water resources trust," and held that "the maintenance of waters in their natural state constitutes a distinct 'use' under the water resources trust."

The Hawaii Constitution (art. X, § 1) reads:

> For the benefit of present and future generations, the state and its political subdivisions shall conserve and protect Hawaii's natural beauty and all natural resources, including land, water, air, minerals and energy sources, and shall promote the development and utilization of these resources in a manner consistent with their conservation and in furtherance of the self-sufficiency of the state. All public natural resources are held in trust by the state for the benefit of the people.

IFC Public Trust Policy Statement: Laws, regulations, and/or policies affecting fishery and wildlife resources and the habitats upon which they depend should be based on the state or province's legal stewardship responsibilities to manage those resources for the benefit and enjoyment of present and future generations.

INSTREAM WATER RIGHTS

The rain is plenteous but, by God's decree,
Only a third is meant for you and me;
Two-thirds are taken by the growing things
Or vanish Heavenward on vapour's wings:
Nor does it mathematically fall
With social equity on one and all.
The population's habit is to grow
In every region where the water's low:
Nature is blamed for failings that are Man's,
And well-run rivers have to change their plans.
— Sir Alan Herbert, *Water*

Acquisition of instream water rights or permits is often the only mechanism available to ensure protection of instream flow needs, particularly on a long-term basis. As Estes (1998) noted, "It is better to reserve water today as opposed to attempting to restore a fraction of whatever water is remaining in the future. The latter is a losing

proposition and, more often than not, irreversible." Some states and provinces provide at least partial legal mechanisms for allocation of instream flows, but many do not.

Streamflow affects a stream's form and function and is fundamental in determining the ecological health of aquatic and riparian systems. In many states and provinces, short- and long-term certainty of inter- and intraannual streamflow is often tenuous. Moreover, the struggle to maintain streamflow in specific systems often recurs with each new proposal for an off-stream water use.

It is better to reserve water today as opposed to attempting to restore a fraction of whatever water is remaining in the future. The latter is a losing proposition and, more often than not, irreversible.

Acquisition of permanent instream water rights or reservations would provide certainty for protection of stream and riparian resources and habitats. It is important for states and provinces to have and exercise the power to hold instream water rights or reservations for the express purpose of managing fishery and wildlife resources to fulfill their stewardship responsibilities.

Providing opportunities for organizations, groups, or individuals to acquire, dedicate, or hold instream water rights in some settings would also increase the potential benefits to fishery and wildlife resources and habitats as well as to private property owners. Such water dedicated for instream purposes, however, should be consistent with the stated or implied goals of state or provincial fishery and wildlife management agencies for aquatic and riparian fishery and wildlife resource needs and habitat requirements.

In this book we focus on fishery, wildlife, and water management practices and philosophies from the perspective of the states and provinces. Agency stewardship responsibilities and statutory authorities often differ from the responsibilities of private individuals and other levels of government. However, opportunities for acquiring or managing instream flows exist at several levels. These may include opportunities for private individuals or entities to manage water supplies to achieve their personal or economic goals. They may also include opportunities to manage waters under federal authorities. In the discussion that follows, we address some of the issues associated with instream flow management by and for these various sectors.

FEDERAL LAWS

The states and provinces share many common objectives when it comes to maintaining, rehabilitating, or restoring riverine resources. Over the past 30 years, several laws have been developed at the federal level to address the protection, rehabilitation, and restoration of riverine resources in the United States and Canada; examples include the Fisheries Act in Canada and the Clean Water Act (CWA), Endangered Species Act (ESA), and National Environmental Policy Act (NEPA) in the United States. These important laws, although controversial at times, have been reasonably effective in dealing with water quality issues at the national level.

However, federal efforts to address water quantity issues at the state or provincial level have sometimes encountered more difficulty. Certainly, there have been circumstances in which state and provincial laws have been effectively meshed with federal laws to benefit instream resources. The Dosewallips case in Washington State (*Jefferson County Public Utility District Number 1 v. Washington Department of Ecology*, 511 U.S. 700 [1994]) is one such example that allowed the state rather than the Federal Energy Regulatory Commission to use federal law to regulate streamflow for instream resources. Contentious situations are most likely to occur when states and provinces believe that their primacy over administration of water permits and rights is being threatened or usurped by a federal action. The unfortunate result in many cases is painful, expensive, and time-consuming litigation that redirects critically short assets that could be more productively spent managing riverine resources.

Because states and provinces have primacy over water allocation within their boundaries, we contend that the effectiveness of most federal natural resource laws will be greater when they are integrated with state and provincial water law. The current controversy surrounding administration of water in the Klamath River in Oregon illustrates this concept very well. Briefly, under the authority of the ESA, the federal government temporarily redirected water that was allocated to irrigators by the state for habitat rehabilitation of endangered fishes in the Klamath River. Water supplies in this system are not great enough to

meet both the needs of riverine resources and irrigators. The resulting loss of water for one year generated hostile sentiments, acts of violence, and distrust at all levels. The state and federal governments have yet to find an acceptable, permanent solution to this impasse.

The state of Idaho recently faced a somewhat similar situation on the Lemhi River where populations of endangered chinook salmon (*Oncorhynchus tshawytscha*), steelhead trout (*O. mykiss*) and bull trout (*Salvelinus confluentis*) were threatened by low flows caused by irrigation withdrawals from the river (Figure 4-8). Here, in anticipation of federal actions like those on the Klamath, the Idaho legislature passed a statute establishing an instream flow of 35 cfs on a portion of the Lemhi. It also authorized establishment of a natural flow water bank—the first of its kind in Idaho. Ranchers are allowed to place active irrigation water rights in the water bank to be used for instream flow in exchange for monetary compensation. The Bonneville Power Administration provided $8 million to assist with water right acquisition and other habitat rehabilitation efforts. (Cindy Robertson, Idaho Fish and Game, personal communication). The restoration of flows resulting from the natural flow water bank has partially addressed federal resource manage-

FIGURE 4-8. Authorized by statute, the established direct flow water bank for the Lemhi River in northeastern Idaho is one example of how fishery management objectives associated with federal laws and mandates can be addressed within the framework of state water laws (Source: Idaho Fish and Game Department).

ment objectives to rehabilitate critically important habitat for the three endangered fishes and, importantly, was achieved within a legal framework that recognized state water law and administrative authority.

One of the hurdles to finding solutions such as those on the Lemhi is an institutional one in that federal and state or provincial governments often view one another as competitors instead of cooperators. Further, some federal laws are written with little if any reference to the need to recognize and integrate state or provincial water laws into management solutions. Even in such cases as the Lemhi, the solutions are never simple and they still require much time, money, and cooperation. However, institutional hurdles must be overcome if government at all levels is to be a more effective steward for public fishery resources.

Another challenge to using state and provincial laws to address federal resource management objectives is that states and provinces often do not have the laws necessary to administer water properly. State or provincial law does not typically accommodate long-term, temporary change of use or leases. The Lemhi Water Bank required a specific act of the Idaho legislature, and few other states or provinces even have such mechanisms. The few that do, such as California, have generally structured them to facilitate the reallocation of water from one consumptive use to another. In addition, few states or provinces have legal constructs that encourage water conservation. Many western states administer water according to the Free River Principle, which in essence means that whenever one user is not using her water right—either by choice or conservation—that water is "free" to other users on the river. Without the ability to legally manage conserved water for specific purposes, conservation actions or mandates often generate no additional water that can be legally protected for the benefit of riverine resources. The bottom line is that much work remains to be done to improve federal, state, and provincial legal opportunities for protecting riverine resources.

IFC Federal Water Management Policy Statement: Federal agencies should integrate their water and riverine management efforts within the constructs of state and provincial laws, regulations, and policies to protect riverine resources.

STATE AND PROVINCIAL OPPORTUNITIES

Many western states have enacted laws, or established programs, wherein the state may hold instream flows to protect fish, wildlife, recreation, riparian areas, and aesthetics (Potter 1988). Many others states and provinces, however, do not have similar laws or programs. Instream water rights may be obtained, for example, in Alaska, Arizona, California, Colorado, Idaho, Nebraska, Nevada, South Dakota, Utah, and Wyoming. Other jurisdictions, such as Florida, Iowa, Kansas, Minnesota, Montana, Oregon, Pennsylvania, Virginia, Washington, and the province of Alberta allow specific agencies to establish instream flow reservations (Reiser et al. 1989; Lamb and Lord 1992). Whereas water rights and reservations are similar, in many states and provinces a "water right" is defined as a right to appropriate water for a specific purpose (e.g., in- and off-stream uses), and a "reservation" specifies a streamflow or water level below which diversion is prohibited.

Even with the best laws, acquiring and protecting instream flows via water rights or reservations may be a protracted and uncertain process. For example, the Alaska Department of Fish and Game, despite enjoying perhaps the most comprehensive instream flow protection laws in the United States and Canada, is hampered in its ability to secure instream flow rights in many streams primarily due to institutional constraints and low level of administrative commitment within the Department of Natural Resources (Estes 1998). The Alaska Department of Natural Resources (ALASKA STAT. § 46.15) has jurisdiction of streamflows and water allocations (Estes 1998). Although the Alaska Department of Fish and Game has applied for 76 instream flow water rights, the Department of Natural Resources has processed and granted only 10 (Estes 1998).

IFC State and Provincial Water Rights Policy Statement: State and provincial laws, regulations, and policies should provide the authority, opportunity, procedure, and process to enable a state or provincial fishery and wildlife agency the right to obtain and/or hold instream water rights, reservations, or licenses in perpetuity for the specific purpose of protecting, rehabilitating, restoring, and managing fishery and wildlife resources and habitats and other trust resources.

PRIVATE INSTREAM FLOW OPPORTUNITIES

Although some states have provided for acquisition of instream flow water rights, reservations, or licenses, the opportunity to do so is often limited to a specific agency(s). For example, in Nebraska, only the Game and Parks Commission and Natural Resource districts may apply for and hold instream appropriations, and such appropriations must be for fish, wildlife, or aesthetics (NEB. REV. STAT. § 46-2,108). The ability of public agencies to acquire and hold instream water rights is a valuable tool. However, providing opportunities for citizens in the private sector to apply for and hold instream water rights would provide additional opportunities to benefit instream fishery and aquatic wildlife resources and processes and private property.

Some states and provinces provide the private sector the opportunity to hold instream water rights; examples include, Alaska, Arizona, and Nevada (Gillilan and Brown 1997). California (CAL. WATER CODE § 1707) and South Dakota (S.D. CODIFIED LAWS § 46-2A-12) allow private parties to change the purpose of existing water rights from off-stream uses to instream uses. The Fish Protection Act of British Columbia (S.B.C. [1997] Chapter 21) allows a right for instream use to be held by a community organization that has a demonstrated interest in the stream. To date, however, few if any cases exist where this has actually happened.

Any mechanism for allowing private instream flow water rights should be structured to integrate with the state or provincial instream program and with other existing uses. Reservations or licenses should be limited to such waters as may be used without being excessive for the purpose defined in the permit application. Specific mechanisms for providing private ownership should be determined by each state or province according to the particular needs of their citizens and legal systems.

IFC Private Instream Flow Rights Policy Statement: State and provincial laws, regulations, and policies should provide the authority, opportunity, procedure, and process to enable an organization, group, or individual the right to obtain, retain, secure, and/or hold instream water rights for individual streams or rivers, or specific sections of individual streams or rivers, for the specific purpose of benefiting fisheries and wildlife and other in-channel purposes.

LEGAL STATUS OF INSTREAM FLOW PROTECTION

In addition to recognizing instream flows as a legitimate public use on par with other recognized uses, regulatory laws should also ensure that instream flows have adequate priority to protect aquatic and riparian resources and resource needs because they are essentially public property.

Instream flow needs in many states and provinces often receive low priority during water allocation processes. Further, ongoing protection for instream flows on short- and long-term bases is commonly at risk. In many states and provinces, flows that were allocated for instream purposes during previous water allocation proceedings are subject to modification as new demands for off-stream water uses develop. Most other kinds of water rights are not subjected to the same type of modification or review. Without sufficient legal recognition and protection, aquatic resources and habitats will continue to experience adverse impacts due to low priority; thus, uncertainty in maintaining streamflow regimes will continue in the short- and long-term.

The importance of effective rules in protecting streamflows is demonstrated in the Mono Lake, California, cases. For many years, virtually all water had been diverted from four of the lake's major tributaries for municipal water supply and hydroelectric generation (Jones and Stokes Associates 1994). Although these uses are recognized as important beneficial uses of water (CAL. WATER CODE § 1201), the uses did not automatically preempt consideration and protection of instream and riparian requirements. Fishery and wildlife uses are also recognized as beneficial uses of water. But, more significantly, specific protection is provided for fish and instream flows when dams are built (CAL. FISH & GAME CODE §§ 5937 and 5946). This protection was not exercised during the original water allocation proceedings. However, when these sections were linked with the Public Trust Doctrine in proceedings many years later, the combination became a very powerful tool for rehabilitating, restoring and maintaining the streams, streamflows, and lake levels. It should be noted, however, that section 5946, which is the more powerful of the two sections, applies only to eastern Sierra Nevada streams and does not extend to other California systems.

Other states have regulatory laws that recognize instream flows as a beneficial use but designate such uses as a secondary priority or preference and do not require the administering agencies to use due diligence to prevent or minimize conflicts between off-stream uses and trust purposes. For example, Arizona (ARIZ. REV. STAT. § 45-157), recognizes fish and wildlife as beneficial uses of water, but rank this use below domestic and municipal, irrigation and stock watering, power and mining uses, and equal with recreation uses.

The state of Nebraska provides another example where instream flows receive a lower priority than other uses. Previously allocated instream flows and water rights are subordinate to and thus, subject to depletion by, demands for municipal water supply, new storage projects with less than 200 acre-feet per year evaporation losses, and undefined de minimus diversions.

In most of the eastern United States and Canada, the riparian doctrine provides some protection for instream flows. In particular, the doctrine applies to off-stream uses that typically require a physical connection between stream or river front property and the waterway. Although this doctrine may afford some protection, there remains significant concern that existing laws may not allow equitable allocation of water to meet competing uses and that off-stream demands will be given priority over instream needs as competition for water increases (Dixon and Cox 1985). This concern could be alleviated when other laws and regulations are enacted that provide fishery and wildlife agencies other tools to maintain or acquire instream flows.

States and provinces should use any avenue available to (1) promote enactment of statutes that recognize instream and off-stream uses on equal footing with other kinds of water rights, reservations, and licenses; (2) administer regulatory statutes, regulations, and policies to ensure that off-stream uses are managed in a manner that prevents or minimizes harm to aquatic and riparian resources and habitats; and (3) ensure that previously allocated off-stream rights are administered according to the uses and limitations specified in their licenses or permits pursuant to each state's or province's statutes.

IFC Instream Flow Priority and Legal Standing Policy Statement: Instream flow rights, reservations, and licenses to restore, manage, and/or protect the aquatic resources of streams, rivers, and lakes should have priority and legal standing to protect aquatic resources.

WATER RIGHTS AND LONG-TERM CERTAINTY

Insofar as managing instream flow is a fundamental element of conserving public natural resources, instream flow water rights should be perpetual. The only exception should be when future information and an evaluation and conclusion by the state or provincial fishery and wildlife agency indicate that a change in the instream flow right would be appropriate for better management and protection of public fishery and aquatic wildlife resources and processes.

Opportunities to protect instream water rights, reservations, and licenses are limited in many states and provinces. For example, Just (1990) noted that instream rights provided under the instream flow statute in Idaho (IDAHO CODE §§ 42-1501 to 42- 1505) failed to hold the same legal stature as traditional diverted uses because instream flow rights are subject to review or revision every 10 to 15 years or at unspecified future dates. Harle and Estes (1993) expressed the same concern regarding instream rights in Alaska. There, instream uses are at a competitive disadvantage compared to existing and potential off-stream uses because the statute (ALASKA STAT. § 46.15.080[f]) specifies review every 10 years for all instream reservations and allows potential modification or revocation of the right. There is no renewal requirement or potential modification or revocation provision for out-of-stream reservations (Estes 1998).

The state of Nebraska's first instream appropriation (NEB. REV. STAT. § 46-2,115) was granted in 1989 (Aiken 1990; Figure 4-9). Although this statute is a precedent-setting measure that offers the opportunity to advance instream flow protection in the state, permanent protection of instream flow reservations in Nebraska is limited by provisions that require review of instream appropriations for fish, wildlife, and recreation every 15 years. To continue, the appropriation must be in the public interest and for beneficial purposes. Accordingly, instream uses remain at a competitive disadvantage because off-stream uses are not subject to such requirements.

Montana's version of instream flow rights allocation (MONT. CODE ANN. § 85-2-419) involves leasing water to restore instream flows within degraded systems. The lease must be reviewed after 10 years. Moreover, an existing lease may be renewed only once for up to an additional 10 years. A water lease derived from conservation or water storage, however, may be initially leased for up to

20 years (McKinney 1991). As in other states, off-stream uses in Montana are not subject to the same requirements and clearly have long-term certainty and competitive advantage.

There are several examples in which states, such as Wyoming, Arizona, and Texas, afford instream water rights long-term certainty and apparent permanency. Wyoming's instream allocation statutes (WYO. STAT. §§ 41-3-1001 to 1013) do not require periodic review, although, as for any other water right, the State Engineer may make periodic review a condition of the permit. Hence, such rights are essentially permanent once they are adjudicated. In Arizona, instream rights are vested (ARIZ. REV. STAT. § 45-151 et seq.), and as long as the holder of such rights continues to put the water to beneficial use that right is retained (Dishlip 1993). Texas may provide semi-permanency for instream water allocations. The Texas Water Trust was established within the Texas Water Bank to hold water rights dedicated to environmental needs, including instream flows, water quality, fish and wildlife habitat, and bay and estuary inflows (TEX. WATER CODE § 15.7031). Section 15.7031 (d) of the Water Trust states that, "Water rights may be held in the trust for a term specified by contractu-al agreement or in perpetuity." However, at this writing, the Texas legislature has placed a moratorium on granting new instream flow rights with a provision requiring additional studies.

Instream water rights, reservations, and licenses should be granted in perpetuity. Such long-term certainty is necessary if state and provincial fishery and wildlife agencies are to meet their custodial stewardship responsibilities and ensure that aquatic and riparian fishery and wildlife resources and habitats receive appropriate consideration and protection. To this end, states and provinces that have instream allocation statutes, regulations, or policies that provide only temporary status or requirements for periodic review of instream flows should seek opportunities to afford the same level of permanency to those rights as given to other kinds of uses. States and provinces that do not have such statutes, regulations, or policies should explore opportunities to establish statutes and other laws to eliminate inequities that jeopardize the long-term certainty of instream rights.

IFC Water Rights Certainty Policy Statement: State and provincial instream water rights, reservations, and licenses should be afforded permanent status to enable them to fulfill their custodial trust obligations for stream, river, and lake aquatic resources.

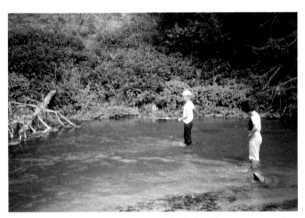

FIGURE 4-9. Mike Ibanez and Jock Davison prepare for fishing on Long Pine Creek in north central Nebraska. Long Pine Creek represents an example in which a public agency applied for and obtained instream flow rights for fish, wildlife, or aesthetic beauty. Long Pine Creek was the first stream in Nebraska that was granted an instream flow appropriation to preserve naturally reproducing populations of brown trout (*salmo salar*) and rainbow trout (*Oncorhynchus mykiss*). Several parties contested the application, and the approval was appealed to the Nebraska Supreme Court. The court affirmed the instream flow appropriation and the constitutionality of the Nebraska instream flow statute (Source: Larry Hutchinson, Division of Aquatic Resources, Nebraska Game and Parks Commission).

BENEFICIAL USE

The principle of beneficial use forms the basis, measure, and limit of water that may be allocated for use by municipalities, industry, or individuals in the western United States. Virtually all states that regulate appropriation of water—Oklahoma and Colorado are notable exceptions—require a determination that a proposed appropriation is in the public interest and a finding that the use is beneficial (Grant 1987), meaning that the allocation is for a recognized use (e.g., irrigation) and that the amount of water claimed is roughly proportionate to the amount required to accomplish the stated purpose. Wyoming's Constitution (WYO. CONST. art. VIII, § 3) states, "No appropriation shall be denied except when such denial is demanded by the public interest." Unfortunately, this requirement is often weakened by exemptions that allow cumulative adverse impacts to fishery and wildlife resources and habitats; for example, water diversions are defined as small projects that are often permitted with little or no consideration of environmental impacts. In Montana, the "small" threshold is a quantity not exceeding 4,000 acre-feet per year or 5.5 cubic feet per second (cfs) (McKinney 1990).

Similarly, regulatory statutes in several eastern states exempt agricultural uses, public water supply, or diversion for steam power plants and oil and gas recovery (Goldfarb 1988). Such exemptions clearly undermine the ability to ensure that offstream uses do not cause unnecessary harm to instream flows. Exemptions also create inequities against regulated uses (Ausness 1983). This is the basis on which the concept of beneficial use was formed. In those states that define beneficial uses of water—either by statute or constitutional law—instream flows are often not included. Thus, in the 1970s, it was common for water users to argue that instream flows could not be considered a beneficial use. Although some uncertainty remains today in a few states concerning instream flows as beneficial uses, that argument seems unlikely to be upheld by most courts or legislatures. Instead, the issues turn on who may claim instream flows, how much water can be claimed, and what constitutes acceptable purposes of instream flows (e.g., recreation, water quality, esthetics, fish and wildlife, riparian habitat).

Most states do not specifically define beneficial use. Rather, they recognize beneficial uses under the broad administrative authorities of their water regulation agencies. Historically, beneficial use included only domestic and municipal use, irrigation, power production, and manufacturing (Grant 1987; Sax et al. 1991). Some early regulatory laws may also have recognized instream flow as beneficial for the purpose of determining whether water was available for off-stream uses (Just 1990). In 1927, the Idaho legislature (IDAHO CODE § 67-4301) directed the governor to " . . appropriate water in trust for the people of the state of Idaho all the appropriated water of Big Payette Lake, or so much thereof as may be necessary to preserve said lake in its present condition. The preservation of said water in said lake for scenic beauty, health and recreation purposes necessary and desirable for all the inhabitants of the state is hereby declared to be a beneficial use of such waters." Oregon legislation (OR. STAT. § 537.170 [8] [a]) enacted in 1929 stated that it was in the public interest to consider the effect of water appropriations on public recre-

ation and commercial and game fishing (Grant 1987).

Legal recognition of instream flow for maintaining aquatic organisms and habitats as a beneficial use in the United States did not become widespread until the 1970s (Shupe and MacDonnell 1993; Sax 1999). Many states, including Alaska, California, and Washington subsequently expanded the list of legitimate instream uses to include recreation, aesthetics, and preservation of fish and wildlife (Sax et al. 1991).

The Alaska Water Law (ALASKA STAT. § 46.15.080 [b]) comprehensively defines beneficial use in terms of the public interest to include the purposes first recognized in the Public Trust Doctrine (Grant 1987; Sax et al. 1991). Briefly, it says that the state has the responsibility "to develop and manage the basic resources of water, land, and air to the end that the state may fulfill its responsibility as trustee of the environment for the present and future generations." Consideration of the impacts on fish and game resources, public recreation, and access to navigable waters is required during public interest review.

In California, "the use of water for recreation and preservation and enhancement of fish and wildlife resources is a beneficial use" (CAL. WATER CODE § 1243). Section 1243.5 states that "in determining the amount of water available for appropriation, the California State Water Resources Control Board shall take into account the amount of bypass flow needed for the protection of beneficial uses."

In the state of Washington, the Department of Ecology is authorized to "establish minimum water flows or levels for streams, lakes or other public waters for the purposes of protecting fish, game, birds, or other wildlife resources, or recreational or aesthetic values of said public waters whenever it appears to be in the public interest to establish the same" (WASH. REV. CODE ANN. § 90.22.010; Figure 4-10).

PUBLIC INTEREST

In Canada, the concept of beneficial use as it applies in the western United States has not become part of the common law other than through rules or policies against wasting water. Instead, water licensing provisions and priority schemes have primarily been set by statute. The issue of public interest is a factor in allocating water but its determination, as in the United States, is broadly interpreted and generally decided according to the circumstances of each application and relevant regulatory authority.

To ensure that they have the authority to issue new water rights, permits, or licenses for instream purposes, it is essential that states and provinces recognize instream uses for fishery and wildlife resources as being in the public interest. Legal recognition of instream flow in the public interest, and the need to protect that interest, is also important when water regulators review applications for new permits for out-of-channel uses or applications for changes of existing uses.

The role of public interest in the formation and application of laws was addressed by The National Research Council (2002):

> Public interest considerations should be included among the third party issues and legal provisions for permitting, conditioning, and denying water transfers. To protect third parties in water rights transfers, the public interest language in western states' water laws should be reviewed, clarified, and, where appropriate, more vigorously applied. States should develop definitions and criteria for assessing what constitutes the public interest, perhaps benefiting from legislative and judicial experiences of the states of Idaho and Alaska. Such definitions should embrace existing water rights holders, environmental water needs for ecosystem protection, and social and cultural values in basins of origin.

Although many states are reluctant to develop definitions or lists of water uses that are in the public interest, the public would be well served by such definitions—if they are lacking in statute— that recognize water uses such as instream flow as equal with other traditional uses.

IFC Public Interest Policy Statement: States and provinces should designate instream uses of water as in the public interest and/or beneficial uses to ensure that riverine resources and processes are considered on an equal basis with other traditional uses of water.

CONNECTIVITY OF SURFACE FLOW AND GROUNDWATER

Streams and rivers and shallow groundwater (or underflow) are often hydrologically linked. When such water is extracted from shallow groundwater aquifers, there may be related short- or long-term reductions in connected surface flows. The potential for such surface flow reductions often is not considered during water allocation processes, and, thus, subsurface water extractions may lead to unmitigated adverse impacts to stream and riparian fishery and wildlife resources and habitats. Consequently, the regulation and allocation of water should recognize the tributary relation between subsurface and surface waters (Sherk 1986).

Some states are beginning to recognize the interconnectivity and potential impacts of subsurface water extraction. Colorado (COLO. REV. STAT. § 37-90-103 [10.5]) now defines groundwater as tributary to surface waters under specified conditions, and this definition "effectively transforms hydrologically connected groundwater into surface water under the prior appropriation doctrine" (Glennon 1995). California also recognizes the interconnectivity and its importance in several sys-

FIGURE 4-10. Since 1971, the state of Washington has provided instream flow protection for fish, wildlife, or recreational or aesthetic values. Tumwater Falls on the Deschutes River near Olympia, Washington, was one of the earliest streams to be afforded public interest protection (Source: Steve Boessow, Washington Department of Fish and Wildlife).

tems and requires evaluation and appropriative permits for subsurface water extractions (CAL. WATER CODE § 1200). In the South, Mississippi has adopted a conjunctive approach to managing its surface and subsurface waters (MISS. CODE § 51-3-1) as has New Hampshire in the East (N.H. REV. STAT. § 485-C:1; Sherk 1986). The Connecticut Water Diversion Policy Act (CONN. GEN. STAT. § 22a-365 et seq.) requires a permit for any withdrawal exceeding 50,000 gallons per day (gpd) from both groundwater and surface water sources. The same criteria, including impacts on fisheries, wildlife, and instream flows, are applied to all applications. Unless the applicant submits convincing evidence to the contrary, the state presumes that groundwater withdrawal creates an equivalent (i.e., 1:1) reduction in surface flow. In addition to state agencies recognizing the hydrologic interconnectivity, other organizations are beginning to recognize the importance. For example, the Susquehanna River Basin and Delaware River Basin commissions, which are interstate commissions, coordinate and regulate ground and surface water withdrawals.

IFC Connectivity of Surface and Groundwater (Legal) Policy Statement: The hydrological interconnectivity between groundwater and surface flows should be recognized, and these waters should be conjunctively managed to protect the short- and long-term fundamental public value of fishery and wildlife resources and habitats.

FISHERY AND WILDLIFE AGENCY ROLE

State and provincial fishery and wildlife agencies are stewards for each sovereign's fishery and wildlife resources. This responsibility, coupled with laws, regulations, and policies, typically empowers these agencies to use the best procedures to determine streamflow regimes that are in the interest of fishery and wildlife resources and habitats and for the short- and long-term benefit of the sovereign's citizens. Some states recognize their fishery and wildlife agency's natural resource stewardship responsibilities and expertise and provide avenues to include agency input during water allocation proceedings. Others do not.

Wyoming's instream flow law (WYO. STAT. § 41-3-1001 et seq.) authorizes the Wyoming

Department of Game and Fish to take the lead in identifying instream flow needs. Specifically, this law mandates that "Subsequent to submission of an application for an instream flow appropriation, the game and fish commission shall conduct relevant studies on the proposal."

The state of Washington requires that all water right applications from the Department of Ecology (the water allocation agency) be submitted to the Department of Fish and Wildlife to determine if issuing the water right would reduce the streamflow below the level needed to adequately support food fish and game fish populations (WASH. REV. CODE § 77.55.020). The director of Ecology may refuse to issue a permit if, in is or her opinion, issuing the permit might result in harm to the fishery.

Similarly, in California, when the State Water Resources Control Board reviews requests to appropriate water, it must consult with the California Department of Fish and Game (CAL. WATER CODE § 1243). The department recommends the amounts of water, if any, required for the preservation and enhancement of fishery and wildlife resources and reports its findings to the board. Furthermore, sections 10001 and 10002 empower the Department of Fish and Game to determine instream flow standards on a stream-by-stream basis.

The mandatory involvement of the California Fish and Game Department in instream flow issues implies that aquatic habitats and fisheries will be effectively maintained and protected. The Water Resources Control Board, however, has not been provided a legal directive to protect instream uses. It is only directed to consider instream values in the water allocation process (Gray 1993). As a result, instream flow rights—compared to off-stream appropriations—are granted second-class status (Meyer 1993) and this status often results in adverse impacts to fishery and aquatic wildlife resources and processes.

Because state and provincial fishery and wildlife agencies are vested with the stewardship authority to manage public fishery resources, it is imperative that they also be accorded the primary responsibility for determining instream flow needs within their jurisdictions. Accordingly, regulatory mechanisms and administrative policies should recognize the stewardship responsibility of state and provincial fishery and wildlife management agencies and grant them the primary responsibility for identifying and using appropriate methods to quantify instream flow needs.

IFC Fishery and Wildlife Agency Role Policy Statement: State and provincial fishery and wildlife agencies should have the primary authority for determining appropriate stream and river flow quantity, quality, and other needs and requirements necessary to restore, manage, and protect fishery and aquatic wildlife resources and processes.

WATER CONSERVATION AND INSTREAM FLOW

Stream and river flows vary within and across years, but are finite resources. Past demands for off-stream water uses have resulted in flows of many streams and rivers being fully or nearly fully allocated or dedicated for off-stream uses. In both the United States and Canada, water allocation processes have historically been based on a principle of taking no more water than can be used. In that setting, the instream needs for rehabilitating, restoring or protecting riverine species and habitats often received little consideration. In today's water management climate, managers are gradually modifying the historic water use paradigm to one of permitting no more than is needed. As this transition progresses, the principles of water conservation should be used to proactively address the instream needs of riverine species and habitats.

This same approach applies when jurisdictions oversee the transfer of water rights. Transfers provide a prime opportunity to reallocate a portion of the water being changed to instream flow purposes. Some jurisdictions have already taken advantage of such opportunities. Alberta, for example (Alberta Water Act § 83; Appendix D), allows the regional director for water management in the Department of the Environment to reallocate up to 10% of the original allocation of water that is being transferred to protect the aquatic environment or to implement a water conservation objective. The reallocation must have been authorized in an approved water management plan, or in a Cabinet Order, and the water withheld may not subsequently be granted to any other person. The government may, however, issue a license to itself for that quantity of water, and the new license would have the same priority as the original water license.

Historically, the transfer of water rights in the United States has protected the rights of existing water users but paid little attention to the public needs of maintaining ecologically healthy river systems. Even with the increasing attention given to environmental matters in recent years, water rights transfers do not allow most water regulators to make involuntary reallocations of water for instream purposes unless it is required under the terms of specific legislation or permit conditions. In contrast to Canada, many U.S. laws require that specified flows be maintained in designated areas in priority relative to other existing water rights. Oregon and Australia provide examples of opportunities for reallocating water. In both jurisdictions, the transfer of water rights is used to restore instream flows.

Historically, the transfer of water rights in the United States from one use to another has reflected greater concern for protecting the existing rights of private water users than for addressing needs of ecologically healthy river systems for the general public.

In Oregon, the process depends on one of the unique characteristics of the prior appropriation doctrine. Users only have a legal right to the quantity of water they actually put to beneficial use. If they cease to use some of the water they have been appropriated, they lose that portion of their right. This principle creates a perverse incentive, because a user who invests in technology to conserve water would lose the right to any water that is no longer put to beneficial use.

Under special circumstances, Oregon allows the holder of the right to sell or lease a portion of the amount of water saved through conservation (Reed 1990; Figure 4-11). If the holder of the right wishes to retain the right to conserved water, the holder must first submit a conservation plan to the Oregon Department of Water Resources. The proposal must show, among other things, the difference in the amount or water prescribed by the holder's water right and the amount that will be used after conservation. Upon approval of the proposal, the agency is required to allocate 25% of the saved water to the state for instream purposes and 75% to the applicant. A higher percentage can be allocated for instream needs if state funds are used in the project. The allocations of the saved water to both the state and the original appropriator are given a priority one minute junior to that of the original water right and the original appropriator is then free to transfer his or her portion of the new allocation. An appropriator who implements conservation without prior approval loses the right to all the water conserved, as provided by the ordinary application of the prior appropriation doctrine.

A more direct reservation of water in the transfer process occurs in Australia. In 1983, the regulations under a preexisting Act (The Water Resources Act 1975) were interpreted in South Australia to facilitate provisions that encourage the trading of water rights (McKay 1994). New South Wales and Victoria followed some 5 years later. As a result of the Council of Australian Government reforms starting in 1995, all jurisdictions have, as of 2001, amended their water acts to promote a separation of water from land and to promote trading within sustainable limits (Australian Water Association 2001).

All of these new statutes provide for an instream flow reservation when transfers occur; however, this is expressed in various ways (Jones et al. 2001). In South Australia, for example, the Minister for Water Resources is entitled to allocate to the transferee a lesser quantity of water than was allocated in the original license. The power to reduce the allocation is found in a number of sec-

tions, notably 39(3) and 39(4). The power may be exercised for any purpose consistent with the Act. The Act aims to provide sustainable water allocations and involve the community in setting up plans for regions. This type of reservation is now recognized in the rules established for a pilot project that encourages interstate water trading in one small section of the much-used Murray-Darling Basin (Figure 4-12). In that system, exchange rates have been established that require any transfers upstream from South Australia to New South Wales or Victoria to leave 10% of the original allo-

FIGURE 4-11. Little Creek in northeastern Oregon represents an example in which the ability of a private landowner to transfer a water right to instream flow was challenged by other water right holders but, ultimately, was upheld as a beneficial use.

FIGURE 4-12. On the Murray-Darling River at Albury-Wodonga, Australia (circa 1977), water right transfer rules for a pilot project that encouraged interstate trading of water require that transfers leave 10% of the original allocation in the river system (Source: Jerry I. Nelson, Maclean, Virginia).

cation in the river (Murray-Darling Basin Commission 2000a, 2000b). The exchange rate has been set at 0.9, or a reduction of 10%. Thus, a sale of 10 cfs of water by a licensee in South Australia would result in an allocation of 9 cfs, minus any losses accrued due to conveyance from the point of acquisition to the point of use, to the buyer in New South Wales or Victoria (Murray-Darling Basin Commission 2000b).

Water conservation is also addressed in Montana. "Salvage means to make water available for beneficial use from an existing valid appropriation through application of water saving methods" (MONT. CODE ANN. § 85-2-102 [14]). The Montana legislature deviated from prior law that disfavored the concept of salvage when it enacted section 85-2-419 (Stone 1990), which says that it is the policy of the state to encourage conservation and full use of water. Future use of salvaged water must be consistent with the original place and purpose. Any proposed use elsewhere, or for another purpose, requires state approval. An apparent weakness of this law is its failure to require that conserved flows be dedicated, even in part, to instream flow. Not only does the law fail to require instream flow protection, it also shifts water management benefits away from the public in favor of private privilege by enabling new consumptive uses to acquire historic priority dates (Stone 1990). Such a practice appears at odds with the duty of the states and provinces to protect public natural resources.

These, or other incentive-based opportunities, should be developed and implemented to encourage off-stream water users to conserve water and legally dedicate conserved or unused water to instream purposes. Such programs could substantially contribute to rehabilitation, restoration, management, and protection of public fishery and aquatic wildlife resources and processes. In addition, states and provinces should also review existing allocations and permitted uses for opportunities to encourage water conservation and other opportunities to change the use of existing rights and reservations to instream flow.

IFC Water Conservation Policy Statement: State and provincial governments should develop and implement legal opportunities to enable consumptive water users to conserve water and dedicate conserved or unused water to instream purposes.

WATER QUALITY STANDARDS

In the United States, the federal Clean Water Act (33 U.S.C. § 1251 et seq.) provides that the beneficial uses of navigable waters and their tributaries include environmental quality and recreation. It directs that all beneficial uses will be protected against impairment. It authorizes states to implement the federal program under their regulatory laws upon approval of the U.S. Environmental Protection Agency. It generally provides two opportunities for implementation of the Public Trust Doctrine.

First, pursuant to section 303 of the Clean Water Act, a state may adopt water quality standards that include or support instream flow requirements. For example, the state may designate a specific fishery as a beneficial use of a given stream, and the standard may even specify the distribution and population of that fishery. Further, the implementing standards, known as numerical or narrative criteria, may establish flows and/or physical conditions necessary to attain that beneficial use.

Second, when implementing standards through regulatory approvals for individual federally approved facilities or activities (i.e., section 401 of the Clean Water Act), the state may again specify minimum flows. Although federal law provides this opportunity to the states, it does not require that it be implemented. An example of such an opportunity is the certification of a federally licensed hydropower project that may include such a flow requirement (*Jefferson County Public Utility District Number 1 v. Washington Department of Ecology,* 511 U.S. 700 [1994]; Figure 4-13).

State and provincial fishery and wildlife agencies should recognize the importance of, and opportunities for, considering instream flow needs when addressing water quality standards and requirements. Agencies should also review their water quality laws, regulations, and policies for opportunities to address instream flow issues.

IFC Water Quality Standards Policy Statement: State and provincial fishery and wildlife agencies should include stream and river flow quantity and other needs and requirements necessary to restore, manage, and protect aquatic and riparian fishery and wildlife resources and habitats within water quality standards and permitting processes.

PUBLIC PROJECT FUNDING

States and provinces often provide grants, loans, or other public funding for construction of water management projects. Public funds are also part of a public trust. As such, the trustee of these funds, acting in a regulatory or other capacity, has a duty to oversee their management. Consequently, such funding should stipulate that project construction and operation is consistent with trust purposes and that the benefits do not unreasonably impair the values of other public trust resources.

Unfortunately, in making decisions regarding allocation of funds, states often fall short of fulfilling their public trust responsibilities because they base some actions more on the public interest than the public trust. Provinces, on the other hand, must rely almost entirely on the public interest criterion in the allocation of public funds and have no legal requirement to consider Public Trust Doctrine limitations.

But in those jurisdictions that do recognize the Public Trust Doctrine, the public interest does not subsume the doctrine. Public interest is generally defined in regulatory laws or other statutes in a manner that vests broad discretion in the administering agencies. The Public Trust Doctrine creates a duty to manage trust resources for trust purposes, not additional purposes that are in the public interest. Just as a trustee for an inheritance is required to protect the corpus, the states and provinces are equally bound to manage trust resources for all beneficiaries, including future generations (Sax et al. 1991). Water development projects that rely in part, or whole, on the use of trust financial resources and that have the potential to damage fishery and wildlife resources should include provisions to provide instream flows and other habitat mitigation features.

IFC Public Funding Policy Statement: Public funding for water management projects should include conditions for the protection of instream flows necessary to meet the needs and requirements of aquatic and riparian fishery and wildlife resources and habitats.

FIGURE 4-13. Streamflow on the Dosewallips River near Olympia, Washington, was the subject of a U.S. Supreme Court decision, 31 May 1994, which established that water quantity is an element of water quality under the Clean Water Act and, hence, Section 401 water certification may be used to establish mandatory instream flows for federally licensed projects (Source: Steve Boessow, Washington Department of Fish and Wildlife).

There is only one nature—the division into science and engineering is a human imposition,
not a natural one. Indeed, the division is a human failure; it reflects our limited
capacity to comprehend the whole
                                        —Professor William Wulf, University of Virginia

CHAPTER FIVE

Instream Flow Programs and Site-Specific Prescriptions

Instream flow management is a complex process under any conditions—made more difficult by a highly technical and evolving science, a public with diverse interests, and a maze of legal and institutional hurdles. To be most effective, state and provincial fishery and wildlife agencies must expand their roles to include specific instream flow protection programs that are administered by trained personnel whose primary job is to work with instream flow issues. Such a focus is essential so that agencies can (1) keep current with new methodologies, developing legislation, and institutional arrangements and opportunities; (2) create public awareness programs; and (3) provide opportunities to solicit community feedback and respond to public and stakeholder interests. The concepts presented in this chapter provide guidelines for developing effective instream flow programs and steps for recommending site-specific prescriptions. Information on legal and institutional elements and the role of the public—although discussed briefly in this chapter—are detailed in other chapters devoted specifically to those topics.

This chapter is divided into two parts—the first addresses instream flow program development and the second deals with the establishment of site-specific prescriptions.

PART I: DEVELOPING INSTREAM FLOW PROGRAMS

The states and provinces have established mechanisms that allow their citizens the right to use the waters within their state or province for legally recognized purposes. Most of those purposes have been and remain ones that remove water and alter the form and function of rivers. However, there is growing recognition that rivers should be managed to conserve their ecosystem function to the greatest extent possible. Because of the limited supply of flowing water, it is important that society continue to evaluate the uses of riverine resources in terms of their own values and not leave the issue of how much flowing water is needed to traditional bureaucratic permitting processes.

There is a long-held belief that resource management decisions require a choice between the economy and the environment. However, this traditional belief is being replaced with a more realistic perspective that the long-term health of an economy is compatible with, and likely depends on, the long-term health of the environment. A growing body of evidence now suggests that the simple trade-off myth is just that—a misconception based largely upon economic models that were either misapplied or based on erroneous assumptions or both (Templet 1995; Goodstein 1999; Whitelaw 2003).

Impacts to the economy are routinely assessed with "economic-based" models that assume a particular resource product forms the foundation of the economy (Quigley et al. 1996). The strength of other economic sectors is determined by what happens to the basic industries. Hence, resource versus economy is defined largely by demand for the extracted resource (Johnson et al. 1991). Economic models also often assume that the economy is static and that change in the basic industry is constant over time. The underlying assumption of such an approach may have been acceptable when demands on natural resources were less complicated, but today there are competing demands for most natural resources that did not exist in earlier times. As with any commodity, competition tends to have a great influence on its relative value. To characterize the issue of "water for fish" versus "water for people" as a simple one is a great oversimplification of a complex situation, in part, because instream flow is just another water use that meets the needs of people—much like domestic use or agricultural supply. The only difference is that the benefit or value of instream flow

The argument of instream flow as an issue of "water for fish versus people" is a commonly heard complaint—often used to elicit a more "common-sense" belief that instream flow practitioners are advocating natural conditions in rivers at the expense of other water users. This idea, however popular, is in essence a red herring. All water uses, whether for industry, municipalities, or instream flow are for the benefit or enjoyment of people. But ultimately, reservation of water for instream flow is about use and enjoyment of riverine resources by future generations. Since these future users are not available to express their needs or desires, fish—like the canary in the coalmine—often serve as a surrogate for healthy riverine conditions. Preserving instream flows (and fish) in effect preserves water management options for future generations.

is based on people's enjoyment of, or welfare derived from, a healthy environment.

The value of flowing water to society can be thought of as three ecosystem-level building blocks that include (1) goods and services, (2) functions, and (3) states (Quigley et al. 1996). Ecosystem goods and services are specific components that can either be extracted or remain in place, such as when water is diverted for consumptive use or rivers are used for recreation. Ecosystem functions are processes, such as the stabilization of a stream bank or a riparian zone's filtration of sediment from overland runoff. Ecosystem states are systemic or integrated characteristics, such as scenic landscapes or watersheds with low flood risk. Consequently, the interrelated nature of these building blocks illustrates how the effect of humans on any one component is related to the other, which invalidates the either/or argument and clearly shows the intimately linked and highly complex nature of the relationship between economics and the environment.

As demands for commodities and ecological values burden aquatic ecosystems to and beyond their carrying capacities, society will be challenged to manage water resources to achieve the greatest overall benefit from ecological systems. This new paradigm will require not only building bridges between competing groups to keep supply connected to the highest-value demands, but also unprecedented cooperation between scientists, economists, and, most importantly, the public. Continuing to characterize these important decisions as a simple choice of water for fish versus people is a failure to address the hard questions of how to best serve the present or future needs of society and our riverine resources.

It is typically the charge of state and provincial fishery and wildlife management agencies to conserve, protect, rehabilitate, and restore aquatic resources in accordance with the laws of their jurisdictions. However, this role does not necessarily place them in a position of assigning fish a higher priority than people. Rather, the charge of all state and provincial fishery and wildlife management agencies is to provide sustainable riverine resources, including viable and diverse populations of native species and abundant fishing and recreational opportunities for current and future generations. These objectives are consistent with the responsibilities of other state and provincial agencies to provide good quality drinking water, water quality to maintain public health, and natural systems to attenuate flood damage. However, for society to decide how best to allocate its limited water resources, agencies must strive to fully and credibly document the consequences or potential effects of water management decisions on river systems.

Bovee et al. (1998) described a five-step process that we adapt to help resource managers develop and implement an effective instream flow program and achieve desired goals and objectives for individual rivers or projects. These steps include (1) determining and reporting instream flow status, (2) setting program goals and objectives, (3) establishing the institutional process for determining instream flows, (4) supporting protocols designed to mimic the magnitude, timing, and duration of the natural flow regimes, and (5) documenting the rationale for program prescriptions. Steps 1 through 3 relate primarily to program development (discussed in Part I) and steps 4 and 5 identify objectives for individual projects (addressed in Part II).

DETERMINING AND REPORTING INSTREAM FLOW STATUS

The IFC recognizes the importance of a holistic approach to river corridor management—

an approach that is designed to protect, rehabilitate, or restore the ecological integrity and biodiversity of aquatic systems. Given the many different U.S. and Canadian legal and institutional arrangements, the first step in any instream flow program is to assess the status of state or provincial instream flow protection on all streams and rivers.

It is best if the general status of aquatic biota and extent of instream flow management for all stream resources is regularly communicated to citizens and policy makers. Such a reporting system would not only describe the status of stream resources but also identify instream flow issues that are currently being considered in water management decisions.

The suggested reporting system is not an end in itself and does not diminish the need for management agencies to determine instream flow needs based on ecosystem-level analysis involving all five riverine components (hydrology, geomorphology, biology, water quality, and connectivity). Instead, the intent should be, as much as possible, to establish priorities and plans for moving instream flow management of all streams within a state or province to ecosystem-based management. This strategy provides natural resource agencies the opportunity to develop periodic reports to document the status and overall trends (either toward improvement or further decline) of streams within its jurisdiction. The status of stream segments should be described regardless of whether or not the natural resource agency has legal authority to identify and set instream flow water management levels.

...the intent should be...to establish priorities and plans for moving instream flow management of all streams ... to ecosystem-based management.

A proactive program might reserve some of the least impacted or most unique streams from future water withdrawal. The strategy for remaining streams could be directed toward developing water management plans that incrementally move a stream closer to ecologically based instream flow standards under the framework described in this document. Whereas such a reporting system would be most useful for helping natural resource

agencies develop priorities for directing instream flow studies and conservation actions, a dual purpose would be to inform the public about the status of their resources and reinforce the notion that agencies are attempting to fulfill their legal stewardship responsibilities to wisely manage those resources for present and future generations.

To facilitate a system of communication, all stream segments throughout a state or region should be inventoried and the instream flow status described. The five reporting categories that we suggest include (1) full instream flow protection, (2) comprehensive ecologically based instream flow management, (3) partial ecologically based instream flow management, (4) threshold level instream flow protection, and (5) no instream flow conservation.

Full Instream Flow Protection

No allowances for additional water withdrawals and/or flow manipulations would be permitted for streams in this reporting category. Management is essentially confined to a hands-off strategy. This level of protection is often assigned to stream segments within designated wilderness areas and to state, province, national wild and scenic rivers, or other reserves. This can vary from complete protection when the area is designated before any permitted uses have taken place (as in headwater wilderness areas and undeveloped areas of Alaska and Canada) to protection of the level of use at the time of designation. In some instances, the natural resource agency may have a goal of complete protection for a stream segment that is presently under some low level of diversionary use. Such a stream could be provisionally identified for full protection with the stipulation that no further water withdrawal be allowed and existing water uses be considered for retirement, purchase or lease, and converted to instream use.

Comprehensive Ecologically Based Instream Flow Management

An ecologically based instream flow program will address all five riverine components that vary with the season of year (intraannual) and with the water supply or watershed condition (interannual). Flow regimes will vary for wet, average, and dry conditions (interannual). Off-stream users are permitted to withdraw water only when streamflow exceeds the specified instream flow. The required instream flow level may be administered so it predetermines the level of withdrawals allowed.

Partial Ecologically Based Instream Flow Management

Streams in this category are those for which instream flow requirements have been determined on the basis of one or more of the five riverine components. Over the past 20 or more years, some instream flow studies have become more sophisticated by targeting multiple components of river resources. These studies are most often based on analysis of streamflows and habitat, primarily for fish (particularly game fish), and sometimes include temperature. Seasonal flows address life stage requirements (i.e., spawning, incubation, and rearing) and ensure intraannual variability. Expansion of the habitat requirements to include all fish species (or guild representatives) and invertebrates ensure a more complete accounting of aquatic community needs. Some instream flow prescriptions may address only historical hydrology and provide recommendations to maintain channel morphology or sustain some level of seasonal (intraannual) variability. Although these efforts represent a significant improvement over flat-line, threshold level instream flow management approaches, they still fall short of strategies that are needed to achieve full fishery or riverine resource protection.

Threshold Level Instream Flow Protection

The phrase "instream flow protection" is often misinterpreted to mean protection of the aquatic resource. In reality, instream flow protection refers only to the amount of water that is protected from withdrawal; it does not guarantee that the level of protection for the aquatic organisms present in the stream is adequate. In many cases, a minimum, or baseline, instream flow protection (flat line) results in considerably less than the average natural flow of the stream remaining in the channel. A stark example of minimum flow management is the use of the $7Q_{10}$ low flow statistic as the default flow in some eastern and southeastern United States. This management level has been used under various guises (e.g., Q_{90}, median base flow) when a single value (flat line) instream flow standard is deemed appropriate (usually by engineers or developers) on the mistaken basis that the organisms in the stream have evolved under such limitations. Although it is true that aquatic organisms must periodically endure droughts, the imposition of a "permanent drought" by reserving only that level of flow would greatly alter the natural riverine resource.

Whereas existing "minimum flow" regula-

tion may have serious effects on some streams, other streams may retain a relatively high level of ecological health and social value. As a means of improving their management and ensuring their ecological health in the future, these healthier stream segments could be identified as such and further permits or allocations for water withdrawal or manipulation could be denied or limited to set amounts if they were shown to cause potential harm to riverine resources. A variable instream flow prescription could be developed based on analysis of the riverine components and opportunities sought for converting some existing water uses to instream flows. Reporting to the public that these streams are minimally managed or over-allocated and setting ecologically based instream flows as goals helps to focus attention on these resources. This situation is representative of many instream flow management efforts in the arid western states and provinces.

No Instream Flow Conservation

In many cases, states and provinces have rivers with no legally recognized protection for instream flows. Identifying the status of rivers in this category does not necessarily mean that the streams are in immediate jeopardy; however, if no management plan is proposed to preserve their ecological health, these streams are at risk for future degradation. It may be that all of the water is withdrawn at times and riverine resources are degraded in terms of some or all of their ecological components. This situation is perhaps representative of many bypass reaches below hydropower dams and streams in the arid states and provinces where previous policies did not provide for instream flow. On the other hand, some rivers that are identified in this category are not currently threatened by water withdrawals—either as a result of their remoteness and inaccessibility or lack of interest in development for whatever reason. These healthy streams are potential candidates for a higher level of instream flow conservation.

IFC Riverine Resource Stewardship Policy Statement: All streams and rivers should have instream flows that maintain or restore, to the greatest extent possible, ecological functions and processes similar to those exhibited in their natural or unaltered state.

SETTING PROGRAM GOALS
AND OBJECTIVES

Instream flow programs should incorporate a broad ecosystem perspective that allows aquatic resource goals and objectives to be designed according to the unique characteristics of each instream flow issue. Knowledge of state and provincial water allocation policies can guide managers in defining realistic goals and objectives for specific stream segments. Managers can then identify the technical approaches to be used and plan studies to gather the information necessary to set appropriate flow regimes, evaluate the potential effects of proposed development schemes, or develop restoration or rehabilitation plans. A comprehensive ecosystem approach can also facilitate communication between natural resource agencies, stakeholders, and the public by keeping interested parties informed about the status of the stream's resources, threats from development, opportunities for improvement, and restoration or rehabilitation plans.

It is essential to know what outcomes are expected before embarking on a course of action. Once these goals are stated, objectives can be identified to best secure instream flows. In the initial stages of an emerging instream flow program, particularly in situations where extensive water use and over-allocation is the norm, the agency's objective may be to attain a permanent instream flow where dewatering had been prevalent or to set a water use limit to halt continuing decline. Although obtaining a single value minimum flow may be a positive step forward, the IFC promotes establishing or expanding program opportunities that move beyond the simple watering of dry stream channels toward sustaining healthy aquatic communities in all streams by prescribing variable flow regimes.

Agency Mission Statements

An agency's mission guides its goals and objectives. The following excerpts from mission statements of several states and provinces illustrate the stewardship responsibilities shared by most states and provinces (Organization of Wildlife Planners 1995):

The wildlife and their environment are to be preserved, conserved, managed, protected and enhanced, for the use, benefit, and enjoyment of the people of this state and its visitors (*Tennessee Fish and Game*).

To manage freshwater aquatic life and wild animal life and their habitat to perpetuate a diversity of species with densities and distributions, which provide sustained ecological, recreational, scientific, educational, aesthetic, and economic benefits (*Florida Game and Freshwater Fish Commission*).

...to manage in a sustainable fashion, the use of Manitoba's fisheries resources and produce a net gain in their supportive habitats for maximum benefit of all Manitobans (*Manitoba Fisheries Branch*).

...the integrity, diversity, and vitality of all natural systems must be protected (*Vermont Department of Fish and Wildlife*).

Conserving wildlife—serving people (*Wyoming Game and Fish Department*).

These mission statements are consistent with the Public Trust Doctrine and the concept that government owes its citizens special duties of stewardship regarding common property fishery and wildlife resources that are held in trust for the public. Advocacy for the principles of the Public Trust Doctrine and related laws are among the fundamental guiding principles of an effective instream flow program. Agencies should specifically identify these resource protection responsibilities in all of their governing documents (e.g., mission statements, strategic plans) to help assert their authority in the many contentious settings they often encounter. The priority should be to protect fully functioning aquatic resources now, before restoration or rehabilitation is needed. Degraded resources warrant protection as well—regardless of their current condition—so that they can be enhanced, rehabilitated or restored, and returned to maximum ecological function and public benefit.

Historically, fishery and wildlife agencies primarily managed game species. Today, aquatic scientists recognize the interconnected nature of all organisms in riverine systems and, thus, have developed a broader focus for managing ecosystems and their component species and processes. Long-term sustainability is a common goal as is establishing a higher profile for nonconsumptive uses such as recreational boating and watchable wildlife.

The statutes and policies that establish agency responsibilities do not value one particular resource over another. Although some streams or stream segments may naturally contain low numbers or no "desirable" fish species, have naturally low flows or human-caused low streamflow, or exhibit impaired water quality that negatively affects the presence and abundance of aquatic organisms, that status does not diminish agencies' responsibility to manage them all as effectively as possible for the public's benefit—now and in the future.

Certainly, many streams and rivers have been severely degraded from their natural condition. Similarly, many other streams and rivers offer numerous benefits to the public for recreational enjoyment, provision of livelihood, opportunities for commerce, and other values. The reality of limited fiscal and personnel resources dictates that agencies should prioritize the investment of their efforts based on criteria that are relevant to their unique situation. However, priorities must also include long-term plans that address public demands for ecosystem protection within the existing legal and institutional framework for public use of streams, lakes, and rivers in the face of public needs for consumptive and other water uses.

IFC Public Trust Advocacy Policy Statement: Advocacy for and protection of the principles of the Public Trust Doctrine must be among the fundamental guiding principles of an effective instream flow program.

General Aquatic Resource Goals

Resource agencies' goals emanate from their legal mandate and mission as well as input from the public. They are further guided by a variety of other state/provincial and federal laws, including, but certainly not limited to, the Public Trust Doctrine, NEPA, and the U.S. Clean Water Act of 1973, as amended. One goal of the Clean Water Act is to protect the biological integrity of waters of the

...the IFC promotes ecological integrity... This goal should form the foundation of a natural resource agency's approach to natural resource stewardship...

United States. Programs should be based on aquatic resource management goals that reflect a commitment to implement these mandates and provide a sequential process as the means of achieving the goals.

What are the instream flow related goals of fishery and wildlife agencies charged with the protection of aquatic resources? A healthy aquatic community? Abundant sport fish populations? Recreational opportunities? All of the above? Complex and differing systems make simple answers difficult. However, the IFC promotes the philosophy of an overarching goal to achieve ecological integrity—"the ability to support and maintain a balanced, integrated, adaptive community of organisms having a species composition, diversity, and functional organization comparable to that of the natural habitat of the region" (Karr and Dudley 1981). This goal should form the foundation of a natural resource agency's approach to natural resource stewardship and its instream flow applications should be driven by specific objectives that move the resource toward this overarching goal. Lackey (1998) defined ecosystem management, as "the application of ecological and social information, options, and constraints to achieve desired social benefits within a defined geographic area and over a specified period." State and provincial resource agencies are often in the position of providing ecological information within a decision-making context that is based on public input. As a consequence, ecosystem management may, but often does not, result in an emphasis on biological diversity. Scientific information is important for effective management, but is only one element in a decision-making process that is fundamentally one of public choice. Lackey (1998) further stated that "there is no `right' decision but rather those decisions that appear to best respond to society's current and future needs as expressed through a decision-making process." It is the resource agency's role to describe the ecological consequences of the various alternatives proposed during the decision-making process.

Instream flow practitioners have often focused on a limited number of important sport fish species. There are several significant shortcomings to such a narrow approach. First, it may not mesh with the agency's mission. Perhaps endangered mussels need consideration. Second, addressing instream flow needs for an isolated species or species life-stage may result in failure to consider system processes that are essential for creating and sustaining the overall habitat. Third, it may fail to consider important biological community interactions. Focusing on a single fish's habitat may fail to consider the needs of its prey species and competitors and, therefore, not adequately address the needs to sustain the fish species of concern.

It is often appropriate to manage a diverse aquatic community and important sport fishes or endangered species. Fishing is an important public use of aquatic resources that is protected by the Public Trust Doctrine and some state constitutions. Attention to specific sport fish or endangered species is frequently warranted, but other components of the aquatic ecosystem must be considered as well. Failure to address all ecosystem components and processes ultimately may lead to alteration or decline of existing riverine resources.

Specific Instream Flow Program Objectives

The goals discussed above are admittedly broad and relate primarily to the stewardship duties of the resource agency. Program objectives must be determined in relation to instream flow opportunities. However, it is important to identify instream flow program objectives in order to move toward the agency's legal stewardship goals, or at least achieve no net loss (status quo). When water allocation or reservation decisions prevent the agency from achieving its stream specific objectives, the agency should report those limitations to the public and seek strategies to expand those opportunities.

Objectives need to include the details of what a resource management goal like "healthy, diverse aquatic communities," means for a specific stream. They might address such things as riparian vegetation, fish and wildlife species or communities, and recreational fishing. Indicators of ecosystem health should include sufficient detail for others to clearly understand what the resource agency is trying to accomplish. Periodic reporting of the status of instream flow management can help communicate and aid in achieving agency goals. Particular areas of concern that should be addressed as part of the objectives, include, but are not limited to, stream communities and native species, reservoir management, and dam removal.

Fisheries management program objectives are an important component of selecting target species for instream flow studies, but the needs of the entire biotic community, including all native species, must be accommodated. The issue is how flow-dependent physical habitat characteristics (e.g., depth, velocity, substrate, cover) influence fish community structure (Gorman and Karr 1978; Schlosser 1982a; Moyle and Vondracek 1985) and whether changes in these variables will cause shifts in species community composition (Moyle and Baltz 1985; Bain et al. 1988).

A guild has been defined as "a group of species that exploit the same class of environmental resources in a similar way" (Root 1967). The guild approach (Landres 1983; Verner 1984; Szaro 1986; Leonard and Orth 1988) is one way to simplify the species selection process especially when high species richness is an issue. Resource use by stream fishes has been summarized on the basis of feeding guilds (Horwitz 1978; Grossman et al. 1982; Angermeier and Karr 1983), habitat-use guilds (Finger 1982; Lobb 1986; Bain et al. 1988; Aadland 1993), and reproductive guilds (Balon 1975).

The priority should be to manage instream flows for communities of native species. However, there are exceptions. In drainages where native fish species have been extirpated, or perhaps development has obviated habitat conditions for native species, some fish and wildlife agencies have stocked nonnative fish species. These nonnative species now provide popular fishing opportunities for the public. Protection of these nonnative fish species is often socially desirable. However, in cases where native and nonnative species coexist, and the agency is managing flows for the nonnative species, agencies should continue to look for opportunities to protect and enhance native species populations.

IFC Native Species Policy Statement: Instream flow programs should acknowledge the importance of and need to manage stream communities and indigenous aquatic biota. Management of nonnative species should not threaten the long-term health or survival of native species and their habitat.

The effects of reservoirs on riverine resources over the past 200 years have been such a significant factor that programs must specifically include ways of addressing riverine resources associated with existing facilities as well as the effects of new projects. Protecting aquatic resource needs within the legal and political framework of states and provinces is a particular challenge considering that almost all human intervention in streamflow patterns and processes can change the basic nature of aquatic resources. Even when actions are taken to mitigate these effects, the best that can be achieved from most mitigation efforts is to minimize negative effects to riverine resources. This is perhaps most true with the construction of dams and other in-channel barriers.

Essentially all impounds affect the five riverine components to some extent, depending on the design and operation of the storage facility (Williams and Wolman 1984; Friedman et al. 1998; Rood et al. 1999; Polzin and Rood 2000).

To minimize negative effects to aquatic resources, programs must allow managers to address the full range of potential impacts to stream channel characteristics below proposed new dams, as well as existing dams, and design management strategies accordingly. In fulfilling this charge, however, it is important to keep in mind that even if the predam flow regime is duplicated exactly, conditions below the dam will differ from preconstruction conditions because of sediment trapped in the reservoir and other water quantity and quality changes (Williams and Wolman 1984; Collier et al. 1996; Kondolf 1998).

IFC Reservoir Management Policy Statement: Instream flow programs should acknowledge the effects of new and existing dams on sediment transport and allow managers the ability to recommend strategies for water releases and sediment management that minimize negative effects to existing channel, riparian, and floodplain properties and processes below the dam.

Whereas government agencies and the public at one time focused on the direct benefits of dams and other in-channel barriers, there is now greater public recognition that all dams provide positive and negative consequences and not all are quantifiable on the same bases. Although many dams still serve useful functions, others no longer serve their original purpose. All dams cause significant change to riverine resources, which may conflict with the stewardship responsibilities of fishery and wildlife management agencies. As a consequence, dam removal may be appropriate when individual dams or barriers no longer provide societal benefits that outweigh their negative effects to streams, wetlands, and floodplains. Dam or barrier removal is not a simple process and must be

based on thorough assessments of aquatic resource benefits and costs that include assessments of short- and long-term effects on stream hydrologic patterns, geomorphologic processes, biologic factors, hydrologic and biologic connectivity, and water quality. A unique mix of physical, ecological, sociological, economical, and legal characteristics apply to each dam. Thus, the issues associated with dam management or removal are unique and no single strategy can be applied in all situations. The goal of any removal project should be to restore affected stream segments to an ecological condition that more closely resembles its natural structure and ecological function (Figure 5-1). (For more information on dam removal, see Baxter 1977; Edwards 1978; Ward and Stanford 1979; Petts 1984; Nilsson and Dynesius 1994; Ligon et al. 1995; American Society of Civil Engineers 1997, and Aspen Institute 2002).

FIGURE 5-1. Kidder Dam in Wahpeton, Minnesota, before and after dam removal. The dam originally presented a safety hazard and fish barrier on the Red River of the North, flowing between Minnesota and North Dakota. The dam was ultimately converted to rapids, thereby enabling fish passage, removing a safety hazard, and maintaining the reservoir pool (Photograph courtesy of Ian Chisholm and Dr. Luther Aadland, Ecological Services Division, Minnesota Department of Natural Resources).

IFC Dam Removal Policy Statement: Instream flow programs should support the removal or modification of dams or in-channel barriers and restoration or rehabilitation of affected riverine resources to more natural conditions and functions when those structures' benefits no longer outweigh their societal costs.

ESTABLISHING THE INSTITUTIONAL PROCESS FOR DETERMINING INSTREAM FLOWS

Effective instream flow programs should at least generally identify a range of tools and strategies that are appropriate for assessing riverine resource management needs within their jurisdiction. Such tools are necessary to determine potential loss to habitat quality or quantity and develop mitigation plans when a project appears likely to

---

Appropriate instream flows are those that provide or maintain ecological functions and processes similar to those exhibited in their natural or unaltered state.

---

violate an established standard or otherwise negatively affect the aquatic resource. Analyses should be conducted to compare alternative development schemes with historic baseline conditions and natural resource agency goals. Whereas it is helpful for programs to generally identify a range or class of tools judged to be appropriate, such specificity should not limit managers' abilities to use any method or strategy necessary to answer particular resource management questions.

Instream flow techniques designed to evaluate such impacts are often referred to as incremental methods (Trihey and Stalnaker 1985). These techniques are site-specific and data intensive. The emphasis on incremental analysis is a result of the National Environmental Policy Act as well as state environmental policy acts in the United States and the No Net Loss Policy of the Canada Department of Fisheries and Oceans. However, the force fitting of incremental methods into emerging instream flow programs at the state and provincial levels often led to misapplications. Because managers were required to defend any flow recommendation on ecological bases, they turned to incremental

methods even when they were not appropriate. Because of the lack of accepted protocols or methods for many of these new programs, attempts were made to capture the credibility of sophisticated incremental methods by using single component models such as the Physical Habitat Simulation (PHABSIM) system taken out of context from the integrated suite of instream flow incremental models (IFIM). Attempts to define a single base flow level using incremental methods are simply another way to get at a number and may not be superior to other (threshold) methods that are designed to yield only a single recommended flow level (Castleberry et al. 1996).

Securing appropriate instream flows for protection of fisheries, wildlife, cultural, and societal resources requires the implementation of study plans that are guided by an approved process and procurement of instream flows within the regulatory framework. Appropriate instream flows are those that provide or maintain ecological functions and processes similar to those exhibited in their natural or unaltered state. The decision to address instream flow issues can be made in response to a proposed water development project, change in an existing permitted project, development of water management plans, and state water planning documents for determining instream flow needs for reservations/permits, public trust issues, and/or establishing regional guidelines for instream flow protection. There are basically two approaches for determining instream flow needs: field-intensive methods and office-based (nonintensive) evaluation methods, which form a continuum defined by effort, defensibility, and need. The appropriate approach depends on the present state of the resource and the level of controversy of a particular project or purpose (i.e., planning versus permitting), constraints and range of possibilities, complexity (i.e., how many issues an instream flow must address), and resource availability (e.g., money, personnel), among other factors. Stalnaker et al. (1995) provided a thorough examination of issues relevant to the selection of appropriate tools for instream flow assessment.

When data have been analyzed and feedback has been received from all stakeholders, it is appropriate that the state or provincial fishery and

---

The first step in scientific endeavors is to clearly identify the problem to be resolved.

---

wildlife management agency have the primary opportunity and authority to approve, modify, or reject the conclusions. After the agency agrees that the studies and conclusions are valid, negotiations with stakeholders may be conducted if they are required or necessary. The final flow strategy should be implemented according to the limits and constraints of each state or province's legal guidelines or other legal requirements.

> *IFC Process Development Policy Statement:* Instream flow programs should establish a process for quantifying instream flow needs that allows the state, provincial, or territorial fishery and wildlife management agency to identify or approve study needs, study design, data analysis, and flow implementation.

Problem Identification and Issue Description

The first step in scientific endeavors is to clearly identify the problem to be resolved. Once the problem has been stated, the geographic context should be established to identify study boundaries and provide a sense of the scale and dimension of the instream flow problem. In some cases, this will require an assessment of potential changes in the hydrological, physical, and chemical characteristics of a watershed due to a proposed development project. Resource issues can then be identified and classified based on the status and characteristics of each watershed. Whether or not a particular resource issue is found necessary for a specific instream flow analysis, the rationale used to decide the relevance of and course of action for a given issue should be documented.

Natural resource (biological) issues are nearly always inherent in instream flow studies and may interact with or be influenced by any or all other issues. Bovee et al. (1998) recommended that two important steps be undertaken in identifying issues: a comprehensive analysis of potential impacts to all stakeholders, and an attempt to filter trivial issues that may impede progress. They also discussed strategies for organizing issues, ranging from simple checklists to more complex and defensible cause and effect diagrams. It is helpful if issues and desired outcomes can be identified early on in discussions to generate as many viable solutions as possible as well as highlight obstacles and constraints. For example, if flow needs to be increased during a season, are there legal or technical mechanisms to allow it? If not, are there mechanisms to address other possible outcomes? Such an approach may avoid redundant or unnecessary work at later phases of project development.

Sufficient information to address each issue is also necessary. This will help to determine the availability or lack of information, formation of an interdisciplinary team, development of objectives, and study design.

Regulatory Framework

To secure instream flows and work effectively within the regulatory framework, managers must have an understanding of the laws, regulations, and policies that can affect instream flow issues (see chapters 2 and 5). In the United States, the Public Trust Doctrine, which protects the public's use of tidal lands, coastal waters, and navigable streams and lakes, and federal laws and regulations may be applied to instream flow problems. Although the states usually control fish and wildlife and manage water, the federal government has responsibilities for endangered species and interstate commerce as reflected in such laws as the National Environmental Policy Act (1969), the Federal Water Pollution Control Act (1972) and the Clean Water Act amendment (1977).

In Canada, the Fisheries Act prohibits activities that interfere with fish habitat or will result in the emission of a deleterious substance into waters frequented by fish without a permit or regulatory authority. However, the provinces regulate water rights and are the main regulators of water quality. Instream flow levels are mainly dealt with by provincial agencies when carrying out duties in respect to water rights. For example, in Alberta, the Water Act (S. A. 1996. c. W-3.5) regulates water rights. Under the statute, the director issuing water rights may set conditions relating to minimum flow. State and Provincial constitutions, statutes, and other laws that can affect instream flow decisions include water allocations laws, interbasin transfer statutes, agency authorities, and environmental protection statutes. An example of provincial statutes is provided in the Alberta Water Act (Appendix D).

In some cases, the Canadian federal government has authority over aspects of ecosystem protection although there typically is no "overlap" or shared responsibility with the provinces. Typically, the federal government is interested in migratory birds and fisheries wherever they occur.

Otherwise, protection of fishery, wildlife, and water resources is a provincial interest. In this regard, it should be noted that in Canada, in contrast to the United States, most public lands and resources are provincial, not federal (i.e., Crown) property. Accordingly, resource development, such as oil and gas, forestry, and grazing are provincial concerns. Moreover, in most, if not all provinces, legislation provides that the provincial Crown is the owner of the bed and shores of all naturally occurring watercourses and water bodies. In Alberta, the relevant law is section 3 of the Public Lands Act (R. S. A. 1980, c. P-30). Because of this ownership, the Crown in right of the province has considerable power to control water resources. In exercising its power, however, the Crown recognizes the rights of those who hold licenses, permits, or approvals.

Understanding legal and institutional authorities and responsibilities should not be limited to those of one's own agency. The responsibilities and authorities of other agencies that affect instream flow decisions must also be understood. Applicable agencies include water development or allocation boards, water quality agencies, water resources commissions, and other federal, state, or provincial natural resource agencies.

Fostering communication among agencies that have instream flow responsibilities is integral to understanding the authorities affecting instream flow decisions. Meeting regularly with federal, state, or provincial agencies, and other appropriate entities to discuss current instream flow issues and instream values not only helps agencies better understand protection challenges and opportunities, but builds trust as well as important lines of communication among participants.

State and provincial agencies also bear the responsibility of educating the public about the legal authorities governing the protection of public natural resources. This can be accomplished via targeted public involvement campaigns and by including this information in public reports, policies, and documentation of instream flow decisions (see Chapter 3 and Appendix B).

IFC Legal Authority Policy Statement: Effective instream flow programs must be based on a clear recognition of legal authorities to protect, enhance, and restore instream flow for public riverine resources

The Role of Legal Counsel

Instream flow programs should include staff adequately trained in appropriate law, legal procedures, and negotiation strategies or have access to legal counsel. Water law and water resources management are complex fields—subject to the precedent of case law, statutes, rulings, and interpretations within a state or province. Rules and regulations of various federal agencies, such as the Corps of Engineers, Bureau of Reclamation, and Federal Energy Regulatory Commission (FERC) in the United States, and the Canadian Ministry of the Environment, add to the complexity. Such laws and regulations as well as their continual changes and judicial interpretations are typically beyond the professional scope of most fishery and wildlife agency personnel.

Legal counsel specifically trained in water and environmental law is often necessary to advise natural resource personnel and the public on instream flow issues and to ensure that properly conducted studies and negotiated strategies are fully implemented within the opportunities and constraints of applicable laws. Attorneys specializing in enforcement of hunting and fishing regulations, for example, should not be expected to intuitively understand the intricacies of instream flow or water law cases. Likewise, rotating instream flow assignments among several different staff members or assigning different elements of the same settlement to different staff members may also lead to confusing and disappointing results.

Legal staff should also have some knowledge of the science of instream flow and fisheries biology. A basic appreciation of how streams, lakes, and aquatic ecosystems function is often helpful to attorneys in crafting legal documents. Perhaps the best way to develop an appreciation is to interact with agency biologists, hydrologists, and geomorphologists. This approach not only facilitates a better understanding of specific issues affecting local resources, but fosters a working relationship between legal counsel and agency staff as well.

IFC Legal Counsel Policy Statement: Instream flow programs should have ready access to specifically trained legal counsel familiar with water law statutes and instream flow programs in order to obtain consistent representation and maximize instream flow benefits under existing laws and regulations.

Stakeholder Involvement

In many instances, the determination of instream flows requires the interaction of natural resource managers and various stakeholders, such as water developers, water resource managers, planning and/or permitting agencies, and interest groups who may be affected by instream flow decisions. Subsequently, it is important that state and provincial instream flow programs be designed to involve legitimate stakeholders in developing and implementing a study plan and following through with negotiation and procurement of instream flow amounts and conditions. Stakeholder involvement consists of several key features. Foremost among these is the need to establish open lines of communication and develop a sense of trust and understanding of respective roles (Bovee et al. 1998). Although the role of each stakeholder cannot be determined a priori, all stakeholders should assume the responsibility to ensure that resources are expended equitably and that all stakeholders have appropriate investment in the process. The relative power or authority of the interested parties depends to some extent on laws, financial backing, and other factors. (see chapter 3 for a discussion of stakeholder involvement.)

The Role of Negotiation

Developing instream flow recommendations on the best available science in concert with effective interdisciplinary teams and informing the public does not always guarantee that flows will actually be implemented. In many situations, desired outcomes to these efforts will not be achieved if the final decision has not been successfully negotiated. Negotiation or problem resolution is one of the major phases of instream flow studies and is explicitly recognized as such in the IFIM and other instream flow study procedures. Although negotiation often occurs during the latter phases of instream flow decisions, it also may be useful in selection of study methods, habitat suitability criteria, and other technical decisions. Negotiating to protect public aquatic resources is integral to establishing and managing instream flow programs. Perfecting these skills requires training in natural resource negotiation.

Keys to successful negotiation include early involvement, cooperative relationships among parties, defensible positions, and the use of appropriate technology to evaluate instream flow needs (Cavendish and Duncan 1986). Lamb et al. (1998) cited four elements of a successful negotiation (1) preparation, (2) concentration on the problem rather than personal considerations, (3) knowledge of the process, and (4) knowledge of one's own role and level of power. Understanding the values of other parties and using that knowledge as leverage is key to successful negotiation outcomes. Preparation includes knowledge of, and experience in, different strategies that may be used during a negotiation. Forming alliances with instream flow advocacy groups, such as environmental, fishing, and hunting organizations, downstream landowners, canoe and kayak clubs, and the like, can strengthen the position for instream flow advocacy (Potter 1988) and increase an institution's negotiating power.

Effective instream flow programs include staff that recognize the value of negotiation to the management process and understand the importance of competent negotiation skills. Such programs (1) emphasize that strong technical data alone will not lead to successful instream flow decisions, (2) include personnel who are properly trained in negotiation skills, (3) conduct necessary planning and negotiations at the start of projects, and (4) establish a firm understanding of institutional values and the "bottom line" for each negotiation. Staff negotiators, if different from those who collect and manage the data, should be involved throughout instream flow studies so that the process and technical decisions are better understood.

In negotiations, compromise must be weighed against risk or impacts on resources (Figure 5-2). Fishery and wildlife agencies must not be too conciliatory to the detriment of natural

FIGURE 5-2. Instead of casting blame, opposing parties should work together cooperatively to solve common problems (Source: Lorne Fitch, Alberta Sustainable Resource Development, Fish and Wildlife Division).

resources. Where NEPA-like legislation exists at the state or provincial level, impact analyses and prevention of losses from proposed development must be the focus of instream flow studies. Natural resource managers must not assume the role of developing recommendations that simply facilitate project implementation. Rather, their responsibility is to oversee studies that lead to variable flow regimes and an understanding of the range of consequences that the proposed action may have on riverine resources.

IFC Negotiation Policy Statement: Effective instream flow programs should include personnel who are trained in negotiation skills, supported by their agency administration, and engaged in appropriate negotiation from the start of projects.

Interdisciplinary Teams

Instream flow decisions are complex and must consider the five riverine components of hydrology, geomorphology, biology, water quality, and connectivity. Recreational issues, economic values, and legal precedents can also affect instream flow decisions. If budgetary resources allow, fishery and wildlife management agencies should retain specialists in these areas or provide sufficient training to improve the skills of existing staff (Figure 5-3). Assistance with training may be obtained through interagency cooperation, univer-

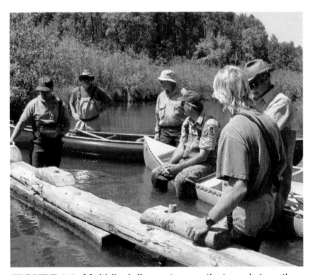

FIGURE 5-3. Multidisciplinary teams that work together and share different perspectives can best address riverine management (Source: Mark Ebbers, Minnesota Department of Natural Resources, Fisheries Division).

sity specialists, or other outside experts. The interdisciplinary team should be under the direction of fishery and wildlife agency instream flow coordinators because of those agencies' primary role as resource stewards. Interdisciplinary teams should cooperatively develop objectives, design studies, select appropriate methods and data collection protocols, implement study plans, analyze data, perform alternatives analysis, negotiate, monitor environmental response, and develop instream flow prescriptions while maintaining stakeholder involvement.

Inclusion of fishery and wildlife managers on interdisciplinary teams should be coordinated by a central person or office on a state- or province-wide basis to ensure consistency of instream flow assessments and applications. Assignment of instream flow coordination to agency staff without specific, up-to-date training in the science of instream flows and permitting processes is typically less effective than to fully trained, permanent staff.

IFC Interdisciplinary Team Policy Statement: Effective instream flow programs require a well-coordinated, interdisciplinary team with adequate staff, training, and funding to address all instream flow and related issues that fall under the agency's responsibilities.

Comprehensive Water Resource Planning

Water planning is another important component of effective instream flow programs. The water planning process is especially useful for dealing with uncertainties related to long-term issues associated with water use and instream flow management and developing strategies for riverine resource stewardship action. Such planning must address opportunities, procedures, and actions necessary to meet all water uses including instream flow needs identified by the public as well as state or provincial fishery and wildlife management agencies.

Comprehensive planning should include (1) accurate assessment of existing water uses, needs, and quality; (2) consideration of all surface and groundwater resources; (3) prioritization of competing water needs; (4) projection of future water needs; (5) identification of opportunities and strategies to accommodate future needs while protecting instream flows; and (6) legal and institutional opportunities to manage water to maximize public benefits. The 1998 South Carolina Water Plan provides an example of comprehensive planning that encompasses many of these characteristics. It establishes instream flow requirements as an essential use of water for navigation, water quality, or fish and wildlife habitat.

Water management plans should address the obvious finite ability of water resources to support present and future needs. In consideration of this reality, future use patterns should place special emphasis on opportunities to maximize multiple uses to accommodate as many societal needs as possible. They should also identify areas where water resources can and cannot support additional consumptive or diversionary uses. Strategies must also emphasize the role of water conservation. In addition, plans should specifically acknowledge that any future water development activities could as easily create negative environmental effects as they provide positive benefits.

Water planning is typically most effective when it is sanctioned by statute or administrative policy and includes meaningful authority, funding, and staff to implement identified strategies within a specific time frame. Although local water planning can be important for communities to formally identify their priorities for water uses, such efforts generally lack enforcement or implementation authority.

> *IFC Comprehensive Water Resource Planning Policy Statement:* Comprehensive water resource planning that includes recognition of instream flows as an essential water use is an important part of an effective instream flow program.

Drought Planning

Droughts are natural and necessary components of an instream flow regime. Although these periods of natural dewatering may have negative, short-term consequences for some aquatic organisms, like fish, they are also important hydrological events for maintaining long-term physical, chemical, and biological processes of the overall fishery (Trush and McBain 2000). Just as high flows are needed to scour the stream channel, prevent encroachment of stream banks, and deposit sediments to maintain a dynamic alternate bar morphology and successionally diverse riparian community, drought flows also serve an essential function. Low flows allow establishment of riparian

seedlings on bars deposited in preceding high flow periods (Figure 5-4). The natural interaction of high and low flows maintains riparian development and aquatic habitat by allowing some riparian development in most years (preventing annual scour that might occur from continuous high flow) while at the same time preventing encroachment by riparian vegetation that would occur if flows were artificially reduced at all times (Leopold et al. 1964).

> Consistent or regular dewatering that essentially creates a condition of annual or permanent drought...changes the structure and function...of stream segments over time...

This dynamic interaction of high and low flow periods also is an important mechanism for maintaining natural assemblages and dynamic processes of native fishes and other aquatic organisms. Consistent or regular dewatering that essentially creates a condition of annual or permanent drought does not offer these benefits and, instead, changes the structure and function of affected stream segments over time (Hill et al. 1991). It is important to understand that the survival of aquatic organisms during periods of low flow or drought does not imply that these are preferred flows or that they should be used to set long-term instream flow conditions. The magnitude, timing, frequency, and duration of low flows are critical aspects of hydrology. Changing any of these aspects will reset many ecological processes and affect structure and productivity of the system. Instream flow alterations exacerbate stresses caused by drought conditions and can negatively affect public fishery and wildlife resources beyond levels that would occur naturally. Recovery of aquatic and riparian communities from these exacerbated effects can take several years, or longer. Due to the effects of extreme low-flow conditions, plans to balance instream and out-of-stream water uses during droughts, and, thereby, minimize the effects on public fishery and wildlife resources, should be developed and implemented. Drought plans that are developed to eliminate natural low flow conditions may resolve human needs in the short-term, but may have long-term ecological consequences.

Drought response plans developed by states and provinces should define essential and nonessential uses with instream flow deemed to be essential because of its public ownership nature. Failure to prioritize uses—and to minimize negative effects to essential uses, including instream flow—will inevitably result in inequitable water allocation during periods of drought. Historically, instream flow and public fishery and wildlife resources dependent on those flows have borne the brunt of such inequitable allocations.

South Carolina has addressed this problem by passing the Drought Response Act of 1985 (§ 49-23 et seq.), which designates instream uses as essential. Section 49-2370(c) reads, in part:

> The department may promulgate regulations to specify categories of nonessential water use. Water used strictly for firefighting purposes, health and medical purposes, maintaining instream flow requirements, and the use of water to satisfy federal, state, or local public health and safety requirements is considered essential water use. The departmentby regulation may provide for the mandatory curtailment of nonessential water uses during periods of severe or extreme drought in drought management areas.

Drought planning could also be included as part of general water planning. As part of these plans, participants should identify legal and institutional opportunities and strategies for maximizing traditional and public fishery and wildlife water uses during water-short periods. As such, participants should have a good understanding of water law and administration or, otherwise, involve specialists who have such knowledge.

IFC Drought Planning Policy Statement: State and provincial instream flow programs should support and participate in development of mechanisms or plans to implement water use reductions during drought periods to protect essential instream flows.

FIGURE 5-4. In unregulated streams, sediment is deposited on point bars during periods of high flows that are colonized by seedlings during natural periods of low flows. This picture of Savery Creek in south central, Wyoming, shows establishment of vegetation resulting from four distinct depositional cycles that are indicated by the arrows.

PART II: ESTABLISHING SITE-SPECIFIC INSTREAM FLOW PRESCRIPTIONS

Fishery and wildlife agencies have a duty to protect or restore instream resources and values. Specific actions are often focused on the management of water quantity to mitigate, protect, or rehabilitate instream resources. If they are to meet the charge of maintaining existing fisheries and riverine resources, agencies should plan water management measures that address the complexity of stream and watershed ecology and integrate diverse physical, chemical, and biological processes. These processes change over time. However, the rate of change is an important consideration in the development of plans. As humans modify rates of change, consequences may be manifested in many parts of a watershed or stream system. For this reason, instream flows should be established in conjunction with complementary watershed management measures that address the rates of change. This section outlines protocols for prescribing instream flows and includes policies that should be considered as part of an effective site-specific instream flow application.

Because stream and watershed ecology is a relatively new discipline (the classic treatise by Hynes was published in 1975) and instream flow is similarly a new practice (Orsborn and Allman 1976; Stalnaker and Arnette 1976; Bovee 1978; Wesche and Rechard 1980; Milhous et al. 1984), there are many uncertainties in the field. To account for those uncertainties and to improve the instream flow specialist's ability to mitigate, protect, rehabilitate, or restore instream resources, management measures need to include goals and objectives, determination of baseline conditions, monitoring, and evaluation, as well as data collection, analysis, and decision making.

DEVELOPING ECOLOGICALLY BASED INSTREAM FLOW PRESCRIPTIONS

The more we study riverine ecology, the better we understand the importance of the interactions and interconnections of its many parts. Regardless of how much information we acquire, however, many other interconnections remain to be discovered and described. It is unlikely that any change to a watershed is neutral; almost any change to one part of a riverine ecosystem forces a reactionary change to other parts (Leopold et al.

1964). Some changes may be immediate while others will be delayed; some will be obvious, others masked—even to the trained scientist. In addition, detection of change may be difficult because of nat-

> ...it should be an ultimate goal of all state and provincial natural resource management agencies to reestablish and sustain the natural flow-related processes.

ural variation and the process-oriented nature of ecosystems (Figure 5-5). Even in completely natural systems, true equilibrium does not exist. The concept of naturally dynamic riverine ecosystems does not justify any particular management option; rather it illustrates the challenge for natural resource managers to properly describe the condition and trend of riverine systems and prescribe solutions that are consistent with their stewardship responsibilities. Figures 5-6, 5-7, and 5-8 offer examples of projects that provided opportunities for maintaining or restoring inter- and intraannual flow variation that approximates natural dynamic processes.

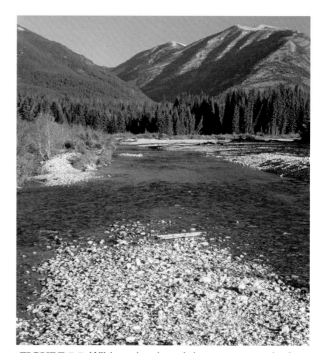

FIGURE 5-5. Wild, undeveloped rivers serve as the best teachers of stream ecology and the importance of natural processes for maintaining the form and function of riverine resources (Source: Lorne Fitch, Alberta Sustainable Resource Development, Fish and Wildlife Division).

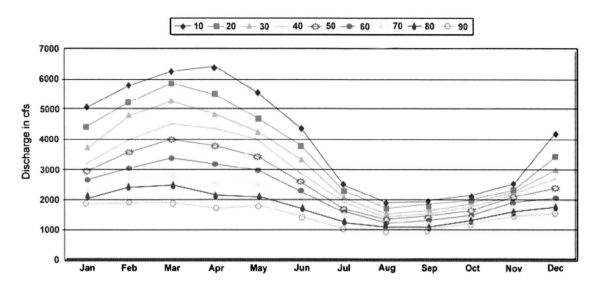

FIGURE 5-6. Monthly time-step instream flow recommendations for the Klamath River, California, in the Shasta River to Scott River reach. These flow recommendations preserve the interannual variability of naturally occurring flows. Recommendations are provided for nine different natural flow exceedence values or water year types (e.g., 10% exceedence = extremely wet year; 90% exceedence = critically dry year. Under these flow conditions the recommended flow is 4,000 cfs (From Hardy and Addley 2001).

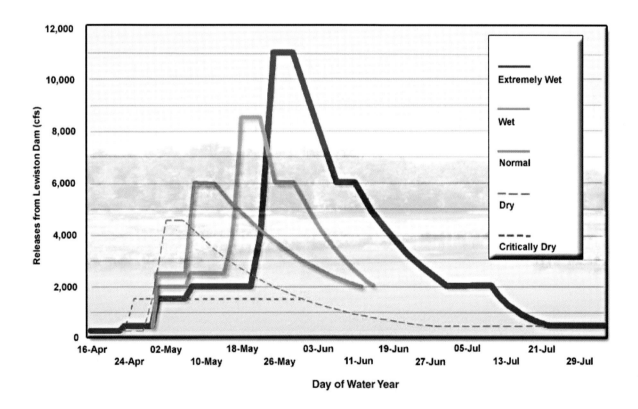

FIGURE 5-7. Recommendations for interannual variability proposed for the Trinity River, northern California (Source: U.S. Fish and Wildlife Service and Hoopa Valley Tribe 1999).

Human alteration of river flow has resulted in widespread geomorphologic and ecological changes throughout North America. Rivers with highly altered watersheds or regulated flows often experience modified hydrographs and may also lose the functional longitudinal and lateral connectivity to floodplains and riparian areas as well as the ability to support natural processes and native species at historic levels. Today, there is a much broader appreciation for the value that aquatic ecosystems and, specifically, free flowing rivers provide to society. Even though many rivers have been highly modified, it should be an ultimate goal of all state and provincial natural resource management agencies to reestablish and sustain the natural flow-related processes.

In the case of pristine rivers, conserving the natural hydrograph should be the goal. The policy of the American Fisheries Society (Rasmussen 1996) is to "insist that the operation of federal flood control and navigation projects be periodically evaluated to find opportunities for restoring

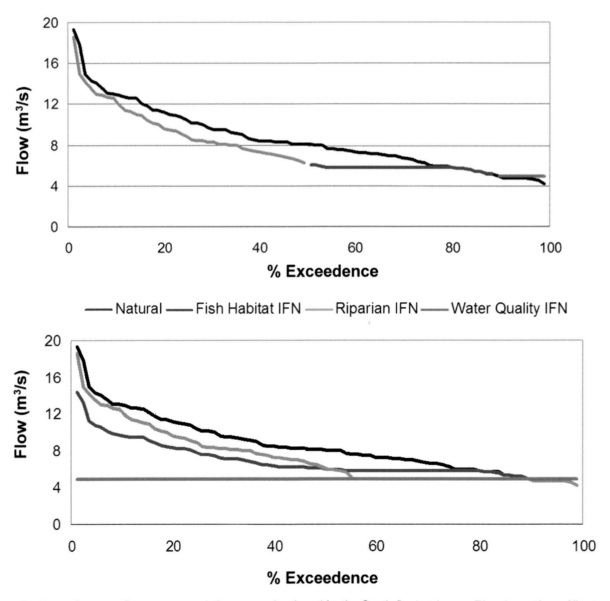

FIGURE 5-8. Instream flow recommendations were developed for the South Saskatchewan River in southern Alberta, Canada, by identifying instream flow needs (IFN) for various ecological functions and patching them together (From Clipperton et al. 2003).

flows that more closely mimic natural hydrographs, and to encourage managers involved in implementing federal environmental management to develop techniques that restore or rehabilitate natural riverine functions by enhancing natural riverine hydrographic features and sediment transport mechanisms."

Great care must be taken to ensure that any flow prescription, including one that approximates the natural flow regime, is logical. All factors that cannot be effectively reversed, such as physical changes that have occurred in the river channel or floodplain, interruption to the sediment supply, or the presence of exotic species must be considered. Managers must recognize the roles of the natural variability of river flow and the five elements of the natural flow regime: magnitude, frequency, duration, timing, and rate of change. In some cases, simply mimicking the shape of the natural hydrograph may be non- or counterproductive if the prescription exhibits the same general shape as the natural hydrograph, but at a much lower or compressed level. This simplistic approach will not ensure the specific flows and duration necessary to drive the dynamic physical and biological processes in the natural or present channel. Maintaining, rehabilitating, or restoring ecological processes are the underpinning of an ecologically based instream flow prescription and hydrologic processes that approximate natural flow regimes and quantities typically provide these processes.

Typically, providing a healthy aquatic community involves attention to the magnitude and duration of the natural flow regime's seasonal patterns (Poff et al. 1997). Flow conditions that vary in a manner similar to natural conditions will establish a variety of habitats and diverse fish communities. Different flow needs can be met by providing them all—separated by time. Variable conditions allow different species to flourish at different times. A temporal and spatial mosaic is a necessary component of riverine ecosystem integrity.

River ecosystems are complex and require variable flows. For example, high flows form and maintain the shape and characteristics of the river channel and floodplain, flush sediment from spawning gravels, maintain riparian vegetation and stream bank stability, provide habitat critical to the life history of certain fishes, and provide cues that initiate fish migration and spawning. One particular flow might provide enough habitat for some fish species and life stages, but it may fail to meet the long-term needs of these species by short circuiting critical physical processes (Poff et al. 1997). Hydrological, physical, biological, and chemical processes and their timing must be considered because all play a role in shaping a river and its aquatic resources.

Although river flows have been modified over time, they can also be restored over time. A summary of recent efforts to restore various components of the natural flow regime is provided in Table 5-1. The list is growing. In an article about the future of habitat modeling and instream flow assessment techniques, Hardy (1998) provided a broad and comprehensive view of the river corridor as an integrated ecosystem. This view provided an opportunity for research on methods and frameworks for delineating the process-driven linkages between flow, sediment transport, channel structure and the riparian community. Richter et al. (1997) proposed the "Range of Variability Approach" based on aquatic ecology theory concerning the role of hydrological variability. This method is intended to be used on rivers where the "conservation of native aquatic biodiversity and protection of natural ecosystem functions are primary river management objectives." In Alberta, the Fish and Wildlife Division has been making flow prescriptions that account for the natural variability of water supply since the early 1980s (Locke 1989).

IFC Flow Variability Statement: Instream flow prescriptions should provide inter- and intraannual variable flow patterns that mimic the natural hydrograph (magnitude, frequency, duration, timing, rate of change) to maintain or restore processes that sustain natural riverine characteristics.

There are scientific and social limits to what can be included in an instream flow prescription. In some watersheds, there may not exist enough recorded hydrologic data to reconstruct the natural hydrograph. There are also confounding factors such as land use and climate change. With any study that involves natural sciences there is uncertainty. Some of the uncertainty can be addressed, in part, by following prudent practices and agreed to protocols (Railsback 1999). In other situations, it is necessary to make clear statements that acknowledge the limitations of our knowledge, methods, and models to explain the complexity and interconnectivity of the real world.

TABLE 5-1. Recent projects in which restoration of some component(s) of natural flow regimes has occurred or been proposed for specific ecological benefits.

Project and water body names and location	Flow components	Ecological purpose(s) for flow regime	Reference
Klamath River	Prescribe inter- and intra-annual flow regimes that mimic the natural hydrograph	Maintain riverine processes to protect aquatic habitats for anadromous and other aquatic species	Hardy and Addley (2001)
Trinity River, California	Mimic timing and magnitude of peak flow	Rejuvenate in-channel gravel habitats; restore early riparian succession; provide migration flows for juvenile salmon	Baringa (1996)
Truckee River, California	Mimic timing, magnitude, and duration of peak flow, and its rate of change during recession	Restore riparian trees, especially cottonwoods	Klotz and Swanson (1997)
Owens River, California	Increase base flows; partially restore overbank flows	Restore riparian vegetation and habitat for native fishes and nonnative brown trout	Hill and Platts (1998)
Rush Creek, California (and other tributaries to Mono Lake)	Stream channel response to reestablishment of flow regimes and channel maintenance flows.	Restore riparian vegetation and habitat for waterfowl and nonnative fishes	Los Angeles Dept. of Water & Power (LADWP) (1995)
Oldman River and tributaries, southern Alberta, Canada	Increase summer flows; reduce rates of post-flood stage decline, mimic natural flows in wet years	Restore riparian vegetation (cottonwoods) and coldwater (trout) fisheries	Fernet et al. (1990); Rood et al. 1995
San Juan River, Utah and New Mexico	Mimic magnitude, timing, and duration of peak flow; restore low winter base flows	Recovery of endangered fish species	Holden (1999)
Green River, Utah and Colorado	Mimic magnitude, timing, and duration of peak flows; mimic duration and timing of nonpeak flows	Recovery of endangered fish species	Muth et al. (2000)
Rio Grande River, New Mexico	Mimic timing and duration of floodplain inundation	Maintain ecosystem processes (e.g., nitrogen flux, microbial activity, litter decomposition)	Molles et al. (1995)
Pecos River, New Mexico	Regulate duration and magnitude of summer irrigation releases to mimic spawning flow "spikes"; maintain minimum flows	Determine spawning and habitat needs for threatened species	Robertson, unpublished paper
Colorado River, Arizona	Mimic magnitude and timing	Restore habitat for endangered fish species and scour riparian zone	Collier et al. (1997)
Roanoke River, Virginia	Restore more natural patterning of monthly flows in spring; reduce rate of change between low and high flows during hydropower cycles	Increased reproduction of striped bass, restore bottomland forest community	Rulifson and Manooch 1993
Kissimmee River, Florida	Mimic magnitude, duration, rate of change, and timing of high- and low-flow periods	Restore floodplain inundation to recover wetland functions; reestablish in-channel habitats for fish and other aquatic species	Toth 1995
Housatonic River, Connecticut	Restore natural hydrograph on a daily time step basis	Restore habitat for native fluvial specialist fish spawning and juvenile develop	Normandeau Associates 1999
Farmington River, Connecticut	Preserve base flows	Restore Atlantic Salmon, maintain native and nonnative coldwater sport fishes (brook and brown trout) and other native fishes	Normandeau Associates 1992
Susitna River Hydroelectric Project, Susitna River, Southcentral Alaska	Preserve natural flow characteristics including seasonal flow patterns, channel geometry, sediment transport, water quality, and creation of large-scale reservoirs.	Prevent degradation to aquatic, riparian, and terrestrial species, habitat, recreation, navigation, aesthetics, socio-economics, in the Susitna River, tributaries, and connected lakes.	Alaska Power Authority 1988a, 1988b

DOCUMENTING THE RATIONALE FOR PROGRAM PRESCRIPTIONS

Perhaps the most critical aspect of making an instream flow prescription is to routinely and formally document how each of the five riverine components is addressed. One element of documentation is to establish the context of an instream flow prescription. Stating the context in terms of the riverine components allows those who must implement the decision, as well as specialists working in other streams, to accurately judge and replicate the approach taken. To be most effective in developing strategies, prescriptions must acknowledge the importance of the five riverine components and include an explanation of the need, or lack thereof, to include them in a study plan.

IFC Riverine Components Statement: Instream flow studies must evaluate flow needs and opportunities in terms of hydrology, geomorphology, biology, water quality, and connectivity.

Riverine Components

In addressing the riverine components, the following elements should be considered:

Hydrology: Stream Gaging. Stream gages provide basic information on hydrology: how much water, when, and how variable? Gage records are important to quantifying and monitoring instream flow needs. Information may be obtained regarding the annual hydrographs of stream and lakes, water budgets, annual and seasonal flow variations, flow response to precipitation or snow melt. Information from gaged streams may be transferable to streams with similar characteristics. However, the greater the geographic separation and the more different watershed characteristics, the less applicable data from another stream gage become (Lowham 1988).

Gaging stations are essential for monitoring compliance and enforcement of instream flow requirements. Project developers should fund placement, operation, and maintenance of these facilities. Where they are absent, gage stations should be installed as a condition of permits or licenses.

Instream flow programs and their administering agencies should be strong advocates for establishing and maintaining individual gages and gaging networks on appropriate streams and lakes. This support can include providing partial funding of gaging stations in key locations, or providing personnel or equipment. Agencies should seek opportunities to cooperate with other entities needing gaging information to reduce costs to individual agencies and expand coverage of the region's water resources.

IFC Stream Gaging Policy Statement: Instream flow programs must support individual gaging stations and networks of gaging stations necessary to quantify hydrographs, make and defend instream flow prescriptions, and monitor and enforce compliance.

Hydrology: Streamflow Measurement Protocol. When collecting stream discharge information for data analysis, compliance monitoring, adaptive management, or any instream flow-related purpose, data should be collected with appropriate equipment and according to approved processes and techniques. To standardize the calculation of stream discharge, flow meters and stream gaging devices and data collection protocols should be used according to accepted practices established by the U.S. Geological Survey (Rantz et al. 1982a, 1982b) and/or Environment Canada (Terzi 1981). The FERC used to make this an automatic license condition and some hydroelectric power licenses still contain this requirement (Christopher Estes, personal communication).

IFC Discharge Measurements Policy Statement: Discharge meters, stream gaging devices, and flow data collection protocols should meet accepted standards of the U.S. Geological Survey and/or Environment Canada.

Hydrology: Developing Synthetic Hydrologic Information. In many situations, appropriate gaging data are either lacking or incomplete. In these cases, hydrologic streamflow information is often developed synthetically using one or more hydrologic simulation models.

One technique to develop or extend a short period of record (less than 10 years) is to develop a regression between the daily flows of the streams with short records and related streams with longer records. If the stream has a short record, corresponding daily flows should be periodically sampled for the entire period of the shorter record. If the stream has a series of miscellaneous measurements, each measurement should be used as a data point in the regressions. If possible, regressions of flows for several streams with long-term gaging records can be developed and the one with the best fit selected. Figure 5-9 shows a regression of daily flows for the Terror and Uganik rivers in Alaska. The Uganik River has the longer period of record.

Once the regression has been performed to the satisfaction of the team, flow events of a particular frequency can be determined for the stream with the partial record. Annual hydrographs of different frequencies can be assembled using either the monthly flow duration or the total annual volume method. However, time steps of less than a month are of limited value because of the errors introduced through correlation.

Unfortunately, many important stream segments in the United States and Canada are not gaged. Several techniques can be used to estimate an annual hydrograph. The selection of any technique will depend more on the amount of hydrologic and meteorological data available than on the merits of the technique itself. The process of estimating an annual hydrograph can be simply stated as two steps. The first is to determine the total annual runoff for a specified water year. The second is to apportion the total runoff into appropriate percentages by month. The most difficult part of the process is usually the estimation of the annual runoff. Because, in most cases, only average annual runoff can be computed, only the average annual hydrograph can be synthesized with much accuracy.

If no gage data are available to generate hydrologic information by correlation, other techniques may be used—such as those based on water balancing equations. Water balancing refers to the balance between inflow of water from precipitation and snowmelt and the outflow from evaporation and streamflow. The difference between inflow and outflow is termed storage and may be positive (if inflow is greater than outflow) or negative if inflow is less than outflow (Thornthwaite and Mather 1955). One technique used to address the lack of detailed data for water balance equations is to use area-precipitation product method (Bovee 1982). The basic approach of this technique is to determine the drainage area upstream from all gaging stations in several watersheds in the same hydrologic unit. The mean precipitation for each area is then determined and multiplied by the appropriate drainage area. Next, a regression line is computed for the drainage area-precipitation product versus the mean annual volume for the gage at the bottom of each drainage area in the regression as shown in Figure 5-10. To determine the mean annual volume for an ungaged stream in the same hydrologic unit or area, it is necessary to determine the area-precipitation product in order to read the mean annual volume from the regres-

FIGURE 5-9. Correlation between mean daily flows of the Terror and Uganik rivers near Kodiak, Alaska (From Bovee 1982).

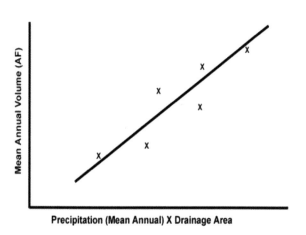

FIGURE 5-10. Regression of average annual volume versus area-precipitation products for several gaging stations in a watershed (From Bovee 1982).

sion line. This technique is less precise in watersheds having large elevation changes and corresponding precipitation gradients. The nature and origin of flows will also affect the precision and accuracy of the hydrologic simulation (Figure 5-11).

Flow estimation can be highly variable depending on the model used and data referenced. For example, Lowham (1988) provided flow estimation models of generally accepted approaches for quantifying hydrologic patterns in ungaged mountainous streams; however, the models typically generated confidence intervals that can be several times larger than the estimated hydrologic value. Any estimating technique should document assumptions, limitations (standard error factors), and context of technique and data used. Although synthetically derived flow information is acceptable in some situations, such as project planning, the data should be considered an interim solution until field data can be collected to refine estimates.

IFC Synthetically Derived Hydrologic Data Policy Statement: Instream flow assessments based on synthetically developed hydrologic information should acknowledge the source of data and its quality. Final decisions or agreements should be based on collection and use of appropriate field data to refine the precision of the original estimates.

FIGURE 5-11. Paradise Ice Cave on Mt. Rainier was a source of flow to the Cowlitz River in southwestern Washington. This glacier cave—known to exist for decades—and the water it once provided has now receded in response to warmer climatic conditions.

Hydrology: Land Use Practices. Rivers function as a part of the valleys they drain (Hynes 1975). The relations between flowing water, sediment, and nutrient transport link instream flows to land use practices throughout the watershed. Evidence of this is that water use and land use practices associated with urbanization, agriculture, forestry, and other land use practices have had a significant impact on groundwater attributes, and the frequency, timing, magnitude, duration, and rate of change of streamflows. Moreover, the widespread degradation of these resources indicates that many land use decisions have been made with little understanding or regard for the effect on adjacent or distant extents of the watershed (Schlosser 1991).

Many human-induced factors can alter instream flows, flow regimes, and groundwater. Land use practices such as removal of permanent cover (including upland forests), grazing, row crop agriculture, and urbanization (watershed hardening) usually accentuate high and low flows, decrease habitat diversity, and reduce the length of the lateral edge between terrestrial and aquatic boundaries (Brooks et al. 1991; Schlosser 1991). Most of these activities are necessary features of human habitation; however, the effects of some on the natural structure and function of riverine systems can be attenuated with adequate planning and consideration of project effects beyond the often-limited boundaries of a particular activity.

IFC Land Use Policy Statement: Instream flow practitioners should recognize the effects of land use practices on instream flows and work with land managers to promote land use practices that maintain or restore the natural hydrograph and avoid or minimize those that negatively affect the natural hydrograph.

Biology: Habitat. Prior to the implementation of instream flow tools that require habitat-discharge relations (e.g., PHABSIM and spatially-explicit two-dimensional habitat models), the identification of target species and their habitat requirements are necessary. Common approaches to the selection of target species may involve any one of a number of approaches including single species, mixed species, restriction to obligate riverine species, habitat guilds (Leonard and Orth 1988, among others), or any combination of vertebrates, invertebrates, and floral components. Many approaches have been developed to derive habitat requirements but most involve some form of habitat suitability criteria that defines some aspect of suitable habitat (e.g., suitable, marginal, preferred). Greater attention should be paid to the flow needs of fluvial habitat specialists. When sufficient data are available it may be possible to identify habitat

---

Many approaches have been developed to derive habitat requirements but most involve some form of habitat suitability criteria that defines some aspect of suitable habitat...

---

bottlenecks that constrain one or more species. These limiting conditions can then be factored into the development of instream flow prescriptions. Complexity is inherent in the development and use of habitat utilization data (see Orth 1987). Bovee et al. (1998) discussed these complexities in relation to behavioral and temporal shifts in habitat use, transferability issues (see also Thomas and Bovee 1993; Freeman et al. 1999; Williams et al. 1999), and interpretation. Habitat suitability analyses should focus on biologically relevant variables. It is typically improper to merely choose a generic (standard) method to describe the habitat under the assumption that target species can be selected at a later date.

Habitat is the site where an organism (or population) lives and is comprised of the biotic (e.g., riparian vegetation, aquatic macrophytes) and abiotic surroundings (e.g., depth, velocity, substrate materials, temperature, water quality). Habitat provides the life requirements of an organism such as food and shelter. Properly functioning stream channels maintain diverse habitat types necessary to sustain the natural aquatic community structure. However, the abundance of aquatic organisms is also related to the availability of habitat through time. Naturally occurring wet or dry periods can limit some populations of native species whereas other species adapted to those flows will flourish. Moreover, maintenance of diverse channel features is not obtained by a single threshold flow. Rather, a dynamic hydrograph of variable flows including both floods and droughts is needed for continuation of processes that maintain and create stream channel and habitat characteristics (Gordon 1995; Trush and McBain 2000; U.S. Forest Service, unpublished paper) and addresses critical time periods.

IFC Habitat Policy Statement: Instream flow prescriptions must maintain spatially complex and diverse habitats, which are available through all seasons.

Biology: Ice Processes. Habitat availability during the various stages of ice formation, presence and break-up, can be one of the most limiting factors to fish and other riverine organisms. Needham et al. (1945) was among the first to report winter fish mortality by documenting that the over-winter loss of brown trout (*Salmo trutta*) averaged nearly 60% in a 4-year period in Convict Creek, California. Zafft et al. (1995) documented trout losses approaching 90% in the tailwaters of Fontenelle Reservoir on the Green River, Wyoming. More recent studies (Maki-Petays et al. 1999; Whalen et al. 1999) have shown that winter habitat availability in ice-covered streams can be one of the most limiting factors to populations of trout. As a consequence, agencies that manage streams in temperate regions where ice formation is prevalent need to consider how winter water management decisions affect ice forming processes and associated habitat characteristics in terms of the hydrology, geomorphology, biology, water quality, and connectivity of streams (Figure 5-12).

Formation of frazil ice (suspended ice crystals formed from super-chilled water) can cause trout mortality through gill abrasion and subsequent suffocation (Maciolek and Needham 1952). Frazil ice may also increase trout mortality as resultant anchor ice limits habitat, causes localized dewatering, and results in excessive metabolic demands on fish forced to seek ice-free habitats (Brown et al. 1994; Simpkins et al. 2000). Pools downstream from high gradient frazil ice-forming areas can accumulate anchor ice when woody debris or surface ice provides anchor points for frazil crystals (Brown et al. 1994; Cunjak and Caissie 1994; Annear et al. 2002) described significant trout losses associated with repeated frazil ice events in the Bighorn River, Wyoming. Losses may also result from stream dewatering due to ice jams and hanging ice dams. Unfortunately, the tools to quantify the relation between flow and favorable ice conditions, and habitat, are limited at this time. In the face of this uncertainty, managers should take a conservative approach when their actions or those of others will result in modification of winter flow regimes, either by additions or depletions.

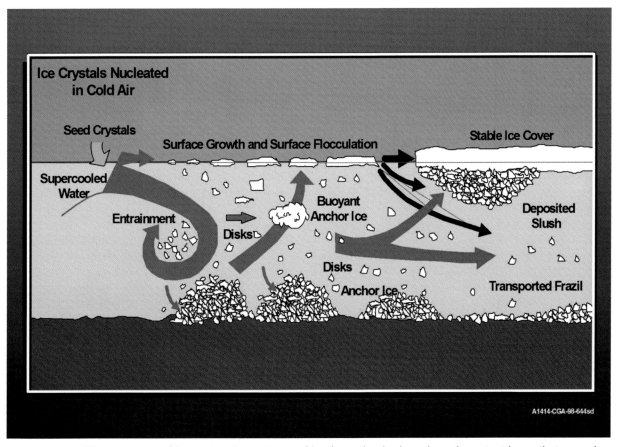

FIGURE 5-12. The presence of ice and various stages of ice formation in rivers is an important issue that agencies should consider when managing winter water withdrawals in northern states and Canadian provinces (Published with permission of Dr. Steven F. Daly, U.S. Army Corps of Engineers, Cold Regions Research and Engineering Laboratory, Hanover, New Hampshire).

IFC Ice Processes Policy Statement: Water management decisions for streams that are prone to ice formation should document the potential effects that the proposed action might have on the stream channel or associated aquatic organisms and, where appropriate, include measures to minimize or avoid potentially negative effects of project-related ice forming processes.

Geomorphology: Channel Form. Natural stream channels in a state of sediment equilibrium typically exhibit a high degree of channel stability over time as they seek and maintain a dimension, pattern, and profile that reflects the various physical attributes of the land through which they pass and the sediment and water that they carry down-

stream. Even "active" or "dynamic" streams that exhibit lateral migration are considered stable if they remain in a condition of sediment equilibrium and maintain their bankfull width, slope, and the same width/depth ratio (Rosgen 1996). The shape of the cross section of any river channel is a function of the flow, quantity, and character of the sediment in motion through the section and the composition of the materials (including vegetation) that make up the bed and banks (Leopold 1994). For alluvial streams, the channel is in dynamic equilibrium when the sediment load is in balance with the stream's transport capacity over time (years) (Bovee et al. 1998). Streams maintain their form and function by consistently transporting the entire sediment load that enters any particular segment of the stream (Figure 5-13).

Channel instability is the result of actions that upset this balance by either increasing or decreasing the sediment transport capability of the

107

stream or the sediment load. When transport capacity exceeds sediment load, the channel adjusts through either channel enlargement or degradation of the bed. When sediment load exceeds transport capacity, aggradation or channel reduction will occur. Many streams naturally exhibit periodic lateral movement across their floodplains; however, they are still considered "stable" if they remain in sediment equilibrium over time and maintain their natural or proper physical characteristics (e.g., bankfull width, sinuosity, slope). (Rosgen 1996). Leopold et al. (1964) noted that "Natural rivers, which are self-constructed and self-maintained, constantly seek their own stability." The science is very clear that alteration of flow regimes (Schumm 1969; Bohn and King 2001), sediment loads (Komura and Simmons 1967), and riparian vegetation can cause changes in the morphology of stream channels.

The dimensions and hydraulic capacity of all rivers are largely determined by the magnitude and duration of the annual high flow level and its ability to transport sediment (Leopold 1994; Carling 1995). This flow level is known as the dominant discharge or effective discharge and is technically defined as the flow that transports the majority of sediment in the long-term. Evidence suggests that bankfull flow approximates the effective discharge in stable stream channels, which indicates the adjustment of the channel to the range of discharges that transport the bulk of the sediment load (Andrews 1980; Leopold 1994; Doyle et al. 1999).

FIGURE 5-13. Effects of flushing flow prescriptions on the Colorado River below Glen Canyon Dam. Views are from the left bank of the river looking at National Canyon debris fan. *Top photo*: Flow rate is approximately 9,000 cfs on 26 March 1996. *Middle photo*: Flow rate is approximately 46,000 cfs on 1 April 1996. *Lower photo*: Flow rate is approximately 12,000 cfs on 5 April 1996. The additional deposition of sediment in the lower photo compared to the top photo is noted by the arrows (Source: Ted Mellis, U.S. Geological Survey, Flagstaff, Arizona).

However, this may not always be the case—especially in streams with disturbed watersheds and stream channels (Doyle et al. 1999).

In streams that have a wide range of sediment size on the channel boundary, a range of flows may best represent the dominant discharge because different flow velocities are needed to mobilize different sizes of bed load and sediment. As Kuhnle et al. (1999) noted, "A system designed with one steady flow to transport the supplied mass of sediment would in all likelihood become unstable as the channel aggraded and could no longer convey the sediment and water supplied to it. A system designed with one steady flow to transport the supplied sediment size distribution would in all likelihood become unstable as the bed degraded and caused instability of the banks."

For many species, completing the life cycle requires an array of diverse habitat types whose availability over time is regulated by the flow regime (Sparks 1995; Greenberg et al. 1996; Reeves et al. 1996). In many stream types, the channel maintenance flow provides an ecological function that directly affects biological and physical stream processes. If water and watershed managers are to avoid future negative ecological effects to unimpaired streams, or employ effective efforts to restore or rehabilitate degraded streams, it is important to understand and embrace the concept that variable flows up to at least bankfull are needed to maintain the form and function of rivers and associated fisheries.

We emphasize that although scientists now have a better understanding of the physical concepts and processes of channel maintenance flows in natural rivers, much remains to be learned about using this information to repair previous riverine damage and rehabilitate or restore river functions that have been disrupted. Likewise, considerable research is needed to allow us to better understand and describe the complex relations between biological processes and variable channel forming flows.

IFC Channel Maintenance Policy Statement: Channel maintenance flow is an essential component of instream flow prescriptions for alluvial channels and maintenance, rehabilitation, restoration, and preservation of stream channel form and associated biological communities.

Geomorphology: Flushing Flows. Flushing flows are naturally occurring short-term flows that remove fine sediments from gravel (Reiser et al. 1989). A successful flushing flow would reduce fine sediments to rehabilitate or restore an important spawning and egg incubation area. By comparison, channel maintenance flows imply a longer time frame to determine success, which entails management of the entire channel and requires an understanding of the complex set of factors that influence channel morphology. Flushing flows are a subset of channel maintenance flows and conventional thinking has long held that if channel maintenance flows have been provided, then so, too, have flushing flows. However, as noted above (see also Kuhnle et al. 1999), a single steady discharge will not transport the same distribution of sediment sizes as a range of flows. Therefore, managers who assume that providing channel maintenance flows will also provide the needed ecological function of flushing flows may, in fact, be prescribing actions that result in detrimental effects to the form and function of the stream channel and habitat.

The movement of sediment depends on availability of sediment and sediment transporting ability (competency) of the stream (Reiser et al. 1989). Deep, fast, turbulent water has greater competency than shallow, slow water; deposition occurs when competency decreases. Artificially reducing peak flows reduces stream competency. Decreasing stream competency can have direct and serious effects on aquatic biota, including fish (O'Brien 1984). The net effect is that sediment inputs accumulate rather than being periodically removed during higher flows. Specified flushing flows may be necessary to mitigate those impacts (Wenzel 1993). Moderately high flows transport sediment through stream channels (Leopold 1994). Studies assessing the impact of sediment on aquatic biota generally demonstrate an inverse relation between the accumulation of fine sediment in fish spawning and rearing habitats and fish survival and abundance (Bjornn 1969; Phillips et al. 1975; Beschta and Jackson 1979; Tappel and Bjornn 1983; Reiser and White 1988; Osmundson et al. 2002). Duration, frequency, and sediment recruitment are related issues. Consistently providing flushing flows (e.g., in a regulated stream) can constantly remove sediment resulting in paved (armored) substrates in areas where sediment is no longer imported, such as below a dam where sediment is stored in the reservoir (U.S. Forest Service, unpublished paper).

IFC Flushing Flow Policy Statement: For many stream types, a flushing flow for removing fine sediments is a necessary component of instream flow prescriptions.

Geomorphology: Channel Modification. Stream channels have been and continue to be physically altered through straightening, widening, lining, reshaping and relocation, with profound effects on the stability and integrity of natural systems (Rosgen 1996). The occurrence of long, straight channel reaches in nature is rare (Leopold et al. 1964). Even where a channel appears straight, it is usual for the thalweg to wander from bank- to-bank. Braided or meandering channels offer greater resistance to flow than do straight channels (Leopold et al. 1964). This resistance dissipates energy, which can help minimize flooding downstream; transports sediment, which helps maintain sediment equilibrium; and forms aquatic habitat.

Stream channelization is a short-term solution to flooding or land management, which results in long-term increases in flow velocity and stream bank erosion (Waters 1995). The deliberate straightening, deepening and widening of natural channels not only removes instream habitat, it can set in motion a sequence of unnatural channel modifications (bank erosion, channel down-cutting). The primary and long-term secondary effects of stream channelization destabilize aquatic ecosystems both upstream and downstream from channelized sections. Some have argued (Brookes 1998), with good basis, that channelization has caused as much or more degradation to riverine resources as has hydrograph alteration (Figure 5-14).

Channelization should be considered only as the last solution to a flow management problem. Changes in watershed and floodplain land use and changes in perceptions and understanding of flooding are the best solutions. In situations where all other alternatives are rejected and channelization must occur, the project should be designed and constructed to maintain natural function and form of the channel to the greatest degree possible. Adequate numbers of channel roughness elements (angular rocks, woody revetments) and channel meanders should be included in the design and smoothing features (concrete or gabion-lined sides and bottoms) should be avoided.

Over much of the past 50 years, fishery and wildlife management agencies and others have worked extensively to develop fish habitat improvement and bank stabilization techniques. Although short-term goals were achieved, much of the work did not reflect an understanding of the importance of geomorphic process and longitudinal and lateral connectivity of the project area to the watershed. Consequently, the long-term success of many projects was compromised and some projects may have resulted in more harm than good. Some examples include bank stabilization projects that lined eroding banks with velocity enhancing structures like rock gabions and habitat improvement structures that created plunge pools on streams with high sediment loads.

It has only been in the past decade that some managers have begun incorporating the established principles of fluvial geomorphology into the design and construction of channel rehabilitation projects. Solutions should be developed that reflect an understanding of the character and func-

FIGURE 5-14. The West Prairie River, near the town of High Prairie in north-central Alberta, Canada, shows a channelized section alongside the natural channel. Channelization has altered all five riverine components. Note the meandering pattern occurring within the banks of the straightened river reach (Source: Lorne Fitch, Alberta Sustainable Resource Development, Fish and Wildlife Division).

tion of the watershed and floodplain and be based on attributes such as sediment transport rates, stream sinuosity, channel slope, hydraulic roughness and natural habitat features.

IFC Channel Modification Policy Statement: Any proposed stream channel modification should document the hydrologic and geomorphic character and function of the watershed and floodplain and incorporate principles of applied fluvial geomorphology and natural habitat features.

Geomorphology: Instream Mining. Instream mining of gravel and minerals typically interferes with sediment transport and can significantly affect biology, hydrology, habitat, water quality, and connectivity (Figure 5-15). In some situations where development in the watershed has caused excessive amounts of sediment to enter the stream, instream mining may actually help restore a stream to a more functional state if properly regulated (Martin and Hess 1986). However, the mining must be regulated to ensure that only material in excess of the normal sediment load of the natural channel is removed. The preferred alternative is better watershed protection because any extraction of instream mineral resources can cause stream channel and bank instability, aquatic habitat loss, water quality degradation, and direct mortality to aquatic organisms.

Instream mining takes advantage of the natural process of bedload transport in streams. Most streams in their natural condition exhibit a state of sediment equilibrium where the quantity of bed materials entering a particular segment is equal to the amount being exported over time (typically many years). In some river systems, sand and gravel may accumulate in some areas. Sand and gravel operations routinely mine these areas and allow the natural transport of bedload material to replenish the site. If this type of activity removes material in excess of the natural deposits at the site, it will create a condition of sediment disequilibrium. To compensate for this sediment-starved condition, water flowing through downstream segments of the stream often acquires bed material from the stream channel, which leads to down cutting or armoring. In other situations, the water flowing beyond mined segments may acquire sediments from stream banks leading to increased erosion, channel widening or channel movement.

If excessive sediments are removed from a mined area, accelerated velocities result that lead to an increase in head cutting upstream from the affected area. Head cutting is the process by which the upstream portion of a stream channel becomes destabilized and erodes progressively in an upstream direction. Head cuts may continue until they reach a point of geologic resistance, or the channel slope is otherwise able to reach a point of equilibrium (Rosgen 1996). The sediment produced by the head cutting directly affects fish, mussels, and other aquatic species throughout various phases of their life cycles.

FIGURE 5-15. The Oldman River in southern Alberta (*left photo*) and the Spavinaw Creek in extreme northwest Arkansas (*right photo*) depict gravel mining from stream channels. Instream mining for gravel and minerals can have significant effects on stream channel form and function. Upstream consequences include bed instability and increased erosion from head cutting.

Excessive instream mining can also cause potentially significant negative effects on floodplain function. As stream bank and bed material moves into the depression caused by mining from upstream, the upstream bed level may be lowered. As the bed level is lowered, the existing floodplain becomes less accessible to flood events. During subsequent floods, the river may adjust to the change in the bed level. Because rivers develop floodplains at an optimum level above the bed, lowering the bed or raising the floodplain causes the near-bank shear stresses of floodwaters to increase. The result is often severe stream bank erosion because the river must build an entirely new floodplain at the lower level and reestablish equilibrium among sediment conveyance, flood flow, and valley slope (Rosgen 1996). Because the former floodplain may be inundated with less frequency, it appears safer for development and encourages human encroachment. The combination of changed flood occurrence and human encroachment means that long-term effects of these physical changes are often worse than before the floodplain was altered.

Understanding the natural processes that occur in waterways with sand and gravel deposits is important. These complex processes are usually hard to predict and manage once disturbance has occurred in the channel. As a consequence, in-channel mining should be the last option considered. In situations where instream mining is the only option, extraction should occur at a level less than or equal to the long-term import of materials to a site to minimize potential negative effects beyond the extraction area.

IFC Instream Mining Policy Statement: Instream mining as a source of sand, gravel, or other materials should only be considered as a last option, and the mining operation should only be allowed to remove material in excess of the normal sediment transport carrying capacity of the stream.

Water Quality. The quality of water in streams is closely related to the quantity and origin of water as a function of the timing, amount, and types of discharges and effluents from natural and man-made sources. Unfortunately, many studies of flow needs have traditionally overlooked including specific analyses of the effect of flow change on temporal and spatial characteristics of water quality including temperature, dissolved gasses, sediment, and concentrations of various chemical constituents. Dams, diversions and water transfers in combination and independent of adjacent land use activities all affect the thermal and chemical character of flowing waters and the effects on riverine processes can be wide ranging and significant depending on the specifics of flow change involved (Hynes 1975; Leopold 1994).

Water quality models that simulate temperature dynamics require empirical data on stream geometry, meteorology, hydrology, and water temperature; for example, Stream Network Temperature model (SNTEMP; Bartholow 1989). Stream geometry data requirements can usually be met through field collection activities associated with characterization of physical habitat. Additional information is needed on stream shading. Meteorological data can be obtained through the National Climatic Data Center as well as from local weather monitoring stations. Hydrological data records are published by the U.S. Geological Survey, and Environment Canada, and stream temperature records are available from state or provincial and federal water quality regulatory agencies, among others, and from collection of empirical stream temperature data.

IFC Water Quality Policy Statement: Instream flow prescriptions must recognize the relation between the quantity and quality of water in streams, document the effects of water quality changes on riverine resources, and implement prescriptions that maintain or improve water quality characteristics for natural riverine resources.

Connectivity: Lateral (Riparian Zone). For some streams, naturally occurring low flow years allow for the establishment of riparian seedlings on bars deposited in the years immediately preceding wet years (Trush and McBain 2000). Frequently occurring small floods may present recruitment opportunities for riparian plant species in regions where floodplains are frequently inundated (Wharton and Brinson 1979; Wharton et al. 1981). Intermediate-sized floods inundate low-lying floodplains and deposit entrained sediment, allowing for the establishment of pioneer species (Poff 1997). Larger floods that recur on the order of decades inundate the aggraded floodplain terraces where later successional species establish. Rare, large floods can uproot mature riparian trees and deposit them in the channel, creating high-quality habitat for many aquatic species. Scouring of floodplain soils rejuvenates habitat for plant species that germinate only on barren, wetted surfaces that are free of competition (Scott et al. 1996) or that require root access to shallow water tables (Stromberg 1997).

Duration, timing, and the rate of change of flow events often determine ecological significance

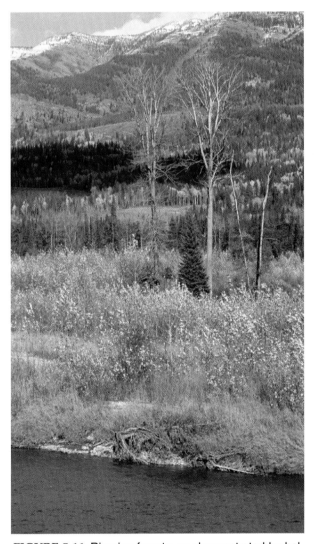

FIGURE 5-16. Riparian forests, as demonstrated by balsam poplar trees (*Populus balsamifera*) along the Elk River, in southeastern British Columbia, require lateral connectivity to ensure that the natural timing of high flows affords natural rates of flow inundation and recession for seed bed rejuvenation, germination, root growth, and tree development (Source: Lorne Fitch, Alberta Sustainable Resource Development, Fish and Wildlife Division).

(Poff 1997). Tolerance to prolonged flooding in riparian plants allows some species to persist in locations from which they might otherwise be displaced by dominant, but less tolerant species (Chapman et al. 1982; Hupp and Osterkamp 1985). Many riparian plant emergence phenologies (the sequence of flowering, seed dispersal, germination, and seedling growth) interact with temporally varying flooding or drought to maintain diversity (Streng et al. 1989; Figure 5-16). Seasonal rates of change of flow conditions regulate the persistence of cottonwoods (*Populus spp.*) (Rood and Mahoney 1990).

For many stream types, riparian vegetation is an integral component for stream function and processes and the related biotic community. Riparian vegetation depends on a range of streamflows to establish or reestablish conditions suitable for riparian vegetation to grow, replenish soil, and trigger emergence phenologies and to maintain plant diversity.

IFC Riparian Connectivity Policy Statement: Instream flow prescriptions must recognize the connectivity between instream flows and riparian areas, and maintain or establish riparian structure and functions.

Connectivity: Lateral (Floodplains). Interrelations between overbank flows and the floodplain provide a conduit for the exchange of nutrients and energy, maintain physical habitat components, and create conditions for establishing and maintaining riparian vegetation. Overbank flows import woody debris into the channel (Keller and Swanson 1979), creating high-quality habitat (Wallace and Benke 1984; Moore and Gregory 1988). Aquatic and floodplain biota are adapted to a range of naturally occurring high flows and the timing of these flows in relation to temperature and predictability of flows (Petts 1987). Floodplain wetlands provide important spawning and nursery grounds for fish (Welcomme 1979; Junk et al. 1989; Sparks 1995) and some fish adapted to exploiting floodplain habitats decline in abundance when floodplain use is restricted (Ross and Baker 1983; Finger and Stewart 1987). It is now widely recognized that the maintenance and restoration of the lateral connectivity across the floodplain is vital for sustaining the ecological integrity of rivers (Junk 1989; Petts 1989; Welcomme 1995) (Figures 5-17 and 5-18).

113

FIGURE 5-17. A common strategy to reduce flood damage is to separate the channel from its floodplain by constructing high dikes, as pictured here along the Elbow River in southwestern Alberta. The resulting loss of lateral connectivity will also reduce the ecological functions provided by the floodplain and may cause the channel to aggrade, ultimately resulting in higher flood stages and greater risks (Source: Lorne Fitch Alberta Sustainable Resource Development, Fish and Wildlife Division).

IFC Floodplains Connectivity Policy Statement: Instream flow prescriptions should maintain or reestablish connectivity between instream flows and floodplains.

Connectivity: Vertical. Streamflow results from a combination of surface water, soil water, and groundwater (Poff et al. 1997). During a wet season, precipitation separates into that which infiltrates, immediately evaporates, or runs over the ground surface (Leopold 1994). Much of the water in rivers first infiltrates the ground after falling as precipitation, flows underground and discharges into streams where the water table intersects the soil surface (Figure 5-19). In rivers above permeable alluvial aquifers, groundwater upwelling produces clear ecological patterns in rivers (Maddock et al. 1995) that influence the distribution of benthic fauna at the river reach (Creuze des Chatelliers and Reygrobellet 1990) and individual riffle scales (Sterba et al. 1992). Infiltration and percolation is also a form of storage and sustains base flows during nonstorm or dry periods (Leopold 1994). However, the water table can drop in dry periods so that springs no longer flow. Groundwater elevation fluctuates naturally in floodplains, terraces, sloughs, and adjacent wetlands seasonally and from year-to-year and is an important component of a functioning river ecosystem (Findlay 1995; Bouwker and Maddock 1997; Trush and McBain 2000).

FIGURE 5-18. The east bank of the Mississippi River, south of Baton Rouge and opposite Manchac Point, Louisiana. The two pictures show the water level inside of the levee (*left photo*) and the highway outside (*right photo*). Looking across the river from the east bank toward Manchac Point (*left photo*), a towboat and barges can be glimpsed through the submerged trees. The trees are growing on what is locally called the batture, which is dry land when the river is at or below mean flow (Source: Blue Watson, Louisiana Department of Wildlife and Fish).

Another concern is watershed inhabitants that become overly dependent on amounts of groundwater that are insufficient to support long-term, sustained demand (Brooks et al. 1991). Pumping water from an aquifer lowers the water table around the withdrawal site creating a cone of depression, sometimes extending for miles (Figure 5-20). Locating wells too close together causes them to interact, which can lower the water table more than if the wells were spaced farther apart depending on the rate of recharge. Stream base flow can be reduced if excessive withdrawals lower the water table. The consequences of reduced natural streamflow are amplified during dry years. Instream flow managers should consider surface waters and shallow groundwater as a single resource and be aware of potential impacts from excessive pumping of groundwater on stream resources.

Some studies have documented a connection between surface stream water and shallow groundwater in alluvial settings and assumed that stream stages approximate water tables in alluvial aquifers (Castro and Hornberger 1991; Stromberg and Patten 1996), but the connection is typically not a simple one. Rather, the connection is often more correlative than causative because the interactions between streamflow and shallow groundwater are complex. Streamflow as a function of shallow groundwater can vary rapidly over relatively short distances and at different times of year

FIGURE 5-19. Cross-section of the Edwards Aquifer in central Texas. Recharge into the aquifer occurs when streams and rainfall runoff enter the fractured limestone outcrops in the recharge zone. Water in the artesian zone is confined under pressure-forming artesian springs and wells. Springs form the base flow for rivers and streams that eventually provide freshwater inflow into bays and estuaries. These spring systems also support unique aquatic communities in an otherwise hot, dry area (Published with permission of Margaret Garcia, Public Affairs, Edwards Acquifer Authority, San Antonio, Texas).

as a function of underlying geology, precipitation, temperature, vegetative cover and other factors (Rains and Mount 2002). Although numerical modeling can sometimes provide a general sense of the effects of shallow groundwater depletions on surface water flow, the ability to model long reaches of streams is generally limited without collection of additional site-specific data (Rains 2003).

IFC Groundwater Connectivity (Management) Policy Statement: Instream flow prescriptions should recognize and describe the extent and nature of connectivity between instream flows and groundwater and manage groundwater withdrawals to avoid potentially negative impacts on instream flows and riverine resources.

Connectivity: Longitudinal. The ability of fish and many other aquatic organisms to migrate within their environment is, at a minimum, important to their survival, and at most, essential to it (Hynes 1970). Aquatic organisms move upstream and downstream to meet a variety of habitat needs (Figure 5-21). These movements may be localized or involve migrations of hundreds of miles. For example, during warm periods in the summer trout often migrate to cool water refuges such as the mouths of tributary streams or to areas of groundwater inflow. Likewise, trout may migrate in the fall to areas that provide over-wintering habitat (Cunjak and Power 1986). Observations of individual brown trout (*Salmo trutta*) inhabiting different segments of a stream system during dif-

ferent seasons led Meyers et al. (1992) to stress the importance of barrier-free streams and a fisheries management approach that focuses on the entire drainage system. Bovee et al. (1994) described the importance of habitat variability and connectivity for smallmouth bass (*Micropterus dolomieu*) and rock bass (*Ambloplites rupestris*) in Michigan's Huron River. In Vermont, the importance of maintaining unimpeded passage was recognized by the legislature, which passed a law making it illegal to obstruct the passage of fish without the permission of the Fish and Wildlife Commissioner (VT. STAT. ANN. TIT. 10, § 4607).

Longitudinal connectivity can also be important to the life history of other invertebrates such as aquatic insects and mussels (Dillon 2000). Each mussel species utilizes specific fish host species. Some can use a number of different fishes whereas others can use only one or two. For example, the only fish host that has been identified for the pink heelsplitter (*Pleurobema sintoxia*) and fragile papershell (*Leptodea fragilis*) is the freshwater drum (*Aplodinotus grunniens*). (Dillon 2000). Barriers such as dams that impede upstream movements of host fish will also constrain the use of upstream areas by mussels that rely on these fish as hosts. Conversely, enabling the movement of host fish to upstream habitat will in turn also allow colonization of these areas by associated mussel species.

If not properly designed, culverts can create significant barriers to upstream movement of fish and other species. Baker and Votapka (1990) cited many fish passage problems associated with culverts and offered some solutions for mitigating those effects. Bottomless culverts and bridges generally pose fewer barriers.

Interface of groundwater-flow system, hyporheic zone and stream

FIGURE 5-20. As illustrated in this cross-sectional view, streambeds are unique environments where groundwater that drains much of the subsurface of landscapes interacts with surface water that drains much of the surface of landscapes. Mixing of surface water and groundwater takes place in the hyporheic zone where microbial activity and chemical transformations commonly are enhanced (From Winters et al. 1998).

Natural and manmade barriers can serve important functions to prevent unwanted aquatic organisms from reaching some habitats. In certain instances, barriers have been constructed to exclude undesirable species from becoming established in portions of some streams. Opportunities to use this strategy as a fishery management tool are usually limited and typically involve considerable planning, coordination with other agencies, and input from the public.

IFC Longitudinal Connectivity Policy Statement: Instream flow prescriptions should recognize and document the importance of connectivity within defined stream segments and the stream system in general. Management actions should avoid creating longitudinal disconnectivity where appropriate and restore connectivity where needed.

Determination Process

Another important element of documentation is to establish the decision rationale. Providing a clear, written rationale for the methods and decision process will help defend the prescription against challenge. A statement of rationale presents the reasons for a decision, including which of the five riverine components is addressed, which is excluded and why, and describes the physical setting, legal constraints, expected water use, study objectives, tools or methods used, study implementation, alternatives analysis, and problem resolution.

An ideal instream flow study would analyze all five riverine components; however, in practice, many instream flow studies do not. Nevertheless, each component must be addressed in some way. In some cases, this may require no more than stating the assumption that a component is not expected to change as a result of the proposed action. Documenting the decision reinforces the need for a

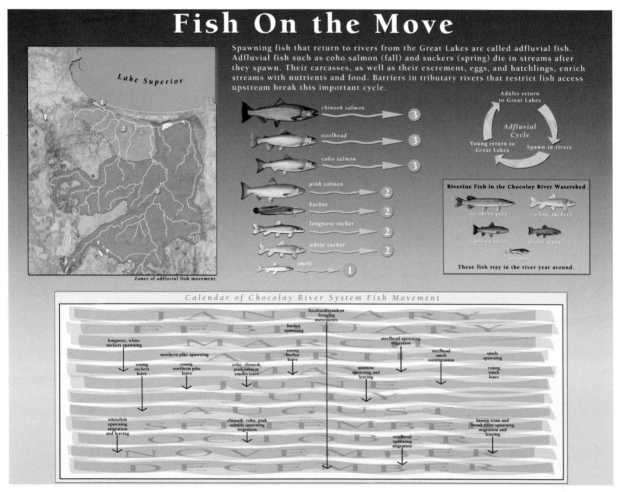

FIGURE 5-21. As evidenced by this poster, longitudinal connectivity of rivers from their headwaters to their mouths can be critically important for many different organisms (Source: Michigan Department of Natural Resources).

comprehensive study, puts the rationale in the record, and allows more effective implementation.

Physical Setting and Baseline Information. Physical setting establishes a brief description of the location of the stream segment, historical trends, and present classification, including the hydrology, type of channel, water quality (e.g., temperature regime) and the biota that will be affected. When do peak flows and bulk of flow occur (months) and what are the sources (springs, rainfall, snowmelt, glacier)? When do lowest and highest flows occur? What is the rate of change between base and peak flows? What is the relation between demand and availability of water for different uses, including instream flow needs? Is the channel alluvial, bedrock, canyon, valley, floodplain, or estuary? Do the species affected include fish, freshwater or estuarine mollusks, insects, riparian trees, floodplain vegetation, estuarine vegetation? If an estuary is affected, is salinity distribution influenced?

Reconnaissance studies or assessments may be needed to address baseline conditions and information gaps and should be built into the study plan (Figure 5-22). Such studies typically answer biological (e.g., community composition), hydrological (e.g., how might existing river regulation affect data collection), water quality (e.g., identify spring sources or cooling reservoir releases that might influence temperature regimes) and/or physical habitat questions (e.g., what current velocities or icing processes might be expected). In essence, a reconnaissance effort will help to familiarize study participants with field conditions, biological communities, channel conditions, unknown features of a river, and riverine components that are most likely to be impacted by water allocation or regulation.

Another study design consideration is the development of baselines that will be used as benchmarks for alternatives analysis and pre-and post-project monitoring plans (Figure 5-23). A detailed discussion of baselines (hydrologic, water

FIGURE 5-22. Example of mesoHABSIM analysis—a method that is gaining popularity, particularly in the eastern United States. *Upper left photo:* The habitat survey delineates hydro-morphologic units and their physical attributes. *Upper right photo:* The fish survey information identifies key habitat attributes affecting fish. *Lower photo:* The model calculates the relative probability of fish presence in each habitat and delineates suitable areas (*shown in green*) (From Parasiewicz 2003).

quality, biological, and geomorphic) is provided in Bovee et al. (1998). Hydrologic baseline conditions, developed from naturalized, synthetic, or historical records are critical to alternatives analysis in intensive studies and hydrologic evaluation methods (e.g., Index of Hydrologic Alteration; Richter et al. 1996). However, extreme caution is warranted when working with altered hydrographs (i.e., records that reflect significant human-caused alteration) in alternatives analysis or descriptive statistical techniques, such as flow duration curves.

Although flow duration curves (also called percent exceedence curves) can provide useful information about flow availability and help managers develop or assess the practicality of recommendations, prolonged depletions can, over time (decades), gradually shift duration curves downward. The net result is that flow duration curves may at some point no longer provide appropriate information about the natural flow patterns that formed the channel and under which conditions the fishery developed. Instead, they can actually show that less water is available (or needed) for instream flow needs.

Setting instream flow needs based on flow duration curves warrants at least two cautions. One caution involves strategies that identify a cap or limit to the amount of water that is allowed for diversion (Figure 5-24). Protective measures to allow a defined reduction in flow from natural levels must actually be based on natural or virgin flow duration levels. Another caution is that a protected base flow is necessary to identify a portion of the hydrograph below which further depletions are discouraged or prohibited (Figure 5-24). Monitoring is essential to ensure that the hydrograph is not affected by demand under this flow protection strategy. Strictly speaking, base flow recommendations do not mandate that water be supplied up to that point, but specify that all flow up to that point should remain in the stream, regardless of the frequency of its availability. Unless the impact of water withdrawals on natural (virgin) flow is documented and accounted for, incremental allocation may at some point reduce flow duration curves such that the percent exceedence level recommended for maintaining the fishery is less than the requirement for biological viability, which the approach is designed to provide. To be most effective, flow duration curve assessments should include reference to both current flow exceedence levels as well as the natural or virgin flow conditions.

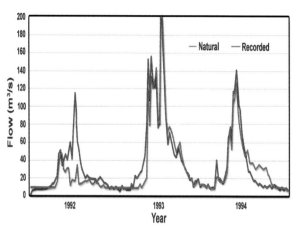

FIGURE 5-23. Hydrograph of regulated (recorded) and unregulated (natural, simulated) flow on the Oldman River in southern Alberta.

FIGURE 5-24. Flow duration curves are sometimes used to identify or assess the availability of instream flow needs but they can be artificially reduced by prolonged depletions. Whether used to identify or assess the availability of a maximum amount of water for diversion (upper) or a base flow below which further depletions are prohibited or discouraged (lower), they should reference natural (virgin) flow conditions.

119

Legal Constraints. Legal issues may either preclude or require certain levels or types of instream flow protection. The Endangered Species Act mandates that when an aquatic, riparian, or floodplain-dependent organism is listed as threatened or endangered there must be a special emphasis on instream flows. Federal reserved water rights under the Winters Doctrine (Shurts 2000) or other federal reservations give priority to the uses necessary to maintain the purposes of the reservation, which often include instream flows.

All these factors might lead to instream flow prescriptions that would not necessarily pertain to all other water uses, even at the same location. Documenting the rationale in the context of a particular legal constraint is the best defense against being forced to meet all situations with one approach.

An important step in all instream flow applications is problem identification (Stalnaker et al. 1995). Initiating the documentation of the decision framework with problem identification is not unique to the IFIM and can be employed with any instream flow method.

Problem identification must begin with a broad ecological perspective. Initially, it is not so much about the "problem" as it is about natural resource management goals. Fishery and wildlife agencies should begin from the perspective of their legal stewardship role over public fishery and wildlife resources. For any instream flow application, there is a need to consider legal and institutional constraints in addition to the ecological aspects, but such thinking should always be related to the effect on the public natural resources and should inform the public of the ecological consequences of any water management decision.

Expected Water Use. Documentation must also provide a record of assumptions, limitations, and context. Consider a water use project whose diversion capacity is small compared to the natural streamflow. Higher flows will dwarf the diversion capacity. In this situation, it may be acceptable to establish a flow regime based only on water quality and aquatic habitat needs, if we can assume the project will not significantly change the natural hydrograph except during low flow periods. However, the permit document should clearly state that the flow prescriptions are conditioned upon the project's proposed configuration and by the stated assumption(s). The same prescription would not be appropriate for a large capacity diversion because the influence on the hydrograph

would be different. Similarly, if the assumption of minimum impact on other, neglected components was later revealed to be unfounded, the prescription must be revisited.

Overall demand and the type of anticipated water use will affect the flow prescription. Hydroelectric diversion often will return all water to the stream. If we disregard increased evapotranspiration rates and the hydroelectric project does not store water, it might be considered nonconsumptive, except in a bypass reach between diversion and powerhouse tailrace. Still, hydroelectric projects may affect temperature, dissolved oxygen (DO), sediment transport, habitat, and connectivity. Therefore, in some respects such a project can be thought of as consuming natural resources. Irrigation, municipal, and industrial water supplies are generally considered consumptive uses. Some dams differ seasonally in their operation, including flood control dams, storage dams, and municipal water supply dams. Sometimes several of these purposes are combined in a single dam and would clearly present changes to the natural hydrograph. Withdrawals from groundwater wells also may affect surface flow during a different season than when water is withdrawn.

Study Objectives. The development of study objectives, as suggested by Bovee et al. (1998), should be guided by agency aquatic resource goals, identified issues, and information needs. They emphasized that "(O)bjectives should be precise, measurable, and achievable." However, objectives also need to be flexible to allow innovations to be discussed and incorporated as warranted. This is especially true when a proposed development is allowed to go forward and mitigation is

---

"Objectives should be precise, measurable, and achievable."

---

the only remaining option. At this point in the process, the lead participants should be familiar with information needs, the geographic boundaries, study objectives, scale, and dimension of the instream flow problem. This foundation will allow agencies to determine which of the five riverine components must be studied given available resources and risks. Other factors will help identify hydrologic, hydraulic, physical habitat, water quality, and biological models and data requirements for each model component.

Often pertinent plans already exist
that can provide guidance in setting
objectives.

Often pertinent plans already exist that can provide guidance in setting objectives. Examples include fisheries management plans, wild and scenic designation, watershed plans, water quality standards and recovery plans for endangered species. Fisheries management plans often include detailed information about a species or groups of species, their habitat and human use. These plans may cover an entire state or province, or they may be watershed-specific. For example, the Strategic Plan for the Restoration of Atlantic Salmon to the Connecticut River (Connecticut River Atlantic Salmon Commission 1998) described what parts of the watershed were managed for wild reproduction or rearing habitat for stocked fish. Fish passage requirements at dams within the watershed were also described. Water quality standards may provide guidance in determining management objectives. These standards often categorize state waters into a number of classes with different designated uses and management objectives. Designated uses often include aquatic life, aquatic habitat and fishing. In some cases, there are numeric criteria; DO is a common example.

The rationale must describe the context
and scope of the prescription so that it
is obvious what the method was
designed to do as well as what it was
not intended to address.

Specific objectives are typically developed during the study-planning phase. Goals and important natural resources are coalesced into specific tasks with specific purposes. In reference to a California law requiring fish below a dam to be maintained in "good condition," Moyle et al. (1998) described a definition that includes three planning levels: individual, population, and community. In addition to fish habitat measures, this approach includes measures such as fish condition, age and growth, presence of outwardly detectable disease or lesions, age class structure, population size and Index of Biotic Integrity. These additional measures are useful for characterizing an existing condition as it relates to fish populations (biology).

Tools. Methods for evaluating and recommending instream flows may range from simple desktop or planning methods to detailed incremental analysis. Rationale for using a particular method or

---

Information regarding choice of
methods, data, assumptions, analytical
procedures, results, and the logic
supporting the outcome are critically
important elements of any instream
flow application.

---

analysis might include scale of impact, cumulative impact, season of impact, ability to regulate use, or legal-political considerations. These must be documented so resulting instream flows are enforceable and one flow analysis method is not forced to fit all future flow prescriptions. For example, someone might propose to irrigate a small garden from a major river through use of a garden hose and small pump. Use would be limited to the growing season and might represent an immeasurable change based on standard gaging data. The cost of doing full studies to determine flow needs at the point of diversion would far exceed the value of the garden. It is possible that a de minimus impact determination might be made and a generic prescription provided for such a project to protect against cumulative impacts, recognizing that the project would not affect winter conditions at all. It would be inappropriate and probably inadequate to hold an irrigation/flood control project at the same place to the same standard of analysis or instream flow requirement. At the same time, the cumulative impact of lawn and garden watering for a major metropolitan area can be very significant during summer drought conditions, even to a very large river. The rationale must describe the context and scope of the prescription so that it is obvious what the prescription was designed to do as well as what it was not intended to address.

Study Implementation. Study implementation encompasses data collection, model development, calibration and simulation, and integration of various models (e.g., channel form, water quality, habitat, habitat utilization). The application of quality control and assurance measures throughout the implementation of the study plan is critical to the credibility of results (i.e., how well they represent reality) and to the defensibility of instream flow prescriptions. Empirical data are necessary to

121

calibrate the models used and set appropriate limits to extrapolation of results. Practitioners should also collect sufficient data to validate the assumptions and predictions of the models they use and assess model sensitivity.

Alternatives Analyses. Analyses of alternatives and data needs must be well thought out and described in sufficient detail to adequately inform decision makers and the public about the agency's position, recommended prescriptions, and consequences of proposed actions. Information regarding choice of models, data needed, assumptions made, analytical procedures, results, and the logic supporting the outcome are critically important elements of any instream flow application.

Methods for determining instream flow needs have been presented in Bovee et al. (1998) and Wesche and Rechard (1980), among others. New methods will be developed. All aspects of the determination process should be clearly identified (i.e., issues, objectives, study plan, methods for data collection, analysis) and well documented. Goals and objectives of studies must be identified at the start of any project to identify the questions about all potentially affected resource components for which detailed answers are needed (see IFC Riverine Components Policy Statement). Then appropriate methods can be selected and data collection planned. Concurrent with this step should be documentation of the assumptions, limitations, and context of the studies. State or provincial fishery and wildlife agency personnel should either direct or be actively involved in the study to ensure that appropriate data are collected and properly analyzed. Agency oversight should include the ability to approve or disapprove of the personnel selected to conduct the studies, details of data collection, methods of data analysis, and other factors that may influence the quality of the studies and subsequent prescriptions.

Data analysis may require output from various models or equations. In most applications of instream flow tools, habitat-discharge relations are developed by modeling or measuring suitable habitat at different discharge levels using biological criteria, channel structure data, and hydraulic simulation or empirical relations. Biological criteria are developed from habitat utilization and availability data. Channel structure data include characteristics of habitat such as substrate, current velocities, depths, instream cover, and a representation of the channel form (i.e., cross-sectional profiles or spatially explicit bathymetry). Hydraulic

simulation generally involves modeling how velocity and depth change with respect to changes in discharge or stage. The Physical Habitat Simulation system (Bovee et al. 1998) contains various routines/models (e.g., stage-discharge models and velocity calibration) to integrate these three components to derive habitat-discharge relations. Another emerging approach involves multidimensional hydrodynamic modeling (Leclerc et al. 1995) coupled with GIS applications and query tools (see Hardy 1998).

There are situations where very stable flow conditions allow certain species to flourish, including natural springs and tailwater fisheries that exist downstream of some large dams. Tailwaters are typically simple ecosystems characterized by invertebrate and fish communities consisting of only a few species that are found in abundance. Given the right water quality and habitat conditions, tailwaters can support abundant, fast-growing trout populations. Does managing for this condition violate an ecosystem-focused mission? Such altered systems may provide mitigation for unavoidable development, but should be considered in the context of watershed-wide plans or assessments. The IFC encourages agencies to pursue a goal of sustaining native species in their instream flow programs. State or province-wide plans delineating stream segments along with stated goals and objectives to move toward ecologically sound instream flow management of all streams is encouraged by the IFC.

Problem Resolution and Dealing with Uncertainty. Because the flow regime exerts a dominant influence on flowing water systems (Poff et al. 1997), its alteration should be expected to result in corresponding ecological changes. These expected changes should be documented. Although there are many cases where considerable, specific effects have been documented, some effects are not readily apparent. Ecological systems are complex and their workings and interrelations are not completely understood. As Dasman (1973) put it, "Today natural diversity still baffles us. Even the simplest natural communities escape our comprehension. We abstract and simplify them intellectually with energy flow charts or system diagrams. When we understand the pictures and formulae, we delude ourselves into believing we understand reality."

Fishery and wildlife agency personnel are often asked to evaluate a water use project and recommend a flow regime that will preserve the ecological health of the aquatic community. Such a prescription cannot be made without adequate information. Therefore, the IFC recommends that water users adopt the following guidelines for projects they initiate:

1) Collect appropriate information necessary to conduct a comprehensive evaluation of the project. A lack of information demonstrating the effects of a project should not be equated with a finding of no impact.
2) Recognize that the greater the level of uncertainty (or the less information available), the more resource conservative the flow prescription should be.
3) Conduct monitoring to aid learning, resolve scientific uncertainties, and adjust project features, if necessary.

Whereas flow requirements depend on the legal context, permit processes usually require applicants to provide sufficient information for an analysis of environmental effects. In some cases, applicants must provide sufficient evidence to demonstrate that their project will not adversely affect fishery and wildlife resources. Natural resource agencies should determine what information they need and request that the project developer provide it. However, the money and time available varies considerably with the instream flow application. As a result, the information available may not be comprehensive or of high quality. Given this fact and the difficulty in assessing biological populations (Hall and Knight 1981; Platts and Nelson 1988; Francis and Shotton 1997), decisions must often be made at some level of uncertainty. These decisions should consider the (1) value of the natural resource; (2) potential risk to the natural resource; (3) ability to reverse unanticipated, negative changes; (4) ability to monitor impacts; and (5) flexibility to modify project operation based on monitoring results.

In the absence of information, it cannot be presumed that water- use projects have no environmental impact. Absence of proof is not proof of absence of effect.

For example, a small project may not be able to provide much information for decision making or institute a monitoring program. Lack of information and any follow-up assessment mean that a more conservative (protective) flow prescription is appropriate. This conservatism may be offset, in part, if the project's potential impact is small.

A large project may provide detailed information and monitoring, but its potential impact may be considerable. The use of "best available science" to develop a flow prescription reduces uncertainty and risk. However, a potential for considerable impact heightens the need for monitoring coupled with the flexibility to modify operations, if necessary. In the absence of information, it cannot be presumed that water use projects have no environmental impact. In fact, a precautionary approach often reverses this burden of proof to presume that a project is harmful until proven otherwise (Food and Agriculture Organization 1995). Absence of proof is not proof of absence of effect.

Rule-of-thumb minimum flow standards—like those based on hydrologic statistics—fall at the low end of the scale for project-specific information and typically lead to a one-size-fits-all prescription for streams that have a wide range of channel characteristics and flows. Furthermore, there is usually no opportunity to assess the biological or geomorphologic effect of incrementally higher or lower flows and adjust the flow regime later. As a result, the level of uncertainty and risk is high and a greater level of conservatism must be built into the standards. The IFC discourages the use of rule-of-thumb methods for building site-specific prescriptions.

Monitoring. After an instream flow regimen is implemented, monitoring can be an effective way to address critical uncertainties in regulated river systems. Monitoring may be appropriate to document the effectiveness of a prescription on a free-flowing river over a period of years depending on related issues and need. Compliance monitoring is almost always appropriate in conjunction with major water development projects to document compliance and mitigation effectiveness. It is likewise a critical component of adaptive management. All parties to an instream flow agreement should keep in mind that even the best skilled personnel and best available science do not guarantee a particular outcome. It should also be noted that monitoring alone is just one part of mitigation.

Traditionally, most monitoring studies have focused on the response of target biological organisms (e.g., pounds per acre of a fish species, number of cottonwood seedlings that sprout). However, programs that focus on single elements or subsets of elements of the five riverine components will only provide a portion of the information needed to address the uncertainty associated with instream flow management. In addition, it is important to acknowledge that each of the five riverine components is best described as a temporal and spatial process. Consequently, monitoring that provides results as static numbers or, worse, as statistical means, does not provide appropriate information to determine the effectiveness of an instream flow prescription.

Petts (1984) categorized the effects of flow modification into three orders of impacts on downstream resources: primary, secondary, and tertiary. Primary impacts occur simultaneously with the change in flow regimen and often include sediment transport and water quality. Secondary responses to flow alterations include changes in channel structure, substrate composition, and primary production. Tertiary order impacts are the responses of fishery and wildlife resources to the above changes.

To be most effective in addressing uncertainty, monitoring should begin several years before implementation of an instream flow. The time frame for monitoring should correspond to the response time of the biotic and abiotic variables to be studied. Studies should continue at appropriate time steps and with appropriate changes in the sampling plan (e.g., they must not compromise the value or interpretation of earlier studies) on a periodic basis to include new techniques as they become available. An excellent example of how such studies should be conducted can be found in Hayeur (2001).

Many institutions dedicate sufficient time and effort to developing instream flow study plans, conducting studies, and analyzing data prior to making instream flow decisions. Once decisions are made, however, few if any resources are identified to assess the appropriateness of instream flow prescriptions or to ensure that instream flow objectives are being achieved. This is especially critical for major water development projects. To address this important need, project sponsors should be required to provide funding and/or personnel to conduct necessary pre- and post-project monitoring as part of the mitigation agreement. Such requirements have been established in Alaska for more than a decade (Christopher Estes, personal communication). The 1996 South Carolina Mitigation Trust Fund is an example of how mitigation (including monitoring) funds can be managed.

IFC Monitoring Policy Statement: Monitoring riverine resource responses to instream flow prescriptions is a fundamental component of effective instream flow programs. Monitoring studies should be based on long-term ecosystem processes as opposed to short-term responses of individual species.

Adaptive Management. Another means of dealing with uncertainty is through adaptive management techniques. The basic premise of adaptive management is that there is considerable room for scientific and technical disagreement regarding the potential effects of a specific action. In situations where competing interests are unable to reach agreement on an instream flow scenario—and time and project flexibility permit—it is increasingly common for the parties to make a best guess based on available information and data, monitor the initial outcome for a defined period, and adjust the strategy accordingly until a scientific consensus results. As with most engineered projects, the adaptive management decision-making process for riverine resources must always err on the conservative side for the resource to ensure that the resource does not "collapse" before the desired outcome is reached.

Castleberry et al. (1996) recommended adaptive management as an important approach for addressing uncertainty associated with instream flow prescriptions and suggested that practitioners undertake three steps as part of the approach: (1) set conservative, resource-protective interim flow standards based on available information, (2) establish a monitoring program that allows the interim standards to serve as experiments, and (3) establish an effective procedure that allows revision of the interim standards based on the new information.

Walters (1986) proposed six steps for conducting an adaptive management exercise:

1) Provide a clear and simple description of the major uncertainties in the form of alternative hypotheses about how the system (or population of interest) will respond to various options. Do not identify every possibility, but do define a likely range of possibilities and a few intermediate possibilities within this range.

2) Assess whether further steps are needed to develop additional models by estimating

---

Mitigation Trust Fund of South Carolina

In 1996 the South Carolina Legislature created the Mitigation Trust Fund of South Carolina (S.C. CODE ANN. § 50-3-180) for the purpose of receiving funds for environmental mitigation projects. The trust fund has been a repository for mitigation and settlement agreement payments related to oil spills and hydroelectric dam operations.

The Mitigation Trust Fund of South Carolina is a good template for developing similar trust funds in other states or provinces. Key features of the trust fund specify that:

1) The purpose is clearly stated.
2) The State Treasurer is identified as custodian of the fund and is required to invest its assets in an interest-bearing account.
3) Deposits and accrued interest may be spent only for the mitigation of adverse impacts to natural resources.
4) Proceeds may be carried forward from year-to-year and do not revert to the general fund of the state.
5) The Board of the Department of Natural Resources (DNR) serves as the fund's Board of Trustees, which has authority over spending and administering the fund.
6) Technical committees consisting of DNR staff, staff of other state and federal agencies, and, in some cases, representatives from the responsible parties review funding proposals and reach consensus on projects before recommendations are forwarded to the DNR Board.

To date, trust fund assets have been allocated for purchase of, and easements on, riparian buffers; studies identifying potential impacts to fish communities; and dam remediation efforts. Other mitigation projects deemed appropriate for funding include instream flow and water quality improvement, dam removal, stream restoration, reservoir shoreline stabilization, sediment control, fish stocking, enhancing fish habitat and fish passage, and environmental outreach programs.

---

the expected value of perfect information. To do this, find the best policy option under the current knowledge level. Then determine how much improvement might occur if it were known for certain which model is correct and if perfect information was available.

3) Develop models for future learning about hypotheses.
4) Identify adaptive policy options.
5) Develop performance criteria for comparing options.
6) Compare options using statistical decision analysis.

He noted that for any particular case, the alternatives must be associated with specific parameter values or whatever models can be used with the available historical data. Often the best way to define a good set of alternative hypotheses is to conduct several independent assessments of the available data and then hold a public meeting to discuss the competing results in a workshop. Such discussions have a way of sorting out trivial alternatives ("your model gives the same results as

mine, just looks different mathematically"). Through this process, discussion is focused on basic differences in policy options, not on trying to find consensus and agreement.

Adaptive management involves compromise by one or more of the parties, the formulation of working hypotheses, assessment, and balancing of risks. An ability to agree on the changes to be made and establish criteria for making such changes is critical to this decision process. Legal constraints, particularly the prior appropriation doctrine and quasi-judicial proceedings such as FERC hydropower licensing processes, may also limit the circumstances in which natural resource agencies have sufficient leverage in adaptive management negotiations. In other cases, federal laws, such as the Endangered Species Act, may serve to maintain a balance.

The key task in adaptive management is to choose the correct action, not to predict uncertain quantities like catch, biomass, or water yield (Kuikka et al. 1999). The simplistic way of making flow prescriptions is to use predictive models to make a statement about flows and what changes can be expected to the hydraulic or water quality measures of habitat. Such an approach assumes a direct correlation between change in physical habitat and the number of fish and/or the general status of the ecosystem. One approach to adaptive management uses various models and measurement technologies and assumes that model output is an effective and acceptable way to identify flow options. Once the habitat objectives and corresponding flow regime are agreed to, monitoring of the new flow regime can be carried out to verify the predictions. This could be thought of as "adaptive management involving a single option," which means that if monitoring does not substantiate the modeled predictions, changes would be made to the models followed by analyses and subsequent alternative recommended flow regimes, but the same physical habitat objectives would be retained.

Another school of thought suggests that the foregoing is not truly adaptive management and that an experimental study should be used to address the uncertainty in achieving long-term goals for instream flows (Walters and Holling 1990; Figure 5-25). This structured process has been referred to as "learning by doing" (Walters 1997), which involves the formulation of hypotheses of the ecological response to alternative flow regimes. Such an approach requires an experimental evaluation period during which time a range of flow alternatives is implemented, either on one system or multiple similar systems, and monitored with replicated years of operation under each alternative. The alternatives tested would include a sufficiently wide range to encompass responses from opposing hypotheses leading to a long-term policy and enough alternatives within this range to determine whether there is a diminishing return (or deleterious effects) for the more extreme, costly alternatives (Walters and Korman, unpublished paper). This approach will fail if monitoring programs are inadequate to measure real responses, unmeasured variables are driving the system, or differences among alternative hypotheses are small compared to other causes of variation in fish populations; however, these objections apply to evaluation of single-option implementations as well.

Testing a range of options offers some possibility for observing response patterns. Walters and Korman (unpublished paper) offered the cautionary note that single-option policy modeling approaches can ultimately lead to a costly type of self-fulfilling prophecy. Whether this assertion is true or not is debatable. The important point is to not restrict the instream flow toolbox and to sup-

FIGURE 5-25. Adaptive management can be a repetitive process of learning by doing until sufficient information and understanding is developed that supports final recommendations

port new and innovative ways to make the best flow prescriptions possible from an ecosystem perspective. This should include applying adaptive management in some watersheds as a complement to the current use of single-option policy-based predictive models. Indeed, the riparian ecosystem of the Grand Canyon, Arizona, has provided a unique opportunity to test various ideas about riparian ecosystem management and the use of adaptive management experiments to help resolve scientific uncertainties regarding best management practices (Walters and Korman 2000).

Another recent example of adaptive management involved the Trinity River in California. The U.S. Fish and Wildlife Service and Hoopa Valley Tribe (1999) presented a well-documented case in which all five riverine components were analyzed. The goal of rehabilitating the Trinity River to provide an anadromous fishery at levels that were present before water development began means that results of decisions about rehabilitating the Trinity River have relatively high certainty and fairly well-known economic implications because the system has been severely degraded. A new management organization was proposed and an adaptive environmental assessment and management approach is now being used in this system.

In some instances developers seek permission to release lower flows than have naturally occurred prior to the project with the offer to increase project flows later if observations prove the proposed releases were harmful. This is a backward approach because the entire burden or risk is

---

> Adaptive management is not an excuse to postpone decisions or to allow decisions to be based on shoddy information.

---

placed on the fishery—not the proposed new use. There is no logic or scientific basis for agreeing to a temporary condition that may harm (sometimes irreparably) the resource even if it would allow for reestablishing higher, more favorable flows later. Flows below the limits of long-term minimum monthly or daily flows should never be permitted until lower flows within the range of preproject variability can be observed and assessed by biologists and hydrologists after the project is operational.

Adaptive management is not an excuse to postpone decisions or to allow decisions to be based on shoddy information (Walters and Holling 1990). If adaptive management is to be part of an instream flow decision, all parties must agree in advance on several points: (1) the objectives for the process; (2) that monitoring of any future changes in the flow regime will be based on credible monitoring information; (3) that increases or decreases in streamflow are possible outcomes of the adaptive management process; (4) the nature of legal or regulatory mechanisms by which future changes can be made (e.g., revocable permits and license articles); (5) adequate funding and other resources (including water supplies) are provided in advance in an independently managed account; and (6) who will manage the account, how interest on the account will be managed, and under what circumstances escrow funds and other resources may be used.

Adaptive management has strengths and weaknesses in respect to instream flow decisions. The method, which can be extremely flexible and responsive to system changes, allows a range of solutions to be examined that will probably capture the variation inherent in most stream systems and reduce the overall uncertainty about a system. If monitoring is properly conducted, practitioners will gain useful information and insights on how these systems function, which should greatly enhance practitioners' technical abilities.

Hilborn and Walters (1992) suggested three basic strategies for addressing uncertainty in management of natural systems over time:

1) *Passive Adaptive Strategy.* Available data are used to develop a "best guess" or "best possible model" based on the data. Managers then act as if this model were true and rely on errors or weaknesses to reveal themselves in the future. This policy is useful when uncertainties are few or when the passive-decision choice is as informative as any other choice would be. Passive policies may cause the system to be locked into a narrow range of strategies without any additional data gathering to help decide whether the optimum is really within this range.

2) *Trial and Error or Evolutionary Adaptive Strategy.* This approach involves trying a variety of alternative policies in an attempt to accumulate evidence as to which one is best. It has the advantage of not requiring the decision maker to make any judgment about which model best fits the data available at any point in time. If the manager has flexibility to try a variety of choices, this strategy may yield a choice that otherwise would not have been identified using rigorous but narrow analyses of historical data. This approach is likely to be wasteful in terms of time, money, and other resources.

3) *Actively Adaptive Strategy.* This strategy involves deliberate construction of a range of alternative models that are consistent with the historical data. The models are then used to identify a policy that balances between probing for information versus caution about losses in short-term services or long-term potential. It involves a great deal of effort in assessment and modeling, much more than in passive policy design. A wider range of alternatives is likely to be tested under this strategy than the passive strategy, but less than under the trial and error strategy.

However, the technique is unlikely to be implemented in quasi-legal proceedings, such as a FERC hydropower licensing, because the parties want and demand certainty as an outcome, not additional studies and other potential license or permit conditions or limitations. This is equally true for proceedings involving other economic interests—such as lending institutions—because they require certainty and minimal risk prior to providing any type of financial assistance to a development project. Developers applying for loans are not likely to be successful if they tell a lending institution they do not know all of the regulatory costs or risks of their actions. The technique can be expensive because effective, long-term monitoring is required throughout the life of the process to allow adequate testing of hypotheses. Ultimately, there may be no exact answer to the problem under consideration and constant adjust-

---

. . . adaptive management is not appropriate for all instream flow decisions, although it can be a useful tool in the right application.

---

ments may have to be made to instream flows to accommodate internal forces (such as new watershed development) and external forces (such as global climate changes). Adaptive management is most effective if the same individuals, or at the very minimum, the same cooperative philosophy, can remain in place over the life of the project (which is very unlikely). Finally, the process requires a long-term commitment by all parties to the adaptive management approach, but such a commitment is often tenuous given the dynamic economic forces that affect public and private entities.

Thus, adaptive management is not appropriate for all instream flow decisions, although it can be a useful tool in the right application. It is best used in situations where (1) fishery and wildlife resource values are high, (2) financial investment in the project is large, (3) project outcomes are uncertain, (4) flexibility exists in project design to accommodate several levels of development, and (5) participants have the time (usually years) and willingness to commit to the project.

IFC Adaptive Management Policy Statement: Adaptive management can be an effective tool but should be used selectively to answer critical uncertainties for instream flow-setting processes.

Developing and Implementing an Instream Flow Study

The discussion of documenting the steps in an instream flow prescription does not cover every eventuality, but it clearly shows that planning and implementing data collection can be a considerable challenge. As we have noted throughout, there is no single way to conduct a study. Each setting will involve its own unique combination of ecological, social, economic, political, and legal characteristics. However, some characteristics are common to most studies. Appendix E provides one possible template or checklist for addressing these factors in developing and implementing a plan of study.

Science can only ascertain what is, but not what should be, and
outside of its domain value judgments of all kinds remain necessary
— Albert Einstein, 1879-1955

CHAPTER SIX

Instream Flow Assessment Tools

Instream flow is not just about fish habitat; it is transdisciplinary. And, it definitely involves more than "just keeping enough water in the stream for the fish". Thus, there is no universally accepted method or combination of methods that is appropriate for establishing instream flow regimes on all rivers or streams. Rather, the combination or adaptation of methods should be determined on a case-by-case basis; that is, choosing the method that is best suited to the particular water

> ...whether a particular method "works" is not based on its acceptance by all parties but whether it is based on sound science, basic ecological principles, and documented logic that addresses specific needs.

body and potential modification under consideration. In a sense, there are few bad methods—only bad or improper applications of methods. In fact, most of the 34 assessment tools evaluated in this section (as well as some that are not) can afford adequate instream flow protection for most of a river's needs when they are used in conjunction with other techniques in ways that provide reasonable answers to the specific questions asked about individual rivers and river segments. Thus, whether or not a particular method "works" is not based on its acceptance by all parties but whether it is incorporated in an overall process based on sound science, basic ecological principles, and documented logic that addresses specific needs.

The development of flow standards must move away from the use of any one tool as a method to obtain a single "minimum" rate of flow and toward the use of a suite of tools that provides variable flow regimes with intra- and interannual variability to maintain or restore the natural form and function of stream channels, their fisheries and riverine resources. Effective flow standards using multiple methods may include a "three rivers concept" (Wald, unpublished paper) where applicable.

> A good prescription must include tools and strategies that identify flow needs for the five riverine components: hydrology, geomorphology, biology, water quality, and connectivity.

The concept derives from three flow processes (water, sediment, and wood transport) that are common to most streams in pre-settlement, protected, or restored conditions. It recognizes inflow, outflow, and storage relationships in that these processes are often inextricably linked by dynamic interactions. Although this multi-method approach is not practical for all situations, it should be the goal whenever possible. A good prescription must include tools and strategies that identify flow needs and the necessary timing and duration to support the processes embodied within the five riverine components: hydrology, geomorphology, biology, water quality, and connectivity. Determining the approach to use for a particular setting is dependent on the nature of the management problem, habitat homogeneity at various scales, data requirements of hydraulic models, and expertise of personnel. The IFC strongly encourages individuals who are intent upon conducting instream flow studies to contact their local fishery and wildlife agency instream flow administrator or IFC representative for help in developing the most appropriate approach for specific projects.

Of the 34 tools reviewed, we evaluate only those that are most commonly used. Omitted are tools that are no longer in use, are just emerging, or are similar to other tools reviewed.

INSTREAM FLOW ASSESSMENT TECHNIQUES

Although the techniques for assessing instream flows can be categorized in a variety of ways, our discussion focuses on three: standard setting, incremental, and monitoring (Table 6-1).

Stalnaker et al. (1995) contrasted standard-setting and incremental techniques as very different approaches to decision making (Table 6-2). Standard setting typically involves desktop, rule-of-thumb methods for setting limits below which water cannot be diverted. Standard setting is often policy-driven. Incremental techniques are site-specific analyses that examine multiple decision variables and enable different flow management alternatives to be explored. Incremental techniques are generally assessment-driven.

Stalnaker et al. (1995) also described "mid-range" techniques that are used like rule-of-thumb flow standards in that they use a predetermined decision-making formula and yield a single flow value. They differ, however, in that some kind of site-specific data, often hydraulic, are usually required. The important distinction is that incremental methods represent a fundamentally different approach to problem solving (e.g., alternative water development schemes, impact analyses, and mitigation plans).

TABLE 6-1. Instream flow assessment techniques, general descriptions, and representative examples.

Technique	Description	Examples
Standard Setting	Sets limits or rules to define a threshold flow regime	Tennant, Wetted Perimeter, R2- Cross, Aquatic Base Flow (ABF), Bankfull Discharge, Salinity-Based Estuary Inflow, Hatfield-Bruce
Incremental	Analyzes single or multiple variables to enable assessment of different flow management alternatives	Instream Flow Incremental Methodology (IFIM), Physical Habitat Simulation (PHABSIM), Two-Dimensional Hydraulic Models, Riverine Community Habitat Assessment Restoration Concept (RCHARC), Stream Network Temperature (SNTEMP), Pennsylvannia/Maryland Model, MesoHABitat SIMulator (MesoHABSIM)
Monitoring/Diagnostic	Assesses conditions and how they change over time	Index of Biotic Integrity (IBI), Indicators of Hydraulic Alteration (IHA), Range of Variability Approach (RVA), StreamNetwork Temperature (SNTEMP), Target Fish Community

TABLE 6-2. A comparison of the two broad categories of instream flow assessment approaches (From Stalnaker et al. 1995).

Standard Setting	Incremental
Low controversy project	High controversy project
Reconnaissance level planning	Project-specific
Few decision variables	Many decision variables
Inexpensive	Expensive
Fast	Lengthy
Rule-of-thumb	In-depth knowledge required
Less scientifically accepted	More scientifically accepted
Not well-suited for bargaining	Designed for bargaining
Based on historical water supply	Based on fish or habitat

Some methods may not fit cleanly into one category and may fit more than one, depending on how they are used. Instream flow problem solving frequently includes the identification of baseline or reference conditions, and there are a number of tools for doing so. For example, surveys are often conducted to characterize populations of aquatic life, natural hydrology, water temperatures, and geomorphologic conditions.

Perhaps the most well-known and widely used incremental method is the Instream Flow Incremental Methodology (IFIM). Whereas the IFIM is often thought of as a collection of computer models, it is really more of a process that can include a multitude of instream flow assessment tools, as necessary, to address the five affected riverine ecosystem components.

As the need for adaptive management has become more widely recognized (Lee and Lawrence 1986; Castleberry et al. 1996; Stalnaker and Wick 2000), monitoring techniques have become important to ongoing evaluations. The Index of Biotic Integrity (IBI) (Karr et al. 1986) is one tool that can be used for this purpose.

Cautions About Standard-Setting Techniques

What is an instream flow standard? In practice, "flow standard" has two common usages: (1) streamflow management rules that are included in a water use permit or river management plan, and (2) a predetermined set of formulas or numeric rules that is used to define a threshold flow regime below which water should not be withdrawn. Because the second is used to determine the first, use of these terms blends together. The second usage is synonymous with a standard-setting policy and is further discussed below.

Ideally, an instream flow standard should identify the resources to be considered, define the level of resource protection intended, and specify assessment criteria (Beecher 1990). It is certainly possible to develop comprehensive standards that fully embody the natural flow paradigm and protect ecosystem integrity. In most instances, however, application of the elements described by Beecher (1990) is either incomplete or inconsistent. Historically, most standards were developed to address conflicts in allocating water between instream and out-of-stream uses. The word "standard" came to mean "minimum"—a line in the sand (sometimes literally) above which all water could be appropriated and below which the water was reserved for aquatic life. Today, most scientists generally agree (Poff et al. 1997) that such a flat-line flow regime does not maintain ecosystem integrity. The IFC asserts that instream flow standards should provide intra- and interannual variability in a manner that maintains or restores riverine form and function to the greatest extent possible. The IFC refers to such variability as "ecosystem-based standards".

Standards offer the advantage of providing decisions that are quick, predictable, and inexpensive. Because they are derived from a predetermined formula, they provide repeatable results. The degree of protection provided by standard setting has varied considerably between and within states (Lamb and Meshorer 1983). Indeed, there are many disadvantages and cautions associated with standard-setting techniques.

Standards have been typically designed to protect fishery resources at some acceptable level. However, it should be recognized that political and economic considerations have usually already been built into the standards during their development. In practice, standards are often more about accommodating water uses than about river conservation. Consequently, many standard-setting approaches provide a minimum flow that offers protection for a lower level of the fishery resource than does the natural condition. Thus, a minimum flow equates to a minimum fishery resource and falls short of goals to maintain existing fisheries, let alone restore them to natural levels. Minimum streamflow standards should be thought of as policy choices rather than fish population or habitat assessment procedures (Stalnaker 1993).

Many standards used today do not provide healthy aquatic ecosystems or fish populations. A case in point is the $7Q_{10}$ method that has been used by a handful of states (Reiser et al. 1989). As a minimum flow standard to sustain aquatic life, $7Q_{10}$ lacks any scientific or common sense foundation and can be expected to result in severe degradation of riverine biota and processes. Even less extreme minimum low flows (such as the 10% mean annual flow) when maintained during much of the year as a long-term condition, cannot be expected to sustain the same fish populations or aquatic life as a natural flow regime, where low flow conditions occur infrequently and for shorter periods (Stalnaker and Wick 2000). A change from a natural flow regime with its inherent variability to the maintenance of a single flow for all seasons will change the ecosystem.

Because the full range of hydrologic conditions shapes a stream and its aquatic community, standards must address more than just minimum flows. Multiple flow levels are necessary to accommodate different needs. For example, high flows can be important to channel maintenance and sediment movement. Atlantic salmon (*Salmo salar*) are behaviorally influenced to move upstream for spawning by flow increases in the fall. Intermediate flows provide optimal conditions for survival and growth of many fish species (Leonard and Orth 1988). Flow setting should also consider the need for intra- and interannual variability, as exemplified by the life history requirements of the Colorado pikeminnow (*Ptychocheilus lucius*), and razorback sucker (*Xyrauchen texanus*) (Stalnaker and Wick 2000). These species require flood flow events for geomorphic maintenance of spawning sites. Flows to accommodate spawning and incubation must be sequentially followed by suitable rearing flows. This sequence does not occur naturally every year, but these fish have unique life histories that are adapted to—and reliant upon—a naturally variable flow regime.

Periodic flood flows of several weeks duration provide access to the floodplain for newly hatched razorback suckers where favorable conditions allow larvae to grow to a larger size before returning to the primary channel with the receding flows. The Colorado pike minnow, on the other hand, is most successful during the average and low flow years when the summer rearing conditions are maximized by warm backwater pockets of zero velocity associated with crossing bars within the primary channel. Conditions that ensure a good year class for both species do not occur in the same year; however, within a 5- to-10-year span one or more years can provide suitable timing and flows for the success of each species. While both species are long-lived (30+ years), one to two good year classes per decade may be sufficient to perpetuate the population of both species.

Historically the most common type of flow standard was derived either in part, or whole, from hydrologic statistics. Methods such as the Tennant (Tennant 1975) and Aquatic Base Flow (ABF)(Larsen 1981) make recommendations that are expressed as a function of average hydrologic statistics. Although hydrology is typically used as a surrogate for habitat conditions, it is important to note that the Tennant method was developed by relating hydrologic characteristics to 12 different habitat and river use attributes in coldwater and warmwater environments at many locations across the eastern and western United States (Tennant 1975). Whereas each method has a rationale (see critique of methods, below), the level of protection

afforded will be inconsistent since habitat is a function of flow and channel shape if recommendations are not calibrated or adjusted to the fishery needs and hydrologic characteristics of each river (Tennant 1975; Bovee et al. 1998). The scientific foundation of these methods continues to be challenged by water users, but the majority of such challenges have been successfully defended (Donald Tennant, personal communication). Standards such as these often provide results that approximate those provided by more detailed, site-specific methods, but they lack the ability to quantitatively assess the trade-offs of habitat at different flows. Given this uncertainty, flow standards derived from these kinds of methods must be conservative in terms of resource protection (Castleberry et al. 1996).

Temporal Considerations

For the most part, these methods are spatial analyses and are temporally static. Many look only at average conditions. In applying these tools, investigators must think in terms of connectivity across time. Riverine organisms have adapted to dynamic flow regimes. Their life histories require seasonal and interannual variability in flows. It is up to the investigator to recognize these biological needs and then put together the pieces of the puzzle provided by the various methods into a cohesive, temporal picture. Biology is the integrator of physical and chemical processes. Therefore, the interaction of the five riverine components over time must be considered in developing a flow regime that will provide the threshold levels and duration and timing of flow necessary to maintain ecological functions. However, even when the most sincere efforts are made to arrive at proper and meaningful instream flow prescriptions, there will probably always be some disagreement

STREAM COMPONENT TOOLS

There are many instream flow assessment tools available for analyzing riverine components. The first step to using any tool is to recognize its intended application, strengths, and limitations. Table 6-3 groups the tools according to their applicability for the five riverine components. Some of the tools, such as the Demonstration Flow Assessment (DFA) and the IFIM, integrate multiple riverine components, but not all. Detailed evaluations for each of the tools follow the format outlined in Table 6-4.

TABLE 6-3. Summary of instream flow assessment tools and a general description of their application.

Stream Assessment Tool	Page	Type of Technique	Level of Effort	Resource Component
Indicators of Hydrologic Alteration (IHA)	134	Monitoring/Diagnostic	Low, but can be difficult (office)	Hydrology
Range of Variability Approach (RVA)	135	Monitoring/Diagnostic	Low (office)	Hydrology
Two-Dimensional Hydraulic Models	137	Incremental	High (field)	Biology
Aquatic Base Flow (ABF) Standard	139	Standard Setting	Low (office)	Biology
Biological Response to Flow Correlations	140	Incremental	High (field)	Biology
Feeding Station	142	Incremental	High (field)	Biology
Flow Duration Curve Methods	143	Standard Setting	Low (office)	Biology
Index of Biotic Integrity (IBI)	144	Monitoring/Diagnostic	High (field)	Biology
Target Fish Community Assessment	146	Monitoring/Diagnostic	Moderate	Biology
Physical Habitat Simulation (PHABSIM)	148	Incremental	High (field)	Biology
MesoHABitat SIMulator (MesoHABSIM)	150	Incremental	High (field)	Biology
Hatfield-Bruce Western Salmonid Regressions	152	Standard Setting	Low	Biology
Pennsylvania/Maryland Model	153	Incremental	Low	Biology
Plunge Pool Method	155	Incremental	High (field)	Biology
Riverine Community Habitat Assessment and Restoration Concept (RCHARC)	156	Incremental	Moderate (field)	Biology
Single Transect Hydraulic Based Habitat Method	158	Standard Setting	Moderate (field)	Biology
Tennant Method	159	Standard Setting	Low (office) Moderate (field)	Biology
Wash. Toe-of-Bank Width (Toe Width)	161	Standard Setting	Moderate (field)	Biology
Wetted Perimeter	163	Standard Setting	Moderate (field)	Biology
Channel Maintenance Flows	165	Standard Setting	High (field)	Geomorphology
Flushing Flow (Empirical, Sediment Transport Modeling, and Office- Based Hydrologic Models)	166	Standard Setting	High (field) Low (office)	Geomorphology
Geomorphic Stream Classification System	170	Monitoring/Diagnostic	High (field)	Geomorphology
Hydraulic Engineering Center--6 Model (HEC-6)	171	Incremental	High (field)	Geomorphology
Hydraulic Engineering Center--River Analysis System (HEC-RAS)	172	Incremental	High (field)	Geomorphology
Enhanced Stream Water Quality (QUAL2E) Method	173	Monitoring/Diagnostic	High (field)	Water Quality
Stream Network Temperature Model (SNTEMP)	175	Incremental	High (field)	Water Quality
Stream Segment Temperature Model (SSTEMP)	175	Monitoring/Diagnostic	Low (field)	
Seven-Day, Ten-Year Low Flow ($7Q_{10}$)	177	Monitoring/Diagnostic	Low (office)	Water Quality
Floodplain Inundation Method	179	Incremental	High (field)	Connectivity
Migration Cue Method	180	Standard Setting	Low (office)	Connectivity
Powers-Orsborn Salmon Barrier Method	181	Incremental	Moderate (field)	Connectivity
Tidal Distributary/Estuary Method	182	Incremental	High (field)	Connectivity
Salinity-Based Estuary Inflow Method	183	Standard Setting	High (field)	Water Quality, Biology
Demonstration Flow Assessment (DFA)	185	Standard Setting	Moderate (field)	Multiple Components
Instream Flow Incremental Methodology (IFIM)	187	Incremental	High (field)	Multiple Components

TABLE 6-4. The components listed below were used to describe and evaluate the instream flow assessment tools. References and other resources are provided for some methods, as applicable.

Summary: A one or two sentence description of the method.

Objective: A statement of the method's purpose.

Type of Technique: Identifies the technique that the method represents. Techniques are categorized as monitoring/diagnostic, standard setting, or incremental.

Description: A general description of the method including equations and overall approach.

Appropriate Scale: The geographic scale(s) that the method may be used to address, and comments as applicable on the temporal scale.

Riverine Component(s) Addressed: The riverine component (i.e., hydrology, geomorphology, biology, water quality, and connectivity) that each method addresses.

Assumptions: Conditions, circumstances or relations presumed by the method to be true.

Level of Effort: Degree of difficulty in applying the method; expressed as low, moderate, or high.

Historical Development: Explanation of how the method evolved; use and testing of the method. Published comparisons with other methods are also discussed.

Application: Characterization of method type(s), data requirements, and recommendations.

Strengths: Identifies advantages of the method.

Limitations and Constraints: Identifies weaknesses and provides other cautionary notes.

Calibration and Validation: Procedures used to calibrate the model and validate its results.

Critical Opinion: The opinion of the Instream Flow Council concerning the method.

HYDROLOGY

INDICATORS OF HYDROLOGIC ALTERATION (IHA)

Summary: Using the Indicators of Hydrologic Alteration (IHA) method, hydrologic records are evaluated to quantify changes in hydrologic regimes.

Objective: The IHA is intended to provide ecologists and hydrologists with a tool to characterize and compare complex hydrologic regimes in ecologically meaningful terms.

Type of Technique: Monitoring/Diagnostic

Description: Daily streamflow values (synthesized or measured) reflecting natural conditions, unaltered by anthropogenic effects (preimpact), and altered (postimpact) hydrological regimes are characterized using 32 parameters. The central tendencies and dispersions of each parameter are compared between the two periods. The 32 IHA parameters are based on five fundamental characteristics of hydrologic regimes: magnitude, timing, frequency, duration, and rate of change. Sixteen of the parameters address the magnitude, duration, timing, and frequency of extreme events, such as annual maxima and minima and the remaining parameters address the magnitude or rate of change of water conditions. Because biologically relevant parameters were selected that were sensitive to hydrologic change, the direction and magnitude of change in each parameter can be used to focus on various aspects of reservoir operations, stream diversions, and the like that may impair integrity or enhance rehabilitation of aquatic ecosystems.

Appropriate Scale: River reach.

Riverine Component(s) Addressed: Hydrology is the only ecosystem component addressed because this method relies solely on hydrologic records.

Assumptions: The basic assumptions of the method are that each IHA parameter has some meaningful biological relevance, the suite of parameters adequately characterizes temporal variation in hydrologic regimes, and central tendency and dispersion of intraannual statistics describe interannual variation.

Level of Effort: This is an office technique. Whereas the level of effort in calculating parameters and deriving statistics is low, developing a "natural" flow record of sufficient length can often be difficult. Software is available to calculate IHA parameters and statistics. Spreadsheet programs can be used to calculate all parameters and statistics.

Application: The IHA can be used in establishing baseline hydrologic conditions and for monitoring/assessment projects. Further, this tool should have some utility for alternatives analysis by comparing preproject hydrology with proposed project hydrology, if available. This could be helpful in planning instream flow studies. Data requirements include a naturalized flow record either from measured streamflow data or from synthesized data. Special attention should be given to measured streamflow records subject to anthropogenic alteration; degraded hydrologic records will influence calculation of parameters and derivation of statistics. Because some of the IHA parameters involve duration as short as one day (e.g., one day minimum) synthesized records that merely distribute monthly records over 30 days will not suffice. Richter et al. (1996, 1997) discussed limitations of various types of hydrologic records and recommendations for the application of parameters to each. Protocols for application of the method are described in Richter et al. (1996).

Historical Development: The IHA parameters were compiled through the Biohydrology Program of The Nature Conservancy. The suite of parameters was developed through a review of ecological literature to identify hydrologic parameters used in ecological research. Additional parameters were identified that would be sensitive to hydrologic alteration. The list of parameters was reviewed by river ecologists from around the world and modified based on their suggestions.

Strengths: The IHA parameters are easy to calculate from appropriate hydrologic records especially with IHA software. The suite of parameters comprehensively characterizes complex hydrologic information. Thus, this method can be used to quickly pinpoint aspects of a hydrologic regime that need to be addressed to restore ecosystem integrity, especially if used in conjunction with other ecological tools such as the Index of Biotic Integrity (see Karr 1981).

Limitations and Constraints: As discussed previously, one constraint is the availability of adequate streamflow records that could limit the application of all IHA parameters and cause uncertainty in the interpretation of statistics, especially for preimpact periods. Further, the IHA parameters reflect conditions associated with intraannual variation in hydrologic regimes; ecosystem processes that operate on longer time frames (e.g., life history of long-lived species and riparian areas) may not be adequately addressed.

Calibration and Validation: There is no known calibration or validation of the method. Ecological research directed toward establishing linkages between various IHA parameters and aquatic ecosystem integrity would be needed to refine and validate this method. Richter et al. (1996) provided a case study application of the IHA on the Roanoke River (North Carolina, USA).

Critical Opinion: Although this technique does not provide an instream flow prescription, it can inform the user about the hydrologic baseline and how to determine what dimensions of the hydrograph have been altered the most. The IHA parameters should be refined to include measures of interannual variation in hydrologic regimes and to derive statistics of central tendency and dispersion. Measures of central tendency and dispersion in IHA parameters have not been related to geomorphology, biology, water quality, or energy pathways. Application of IHA is limited by the ability to develop sufficient hydrologic records for preimpact periods. However, this model is one of the better tools for developing baselines for hydrological regimes, alternatives analysis, and monitoring/assessment level projects.

RANGE OF VARIABILITY APPROACH (RVA)

Summary: Using the Range of Variability Approach (RVA), target streamflows for river management are determined by identifying an appropriate range of variation in each of the 32 indicators of hydrologic alteration (see IHA method evaluation) parameters (i.e., 1 standard deviation from the mean). These targets can then be used to help develop and implement river management strategies, including adaptive management.

Objective: The purpose of the RVA is to provide a framework to guide river management efforts to restore or maintain natural variability in hydrologic regimes for restoration/conservation of aquatic ecosystems.

Type of Technique: Monitoring/Diagnostic

Description: Daily streamflow values (synthesized or measured) from a period of record reflecting natural (unaltered by anthropogenic effects) hydrological regimes are characterized using 32 indicators of hydrologic alteration (see IHA method evaluation). A range of variation in these "ecologically relevant" hydrologic parameters is selected and used to formulate initial instream flow targets for river management. The hydrologic parameters are discussed in the review of the IHA method. Instream flow targets are used in designing management strategies (i.e., reservoir operations and stream diversions) and adaptively refined as indicated by long-term ecological research/monitoring and as needed to conserve aquatic ecosystems.

Appropriate Scale: River reach or basin depending upon the breadth of application.

Riverine Component(s) Addressed: Hydrology is the only ecosystem component addressed because this method relies solely on hydrologic records to develop instream flow targets.

Assumptions: The basic assumption of the method is that the full range of natural variability in the hydrologic regime is necessary to conserve aquatic ecosystems. Whereas the parameters may describe the intraannual variation in a hydrologic regime, the authors state "the dependence of native aquatic biota on specific values of the hydrologic parameters employed in the RVA has not been widely, nor comprehensively, substantiated with statistical rigor" (Richter et al. 1997).

Level of Effort: This is an office method. Although the level of effort in deriving the ranges in variability is low, acquiring a "natural" streamflow record of sufficient length can often be difficult. Implementing the approach can be difficult because it relies on the ability to modify instream flow targets in river management; difficulty arises when appropriated water has been locked up in perpetuity. Software is available to calculate IHA parameters.

Application: Although the RVA was designed to be applied to river systems characterized by sub-stantially altered flow regimes and to allow initial river management decisions to be made when no or limited long-term ecosystem research results are available, particular attention needs to be paid to geomorphic condition of the channel. The RVA appears to be flexible enough to allow for alternatives analysis and can be used to set standards. As with IHA, data requirements include a naturalized flow record either from measured streamflow data or from synthesized data. Because some of the IHA parameters involve duration as short as a day (e.g., one day minimum), synthesized records that merely distribute monthly records over 30 days will not suffice. Richter et al. (1996, 1997) discussed limitations of various types of hydrologic records and recommendations for the application of parameters to each. (see Richter et al. [1997] for a discussion of protocols.)

Historical Development: The RVA is an extension of the IHA. It has not been applied to date or experimentally tested; however, Richter et al. (1998) presented a case study of its application on the upper Colorado River basin (i.e., Colorado and Utah USA).

Strengths: The RVA provides managers with a tool that allows interim flow targets and river management strategies to be developed without long-term ecological data. Application of the RVA requires that strategies and targets be revisited once ecological data have been collected and evaluated.

Limitations and Constraints: As discussed previously, one constraint is the availability of adequate streamflow records that would limit the application of all IHA parameters and cause uncertainty in the interpretation of natural variation in parameters. As the authors note, the default statistical derivation of natural variability (i.e., the mean plus one standard deviation) may not be appropriate for hydrologic records with skewed distributions. Practitioners should pay close attention to the data in large floodplain rivers where flood pulses may last for greater periods and the mean and default variability may not be adequate to capture an important hydrologic phenomenon. Additionally, in situations where the sediment regime also has been altered, restoring the natural hydrology alone cannot be expected to restore the river ecosystem. This may be particularly true below dams, which trap sediment, or in watersheds that have been greatly altered by land use practices. Another constraint is the requirement to amend strategies and targets given regulatory considerations that often require certainty/finality in water right permitting. Further, the IHA parameters reflect conditions associated with intra-annual variation in hydrologic regimes; ecosystem processes that operate on longer time frames (e.g., life history of long-lived species and riparian areas) may not be adequately addressed.

Calibration and Validation: There is no known calibration or validation of the method. Ecological research directed toward establishing linkages between various IHA parameters and aquatic ecosystem integrity would be needed to refine and validate this approach.

Critical Opinion: The primary application of this approach is to set initial river management targets for river systems in which the hydrologic regime has been substantially altered by human activities and the focus is to restore or maintain the regime of natural variability of the hydrologic system. These are worthy goals; however, as with any method, blind application has pitfalls. For example, restoring only a natural flow regime to river channels that have been geomorphologically altered or impounded and no longer in sediment equilibrium may not be in the best interest of aquatic ecosystem integrity. These altered channels may not be able to adequately handle a natural flow regime without prior modification or rehabilitation of the channel itself. The IHA parameters should be refined to include measures of interannual variation in hydrologic regimes. Natural variation in IHA parameters has not been related to biology, water quality, geomorphology, or energy pathways. Instream flow use afforded by this technique is dependent on the scale at which the model is applied and an assurance that the hydrology and sediment balance has not been altered by water and land use practices. Mimicking the shape of the hydrograph alone is not enough if the result is a significant suppression of the hydrograph to a much lower level that does not reach threshold levels and duration necessary to maintain natural ecological processes. The practitioner must ensure, at a minimum, that the low flow period prescribed does not go below, for example, the median flow for the low flow month or the $7Q_{10}$. At the same time, equal attention should be paid to the upper portion of the hydrograph. In unregulated alluvial streams, and those where sediment equilibrium has not been disrupted, the high flows prescribed must equal or exceed bankfull flow; in large floodplain rivers, the infrequent but ecologically significant pulses must be preserved.

BIOLOGY/HABITAT

TWO-DIMENSIONAL HYDRAULIC MODELS

Summary: Two-dimensional hydraulic models are computer models that are useful for simulating velocity patterns throughout a stream reach. They can be linked with hydraulic habitat models (e.g., the habitat suitability submodels of Physical Habitat Simulation [PHABSIM]) to simulate habitat characteristics at unmeasured discharges.

Objective: The purpose of two-dimensional hydraulic models is to simulate water surface elevations, velocity, and depth patterns throughout a stream reach.

Type of Technique: Incremental

Description: Several two-dimensional models have been promoted for use in hydraulic habitat analyses in recent years (Ghanem et al. 1994; Leclerc et al. 1995).

Appropriate Scale: River reaches and segments.

Riverine Component(s) Addressed: Hydraulics are measured as input to habitat models and can be used to address the Biology component.

Assumptions: Assumes that theoretical equations of physical processes along with a description of stream bathymetry (using x, y, and z coordinates) provide sufficient input to simulate velocity distributions throughout a stream reach.

Level of Effort: The level of effort is high because intensive site-specific analyses are required.

Historical Development: Two-dimensional hydraulic models have been around for many years and were developed for describing hydraulics around objects in the water column (such as bridge abutments) and for simulating flood stage in floodplains. As with one-dimensional hydraulic models, accurate and detailed velocity predictions throughout long-river reaches were not the purpose or common engineering practice with two-dimensional hydraulic models. However, two-dimensional hydraulic models can produce velocity simulations in two-dimensions without any empirical velocity measurements on-site. With the development of hydraulic based habitat models and the extensive use of one-dimensional hydraulics throughout the world (as in the PHABSIM model), hydraulic engineers have promoted n-dimensional models as useful supplements to the suite of habitat modeling tools (Bechera et al. 1994; Ghanem et al. 1994; Olsen and Alfredson 1994; Leclerc et al. 1995; Bovee 1996). Claims have been made that fewer data, or more easily acquired data, are needed for two-dimensional models than for one-dimensional models. This has not been demonstrated to be a general rule. However, because two-dimensional models do not need to have point measurements taken along transects for large rivers using boats equipped with GPS, the collection of bathymetric data can be taken relatively rapidly by cruising throughout the stream reach. However, habitats less than approximately 1-m deep require measurement by walking, as does description of the floodplain, and it is time consuming.

Application: Stream reaches and segments. These models are most useful for describing velocity patterns in highly complex channel segments (around multiple islands, braided reaches, floodplains and under unsteady flow conditions) where one-dimensional models are extremely difficult or impossible to build. As a result, most instream flow studies have ignored, or excluded, such areas. For small, wadable streams with single thread channels--and where unsteady flow conditions are not an issue—the two-dimensional models have not been found to be any more time saving in the collection of field data than the one-dimensional models and they give essentially the same habitat representations (Waddle et al. 2000). When used with habitat suitability models (as in PHABSIM), the same constraints apply to two-dimensional models as to the one-dimensional models and independent observations collected on-site are necessary for habitat model validation.

Strengths: Two-dimensional hydraulic models offer several advantages in simulations of velocity patterns throughout long river reaches. They allow (1) simulation of unsteady flow conditions, such as in river rapids (assuming the channel bathymetry can be described); (2) simulation of velocity patterns around complex braided channels and channels with multiple islands and associated backwaters; (3) simulations of depth and velocity patterns over floodplains (again assuming adequate bathymetry throughout the floodplain); and (4) production of highly accurate habitat maps, using spatially explicit habitat metrics as in landscape ecology.

Limitations and Constraints: Model simulations of velocity distribution throughout a study reach are possible without any on-site velocity measurements. However, these can easily provide a false sense of security and lead practitioners to take short cuts in describing the channel bathymetry. Consequently, habitat suitability maps can be produced with few ground elevation measurements (e.g., along a few transects at intervals of as much as a mile) to describe the reach bathymetry. Without proper calibration and validation, individual point velocity predictions can have considerable error while the average velocities may be good (Waddle et al. 2000). Spatially explicit habitat metrics used to generate habitat maps can be misleading in that little research has been completed that demonstrates any correlation with biological responses of aquatic organism populations. This area of research offers much promise.

Calibration and Validation: Simulation of velocity distributions throughout a study reach is possible without any on-site velocity measurements. As in all applications of simulation models, proper calibration and validation are essential to establish scientific credibility. An independent data set of reach velocity measurements taken at a specific discharge is needed to compare with model output for the same discharge. Often velocities in fringe areas and around islands do not match well, and calibration by adjusting roughness, tinkering with the mesh size, etc. is necessary to bring the model output in agreement with the empirical data. Once calibrated in this way, further comparisons of model output at other discharges are necessary for validation.

Critical Opinion: This technique provides hydraulic information that can be used with other data and models (e.g., habitat suitability criteria). It can be very useful for describing complex habitats such as side channels, eddies, and boulder habitats. Claims that fewer data, or more easily acquired data, are needed for two-dimensional models than for one-dimensional models should be taken with a grain of salt. In part, the reduced data requirement is based on the assertion that two-dimensional models can produce accurate simulations without the calibration velocities that are so time consuming with one-dimensional models. Although calibration velocities are not necessary to run the models, large amounts of bathymetric data are needed to accurately simulate the hydraulic attributes in a complex river reach. It is very easy to take short cuts in data collection, and, if independent observations are not taken for model validation, the model output can be grossly erroneous without the user knowing it. Maps produced from carefully measured and modeled stream reaches are virtually indistinguishable from maps produced from scant and poorly measured reach data. Consequently, as with all hydraulic models, calibration and validation data must always accompany the use of two-dimensional hydraulic models. The very strengths of these models often lead to their limitations in habitat mapping in that detailed habitat maps can be produced even with scantily described river channels and floodplains. Through the use of advances in aerial photography and GPS, two-dimensional modeling holds promise for developing the data to address other components, such as lateral (floodplain) connectivity.

NEW ENGLAND AQUATIC BASE FLOW (ABF) STANDARD

Summary: The New England Aquatic Base Flow (ABF) Standard is a standard-setting approach that uses hydrologic statistics as a surrogate for aquatic habitat.

Objective: The purpose of the method is to provide flow releases that ensure the survival of indigenous aquatic organisms.

Type of Technique: Standard setting

Description: Commonly referred to as the ABF, or New England Flow Policy, this method is a component of the broader U.S. Fish and Wildlife Service's (USFWS) New England Flow Policy (Larsen 1981). The method recommends the August median flow (also referred to as the aquatic base flow or ABF) as a minimum instantaneous flow requirement, unless additional, seasonal releases are needed to protect fish spawning and incubation. During the spring and fall/winter periods, the respective recommendations are the April/May median flow and the February median flow.

Appropriate Scale: Reach. The temporal scale is addressed through the use of seasonal median flow values to protect spawning and incubation, as discussed above.

Ecosystem Component(s) Addressed: Biology is addressed using hydrology as a surrogate for habitat. The method addresses aquatic habitat during the summer low flow period and seasonal needs for spawning and incubation.

Assumptions: Aquatic life in New England streams evolved and adapted to the natural flow regime and emulating that regime should provide an adequate level of protection. Low flow conditions during August represent a natural limiting period due to reduced living space, high water temperature and low dissolved oxygen. Because stream organisms have evolved to survive these periodic flow conditions without major, long-term population changes, a base flow equal to the August median flow should perpetuate them. Historical median flows during the spawning and incubation periods will protect reproduction. Gage records come from watersheds where flow is unregulated so that the hydrology is uneffected.

Level of Effort: This is an office technique that requires little effort. It uses gage records or default values. The watershed area at the project must be determined and is usually measured from existing maps.

Historical Development: The New England Flow Policy was issued by the USFWS in 1981 to serve as a water resource planning tool, address numerous water use applications, and provide guidance to USFWS personnel in the New England region on instream flow assessment (Lang 1999). It evolved from a procedure developed by Robinson (1969) for determining instream flow needs for fisheries, which was applied within the Connecticut River watershed. The method divided the year into four periods and prescribed a different percentage of the historic median flow for June of each period. For rivers where the flow records are inadequate, the median flows for April/May, August and February are assumed to be 4.0, 0.5 and 1.0 cubic feet per second per square mile of drainage (cfsm). These "default" values were calculated as the median of mean monthly flow statistics from 48 unregulated, representative New England streams. As a point of reference, the 0.5 cfsm default equates to 26% of the average annual flow (Lang 1999). Kulik (1990) discussed refinements to the ABF.

Application: The August median flow standard is only applicable to the low-flow season during average or dry year condition(s). This method should not be used to derive a single flow for the entire year; it does not address geomorphology and natural hydrologic variability.

Data required include either gage records or use of default hydrologic standards calculated from a collection of unregulated, regional gages. Preferably, at least 25 years of U.S. Geological Survey gaging records for unregulated (basically free-flowing) flow conditions near the project site should be available to apply this refined method.

Some applications in the southeastern United States have calculated the ABF using September rather than August median flow, since September was the month with the lowest median flow in those regions (Orth and Leonard 1990; Evans and England 1995).

Strengths: Fast, inexpensive, consistent, and easy to understand.

Limitations and Constraints: The ABF is based on the New England hydrology. It was developed in the Connecticut River basin and then expanded to the New England area. The default values should not be used in other regions. The method does not directly consider geomorphology, biology, water quality, or connectivity, and it does not address the flow needs of specific species or life stages. It is not appropriate for negotiated decisions in which multiple alternatives are explored. Selection of the August median flow, as opposed to some other flow statistic (e.g., September median flow, August mean flow, 60% exceedence flow for July-September) is somewhat arbitrary. Some water users dispute the exact means for calculating gage statistics and, in turn, suggest alternative flow values. Altered watersheds will exhibit altered hydrographs, gage data, and medians.

Calibration and Validation: Studies have not been conducted that show a relation between ABF and geomorphology, biology, habitat, or water quality. Although some attempts (unpublished) have been made to compare ABF with flow values in hydropower licenses in which the PHABSIM method and other studies were conducted, case-specific special circumstances and differences in negotiation make such a comparison questionable. It would be more useful to examine actual PHABSIM model results to assess the validity of an ABF-based flow regime. Orth and Leonard (1990) made such a comparison for Virginia streams and

concluded that "Aquatic Base Flow recommendations provided variable levels of habitat maintenance among seasons and different size streams."

Critical Opinion: This method relates primarily to the low flow period in the northeastern study streams where it was developed and may not be applicable in other regions. The August median flow should not be used as a year-round flow because increasing its frequency and duration can be expected to impact aquatic life. The additional application of the seasonal flows sometimes required for fish spawning and incubation is an improvement but still only crudely tracks natural hydrologic variability. Using medians for long time periods immediately trades away roughly half the flow. In floodplain/alluvial systems, a flow regime that maintains channel processes is extremely important. The ABF is not applicable in these systems because channel shape is not driven by summer low flows.

For rivers with wide channels (whether natural or altered), aquatic base flows may provide a lower level of habitat protection because more water is required to "fill" the channel. For projects with sufficient storage capacity to maintain a standard flat-line flow for long periods, this method should not be used except as part of a suite of tools that ensures hydrologic variability.

As with other methods that rely on gage records, hydrologic statistics can change over time with changes in the watershed (land use change) and at higher scales (global climate change, weather cycles). Initial analysis using the Index of Hydrologic Alteration (Richter et al. 1996) can be used to quantify the amount of hydrologic deviation from a natural condition before applying this method.

Similar standard-setting methods based on hydrologic statistics have also been evaluated (see Flow Duration Curve methods and the Tennant method).

BIOLOGICAL RESPONSE TO FLOW CORRELATION METHOD

Summary: The Biological Response to Flow Correlation method establishes a relation between biological data or habitat quality and hydrology or other components or combinations of components (e.g., hydraulic habitat, geomorphology, water quality).

Objective: The method identifies correlations between biological response or habitat condition and flow-related variables.

Type of Technique: Incremental

Description: The Biological Response to Flow Correlation method involves tabulation and analysis of biological response (such as population size, habitat condition to flow, or a flow-dependent habitat index), using graphs or correlation analyses. The relation between biological response or habitat condition and flow attributes may be linear or nonlinear and may differ for different streams or types of streams.

Appropriate Scale: Reach, subwatershed, watershed, region

Ecosystem Components Addressed: Biology

Assumptions: The primary assumption is that some independent variable, such as flow, or a combination of variables, exerts a significant enough effect on the biological response or habitat condition that the effect can be described by development of a statistical model. Once developed, the relations can be used to predict the biological response in streams and stream types for which the relation was developed.

Level of Effort: The effort required for this technique is initially moderate to very high. Development of relations or models typically requires collection of data on environmental variables from several streams over one or more years. This method then requires graphing and regression analysis (linear or transformed) of a relation between biological responses, such as fish population, or habitat condition and different flow statistics, or hydraulic variables. After the relation is developed and validated for use, it can be applied from the office in some cases; however, some tools require one or more site visits to collect data.

Historical Development: This method is a standard study approach in science (see Neave 1949; McKernan et al. 1950; Smoker 1953, 1955; Swift 1976; Binns and Eiserman 1979; Mathews and Olson 1980; Frenette and Julien 1984; Anderson and Nehring 1985; Conder and Annear 1987; Bovee 1988; Fausch et al. 1988; Hvidsten 1993; and Nehring and Anderson 1993).

Application: The implementation steps are to gather data on biological response of interest (e.g., population size, year-class strength, average growth, condition) or habitat condition or quality; tabulate corresponding flow statistics or habitat statistic of interest (e.g., peak flow, low flow, average flow over a period); and run regressions of biological response against flow statistic of interest. Once a significant correlation has been established, these regressions can be used for management decisions on that stream to assess the adequacy of existing flow patterns or the potential benefit of modified flows or flow regimes.

This method may be helpful in some cases, particularly in simple systems (few species of fish), to develop adequate flow recommendations or support instream flow prescriptions for part of the biological component for one or more seasons during the year. Refer to standard statistical texts for protocols involved for developing statistical correlations and relations.

Strengths: With sufficient sample size and statistical power, this method can provide support and rationale for a flow recommendation on the system where it was developed or on related stream types.

Limitations and Constraints: Some models may require existing data on flow and an associated biological response for use to be practical. Regression or other statistical tests used to develop the model or relation do not directly identify flows that should be provided or protected, but indicate the effect of flow or some habitat index on biological response. Results are often used in conjunction with river management objectives for population or habitat management to quantify flow need.

Calibration and Validation: In some cases, the biological response from the regression should be tested on a separate set of data to be considered validated. In other cases, practitioners should confirm that the model is being applied to a stream type that is similar to the stream or group of streams used to develop the model. The next step is to forecast biological response and test forecast accuracy, or to try to transfer the approach to a similar stream, watershed, or region, or other types of streams or regions.

Critical Opinion: These methods (regressions) should not be used on streams or systems where they were not developed without testing to show transferability. They can help identify important variables for use in developing appropriate coefficients for a new application. These methods can provide valuable information where correlations are significant, but commonly do not capture all sources of variability affecting the biological or habitat response. They often display general relations and trends (with wide confidence intervals) better than they provide tight estimates of population or habitat metrics. Trends and relations, whether linear or nonlinear, can be useful for identifying thresholds and making management decisions.

Unless a chosen method or approach is specifically designed to address multiple ecosystem components (which most are not), other methods are needed to address geomorphology, hydrologic variability, water quality, and connectivity.

FEEDING STATION METHOD

Summary: The Feeding Station method describes a feeding habitat index based on areas of slow water adjacent to faster water that meets or exceeds depth thresholds.

Objective: The method attempts to identify the discharge that maximizes the number of feeding stations for trout, using hydraulic simulation.

Type of Technique: Incremental

Description: The method serves as an alternative to conventional weighted usable area (WUA), the method relied on concepts of Bachman (1984) to provide a comparison to WUA, which in the early 1980s made intuitive sense but was invalidated.

Appropriate Scale: Microhabitat

Riverine Component(s) Addressed: Biology component is addressed by examination of hydraulic habitat.

Assumptions: The model assumes that trout select feeding stations (microhabitat) based on hydraulic habitat (i.e., consisting of slow water immediately adjacent to faster water as described above). Presence of the described feeding areas enhances salmonid production.

Level of Effort: The model requires a high level of effort in the field and in the office. In addition to hydraulic modeling requirements, the model requires manual review of each cell within a hydraulic simulation and its relation to adjacent cells at every flow of interest.

Historical Development: Snorkeling observations showed little or no use of shallow (<0.5 ft) depths by trout larger than fry. Literature and observations supported the concept (Fausch 1984; Beecher 1987; Washington Department of Fish and Wildlife and Department of Ecology 1996).

Application: This method employs hydraulic modeling from the PHABSIM system and a similar approach has been incorporated as an option in a version of a PHABSIM habitat model. Feeding areas are delineated by examination of hydraulic simulations or repeated measurements over a range of flows. Usually, habitat value (either 1 or 0) is tabulated manually for each cell, according to hydraulic conditions in the cell and the adjacent cells. A cell is considered to be a feeding station if:
1) Depth is at least 0.5 ft.
2) Velocity is less than 1 ft/sec (0.3 m/sec).
3) Velocity in one of adjacent (lateral) cells is at least 1 ft/sec.
4) Velocity in same adjacent cell is at least 0.5 ft/sec faster than in cell.

The number of feeding stations is tabulated at each simulated flow of interest.

Strengths: None relative to alternatives available, such as PHABSIM.

Limitations and Constraints: This method is very scale dependent: distance between verticals (cell width and transect placement) must match the actual search range of the species of interest. Otherwise, you can underestimate actual feeding stations. Although the model simulates the feeding station concept that has been the subject of considerable published energetics research in field and laboratory, it is limited to lateral velocity gradients. It was originally proposed to incorporate a vertical velocity difference, but such applications require the use of three-dimensional hydraulic models and typically have not been used. It was developed when PHABSIM was relatively new and many of the assumptions, particularly that WUA incorporating depth, velocity, and substrate determine microhabitat quality, were untested for salmonids.

Subsequently, more work has demonstrated a correlation between PHABSIM output and fish distributions. If feeding station analysis results match cell suitabilities at a reach level, then the feeding station method adds nothing. If it differs, then the use of PHABSIM is preferred because it has provided more successful validation.

Calibration and Validation: To date, there has been no validation demonstrating a correlation between this method of feeding station analysis and fish distributions. To validate this method, the practitioner should (1) perform standard hydraulic model calibration to ensure that the model reasonably approximates actual depths and velocities at flows of interest, (2) measure fish distribution along PHABSIM transects and identify concurrent feeding stations, and (3) determine if actual fish distribution matches feeding station distribution.

Critical Opinion: This method has resulted in inadequate flow recommendations and should not be used without additional research. The main purpose of the method served as a check on WUA versus flow patterns when there were few tests of assumptions for WUA. If both methods yielded similar trends, then both were assumed to be more likely to be approximately correct. If the two methods differed, then nothing pointed to one method or the other. However, that assumption has changed. Research supports the assumptions behind WUA (Beecher et al. 1993, 1995); thus, the Washington Department of Fish and Wildlife, which developed the Feeding Station Method, now strongly prefers WUA and no longer uses the feeding station analysis. Use of this method has led to inadequate flow recommendations that were rejected by the Washington State Pollution Control Hearings Board (2000), which has initial review of water appeals.

FLOW DURATION CURVE METHODS

Summary: Instream flow methods based on flow duration curves derived from hydrologic records.

Objective: To obtain a single flow value with a minimal amount of effort that has some hydrological relevance to maintaining natural habitat or geomorphologic characteristics.

Type of Technique: Standard setting

Description: Exceedence percentiles or proportions of monthly medians are calculated from flow duration curves derived from hydrologic records. Many approaches have been developed and each uses a different rationale/biological justification for selection and derivation of percentiles and/or percentages. Examples include:

Hoppe Method (Hoppe, unpublished paper)—the flow that is exceeded 40% of the time (Q_{40}) is recommended for spawning and the Q_{80} is recommended for food production and cover. In addition, the Q_{17} is recommended as a flushing flow for 48 hours.

Northern Great Plains Resource Program Method (unpublished report)—Q_{90} recommended for a minimum instream flow on a monthly basis; Q_{90} derived from "normal" or average flows.

Lyon's Method (Bounds and Lyons 1979)—40% of the monthly median (Q_{50}) is recommended for maintaining habitat from October through March and 60% of Q_{50} is recommended for enhancing flows for spawning and during hot summer months (April-September).

Other methods have been developed that derive percentages or percentiles based upon specific (e.g., Arkansas Method, Filipek et al. 1987) or historical biological data (e.g., Texas Method, Matthews and Bao 1991).

Appropriate Scale: Reach. The temporal scale may be addressed through the use of seasonally adjusted flow statistics.

Riverine Component(s) Addressed: Hydrology is the only ecosystem component addressed because this method relies solely on hydrologic records to develop instream flow standards. Consideration of biology is intended in some methods by making adjustments in percentages or percentiles for some times of year (e.g., spawning season).

Assumptions: Each method may have multiple assumptions but the basic assumption is that the identified percentages or percentiles are appropriate for maintaining habitat for aquatic biota.

Level of Effort: These are office techniques. Whereas the level of effort in deriving flow duration curves is low, acquiring a "naturalized" streamflow record of sufficient length can often be difficult. Some methods require a moderate level of effort to collect field data or assimilate historical biological data. Where adequate stream gaging records are lacking, additional effort is needed to develop hydrologic statistics based on appropriate gages in nearby drainages and watershed characteristics.

Application: These are standard-setting methods developed for application within a specific region. They serve as examples only; other research is necessary to establish these types of relations within different regions. Data needs include hydrologic records of sufficient duration. Records that are degraded by anthropogenic change will compromise derivation of flow duration curves and subsequent recommendations. Naturalized flow records would be a preferred alternative.

Historical Development: Varied.

Strengths: Once the relation(s) have been established, and the similarities of the source and target watersheds and biology have been verified, flow duration curve methods are quick, easy, and relatively inexpensive. At that point, they do not require additional field measurements.

Limitations and Constraints: These methods were developed as a way of extending limited research to similar streams, within a geographical region. When applied to streams within the region where they were developed, these techniques may be used as the second step in a more comprehensive instream flow program, where detailed research on the biological relation to discharge is being conducted. The practitioner must verify that the target streams are similar in terms of hydrology, geomorphology, biology, and water quality to the source streams and likely to remain so. Defining acceptable temporal and spatial variability in the established relation is often a stumbling block. The real constraint of these techniques is that considerable research must occur to establish and verify the relations of biology to the hydrologic parameter being proposed for use.

Calibration and Validation: Ecological research directed toward establishing linkages between flow exceedence percentiles (or percentages of monthly median flows) and aquatic ecosystem integrity would be needed to establish the validity of these types of methods. Application of the method requires research that verifies the original relations established in the source streams and that also exist in the target streams.

Critical Opinion: Selection of percentages or percentiles for maintaining habitat quality is difficult to justify and is arbitrary without the site-specific information to develop and then verify use of the hydrologic statistic. For example, in many western Washington streams, flow is flashy. The statistics may indicate that the flow that maximizes coho spawning habitat, for instance, only occurs a small percent of the time. If the 90% and 10% hydrographs are plotted, it may appear that the best spawning flows are "never" there, but when daily flows are graphed they occur regularly enough during the appropriate season that they meet the Washington Department of Fish and Wildlife's developing definition of achievable or feasible (Hal Beecher, personal communication).

The precision of results is only as accurate as the quality of hydrologic data used to obtain the flow standard, which can yield exceptionally wide confidence intervals around some flow recommendations. Unless the underlying relation of hydrology to biology (habitat) is substantiated within the target region (which is seldom done), these techniques are inappropriate by themselves for establishing instream flow levels or assessing the validity of instream flow recommendations that are derived from other methods. These methods and approaches do not provide for the necessary regime of flows that are critical to maintaining natural riverine functions and processes. These techniques may be acceptable for developing preliminary or reconnaissance level recommendations, but they do not provide quantitative information about biological or geomorphologic processes that are important for maintaining fisheries or natural river processes. Where that level of information is needed, other methods should be used. It is not acceptable to use this group of methods to evaluate the adequacy of recommendations derived from other methods that use site-specific data because they contain less detailed, site-specific information.

INDEX OF BIOTIC INTEGRITY (IBI)

Summary: The Index of Biotic Integrity (IBI) is a biologically based multi-metric index used for assessing and monitoring the biotic integrity of a site.

Objective: The purpose of the IBI is to assess and monitor the biotic integrity at a specific site relative to expected conditions for similar streams.

Type of Technique: Monitoring/Diagnostic

Description: The IBI integrates a set of metrics of fish assemblages that fall into three categories: species composition, trophic composition, and fish abundance and condition. New categories of metrics continue to evolve as the method is further tested and expanded to new regions. A benthic invertebrate index of biotic integrity (B-IBI) has also been developed and has had widespread acceptance and use. Initially, 12 fish metrics relevant to midwestern streams were produced. Metrics can be modified, added, or deleted to reflect regional fish communities and still maintain the theoretical underpinnings of IBI. Each metric is rated according to expected conditions at a stream of similar size and geographic region with minimal human impact. Each metric is scored a 5, 3, or 1 depending if the site approximates, deviates somewhat, or deviates strongly from expected conditions. The sum of all of the metrics results in an IBI total score. The integrity of the site (based on a 12 metric index) is defined as Excellent (58-60), Good (48-52), Fair (40-44), Poor (28-34), Very Poor (12-22), and No Fish.

The IBI requires an "expected condition" to evaluate the integrity of a site. The expected conditions are valid for streams of the same size in the same geographic region. The method appears to be appropriate for any size of stream and has also been adapted for other environments such as lakes, estuaries, wetlands, riparian areas, and reservoirs.

Appropriate Scale: Reach.

Riverine Component(s) Addressed: The IBI addresses the Biological component. It uses biological metrics to indicate both chemical and physical degradation of a site caused by human impacts.

Assumptions: The basic assumption in using the IBI is that the metrics that are measured (whatever they are for a particular region) are sensitive to a broad range of environmental degradation and show a consistent quantitative change across a gradient of human influences. Further, the fish IBI assumes that the sample on which it is based reflects the taxa richness and relative abundance of the stream fauna without bias toward size or taxa.

Level of Effort: This is an incremental method that requires intensive field effort (in terms of labor and cost) in the data collection stage, particularly if it is being applied in a new region where site-specific metrics must be defined and tested. Existing data can be used if there is confidence that species composition and relative abundance across all trophic levels (i.e., not just sportfish) can be produced.

Historical Development: The IBI was developed in response to federal U.S. legislation that calls for the protection of the biological integrity of the nation's water. A water quality monitoring approach was initially used, but cleaner water was not stopping the decline of biotic integrity of water resources. Fish were chosen as biological monitors because they are (1) present even in the smallest streams, (2) are relatively easy to sample and identify in the field, (3) occupy several trophic levels in the food web, and (4) can be responsive to a wide range of man-induced environmental disturbances. The metrics initially outlined in the IBI and the criteria for ranking each metric were developed for midwestern U.S. streams. As the application of the IBI widened, it was found that many of the metrics would need to be modified regionally. Examples of its application can be found in Fausch et al. (1984) and Karr (1981,1991).

Application: The IBI has been applied throughout the world. Initial testing was conducted in the northern midwestern United States, where the method was developed. Karr and Chu (1997), among others, discussed fish and invertebrate IBIs and how they have been developed, tested and applied. Although true experimental manipulation of conditions has not been conducted, IBI scores have predicted degradation where known sources of pollution or poor habitat conditions are found. Metrics chosen for use in IBIs have also been tested to show if a predicted response is found over a gradient of human influence using statistical and graphical analysis.

Strengths: The technique is widely used and generally accepted. The IBI quantifies the biological effect of degraded water quality conditions and is more sensitive and thorough than classic methods of monitoring water quality.

Limitations and Constraints: Considerable expertise and sampling is required to develop the "expectation criteria" of species richness and composition against which all other sites of similar size and geographic region will be compared. In areas where the IBI has not been applied, local expertise and preferably existing data are needed to rank and interpret the data and modify the metrics. A classification system may be required to determine if the site being studied is in a different category than other IBI sites in the area. In regions with low species richness, the IBI has been difficult to apply and often requires major modifications. Recent work has found that fish and benthic IBIs do not always result in the same ranking at a site. It has yet to be determined if these differences are a result of sensitivity, sampling effectiveness, water body size, or some other factor.

Calibration and Validation: There are no "cookie cutter" steps to follow to modify (i.e., calibrate) the IBI metrics so that they are representative of local fauna while maintaining the sensitivity of the index to environmental perturbations. Local expert knowledge, and preferably local data, are required to adjust the IBI for a new region and to evaluate what metrics are sensitive to environmental degradation. A set of categories to be measured is generally accepted, but which metrics within each category and how to represent those metrics are issues that need to be addressed at a regional scale. If the proper metrics are not chosen, the IBI will not be an accurate or useful tool.

One method of validation is to conduct an IBI study upstream and downstream of a known source of pollution, or above and below an irrigation diversion, and compare the results. The IBI scores should reflect the expected differences in the biotic integrity of the sites. Statistical validation of IBI results has also been done for some data sets. Validation of the metrics chosen can also be conducted. One commonly used metric is a measure of intolerant species. The generally accepted rule for this metric based on the experience of IBIs developers is that intolerant species should not be present in sites with a rating of "fair" or worse. Similar criteria are available for other metrics, but may be specific to a region.

Critical Opinion: The IBI is not a tool that can be used to develop an instream flow recommendation. It is an assessment and monitoring tool that can be used to give an initial assessment of a site and then track any changes in the biotic integrity of the site after an instream recommendation is made. The method is heavily reliant on expert judgment for many of the steps in the process, which can be a lim-itation in developing, testing, and applying the method in a new region. The IBI can be expensive to implement depending on the site being studied. It would be most cost effective for a long-term moni-toring program that is proposed to evaluate the effects of an instream recommendation.

TARGET FISH COMMUNITY ASSESSMENT

Summary: The Target Fish Community (TFC) method was developed—using regional distribu-tion and local relative abundance data—to describe a community of fish that is appropriate for a natural river when streamflow and biological integrity are maintained. The TFC method is used as a benchmark for comparison to an existing com-munity and identification of departures from the TFC.

Objective: The purpose of the Target Fish Community method is to describe a model fish community that serves as a target for river restora-tion, rehabilitation, or enhancement and as an end-point for evaluating program progress.

Type of Technique: Monitoring/Diagnostic

Description: The TFC method (Bain and Meixler 2000) was developed for use on a defined reach of the Quinebaug River in Massachusetts and Connecticut. This method can be followed, with some modification, on any defined reach of a mod-erate or large river system.

The first step in using this method is to develop a list of fish species known to have historically inhab-ited the subject river basin. The list is then used as a starting point for selecting species to include in the community analysis. In the Quinebaug study, some species were deleted due to their marine or estuar-ine distribution or because they were not listed in detailed historical records as locally present. Others were added because of their recorded recent occur-rence. Selected species are then classified into three macrohabitat classes: generalists (MG), fluvial dependents (FD), and fluvial specialists (FS) based on habitat requirements. Pollution tolerances, tem-perature preferences, and trophic status are also sum-marized for each species when data are available.

To define a target community, fish collections are assembled from several rivers that have been identified by management agencies as being in a desirable fishery. These data are compiled and summarized to identify about 10 species in rank order of abundance using average rank abundances across the quality-rivers. Fish abundance data from these rivers are mathematically converted to the expected proportions of each species in the Target Fish Community.

Once the TFC is developed for a study reach of river (which can be considered the "expected" community), species proportions are compared to those from recent fish surveys on the study reach (which can be considered the "observed" community). The comparisons of target and current fish communities were made using a percent model affinity procedure (Novak and Bode 1992).

Appropriate Scale: Reach

Riverine Component(s) Addressed: Biology

Assumptions: One of the assumptions accompanying the application of this method is that a set of management-specified quality rivers has similar fish communities that would be characteristic of a similar class of rivers in a region. Further, quality rivers are assumed to have fish fauna indicative of a desired condition. Sampling used to document the existing fish community in the study reach and in quality rivers should be comparable and reflect the true fish species composition.

Level of Effort: Field data on fish abundance must be obtained. However, this method is designed to use the data that state agencies currently gather rather than developing independent or more complex sampling schemes. Effort should be focused on sampling free-flowing habitat types in proportion to their availability in the study reach. The level of effort required to assemble the information about quality rivers is fairly substantial and should involve discussions with regional fisheries experts.

Historical Development: The method was first developed to set a measurable target for river rehabilitation. The work was part of a flow study on the Quinebaug River in Massachusetts and Connecticut under the direction of the U.S. Environmental Protection Agency (EPA). In addition to the EPA, participants included New England Interstate Water Pollution Control Commission, Massachusetts Department of Environmental Protection, Connecticut Department of Environmental

Protection, Massachusetts Division of Fisheries and Wildlife, U.S. Fish and Wildlife Service, U.S. Army Corps of Engineers, U.S. Geological Survey, and Millenium Power Partners. Many of these participants continue to meet periodically to discuss standardization of methods for applying this approach to other watersheds and study reaches. The method has been modified for use in the Ipswich River watershed of Massachusetts, and the state plans to conduct a TFC analysis on all its mainstem rivers.

Application: The TFC method can be used to evaluate instream flows, once they have been established or manipulated, for their resource enhancement or protection value. It can also be used to assess other impacts to river systems. Several field sampling standardization criteria have been developed, but most of those criteria are already in place in most agency survey and inventory protocols. Effort should be focused on sampling free-flowing habitat types in proportion to their availability in the study reach. The TFC is not a tool for developing incremental instream flow recommendations.

Strengths: This is a practical approach that is based on some easily understood assumptions. It is presentable to a wide range of audiences. The data requirements are easily attainable by resource agencies using standard survey and inventory procedures. The Target Fish Community method provides decision makers and stakeholders with a reasonable expectation (not a precolonial ideal) of what the fish community should look like and a measurable goal for restoring the fish fauna in the study reach. The use of quality rivers as a surrogate for a more traditional "reference" river is a realistic method for New England waters because true reference conditions rarely, if ever, exist in moderate to large rivers. The method focuses on the most common fish species, which allows the community to be characterized without the need to assure representative sampling of rare species.

Limitations and Constraints: This method can be applied to moderate or large rivers but should not be used in very large rivers or small streams. The sensitivity of the method to detect modest changes in the flow regime has not yet been determined. For rivers with migratory fish species, the timing of fish sampling efforts is a significant issue. The TFC developed for quality rivers appears to be regionally transferable as long as the most common fish in the community are the same.

Calibration and Validation: This is a regional approach that should be repeated and validated for each different region in which it is used. The method is relatively new and has yet to be widely tested.

Critical Opinion: This method employs a readily understandable common-sense approach to fish community assessment and resource monitoring and provides a measurable goal for restoration or rehabilitation. Fish communities, sampled through standardized methodologies, in free-flowing reaches of moderate-sized rivers should consist primarily of fish species adapted to live in lotic conditions (fluvial dependents and specialists). Rather than relying on a single-species approach for resource protection, which tends to accentuate the value of relatively few commercially important species, the TFC method highlights fish community characteristics that are relatively easy to interpret. The method does not provide incremental flow recommendations but does establish a biologically based goal for rehabilitation or restoration and the mechanism by which incremental flow changes can be assessed. By combining this method with other incremental methods (e.g., MesoHABitat SIMulator, Physical Habitat Simulation), predictions can be made about how to improve habitat quantity and quality to attain the TFC.

PHYSICAL HABITAT SIMULATION (PHABSIM)

Summary: The Physical Habitat Simulation (PHABSIM) system is a computer program that is used for quantifying the suitable versus unsuitable hydraulic habitat attributes of selected species and life stages as a function of discharge. Measurements are at the microhabitat level within representative stream reaches or specified mesohabitat types.

Objective: The purpose of PHABSIM is to develop the relation between hydraulic habitat features and discharge for individual species and life stages of fish or macroinvertebrates in specific river reaches. This relation provides input to the total habitat and time series analyses component of the IFIM.

Type of Technique: Incremental

Description: The PHABSIM is a model that is designed to calculate an index to the amount of

microhabitat available for selected species life stages at different discharges. It has two major analytical components: stream hydraulics and life stage-specific habitat suitability requirements. Output is the functional relation between habitat hydraulics and discharge for a stream reach. This is typically presented as a graph of weighted usable area (microhabitat) versus discharge. The PHABSIM was specifically developed as a component module within the comprehensive Instream Flow Incremental Methodology (IFIM). As such, it addresses only the spatial distribution of the hydraulic attributes of the stream habitat. The computer models are designed to provide input to habitat time series programs (Milhous et al. 1989). Only when combined with the hydrologic time series of the streamflow to develop a time series of total habitat are the temporal aspects of the habitat addressed.

Appropriate Scale: Results are based on microhabitat and are applied within mesohabitats to describe river reaches.

Riverine Component(s) Addressed: The biological component is addressed through hydraulic habitat. It is presumed that there is an explicit relation between hydraulic habitat and the spatial distribution of aquatic organisms.

Assumptions: Users of PHABSIM assume that physical-hydraulic habitat variables are important determinants of individual aquatic organisms spatial distributions. Consequently, species are assumed (supported by considerable research) to exhibit preference-avoidance behavior for depth, velocity, and the reach characteristics of cover and substrate. Users thus assume that areas of suitable and unsuitable habitat within the wetted stream channel may change significantly with discharge. Users also assume that the channel geometry does not significantly change from that described in the model for the time period analyzed. Therefore, repeated measurements of the channel geometry are necessary in changing channels.

Level of Effort: This is an incremental method that requires intensive fieldwork (i.e., multiple site-specific measurements within river reaches and mesohabitats) and calibration/verification of both hydraulic and suitability submodels.

Historical Development: The PHABSIM model evolved from early work on the depth and velocity preferences of salmon in known spawning habitats as described and used to prescribe instream flow standards in the State of Washington (Collings 1974) and by Waters (1976) for the life stages of trout in California. These concepts were linked with one-dimensional hydraulic models originally used to simulate water surface elevations in rivers to simulate flood flows. Considerable modification and testing of these hydraulic programs along with regression models produced the library of model options found in PHABSIM where the focus is on the spatial distribution of velocities rather than simply water surface elevations. Habitat suitability criteria comprise the biological input to the PHABSIM model. Considerable work was undertaken to describe and test techniques for developing habitat suitability criteria (Bovee 1986; Thomas and Bovee 1993). Several look-alike versions of PHABSIM have been developed and are in use throughout the world (Dunbar et al. 1998). Recent developments are incorporating n-dimensional hydraulic models with the habitat suitability models of PHABSIM (see separate discussion of two-dimensional hydraulic models and MesoHABbitat SIMulator (MesoHABSIM).

Application: Field measurements of depth, velocity, substrate material, and cover at specific sampling points along transects placed across the stream channel are taken at different flows. The sampling points are termed verticals and describe conditions for some distance around them (cells), judged to be relatively homogenous. Water surface elevations are also collected and are used to calibrate the hydraulic models. Hydraulic models are used to calculate water surface elevations for specified flows (from which the depths are computed) and to simulate velocities at the same flows. Each step uses theoretical equations or empirical regression techniques, depending on the circumstances. Most applications involve a mix of submodels to characterize hydraulic conditions at simulated flows. The habitat component weights each stream cell using indices that assign a relative value between 0 and 1 for each habitat attribute, indicating how suitable that attribute is for the life stage under consideration. These attribute indices are usually termed habitat suitability criteria. They are developed using direct observations of the attributes used most often by a particular life stage of a species, by expert opinion about what the life requisites are, or by a combination (Bovee 1986). Much debate and effort has been expended over

the last decade as to the "most appropriate" sampling and analytical procedures for developing the habitat suitability criteria.

Practitioners must remember that the habitat suitability criteria are "input" to the habitat model and are not the output. The simulated suitable versus unsuitable output in terms of stream area is the important output of PHABSIM. This is the critical product from PHABSIM that forms the shape of the habitat versus flow function of the modeled reach. Therefore, validation of the biological submodel in PHABSIM is done by observation of fish distribution in the field compared with predicted suitable versus unsuitable areas of the modeled stream as indicated by the intermediate output of PHABSIM.

A common practice has evolved among some practitioners for prescribing an instream flow standard by recommending the maximum habitat value from the weighted usable area or discharge graph for a single life stage of a single species or by some aggregation technique of the maximum values from among several species and life stage plots. Although this approach might be considered by some practitioners to be appropriate in certain situations, the primary value of PHABSIM is its ability to identify trade-offs between streamflow and hydraulic habitat as a decision-making tool.

Strengths: The PHABSIM is a rigorous library of models much tested and capable of demonstrating whether or not the changing hydraulic features of a flow regime are likely to have significant effects on fish distribution. The most valuable use of PHABSIM is to identify and quantify those areas within the wetted stream environment that are unsuitable for specific life stages of evaluated aquatic species under various discharges. When coupled with hydrologic time series, the timing, amount, and duration of unsuitable areas can help identify potential habitat bottlenecks induced by natural or managed flow events (e.g., see Bovee et al. 1994) or the relative strengths of one prescribed flow regime versus another.

Limitations and Constraints: The PHABSIM provides a habitat/flow function that is limited to the hydraulic attributes of depth and velocity within fixed channel indexes. Further, it evaluates only the spatial aspects of the hydraulic attributes within stream reaches and requires a well designed stratified sampling procedure for extrapolation to segments and linkage with hydrologic time series to describe the temporal aspect of the habitat hydraulics. Because the habitat-based instream flow models rely on empirical measurements of the stream channel as inputs, adequate understanding of sediment transport and channel dynamics must be incorporated into any simulation for unobserved flow conditions.

The model does not predict the effects of flow on channel change. If a channel is not in dynamic equilibrium, the model users may have to hedge on simulations of future (therefore unobservable) discharge conditions and call for periodic adjustments, with empirical measurements at regular intervals. Likewise, water quality is not incorporated in PHABSIM. Any significant alteration of the flow regime by flow regulation has been shown also to result in alteration of the temperature regime. Small changes in temperature can have very significant effects on egg maturation, incubation, and time of hatching and growth, depending on the species. Stream temperature can also affect the suitability of some habitat types for some species and life stages of organisms. In addition, PHABSIM cannot provide meaningful information on the effects of rapidly varying flow.

Inappropriate selection and use of models, ignoring model assumptions and failure to validate model output can lead to serious errors in application. First-order habitat requirements are well known for only a few high-profile species. Basic habitat requirements are not known for many rare or widely dispersed species, or those that inhabit streams and habitat types that are difficult to sample. Second order habitat requirements (e.g., proximity to food sources or refugia) are largely unknown for many aquatic species.

Calibration and Validation: Procedures for calibration and validation for the hydraulic models are described by Milhous et al. (1989) and by Thomas and Bovee (1993) for the habitat suitability models. Careful calibration and validation of both hydraulic and suitability aspects of PHABSIM are necessary to establish scientific credibility.

Critical Opinion: The PHABSIM is best used as a decision-making tool for evaluations of alternative discharges to quantify the proportions of suitable and unsuitable areas of stream reaches and segments subject to regulation or flow management. Practitioners should place emphasis on developing habitat suitability criteria that closely describes the species of interest's actual behavior.

Output must be measured against what is known to occur for the species of interest. Reach mapping is a critical component of applying this method and can help to ensure against mistakes in applying the habitat suitability criteria. For example, fish that typically spawn or rear along river channel margins and floodplains may select for slow, shallow habitat that the model may indicate occurs at very low discharges in the center of the channel. In reality, only channel margins or overbank areas provide spawning and rearing habitat for these species, and correct interpretation of the results and subsequent recommendations must reflect this biological phenomena. To avoid such mistakes, the modeler must eliminate (set channel index to zero) in-channel areas from consideration as spawning and rearing habitat.

When used, the PHABSIM model must be placed in proper context as to the relative importance and likely change in the other ecosystem components. It does not provide information about the full range of ecosystem components but is useful for helping describe the biological component by assessing hydraulic habitat. Additional analysis, separate from PHABSIM, must be completed to adequately address instream flow needs for hydrologic variability (inter- and intraannual), geomorphology, water quality, and connectivity. Practitioners should not simply prescribe a minimum instream flow standard by recommending the maximum habitat value from the weighted usable area/discharge graph for a single life stage of a single species. Doing so can result in unrealistic recommendations that damage the credibility of the entire study and the study team. Rather, output from the model should be used as input to a habitat time series analysis, which is useful in identifying habitat bottlenecks and the most limited life stages in order to support recommendations that maintain or restore hydraulic habitat conditions that meet defined instream flow objectives (e.g., maintain the existing amount or restore a certain percentage of the limiting habitat in an average year).

MESOHABITAT SIMULATOR (MESOHABSIM)

Summary: MesoHABitat SIMulator (MesoHABSIM) (Parasiewicz 2001) is similar to PHABSIM (Milhous et al. 1990) in that both quantify physical habitat attributes and relate those to the habitat suitability requirements of selected species and life stages as a function of flow. Whereas PHABSIM involves a detailed microhabitat survey within selected sampling locations, MesoHABSIM uses mesohabitat mapping of entire river sections under multiple flow conditions.

Objective: The purpose of MesoHABSIM is to provide a conceptual approach for habitat assessment that can be used to examine river rehabilitation and restoration scenarios, including alternative flow regimes, for an entire river or river section.

Type of Technique: Incremental

Description: MesoHABitat SIMulator uses the widely accepted concept of physical habitat simulation models (such as PHABSIM) but focuses on the mesohabitat scale. The entire river section of interest is surveyed at a number of different flows. Hydro-morphological units (11 are listed, including riffle, run, pool) are delineated at a specific discharge and used in combination with hydraulic and cover attributes to define the mesohabitat type. The suitability of a mesohabitat type for a target fish community (see Target Fish Community method) is assessed based on electrofishing surveys, using multivariate statistics. The results show the variation in the spatial distribution of mesohabitats, and when combined with the biological criteria yield information about habitat quantity.

Appropriate Scale: Results are based on mesohabitat data and are applied to river reaches, up to a watershed level.

Riverine Component(s) Addressed: Biology is addressed through physical habitat measurements at the mesoscale. Fish sampling is conducted to establish the relation between the mesohabitat used and its physical attributes.

Assumptions: This model assumes that the hydraulic and cover characteristics of mesohabitat units are important in determining the spatial distribution of aquatic organisms. The relation between habitat area and flow is derived from representative sites and assumed to be valid for the entire river sections. Habitat use information, typically gathered during summer, is assumed to be valid only for that season.

Level of Effort: MesoHABitat SIMulator requires a relatively high amount of fieldwork. Whereas measurements are simpler and less intensive than those for PHABSIM, they are more extensive in that the entire study reach is surveyed at least once. Parasiewicz (2001) estimated the cost at about 50% of a standard PHABSIM application.

Historical Development: The concept and approach of this method has only been recently published (Parasiewicz 2001). MesoHABitat SIMulator was applied in 2000 as part of a multidisciplinary study of the Quinebaug River in Massachusetts (Parasiewicz and Gallagher 2002) and is presently being applied in other watersheds to determine ecological quality, establish minimum flow standards, and design rehabilitation and restoration measures. The concept presents a framework within which a variety of methodologies can be used. As a new method, further refinement is likely to occur over time. Additional Information about MesoHABSIM can be found at Cornell's Instream Habitat Program website (http://www.dnr.cornell.edu/research/IHP/).

Application: The method requires mesohabitat mapping of the study area at multiple flows and electrofishing or snorkeling to establish mesohabitat-level biological criteria. The objective of fish data collection is to describe habitat occupancy.

Strengths: Although MesoHABSIM is a new and still developing approach, it uses the same conceptual approach as PHABSIM models that are already widely accepted. Because the entire study area is surveyed, MesoHABSIM will adequately represent the study area. In contrast, transect-based studies are often criticized for surveying habitat, in detail, that may not be representative of the study reach (Castleberry et al. 1996; Williams 1996; Railsback 1999). MesoHABitat SIMulator allows large river reaches to be fully assessed and can be used in concert with a GIS analysis. Habitat data collection is simple enough to be performed by either trained technicians or volunteers. In addition to instream flow applications, this method can also be used to predict habitat and fish community responses to other river rehabilitation and restoration projects, such as dam removal or channel alterations.

Limitations and Constraints: Whereas PHABSIM includes very detailed information on a relatively small spatial scale, MesoHABSIM gathers less detailed information on a larger scale. Error may be introduced through inconsistent classification of hydro-morphological units and the determination of unit boundaries. Field measurements must be done at multiple flows in order to construct a habitat-flow curve. How this relates to the long-term fish community that might exist, and variable flow conditions including natural hydrology, is unclear. However, the same can be said for other physical habitat simulation models.

An application from the Quinebaug River was presented as an example in Parasiewicz (2001). The flow regime on this river has been drastically altered, making it easier to demonstrate a biological impact. The sensitivity of MesoHABSIM to detect modest flow differences has not yet been demonstrated.

Calibration and Validation: The method has only been validated on small streams under low flow conditions. It has not yet been tested for high flows.

Critical Opinion: One of the criticisms of PHABSIM is that habitat criteria are developed at a much smaller scale than the cell size commonly used in hydraulic models, introducing error into the results (Railsback 1999). MesoHABitat SIMulator avoids this objection and appears to be a viable alternative to microhabitat-based models. Application of the technique is ongoing for several applications in the northeastern United States, and the method's usefulness will become clearer as scientists have the opportunity to use and evaluate it. At present, MesoHABSIM appears to be a useful way to quantitatively address instream flow applications for river rehabilitation and restoration.

HATFIELD-BRUCE WESTERN SALMONID REGRESSIONS

Summary: Hatfield and Bruce (2000) developed a series of equations to estimate the flow (cfs) that maximizes weighted usable area (WUA) in PHABSIM studies for up to four life stages of brown trout (*salmo salar*), chinook salmon (*Oncorhynchus tshawytsch*), rainbow trout (*O. mykiss*), steelhead trout (*O. mykiss*), and all species pooled—including bull trout (*Salvelinus confluentus*), Dolly Varden (*S. malma*), chum salmon (*O. keta*), coho salmon (*O. kisutch*), cutthroat trout (*O. clarki sp.*), pink salmon (*O. gorbuscha*), sockeye salmon (*O. nerka*), and mountain whitefish (*Prosopium williamsoni*).

The equations use loge of mean annual discharge (MAD), of latitude, and of longitude as predictor variables. Hatfield and Bruce (2000) proposed their method as a reconnaissance level method.

Objective: The purpose of the Hatfield-Bruce salmonid habitat-flow equations is to estimate the flow that maximizes WUA for each species and life stage for which an equation has been developed, including the pooled suite of western salmonids. Thus, it eliminates the incremental element from PHABSIM.

Type of Technique: Standard setting

Description: The Hatfield-Bruce salmonid habitat-flow equations is based on PHABSIM study results. Input variables include MAD, latitude, and longitude; however, only two of these are used for any life stage.

Appropriate Scale: As with PHABSIM, results are based on microhabitat and are applied to mesohabitats and river reaches.

Riverine Component(s) Addressed: The biological component is addressed through hydraulic habitat. It is presumed that there is an explicit relation between hydraulic habitat and aquatic organisms.

Assumptions: Users of these equations make the same assumptions as users of PHABSIM in that (1) physical-hydraulic habitat variables are important determinants of individual aquatic organisms' spatial distributions; (2) aquatic organisms exhibit preference-avoidance of depth, velocity, substrate, and cover; (3) suitable and unsuitable habitat change with discharge; and (4) channel geometry is relatively constant.

Level of Effort: Minimal. The user can look up MAD and latitude and longitude and enter these variables into equations on a calculator or computer.

Historical Development: Hatfield and Bruce (2000) reviewed 127 PHABSIM study results from western North America. Many of the studies included multiple sites, multiple species, and multiple life stages, so that sample sizes approached 500 for some species. Adjusted R^2 for equations are at least 0.598 except for nonnative brown trout. Although independent variables considered in model development included latitude and longitude, mean annual discharge, elevation, catchment area, reach gradient, and distance to the coast, only the first three variables were used in the predictive equations. Smith and Sale (1993) used a similar approach with a much smaller sample size.

Application: Users can look up MAD and latitude and longitude and enter these variables into equations on a calculator or computer. Application is limited to western Canada and the western United States. Hatfield and Bruce (2000) intended this method primarily for project scoping, research planning, and initial steps in adaptive management, with more detailed, site-specific study to refine management decisions.

Strengths: The Hatfield-Bruce equations provide quick estimates of flows that maximize WUA for several western North American salmonids. Although these estimates provide more species-specific information than the Tennant method, they are suitable for the same types of uses as the Tennant method.

Limitations and Constraints: The Hatfield-Bruce equations rely on latitude and longitude and are, therefore, limited to the geographic region in which they were developed: western North America. Unlike PHABSIM, on which it is based, the Hatfield-Bruce method does not produce incremental results. It does not incorporate the details of channel geometry and hydraulics found in PHABSIM. Hatfield and Bruce (2000) emphasized the limitations that should be used with this tool.

Calibration and Validation: Users must determine MAD, latitude, longitude, and species of salmonids of interest at the site. No independent validation has been published, but PHABSIM results generated since November 2000 could be compared to Hatfield-Bruce equation results.

Critical Opinion: The Hatfield-Bruce equations provide an additional level of refinement over hydrology-based methods when used for salmonids in western North American streams. It is a reconnaissance level or office tool that is not a substitute for detailed analysis of watershed and reach.

THE PENNSYLVANIA/MARYLAND INSTREAM FLOW MODEL

Summary: The Pennsylvania/Maryland Instream Flow Model (PMIFM) is a microhabitat impact

analysis method for brook and/or brown trout (four life stages) present in specific stream types located within a region of Pennsylvania and Maryland (Denslinger et al. 1998). The data collection procedures and simulation of microhabitat is based on the Physical Habitat Simulation Model (PHABSIM)(Milhous et al. 1989; Bovee et al. 1998). The PMIFM quantifies changes in available trout microhabitat by comparing proposed water withdrawal alternatives to historic median monthly or mean daily flows using a minimum of a 10-year period of record. Brook and/or brown trout streams with a drainage area less than 100 mi2 were classified into four stream types based on geologic features. Physical microhabitat data from stream type study sites, for each of the four stream types, were aggregated and used to calculate normalized minimum weighted usable area. The microhabitat impact analysis is used in decision making for water withdrawal permits.

Objective: The purpose of the PMIFM is to allow an evaluation of the incremental impacts of water withdrawals on the physical habitat of wild brook and brown trout throughout portions of Pennsylvania and Maryland. The PMIFM was developed with the intention that a site-specific study would not be required.

Type of Technique: Incremental

Description: The PMIFM is based on a geologic classification of brook and/or brown trout streams with a drainage area less than 100 mi2. Stream study sites were selected and physical microhabitat data were collected for each stream type to characterize brook and brown trout microhabitat for similar streams within a region. Ninety-seven stream segments distributed among 72 streams were sampled in the Ridge and Valley and Appalachian Plateau Physiographic Provinces in Pennsylvania, and 12 stream segments distributed among 11 streams were sampled in the Piedmont Physiographic Province in Maryland. The stream segments sampled in each region were selected using a stratified random sampling scheme. Strata were Physiographic Region and length of stream from the headwaters to a potential water withdrawal location (0-5 mi, 5.1-10 mi, 10.1-15 mi, 15.1-20 mi). Weighted usable area (WUA) vs. discharge relations were developed for each study site. The WUA vs. discharge relations are used to compute microhabitat values using historical median monthly flows for a period of record from 10 to 75 years or daily flows for a period of record of up to 2.5 years. Using the monthly median flow example, monthly median flows for each year in the period of record from the candidate stream, are converted to average microhabitat values for each flow using the WUA vs. discharge relations from all study streams that characterize the project stream. Flows are then adjusted per the proposed withdrawal, and microhabitat quantities are estimated using the new flows. Comparisons are made between the historic and proposed condition. The resultant habitat and flow data can be analyzed using various time series and averaging techniques. Habitat suitability criteria used in the model were developed from observational studies conducted on four Pennsylvania streams.

Appropriate Scale: Reach or segment

Riverine Component(s) Addressed: The biological component is addressed through hydraulic habitat. Hydrology is also addressed through model outputs that analyze the flow regime with and without a proposed withdrawal.

Assumptions: This method assumes that the aggregate of the PHABSIM analyses used to develop the microhabitat simulation model are representative of the project stream. The habitat suitability criteria are assumed to be applicable for all study regions.

Level of Effort: This incremental method does not require stream-specific physical microhabitat data. Tables of monthly median flows for a historical period of record of at least 10 years must be available, or developed, using either site-specific or synthesized data from a representative gage. Data can be analyzed by either running the computer model or by examining figures that are available in the study report and that were generated from numerous iterations of running the model for representative stream gages throughout Pennsylvania.

Historical Development: The PMIFM was the result of an interagency study conducted from 1995-1998 (Denslinger et al. 1998). The incentive for the study was an attempt to resolve discrepancies in the ways instream flow protection was being addressed among various agencies with instream flow protection responsibilities. Previously, instream flow protection levels were based on standard-setting techniques (primarily the Tennant and $7Q_{10}$ methods). The PMIFM has

been used to evaluate numerous projects to date. It allows evaluation of various alternatives for water withdrawals and enables decisions to be based on the relative loss in trout habitat among the alternatives.

Application: The method is based on the time series analysis aspect of the Instream Flow Incremental Methodology (IFIM) and, specifically, the Physical Habitat Simulation (PHABSIM) model component of the IFIM. However, it is not a site-specific application of the PHABSIM, but a representation based on regional data. This allows the method to be applied without site-specific data collection, which makes it attractive to regulatory agencies as well as water users. These beneficial aspects must be weighed against the greater confidence that would be possible with a site-specific PHABSIM study. The model is currently limited to use on streams inhabited with wild brook and/or brown trout with a drainage area less than 100 mi2 that are located in Pennsylvania and Maryland within the physiographic provinces evaluated. It has not been applied to warm water streams. Model subroutines that allow evaluations of adult trout have been used to evaluate microhabitat for stocked trout. Use of the approach could most likely be expanded if adapted to other geological settings, stream types, fish species, and the like. Although the method does not address geomorphology, water quality, or longitudinal connectivity, it could conceivably be adapted to address these resource components.

Strengths: This method is well suited to alternatives analyses and evaluation of the relative impacts of various water withdrawals, instream flow reservations, reservoir releases, and, especially, for routine permit reviews by regulatory agencies. It is much less costly to apply than site-specific applications of PHABSIM. It is an incremental method, which makes it much more flexible to apply than a standard-setting technique. The fact that it is based on representative site-specific data from streams similar to the project stream (as defined by the classification approach) makes its use more reasonable in light of criticism sometimes made of methods that were developed in other geographic areas.

Limitations and Constraints: The method, as now developed, is limited in geographic scope and the fish species addressed but it could be adapted to address other fish species or resource components (e.g., geomorphology, aquatic communities, or larger streams). It is a regional representation, and site-specific studies will yield more reliable data. Although the method allows an estimate of the impacts of water withdrawals on fish habitat, the relation between habitat loss and fish population response is not addressed.

Calibration and Validation: The various hydraulic models in the method were developed using the PHABSIM procedure and were calibrated accordingly. Confidence intervals are generated based on the variances from the estimates of historic and impacted habitat generated for each study stream segment used in the analysis. Validation of the habitat impact analysis would require site-specific PHABSIM analysis that could then be compared to the regional analysis. Studies have not been conducted to establish the relation between fish population response and microhabitat impact as estimated from the model.

Critical Opinion: The PMIFM allows various alternatives to be evaluated using an incremental analysis of microhabitat changes compared to a baseline condition (historic median monthly or mean daily flows). The method could be applied to other geographic areas, stream types, and the like, if the considerable work necessary to acquire regional data was done. The method is superior to most standard-setting approaches because it allows proposed withdrawals to be viewed in relation to the actual streamflows and habitat estimates for a site. Certainly large withdrawals will have much greater impacts on habitat than small withdrawals, in most cases, but standard-setting methods are usually inadequate to take this fact into consideration. More accurate and precise evaluations can be made using site-specific studies, which are certainly warranted in some cases, but the PMIFM may be adequate for use in many permit reviews where regional approximations are deemed sufficient.

Because PMIFM does not address geomorphology, water quality, and connectivity, these resource components must be addressed using other techniques. Also, the PMIFM was designed to address the microhabitat needs of wild brook trout and brown trout only. Instream flow needs for other aquatic species or communities may be more or less than those required for these species, and adaptation of the method would be required to properly address these needs.

The primary users of PMIFM—Pennsylvania Fish and Boat Commission (PFBC), Pennsylvania Department of Environmental Protection, and the Susquehanna River Basin Commission—have found that microhabitat is readily accepted as an appropriate decision variable in many instances (Leroy Young, PFBC, personal communication). Being able to evaluate several alternatives in a timely manner allows for a negotiated decision.

PLUNGE POOL METHOD

Summary: The Plunge Pool method is an empirical method designed to provide a mixture of fast flowing, turbulent plume and slow, deep water in steep bedrock channels or channels formed by very large boulders (greater than 1 m diameter).

Objective: The intent of the method is to establish minimum flow standards and operational flow regimes in high gradient, bedrock- or boulder-controlled trout streams.

Type of Technique: Incremental

Description: The basis of the Plunge Pool method is visual observation of the turbulence plume at a range of discharges. Photo-documentation of each flow from fixed photo points is highly recommended. To perform a plunge pool method study, the practitioner:

1) Selects at least three transects across each plunge pool to characterize plunge pool habitat.
2) Measures or determines depth at each selected point along transect at each flow of interest (at least three different flows over a wide range).
3) Determines the edges of turbulence plume (may be distinguished by abrupt change in velocity, foam or white water, or turbulence) at each transect at each flow of interest.
4) Calculates the ratio of area of deep, calm water to area of plume at each flow of interest.
5) Determines the flow that provides greatest area of deep, calm water with a good ratio of plume and associated turbulence, based on the suitability table developed by the practitioner.

The suitability table assigns suitability for various ratios of plume area to deep, calm area.

Appropriate Scale: Mesohabitat, reach

Riverine Component(s) Addressed: Biology is addressed through visual examination and quantification of hydraulic habitat. Longitudinal connectivity is maintained through the use of the method in these stream types.

Assumptions: Although pool area changes little with flow, maintenance of a high velocity plume at the head of a plunge pool transports greater amounts of food and is important for fish production. However, a mix of habitat conditions is critical; low velocity areas are necessary for resting and energy conservation by trout. At extremely high flows that maximize plume, resting areas are reduced or eliminated and the habitat suitability is reduced. Channel maintenance and riparian maintenance are assumed not to be of concern because of bedrock channels and limited riparian soils. Water quality is assumed not to be of concern.

Level of Effort: Moderate to high. Field effort is high but interpretation is simple. Analysis can rely on multiple field measurements or hydraulic modeling from a smaller number of field measurements.

Historical Development: This method was developed in Washington State (Washington Department of Fish and Wildlife and Department of Ecology 1996). Measurements of width, depth, velocity, and plume area showed that a balance of deep, calm water and plume area occurred at moderate discharges in four pools in two streams. Observations of resident coastal cutthroat trout (Salmo clarki) behavior showed that they favored areas of deep, slow water close to the plume in one of two streams; the other stream had no fish.

Application: This method is only appropriate in high gradient stream reaches in cool climates where channel maintenance, riparian maintenance, water quality are not serious concerns. It was developed and is intended for use where one or two species are the only fish present. Other considerations, such as other aspects of connectivity (e.g., migration) or biology (e.g., spawning), need to be addressed by other methods.

Strengths: The method relies on empirical measurements, which can be augmented by hydraulic modeling. It provides results that are intuitively more reasonable than hydraulic/habitat modeling at low flows; that is, one-dimensional hydraulic models do not handle high velocity that develop at higher flows (i.e., unsteady flow).

Limitations and Constraints: The method is only applicable to high gradient, cascading bedrock or boulder streams inhabited by trout. Separate spawning and incubation flow determinations are needed. It does not address other biological aspects such as spawning, incubation, or migration flows, nor does it address any of the other ecological components.

Calibration and Validation: See Method Description. Compare fish abundance in many pools having different configurations and different "best" flows according to the metric. Track the metric over time for each pool. Determine if there is any correlation between fish abundance and minimum, median, mean, or maximum of the metric, accounting for prior conditions and recruitment.

Critical Opinion: This method is only to be used in bedrock controlled, high gradient, cascading streams. It focuses on hydraulic habitat directly and on connectivity in a qualitative way. In such cases, the method adequately provides for instream flow use, but the other components must be considered (e.g., water quality). Applying this method usually results in recommendaitons of low to moderate flows. However, the method is not suitable for streams in which channel maintenance, riparian maintenance, and valley maintenance flows are important. This method only addresses a portion of the biology/habitat ecosystem component, and, if used, should be combined with other biology/habitat models to identify biological needs for other times of the year. It must be combined with other tools to identify flow needs for hydrology, geomorphology, water quality, and connectivity ecosystem purposes.

RIVERINE COMMUNITY HABITAT ASSESSMENT & RESTORATION CONCEPT (RCHARC) METHOD

Summary: The Riverine Community Habitat Assessment & Restoration Concept (RCHARC) method is a transect-based model that examines

156

the spatial and temporal distribution of depth and velocity, as a proxy for habitat conditions, to compare different water management alternatives.

Objective: The model's purpose is to assess depth and velocity distributions among alternative management scenarios.

Type of Technique: Incremental

Description: The method compares depth and velocity distributions at selected time intervals, between a reference river and a target river or flow management alternative. Transects are used to establish the depth and velocity distribution within a reference reach. This distribution is determined for the mean flow for each month, typically with the aid of hydraulic modeling. The same determinations are also made for another river reach or for the same reach under a regulated flow regime. Statistical metrics (such as correlation coefficients) are then used to compare the target reach and water management against the reference condition. The better the target condition matches the reference condition, the higher it ranks for habitat quality.

Appropriate Scale: The method is applied to a stream reach or segment; measurements are obtained to characterize mesohabitat types. The RCHARC uses a monthly temporal scale.

Riverine Component(s) Addressed: This technique uses hydraulic habitat to address Biology.

Assumptions: The RCHARC method is based on the following assumptions:

1) River channels are stable.
2) Transects accurately characterize habitat conditions.
3) Depth and velocity distributions measured in the reference river represent ideal habitat conditions.
4) Depth and velocity distributions adequately represent habitat conditions.
5) The depth and velocity distributions for time series of mean monthly flows adequately represent the intraannual variability.
6) Target rivers are similar to the reference river.

This method is based on the premise that specific species or groups of species prefer certain depth and velocity conditions, that the fish community is determined by the distribution of depths and velocities that occur over time, and that a river with an unaltered channel and natural flow regime provides a reference condition for ideal habitat conditions. This method can only be applied between streams (reference to target streams) with similar fish communities. The method uses physical measurements (depth, velocity) as a proxy for the biological component; that is, habitat necessary to support an aquatic community. The importance of seasonal flow variations is recognized through the use of monthly depth and velocity distributions.

Level of Effort: This is an incremental method that requires minimal fieldwork. Transect data must be obtained. Hydrologic data are necessary to determine the reference condition and develop realistic flow management alternatives. Analysis can be done using commonly available computer software.

Historical Development: This method was originally developed by the U.S. Army Waterways Experiment Station and used on the Missouri River to assess flow management alternatives (Nestler et al. 1993, 1996).

Application: The method is an incremental technique in that it allows the assessment of different alternatives. However, the variables it considers are limited. It is designed to be used as an impact analysis tool in degraded and over-allocated rivers, but its application hinges on similarity between the reference reach (ideal conditions relative to depth and velocities) and target reach (degraded conditions). A typical example is comparing upstream/downstream reaches where the downstream is subject to the management alternatives. By setting predetermined thresholds of deviation from reference conditions, RCHARC could be used as a standard-setting approach. Nestler et al. (1996) used monthly statistics and summed them to produce a single number representing total impact. It would, however, be possible to examine time steps individually and to specify whatever time step is most relevant.

Transect depth and velocity data representative of the different channel types must be obtained so that conditions at each mean monthly flow can be hydraulically modeled. If a different river is used as the reference, data must be obtained for both the reference and target rivers. An historical hydrologic record is needed to establish the reference condition, unless a surrogate, unregulated stream is used. Hydrologic information about the target stream is also required for developing realistic water management alternatives. Nestler et al. (1996) mentioned several statistical alternatives for comparing reference and target conditions.

Strengths: By looking at hydraulic patterns at the mesohabitat level, RCHARC avoids the problem that local or transferable habitat suitability criteria are not available for all organisms.

This method can be used in a monitoring mode to look at long-term changes in the hydraulic environment and channel shape. Interpretation of results is straightforward because a management alternative can be scored with a single value.

Limitations and Constraints: Looking at the overall depth and velocity distribution is in one sense a community approach, but it may be too coarse a measure to accurately represent habitat conditions. It does not, for example, consider the needs of some organisms for special flow events, particularly the high and low flows. For example, some fish may deposit eggs during high flow conditions not represented by mean monthly flows and may require subsequent flows that recede gradually enough that eggs are not dewatered prior to hatching.

The method does not address the needs of specific species and life stages and their special seasonal flow needs if outside the monthly mean. It does not consider flow requirements associated with the channel forming and maintenance process. Changes in water management can change the channel configuration and the depths and velocities; RCHARC does not take this fact into account.

If a different reach or river is used as a reference, the reference must be comparable to the target reach. Because no two reaches are ever identical, part of the RCHARC results will be due to reach differences rather than flow differences.

Calibration and Validation: Hydraulic modeling results must be calibrated and validated. We are not aware of testing that has been done to validate the method or compare results with other methods.

Critical Opinion: The RCHARC method may be too coarse to adequately represent the quality of habitat for aquatic life for three reasons. First,

habitat conditions may not be adequately represented if transects are not located primarily with habitat in mind, are insufficient in number, or measured with a minimum number of verticals. Second, the use of mean monthly flows may not adequately consider specific flow requirements (magnitude and temporal aspects) of certain life stages of aquatic organisms. Third, reach level analysis may mask mesohabitat differences; analysis at the mesohabitat level may be more useful, provided that habitat types and their hydraulic attributes are adequately sampled (Parasiewicz 2001).

Like other methods, the ultimate measure of success is the response of aquatic populations over time. However, comparison of results to other habitat metrics would be informative. Whereas RCHARC is useful for planning and comparing water management alternatives, its level of resolution may not be appropriate for controversial water management situations. The method can be used to look at changes in the depth and velocity distribution that occur over time in association with changes in river morphology. In cases where the goal is to monitor river morphology, collection of substrate data would also be useful.

SINGLE TRANSECT HYDRAULIC-BASED HABITAT METHODS

Summary: Single Transect Hydraulic-Based Habitat methods represent a transect approach for quantifying minimum or base flow values for times of year when streamflow is at its lowest.

Objective: The purpose of the methods is to identify flows sufficient to provide a minimum or basic survival level of fish hydraulic habitat.

Type of Technique: Standard setting

Description: A stage-discharge relation is computed using Manning's equation and the prescribed instream flow is the discharge that provides the percent of wetted perimeter, average depth, and average velocity as specified by the particular method.

Appropriate Scale: River segments (the upstream and downstream boundaries are specified for each flow prescription).

Riverine Component(s) Addressed: Biology is assumed to be addressed using hydraulic habitat.

Assumptions: This method assumes that if adequate wetted perimeter, average depth, and average velocity are maintained over the shallowest portion of stream riffles (the hydraulic control), then the hydraulic habitat will be sufficient to sustain the fishes and macro-invertebrates in all other parts of the stream reach as well. Use of the method also assumes that water quality, sediment transport, and channel geometry are acceptable and will not change or that flows to maintain those functions and processes are provided based on other methods.

Level of Effort: Use of the model requires medium effort. Site-specific data at one or more transects across the stream and computer generated hydraulic characteristics are needed.

Historical Development: The U.S. Forest Service originally developed this method as a single transect approach using the sag-tape technique for computing discharge (Anonymous 1974; Rose and Johnson 1976). The sag-tape data collected at one or more riffles were used to provide input data for a computer program, R2-Cross, which uses Manning's equation for calculating discharge. The AVEPERM program of the Physical Habitat Simulation (PHABSIM) suite of models can also be used to generate the same hydraulic characteristics. The R2-Cross method has been used by the Colorado Water Conservation Board for establishing minimum flows since the passage of instream flow legislation in 1973 (Espergen and Merriman 1995). The Wyoming Game and Fish Department has used a variation of that method for identifying maintenance flow needs in Wyoming since 1983 (Annear and Conder 1984).

Application: This method has typically been used on streams in the western United States. After identifying an appropriate stream segment and visually surveying a reach within the segment, single transects are placed across the shallowest portion (the hydraulic control) of one or more representative riffles. The flow recommendation is subsequently based on a level of flow that will maintain minimum hydraulic criteria standards at one or all of the riffles being modeled (Nehring 1979; Annear and Conder 1984).

Strengths: This a straightforward empirical method that is fairly widely used and accepted in parts of the western United States for determining base flows. The technique does not require any stream gaging and is based on the unique physical characteristics of each stream.

Limitations and Constraints: This method does not consider any ecological components other than biology/habitat and then it only yields a single flow. It does not address flow needs for intra- or interannual hydrologic variability. The selection of study riffles and placement of transects requires a skilled practioner. Otherwise, improperly placed transects can yield inappropriately high or low instream flow prescriptions.

Calibration and Validation: No calibration or validation procedures are indicated.

Critical Opinion: This technique was developed in the western United States where it is generally accepted and still used. As such, issues of water quality, such as temperature, were assumed not to be limiting. Like many other methods, this technique assumes that hydraulic habitat is a surrogate for addressing the biology of the system; however it provides only one recommendation and, therefore, should be restricted to prescribing flows during the low flow season only. It does not provide for the necessary regime of flows that are critical to riverine ecology, but may be a component of a flow regime that includes recommendations for other ecosystem purposes derived from other models. The method should not be used to prescribe a year-round base flow unless other models that address other ecosystem components support that level of flow.

TENNANT METHOD

Summary: The Tennant method is based on percentages of average annual flow (QAA) derived from estimated or recorded hydrologic records, limited field measurements, and photographs taken at multiple discharges. This method is also referred to as the Montana method.

Objective: The purpose of the method is to get seasonally adjusted instream flow recommendations that have some hydrological relevance for maintaining natural habitat, geomorphological, and recreational attributes of streams and rivers with minimal to moderate effort.

Type of Technique: Standard setting

Description: Streamflow records are used to calculate QAA. Various percentages of the QAA are calculated and applied to two 6-month periods (October-March and April-September) to obtain instream flow regimens. Field data and photographs can be used to help verify recommendations or develop site-specific percentages/time periods. Habitat quality for each regimen is listed below. Percents are based on QAA.

Narrative Description of Flow[a]	April to September	October to March
Flushing or maximum flow	200% from 48 to 72 hours	
Optimum range of flow	60-100%	60-100%
Outstanding habitat	60%	40%
Excellent habitat	50%	30%
Good habitat	40%	20%
Fair or degrading habitat	30%	10%
Poor or minimum habitat[b]	10%	10%
Severe degradation	<10%	<10%

[a] For fish, wildlife, recreation, and related environmental resources.
[b] This is only for short-term survival in most cases.

Tessmann (1980) and others (Estes 1984, 1998) adapted Tennant's seasonal flow recommendations to calibrate the percentages of QAA to local hydrologic and biologic conditions including monthly variability. Under Tessmann's changes:

Situation	Minimum Monthly Flow
MMF[a] < 40% MAF[b]	MMF
MMF > 40% MAF and, 40% MMF < 40% MAF	40% MAF
40% MMF > 40% MAF	40% MMF

[a] MMF = mean monthly flow
[b] MAF = mean annual flow

Scale: River segment

Riverine Component(s) Addressed: Natural hydrologic variability is used as a surrogate for biological, habitat, and use parameters that Tennant referenced to develop the method. Those parameters included depth, width, velocity, substrate, side channels, bars and islands, cover, migration, temperature, invertebrates, fishing and floating, and aesthetics.

Assumptions: The basic assumptions of the method are that the various percentages of QAA are appropriate for maintaining habitat quality, that the time periods for providing different levels of flow are appropriate and that if calibrated to the local hydrologic and biologic conditions, the method is transferable from the streams Tennant used to develop the method to those under current study.

Level of Effort: Low. This is often referred to as an office technique; however, field effort is required if the practitioner seeks to calibrate or adjust the method on a site-specific or regional basis (Estes and Orsborn 1986; Estes 1998). Once adequate streamflow records are obtained, QAA can be calculated easily. The QAA annual flow is one of the few hydrologic statistics that can be estimated with little or no hydrologic data; however, its precision and accuracy will be improved with use of long-term hydrologic mean daily flow records (Estes and Orsborn 1986).

Historical Development: The Tennant method was developed based on extensive field observations of 12 habitat and use parameters and measurements of hydraulic conditions at numerous locations across the United States. Data were collected from eastern, western, and midwestern streams. Although often regarded as a method suitable only for the western United States, the method was developed using data from a much wider geographic area and range of stream types in the United States. The method was first applied in the 1950s in the Ohio and Delaware River basins. Reiser et al. (1989) cited it as the second most commonly used method in the United States. Other practitioners have subsequently modified the method (Bayha 1978; Tessman 1980; Estes 1984; Estes and Orsborn 1986; Estes 1998) to address specific considerations (e.g., Tessman's modification has been used throughout the northern great plains and Canadian prairie provinces where it better reflects the flashy nature of prairie streams.) The Tennant method has been thoroughly discussed in reviews of instream flow methodologies (e.g., Wesche and Rechard 1980; Estes 1984; Estes and Orsborn 1986; Morhardt 1986; Stalnaker et al. 1995).

Application: This is a standard-setting method. It assumes a relation to biology that should be validated in the region where it is being applied. The method can be acceptable for use in systems where there is little or no hydrologic and biologic data, and little or no competition for water. It is a tool for planning and reconnaissance level flow determination. When complex flow trade-offs are required, more detailed, site-specific studies using other methods should be conducted to analyze habitat trade-offs with different flows. Research by Estes (1984) and Reiser et al. (1988) suggested that supplemental analyses are required to modify or substitute for Tennant method flushing flow calculations.

Data needs include hydrologic records of sufficient duration (Estes 1998). Records that are not based on natural flow conditions will compromise calculation of QAA and subsequent recommendations. Naturalized flow records would be a preferred alternative for channels that have not been altered.

Strengths: This method is inexpensive, quick, and easy. It does not necessarily require field measurements; however, the optional field efforts to calibrate the model to local situations are not overly burdensome and can add validity to recommendations. Results are relatively consistent from stream to stream and region to region.

Limitations and Constraints: The QAA annual flow is derived from hydrologic data; thus, prescriptions are only as good as the hydrologic records on which they are based. The quality of biologic data, such as fish life phase periodicity, will affect the precision and accuracy of this method. Where hydrologic records are simulated from other drainages, confidence intervals associated with those estimates can be large. Hydrologic data that are substantially altered from historic flow levels will influence the calculation and may not support fishery management objectives. Average annual flow does not often reflect seasonal patterns in hydrology. The 10% of QAA level should never be used as a basis for setting conditions when not a natural flow level. This flow level was intended to indicate short-term survival only and should not be used as an instream flow recommendation unless it represents local existing hydrologic conditions that biological studies indicate will sustain healthy fish populations.

Calibration and Validation: Tennant designed this method to afford its users considerable flexibility in applying it. Regimens (seasons when flow recommendations apply) identified by Tennant may need to be adjusted to fit different geographic regions, hydrologic cycles, or seasonal biologic needs (e.g., to meet the needs of fall spawning fish versus spring spawning fish). The percentages identified by Tennant that describe various levels of flow suitability were derived from data collected at a wide range of streams and river types and sizes across the United States and do not usually require adjustment. They may, however be adjusted or calibrated if local hydrologic and biologic conditions warrant. Field data (i.e., depth, velocity and width along transects, habitat use by aquatic organisms, and human uses of the river) would need to be collected to determine appropriate percentages.

Critical Opinion: The method should be associated with analyses of biological habitat needs at various times of year to be most useful in a specific region. Use of this method should be preceded by hydrologic analysis, such as with indicators of hydraulic alteration (IHA), so the degree of hydrologic alteration that has occurred can be considered along with an understanding of channel morphology and sediment yield. Recommendations should always relate to naturalized hydrographs; otherwise, recommendations will relate to depleted stream conditions and result in less than intended flow protection. Tennant never intended users to select one flow from his table (e.g., 30% QAA) to be used as the only flow needed. If this method is used, it can and should be used to recommend different flows at different times of year to follow the natural hydrograph to the extent allowed by the method. The method does not provide quantitative information about biological or geomorphologic processes. Where that level of information is needed, other methods should be used. Because of its robustness, this method is a reasonable starting point for quantifying instream flow needs to which refinements can be made if needed. It is not acceptable to use this method, or models like it, to evaluate the adequacy of recommendations derived from other methods that use site-specific data because the Tennant method contains less detailed information.

WASHINGTON TOE-OF-BANK WIDTH METHOD (TOE-WIDTH METHOD)

Summary: The Washington Toe-of-Bank Width method (Toe-Width method) is a standard-setting model used primarily in western Washington on alluvial channel streams to determine flows that maximize preferred depths and velocities over suitable spawning gravel. The method employs several equations with channel cross-section parameters for different species and life stages.

Objective: The purpose of the method is to determine flows that provide adequate spawning and rearing habitat for anadromous salmonids.

Type of Technique: Standard setting

Description: The Toe-Width method employs several regression equations with channel cross-section parameters for spawning and rearing of different species of salmon and steelhead. Rearing equations are based on a wetted perimeter approach. This is a standard-setting method used primarily in western Washington on alluvial channel streams to determine flows that maximize preferred depths and velocities over suitable spawning gravel.

Appropriate Scale: Either segment or reach

Riverine Component(s) Addressed: Biology

Assumptions: This method assumes that spawning and rearing habitat are limiting factors for production of anadromous salmonids in Washington, and flows that maximize these habitats can be predicted using regression models. Like many other methods, this one assumes that biological characteristics are represented by hydrology and hydraulic characteristics and that the established relation between toe-width and maximum spawning over gravel bars is valid. The regression equations developed from 18 streams (3 sites each) are assumed to be applicable to any small- to-medium-sized stream in western Washington.

Level of Effort: This method requires a minimum level of fieldwork. The basic method requires only a few minutes to measure channel widths, average them, and enter the average into the appropriate equations.

Historical Development: The model was developed by predecessors of the Washington Department of Fish and Wildlife, in conjunction with the U.S. Geological Survey, for small to medium-sized alluvial streams supporting salmon and steelhead. Depth, velocity, and substrate suitabilities were determined for spawning for five species of salmon and for steelhead. At three study reaches in each of 18 streams, depth and velocity distributions in relation to the distribution of suitable spawning gravel at a number of different flows were evaluated. For each site, the relation between flow and spawning habitat was determined. The relation between flow, which maximized spawning

habitat and a number of watershed and channel variables, was assessed using regression. The best fit was obtained using toe-of-bank width. The equation differs by species. An additional equation was developed for rearing species. The rearing equations relate wetted perimeter at riffles to flow on the assumption that wetted perimeter at riffles reflects the habitat needed for the production of benthic macroinvertebrates, which are necessary to feed fish. This method has been evaluated by Collings et al. (1972), Collings (1974), and Swift (1976).

Application: To apply this method the practitioner must:

1) Locate toes of bank on each side of channel based on change of slope, change of substrate particle size, change in vegetation at five or more riffle (alluvial) transects.
2) Measure width between toes of bank.
3) Average toe-of-bank widths.
4) Use average toe-of-bank width as variable in species and life-stage specific equations for different Pacific salmon and steelhead to calculate recommended instream flows for specific seasons and species.

Strengths: The main value of this method is that the only data requirement is average toe-of-bank width. The method requires minimal effort and provides significant protection against additional allocation in small to medium-sized order streams in western Washington. Results of application of the rearing flow equations of the method have been consistent with regression analysis showing that production of stream rearing anadromous salmonids in western Washington is limited by low summer flows.

Limitations and Constraints: Recommendations resulting from application of the method are within the order of magnitude of naturally occurring flows for the activity (spawning or rearing) in most streams of the size for which the method was developed. In smaller streams, the model generates flow recommendations that exceed typical flows, and in larger streams (>5,000 cfs mean annual flow) the method generates recommendations that are much lower that the lowest flows on record.

Calibration and Validation: Calibration to other species and regions would require determination of preferred ranges of depths and velocities. Those depths and velocities would then need to be applied in a process similar to that used in Washington. Practitioners would then need to compare recommendations to the flow that maximizes spawning weighted usable area for salmon (or other) species of interest.

Critical Opinion: Use of Toe-Width method is limited to small- to mid-sized alluvial streams in Washington State, primarily on the western side of the Cascade Mountains. The method should not be used in other regions; however, the basic approach could be used to develop similar equations for other systems. It has a high error associated with the regression, even on the streams where it is appropriate. It is viewed in Washington as a reconnaissance level method, but not the preferred method when flow recommendations will be controversial. This method is designed for spawning salmon and steelhead (*anadromous salmonids*) and employs several regression equations with channel cross-section parameters for spawning and rearing of different species of salmon and steelhead. Rearing equations are correlated to the breakpoint of wetted perimeter. Other methods must be used in conjunction with this method to address other ecosystem components.

WETTED PERIMETER

Summary: The Wetted Perimeter method uses a graphical representation of the wetted perimeter versus discharge as a surrogate for physical habitat. It selects the breakpoint on this graph as the prescribed instream flow.

Objective: The purpose of the method is to provide an objective means of determining a minimum instream flow prescription for the low flow period.

Type of Technique: Standard setting

Description: A graphical plot of the wetted perimeter versus discharge on which a visual breakpoint (often referred to as the inflection) is selected as the instream flow recommendation. Wetted perimeter is that distance along the stream bottom from the wetted edge on one side to the wetted edge on the other side measured at a given discharge. Discharge is measured following standard practices. Multiple measurements of the ground profile are taken across the channel from bankfull on one side to bankfull on the opposite.

The most common application places a single transect across the stream where the channel is rectangular in shape (usually at the high point of a riffle). For ungaged streams, multiple discharge measurements must be made to develop a stage-discharge relation. More recent practice is to use computer programs based on Manning's equation to compute the stage-discharge relation for a cross section.

Appropriate Scale: River reach. Should only be applied to riffle mesohabitat types.

Riverine Component(s) Addressed: Biology is addressed through consideration of hydraulic habitat.

Assumptions: The method application assumes that the flow represented by the breakpoint will protect the food producing riffle habitats at a level sufficient to maintain the existing fish population at some acceptable level of sustained production. The method further assumes that the stream channel is stable and unchanging over time.

Level of Effort: Several visits to the site at numerous discharges (10 or more) are necessary if empirical relations are to be used. With hydraulic models that simulate stage-discharge relations, less than one day at the site is needed. However, as with all simulation models, two or more additional site visits at different discharges are needed to compare empirical observations with model output.

Historical Development: Initially the model was based on multiple measurements to develop empirical relations. It is now common to use computer programs to analyze cross sections and develop stage-discharge relations and wetted perimeter plots (Grant et al. 1992). Gippel and Stewardson (1996) critically evaluated the "inflection point" and noted that the determination of the breakpoint is highly error prone. They also presented a technique for mathematically defining the point of maximum curvature. Annear and Conder (1983) likewise found considerable variation in using inflection points for determining instream flow levels when compared to other methods. Early reports (Collings 1974) estimated that the discharge represented by the breakpoint protected 50-80% of the maximum available wetted perimeter. The Oregon Department of Fish and Wildlife recommended that at least 50% of available wetted perimeter be maintained (Ken Thompson, personal communication; Stalnaker and Arnette 1976). Tennant (1976b) found that discharges covering 50% of the wetted perimeter in Montana streams represented approximately 10% of the mean annual flow. Nelson (1980) attempted to demonstrate healthy standing crops of trout in Montana streams subject to low flows defined by the wetted perimeter. Gippel and Stewardson (1996) found that the discharge represented by the wetted perimeter breakpoint in two high mountain streams in Australia was similar to the 95% exceedence flow. Dunbar et al. (1998) concluded that the discharge determined by the breakpoint still significantly reduced invertebrate production.

Application: Wetted Perimeter may be used to establish a low flow standard. However, it should be used in conjunction with evaluations of the other ecosystem components so that it only establishes the low flow season recommendation.

Strengths: Easily measured on site for ungaged streams. Useful only if instream flow prescriptions are for the low flow season (such as constraining permits for water withdrawal during summer and fall only) and flow is known to be nearly natural (not effected by water withdrawals) for the other seasons.

Limitations and Constraints: This method addresses only low flows (usually summer/fall) and does not address intra- or interannual variability. The method also does not address channel geomorphology, water quality, or connectivity and should be restricted to streams with well-defined riffle and pool sequences. For channels with cross-sectional shapes that are parabolic or V-shaped, the wetted perimeter versus discharge relation continually rises and does not show a well-defined break point. For braided channels, multiple break points may be observed. The determination of inflection or break points for all habitat types can be somewhat subjective to identify precisely. The method should not be applied to pool cross sections or to alluvial streams that are usually low gradient, meandering, and have pool-crossing bar features.

Calibration and Validation: When based on multiple empirical measurements, no calibration is necessary. On the other hand, when using computer programs that are based on Water Surface Profile (WSP) programs based on Manning's equation to calculate stage-discharge relations, some site measurements are needed to validate by comparing predicted versus observed wetted perimeter for at least three widely spaced discharges.

Critical Opinion: The Wetted Perimeter method uses measurements of hydraulic habitat to derive recommendations and assumes a relation between habitat and biology. Use of this method should be restricted to streams or stream segments where the stage at the chosen transect area is flow-sensitive and represents the geomorphic structure and shape of the river channel throughout the targeted river segment. Such areas are often, though not always, associated with bedrock-controlled high gradient streams with well-defined, rectangular-shaped riffles and no significant floodplains. If used in other streams, it should be considered as only one component of a recommendation that uses additional analyses. In selecting a low flow season discharge with this method, it is recommended that the flow prescribed be that discharge that covers at least 50% of the wetted perimeter in streams that are less than 50 feet wide and between 60 and 70% in larger streams (Nehring 1979) or the breakpoint on the wetted perimeter discharge relation, whichever is higher. The method typically does not provide the necessary regime of flows that are critical to riverine ecology, but it may be a component.

GEOMORPHOLOGY

CHANNEL MAINTENANCE FLOWS IN GRAVEL-BED STREAMS

Summary: This is a bedload-based method for quantification of channel maintenance (CM) flows adapted for use with a wide variety of alluvial streams. The U.S. Forest Service (USFS) has developed this approach to make federal reserved water rights claims designed "to secure favorable conditions of water flows" for which the national forests were originally created.

Objective: To secure favorable conditions of streamflow, the USFS—based on its legislated mandates—sought to identify and reserve certain flow levels in streams on national forest lands. These flows, known as channel maintenance instream flows, are intended to maintain the physical characteristics of the stream channel. Desired channel maintenance occurs when the flow regime can transport the quantity and sizes of sediment imposed on the channel without aggrading or degrading the channel.

Type of Technique: Standard setting

Description: This method is for application in alluvial streams. Some flows are needed in all channels to maintain their natural form and function, but adverse effects are more likely to occur in low gradient alluvial channels than steep nonadjustable channels. Alluvial streams can be subdivided into gravel-bed and sand-bed streams. The approach described here is intended for gravel-bed streams and rivers. Significant bedload transport in gravel-bed rivers begins to take place at moderate discharges approaching bankfull flow. In contrast, sand-bed channels transport sand-sized sediment and adjust their form and resistance constantly through a large range of flows.

Appropriate Scale: River reach (approximately 20 times bankfull channel width).

Riverine Component(s) Addressed: Geomorphology component is addressed using hydrologic information and sediment transport data.

Assumptions: This method is based on the following fundamental premises:

1)   A stream channel adjusts its width and depth in response to changes in flow and sediment.
2)   The sequences of flows that form channels vary in timing and quantity over the long term resulting in a quasi-consistency of channel features that repeat themselves given similar conditions.
3)   The water confined in channels periodically moves the sediments that form the bed and bank of channels.
4)   A certain quantity of water is necessary to transport the bed material and erosion products entering the channel network and thereby maintain channel form.
5)   The amount of water needed to maintain the channel depends on the amount and sizes of sediment entering the channel in the long run.

Measured ratings of bedload discharge as functions of water discharge, by sediment size, are adequate to determine the discharge required to initiate transport of sediment that is not supply limited. All natural streamflows larger than this discharge are required for channel maintenance. This initiation discharge is normally achieved at bankfull (Emmett 1999).

Level of Effort: This is an incremental method requiring a relatively high level of effort and empirical data.

Historical Development: The geomorphic literature has generally established that the discharge at bankfull stage and the flow that moves the greatest amount of sediment over time (effective discharge) have approximately similar values. The scientific basis for the sediment transport part of a channel maintenance flow regime is well summarized in Carling (1995) and the USFS (1997) as follows:

1)   Sediment movement must occur for the channel to change its shape.
2)   For the channel to maintain its capacity over the long term, the inflow of sediment must equal the outflow of sediment (the stream is in dynamic equilibrium).
3)   Sediment transport important for channel maintenance begins at the flow level where bedload sediment begins to move a significant portion of the gravel-size material.
4)   The relation between water and sediment is generally concave upward; higher flows

are the most efficient at moving sediment.

5) For the channel to move the most sediment with the least water, a range of flows is needed to maintain the channel.

Application: Application of this method requires streamflow data (historical daily mean discharge and duration); sediment data (suspended sediment, bedload particle size distribution); and channel geometry data (site map, photographs, cross sections) at the quantification site to compute cumulative sediment transport (bedload transport rating curve). The Helley-Smith bedload sampler (Helley and Smith 1971; Emmett 1980) is commonly used for bedload measurements. The recommended procedure is to conduct two traverses of the stream sampling at least 20 equally spaced cross-channel locations on each traverse with a sampling duration of 30 or 60 seconds at each vertical (Emmett 1981). Normally, cross sections are located in straight reaches between meanders in sufficient number to characterize the variability of the study reach. Wolman pebble counts (Wolman 1954) are useful to characterize the surface particle size distributions of the bed-material making up the study stream. The survey needs to include a longitudinal profile of a stream that establishes the elevation of the existing water surface, channel bottom, and the floodplain (bankfull stage). Normally, longitudinal profiles extend a length of approximately 20 times bankfull channel width along the channel. Details of field techniques for bedload and suspended sediment transport measurements can be found in USFS (1988) and Bunte and Abt (2001).

Strengths: The method is based on strong empirical evidence from gravel-bed alluvial streams. With adequate data collected on site, quantitative flow regimes for maintaining channel form may be established.

Limitations and Constraints: The following situations fall outside the scope of this method:
1) Determining releases below dams.
2) Restoring previous channel capacity or condition. The consequences of returning natural flow regimes to channels with historically reduced capacity require site-specific study and careful evaluation.
3) Determining flow needs in steep or bedrock controlled channels.
4) Determining flow needs in braided channels.

5) Evaluating the consequences of chronically low flow increases.

Calibration and Validation: Where empirical data on flow or sediment cannot be obtained in a reasonable time, models or other extrapolation techniques may be used to develop preliminary or interim flow recommendations. These models and other techniques need to have some field-measured data or hydrologic characteristics to calibrate them to the specific site. Field calibration of bedload sampler may be necessary.

Critical Opinion: This is a science-based method that can be used in gravel-bed alluvial streams and rivers when maintaining the existing channel is the goal. However, the practitioner must first establish the status of sediment transport equilibrium and document that maintaining the existing channel form or restoring the existing channel form to a more natural condition is an appropriate, achievable goal. Channel maintenance flows recognize the primary influence of high flows, sediment transport, and large woody debris on channel morphology (see attributes 8 and 9, in Trush et al. 2000). The method addresses the relation between high flows and sediment. Entrainment, transport, and deposition of large woody debris may be included. Assessment of the current role of large woody debris in channel morphology needs to consider past snagging and wood removal practices, isolation of floodplains by levees and bypass channels, and logging of riparian forests. The cost of collecting data and conducting necessary analyses can be significant. Whereas this method reasonably addresses instream flows for maintaining important geomorphologic characteristics and processes, it does not address the hydrologic, biologic/habitat, water quality, or connectivity riverine components. The model should be used in combination with other methods to develop year-round instream flow needs to maintain all ecosystem functions.

FLUSHING FLOW: EMPIRICAL, SEDIMENT TRANSPORT MODELING, AND OFFICE BASED HYDROLOGIC METHODS

Summary: Each of the three flushing flow approaches is used to determine flows necessary for sediment transport.

Objective: Flushing flow is used to remove accumulated sediments from riverine habitats.

Flushing flows are a management tool that is commonly used for improving spawning gravel quality and fish reproductive success, increasing food production, maintaining pool depth and diversity, and preserving channel complexity by preventing channel encroachment, keeping secondary channels functioning, and preventing embeddedness.

Type of Technique: Standard setting

Descriptions: Reiser et al. (1988) reviewed 15 methods of flushing flow recommendations. We have separated those methods into three groups (1) empirical, (2) sediment transport modeling, and (3) office based hydrologic methods. Flushing flows are achieved when flows are sufficiently high to result in streambed mobilization. When streams have regulated flows, two factors can occur: upstream sources of streambed gravels may be lost to deposition in the impoundment and/or high flows may be eliminated that would normally result in streambed mobilization. When the major sediment sources to a river system are above impoundments and the project area, flow releases may be substantially sediment free and the absence of sediment may create problems. In that case, recommendations for flushing flows may not be appropriate since excessive sediment is not normally a problem. High flows may still be necessary to prevent encroachment of vegetation into the stream channel. However, if major sediment sources are below the project and flows are regulated, the sediment input will likely exceed the sediment transport rate and deposition will occur. When this occurs, recommendations for flushing flows are appropriate.

Empirical Methods

In general, empirical field methods are based upon test flow releases during which changes in bedload transport, suspended load transport, bed composition, and cross-sectional profile are evaluated. Transport samples are collected during the test flow release, movement of painted gravel is evaluated, changes in key bed characteristics—such as percent fines and d50 (i.e., the median size of pebbles larger than 10 mm)—are monitored by core samples and/or pebble counts, and cross-sectional profiles are measured before and after to assess channel widening, deepening, and changes in depth and velocity variability. As tracers are monitored during flow events, determinations are made for minimum flows that result in movement

and maximum flows that do not cause movement. Where the values converge is labeled the threshold discharge. A large number of samples may be required to determine convergence of the two values. O' Brien's (1984) study on the Yampa River described the Effective Discharge Methods. Suspended sediment, bedload, and physical and hydraulic parameters data were collected at 21 channel cross sections. Results were used to develop a theoretical hydrograph necessary for channel maintenance. In this incised stream, the bankfull discharge was a 20-year event whereas the effective discharge was a 1.5 to 2-year event. This technique requires individuals who have sufficient expertise, time, and funding, but results are very thorough and defensible.

Sediment Transport Modeling Methods

Many models exist, but the two most commonly used are modifications of the Meyer-Peter Mueller formula (1948) and the Einstein method (Einstein 1950). The Meyer-Peter Mueller formula has been used in gravel-bed streams whereas the Einstein method is most applicable in sand-bed streams. Neither model addresses the timing and duration of needed flows.

The Incipient Motion Methodology is typically used to predict the incipient motion of particular size sediment. The methodology is based on the Meyer-Peter Mueller formula, which was used in Wyoming studies (Water and Environment Consultants 1980). Field data collected included bed material composition, streambed and water surface slopes, water velocities, and watershed and river characteristics. Flushing flow was defined as the discharge that started a certain sized particle in motion (shear stress). Such a computation can result in removing surficial fines but does not necessarily involve bedload movement. Desired flows were those that occurred at the slowest velocity at the cross sections was equal to the desired shear stress value. A 72-hour duration was recommended but no reference is made for seasonal timing.

Incipient motion is based on Shields entrainment function (Shields 1936; Reiser et al. 1988) and uses sediment grain size and channel slope to recommend flushing flows. Variation of the Shields function from the recommended 0.03 value can result in significant changes in the recommended flows. Subsequent studies have modified the original diagrams, since the original work involved uniform particle size in a flume (Reiser et al. 1988). Streambeds are comprised of mixed particle sizes and to account for nonuniform material, various authors have recommended use of particle diameter at differing percentiles (10, 30 and 50). Reiser et al. (1988) reviewed two studies that concluded a Shields parameter of 0.03 is correct for mobilization of gravel-bed streams. The required discharge as cfs/ft can be predicted from the median grain size and channel bed slope.

Office Based Hydrology Modeling

Several methods are based on channel characteristics such as percentage of bankfull or other flow statistics such as exceedence or variations of average annual flow (QAA). Gage data are needed or must be synthesized for proper use of these methods. Tennant (1975) recommended two times QAA from 48 to 72 hours. Estes and Orsborn (1986) noted that Tennant's recommendation for flushing flows should be calibrated to local hydrologic patterns, which in their studies in Alaska could be in the range of 400-800% of QAA to achieve bankfull discharge. Estes and Osborne (1986) also recommended 60-75% of 2-year instantaneous peak flow for a 3-7-day period. The Hoppe method uses the 17th percentile flow, and Beschta and Jackson (1979) recommended 5% exceedence. These various studies illustrate how the local hydrology and channel geomorphology affect the determination of flushing flows.

The Tennant method is a standard-setting tool for recommending instream flows for resource protection. One component is a recommendation for establishing flushing flows. Mean annual flow (MAF) fills about 33% of the stream channel in many streams. Three hundred percent MAF will fill the channel to the floodplain whereas 200%, Tennant (1975) concluded, will produce sufficient depths and velocities to move silt and bedload materials. Tennant developed his procedures from 20 years of observations on a wide range of eastern, western, and central U.S. streams and U.S. Geological Survey data.

The Hoppe method (Hoppe, unpublished paper; Wesche and Rechard 1980) indicated that suitable flushing flows occur at the 17th percentile of the flow duration curve in the Fryingpan River, Colorado. T The sentence highlighted he duration of 48 hours was sufficient to remove the target level of fine sediments in that system.

Beschta and Jackson (1979) concluded that flushing of fines occurs when the channel bed is disrupted and bedload transport occurs. Their field measurements in Oregon Coast Range streams documented that sand size particles moved on high flows that occurred about 20 days a year. This is the flow that is equaled or exceeded about 5% of the time.

Scale: Reach

Riverine Component(s) Addressed: Geomorphology

Assumptions: The effective discharge, sometimes referred to as the dominant discharge, will remove fines from cobble bars, replenish sand on beach and bar areas, and prevent vegetation encroachment within the channel. Bankfull discharges are necessary to rework and maintain cobble bars, maintain channel morphology, and stimulate riparian vegetation development.

Level of effort: The effort for field-based methods can range from moderate to very high depending on the method. Office-based recommendations will require relatively low effort.

Historical Development: Sediment transport models have been developed since the 1950s. Several refinements have been made since then, but they are essentially unchanged. All involve equations that an engineer appreciates and biologists dread. They are generally based on the shear factor for varying sized bed material. The Meyer-Peter Mueller formula was based on flume studies using mixed and uniform sand to large gravel particles. The same parameters that govern incipient motion also control the sediment transport process (e.g., energy gradient, hydraulic radius, particle size, manning's n value). The Einstein method hypothesized that bedload transport is related to turbulent flow fluctuations rather than the average stresses on a sediment particle. This method estimates transport rate of discreet size fractions that compose the bed material. Changes in bed composition can then be predicted. A bed material transport method was described in Reiser et al. (1988). Leopold (1994) described a similar study to monitor bedload movement.

Incipient motion using the Meyer-Peter Mueller formula involved only a specific size particle. In the study, the particle size was 2-3 mm. As structured, the flows would not result in bedload movement--a condition necessary for channel maintenance. If the particle size chosen was large enough to result in bedload movement, the method would be very useful in establishing flushing flows. Several assumptions were made in this application, which would need to be evaluated in other studies.

Application: All the techniques can be used for standard setting of flows. Incipient motion models can be used for incremental recommendations. Sediment modeling and office-based hydrology methods are most appropriate for standard setting especially in the planning stage. Additional verification would be needed prior to any final recommendation.

Strengths: All of the techniques can be used to generate a flow necessary for planning purposes. Studies would be needed to finalize operating rules. The sediment transport models have been widely used and are accepted in the scientific community.

Limitations and Constraints: The bed material transport methodology requires observation of marked tracers and, therefore, clear visibility systems. Use is limited to gravel-bed streams. Tracers must be fitted carefully into the substrate to replicate an undisturbed streambed. Failure to recover tracers will increase the sample size needed and indicate the extent to which materials are moving. Effective discharge constraints are primarily time and money. Determination of sediment loadings is a time-consuming and costly process.

Despite widespread uses of these models, results will vary significantly. Richardson et al. (1975) reported a 100-fold difference between the predicted sediment discharges from two models. No universally applicable transport model exists. Therefore, verification is necessary because the choice of the transport model used will give significantly different results, even in the same stream.

Sediment transport models can produce highly variable results among the different models that have been applied. This demonstrates the models' sensitivity, complexity, and uncertainly of the many variables. This group of models in combination with office-based hydrology models is best used for preliminary planning purposes. Site-specific validation is needed before flow determinations and recommendations are adopted on a permanent basis.

Calibration and Verification: Verification of sediment modeling and office-based recommendations is a glaring weak point. Evaluation of recommendations is minimal (Reiser et al. 1988). Reiser et al. (1988) recommended several techniques to evaluate sediment changes as a result of flow recommendations and provided descriptions of methods that can be used to assess the effectiveness of flushing flow recommendations. For the sediment transport model, Reiser et al. (1988) reviewed two studies that reported poor correlation between predicted and observed transport rates when channel slopes were above .001. No studies have been conducted to compare the effectiveness of differing methods.

Critical Opinion: Results can be quite variable depending on the method chosen. The effective discharge method is particularly useful for initiating streambed movement and flushing fine bed materials. A primary consideration before recommending flushing flows is to first document the need for the flow, including an analysis of the availability of sediment to transport and the stability of the riparian area. Flushing flows can be detrimental to existing ecosystem function when the riparian area is unstable or the system is sediment-starved. In addition to the magnitude, applications should specify the timing and duration of the recommended flow and make provisions for evaluating or monitoring the results (long-term). Only a few methods recommend duration or ramping rate. Recommendations should be to provide flushing flows during the time of natural high flows because most native species have evolved around the normal annual hydrograph.

Field-based empirical methods can be accurate and highly predictive if they are properly calibrated. Sediment modeling and office approaches can generate relatively wide discrepancies in recommendations (Reiser et al. 1988). These latter kinds of methods can provide reasonable reconnaissance level estimates of flushing flow needs if practitioners document their logic well and retain the ability to refine the flow recommendation prior to implementation. If sediment modeling or office approaches are used for project planning, it is best to ensure that results generate a conservatively high estimate of flow need to ensure that adequate water will be available to maintain ecosystem function if and when field-based studies document a different need.

GEOMORPHIC STREAM CLASSIFICATION SYSTEM

Summary: The Rosgen geomorphic stream classification system (Rosgen 1985, 1994, 1996) involves four levels of hierarchy for river inventory and assessment.

Objective: The method describes and groups similar streams based on their morphology.

Type of Technique: Monitoring/Diagnostic

Description: Level I is a geomorphic characterization process that uses channel slope, shape, and pattern that results in nine stream types (A through G including subtypes). Level II is a morphological description incorporating channel entrenchment, dimension, pattern, profile, and substrate. From this analysis, the quantified reach is assigned a single letter/number classification title (i.e., A2, C1) and stability can be evaluated. A critical component of this analysis involves identification of bankfull stage. Level III is a stream state or condition analysis. It is very data intensive and incorporates factors that influence the current state (riparian vegetation and bank erosion, sediment supply and deposition patterns, and flow regime). Level IV is the validation level and is the result of analysis of sediment condition, streamflow, and stability measurements.

Arend (1999) described two additional classification techniques also based on channel geomorphology: the technique of Galay et al. (1973) and the bed form technique (Montgomery and Buffington 1983; Bisson and Montgomery 1996).

Appropriate Scale: Reach

Riverine Component(s) Addressed: Geomorphology

Assumptions: The method assumes that the classification scheme is valid and useful and that additional classes are not necessary. It assumes that stream behavior can be predicted from its appearance and that bankfull flow is an important, key parameter, which is common to all stream types.

Level of Effort: The method requires intensive effort that increases as the level of analysis increases. Effort can be low at level I, and increase substantially at level IV.

Historical Development: The stream classifica-tion system was first proposed in 1985. It was revised in 1994 and finalized in 1996.

Application: This method is applicable for establishing baseline status and for monitoring changes in stream channel as a result of streamflow changes.

Strengths: This is a widely publicized hierarchical classification system that is generally accepted. Level I analysis examines a limited number of variables and results in a basic stream type designation. This information can be useful for prioritizing which streams to select for instream flow studies and other types of habitat-related work. Subsequent levels require more empirical data and provide more information. This system best serves as a framework for understanding the interrelated geomorphic processes that shape channels.

Limitations and Constraints: Determination of bankfull elevation is one of the most critical steps and can be the most common error in field observation. Improper identification of bankfull stage can influence classification and may be difficult, if not impossible, in streams rapidly adjusting to hydrological and geomorphologic changes or subject to extreme flow fluctuations (e.g., below hydropeaking dams). Levels need to be calibrated to determine if flows approximate the 1.1- to 2.3-year recurrence interval. If not, the process used to identify the bankfull condition needs to be further refined. Proper training and rigorous attention to the procedures and data needs are critical to successful application of this technique. The assumption that bankfull flow is an important, key parameter, common to all stream types, has been questioned as to its applicability on all streams (Miller and Ritter 1996; Goodwin 1999). Streams of the same stream type may have been formed by different processes or may be evolving into different conditions.

Calibration and Validation: Verification is possible by comparing field measurements for bankfull maximum depth, width, and cross-sectional area to regional curves as documented in Rosgen (1996). Regional curves should be developed in a practitioners region to verify and validate information obtained in field investigations.

Critical Opinion: This is a well-regarded empirical system useful for determining current stream channel condition. It cannot be used to recommend instream flows for any time of year. By analyzing stream channel stability, the manager may be able to assess the impacts of environmental changes on the stability of the system with changes in geomorphic factors. The user must still account for timing, duration, frequency, and magnitude, particularly if trying to relate higher flows to biological processes. The method can also be useful in monitoring changes in flow patterns on channel form, function, and stability.

HYDRAULIC ENGINEERING CENTER-6 MODEL (HEC-6)

Summary: The Hydraulic Engineering Center-6 model (HEC-6) was developed by the U.S. Army Corps of Engineers (USACE) to simulate the capability of the stream to transport sediment based on sediment loads and stream discharge. Information and documentation on calibration and validation is available from the USACE website: www.wrc-hec.usace.army.mil.

Objective: The HEC-6 model is a one-dimensional flow and sediment model designed to simulate changes in river profiles due to scour and deposition over long time periods (USACE 2000a). The model has the ability to evaluate a network of streams, channel dredging, levee and encroachment options, and several methods of computing sediment transport rates. When properly calibrated, it can predict channel response to changes in sediment and flow.

Type of Technique: Incremental

Description: Flow records are partitioned into a series of steady flows of varying discharge and duration. Water surface profiles are computed for each flow. For each cross section, the energy slope, velocity, and depth are calculated. Potential sediment transport rates are computed for each section and flow. The amount of scour and deposition are computed based on the flow duration and the channel cross-sectional shape readjusted accordingly. Based on the altered geometry, the next flow cycle is analyzed for changes in bed geometry. The cycle is continued for the duration of records. Sediment calculations are performed by grain size fraction, thus allowing simulation of hydraulic sorting and armoring.

Appropriate Scale: Reach

Riverine Component(s) Addressed: Geomorphology

Assumptions: The HEC-6 model is sensitive to certain data inputs and the selection of the sediment transport function. Extensive experience is needed with these parameters to produce results that will correctly predict channel geometry and sediment transport capabilities.

Level of Effort: The level of effort is high and the amount of data collected is large, which requires efficient data storage methods. Four categories of data are used as input: reach geometry, sediment, hydrology, and special commands. Geometric data includes cross sections, delineation of movable bed areas (deposition and scour), reach lengths, and Manning's n values. Sediment data include inflowing sediment load sorted by size class for a range of flows, streambed material gradation, and selection of sediment transport function. Hydrologic data include discharge, temperatures, downstream water surface elevation, and flow duration. Water and sediment discharges must be defined at the upstream boundary and each local inflow point. Stage must be prescribed at the downstream boundary of the primary stream segment, but can be prescribed at hydraulic control points. Twelve sediment transport functions are available as options and can yield different answers. Reviews are available that rate the sediment transport functions for accuracy (USACE 2000b).

Historical Development: The Hydraulic Engineering Center-6 model was developed by the USACE, runs on the DOS platform, and is probably the best known and most highly used model of its kind in the country (USACE 1991).

Application: The HEC-6 model can be used as an incremental method for establishing flows necessary to establish a state of channel equilibrium.

Strengths: The model has been widely applied and used. Documentation is very thorough for data collection and model calibration and validation. Many variables can be altered to calibrate and validate the model.

Limitations and Constraints: The model does not handle rapidly varying flow but requires a steady state of flow. The model is extremely complex, as would be expected for such a dynamic, multi-variable system. Data needs are extensive and variables complex. The model is very sensitive to certain input parameters. But some of these parameters—such as bed material gradation, inflowing sediment loads, and moveable bed limit--have low or moderate reliability in terms of field collection results. However, these same factors are highly sensitive in terms of output results. Moreover, the user may select from among twelve different sediment transport functions, the choice of which can produce widely varying results in sediment transport rates and channel geometry.

Calibration and Validation: Data sets are needed for calibration and validation. Extensive documentation is available on the USACE web site (see above) regarding model calibration and validation.

Critical Opinion: The HEC-6 model should be used only when accompanied by proper calibration and validation; otherwise predictions may be invalid. To use the model properly, a high level of training and experience is required. Most biologists do not have this level of expertise and should work with a competent sediment specialist or hydraulic engineer. The model, when properly calibrated and validated, can be extremely beneficial in developing flows to handle the sediment transport requirements of the stream and can address the geomorphology ecosystem component of instream flow needs. It should be combined with models that address other riverine components to provide an instream flow regime that addresses all of the needs of a stream.

HYDRAULIC ENGINEERING CENTER-RIVER ANALYSIS SYSTEM (HEC-RAS)

Summary: The Hydraulic Engineering Center-River Analysis System (HEC-RAS) is a model created by the U.S. Army Corps of Engineers (USACE) to develop a water surface profile model.

Objective: The model's purpose is to provide information on river stages over a range of flows, particularly for floods. The IFC encourages its use in recommending flows necessary for channel and floodplain maintenance.

Type of Technique: Incremental

Description: The HEC-RAS model is a water surface profile model for river simulation of steady,

one-dimensional, gradually varied flow in either natural or man-made channels. The basic computational procedure is based on the solution of the one-dimensional energy equation. Energy losses are evaluated by friction (Manning's equation and contraction/expansion (coefficient multiplied by the change in velocity head). The momentum equation is used in situations where the water surface profile is rapidly varied. These situations include mixed flow regime calculations (i.e., hydraulic jumps), bridge hydraulics, and evaluation profiles at river confluences. Data input is performed through interactive graphics and dialog boxes. The HEC-RAS model is capable of modeling subcritical, supercritical, and mixed regime water surface profiles. It has culvert and bridge routines. The program can model a single river reach, a dendritic system, or a full network (looped systems). Version 2.2 has the ability to model floating ice as well as dynamic ice jams. Users can simulate channel modifications to evaluate changes in water surface elevations.

Appropriate Scale: Reach

Riverine Component(s) Addressed: Geomorphology

Assumptions: For this tool to be useful, links will have to be established between the desired ecosystem benefits and the required physical process that produces the benefits.

Level of Effort: Effort can range from moderate to high depending on the detail needed. Surveyed elevations are required for valley cross sections for the reach or segment in question. Longitudinal valley surveys are required when linking multiple sites.

Historical Development: The model was derived from HEC-2 (ASACE 1962). The HEC-2 model was first released in 1968 followed by a PC version in 1984. The next generation was initiated in 1990; the latest version, 4.6.2, was released in 1991; and HEC-RAS was released in August 1995 (version 2.2 plus patch). The HEC-2 model is DOS based and the enhanced HEC-RAS is Windows based. For more information about HEC-RAS, see Dodson and Associates (2000) at www.dodson-hydro.com.

Application: The HEC-RAS model is useful for standard setting when floodplain inundation is critical for physical and biological processes. Segment and reach is the appropriate scale.

Strengths: The model is widely used. Extensive training and documentation is available.

Limitation and Constraints: This model requires a trained hydrologist or hydraulic engineer in most cases. Cross-sectional information will be needed. Important physical/biological processes need to be identified as well as the flows necessary to maintain that component. The model can be used to develop the flow volume necessary for flood-plain inundation. The model cannot be used in high gradient streams and rivers. Timing and duration of flood flows will also need to be addressed by the study.

Calibration and Validation: Comparison to the stage-discharge relation observed in the system is recommended for calibration and validation.

Critical Opinion: This is not an instream flow method; it allows practitioners to establish a stage-discharge relation in unsteady flow situations and provides information that may be useful to establish out-of-bank flows for riparian or floodplain maintenance. Such recommendations can only be made after thorough examination of the existing hydrology, as with IHA, and analysis of the biological requirements. This is a widely used model by the USACE and many private firms. Results are well accepted. The model will provide the flows necessary to achieve certain water elevations. The timing, magnitude, duration, and frequency of floods must be known for the negotiator to develop recommendations necessary to support requested discharges.

WATER QUALITY

ENHANCED STREAM WATER QUALITY MODEL (QUAL2E)

Summary: The Enhanced Stream Water Quality model (QUAL2E) is a one-dimensional water quality model that assumes steady-state flow but allows simulation of diel variations in temperature or algal photosynthesis and respiration.

Objective: The model simulates water quality (i.e., temperature, dissolved oxygen (DO), nitrogen (N), phosphorus (P), chlorophyll a, biochemical oxygen demand (BOD), coliform bacteria, and up to three conservative minerals) as a function of discharge in stream channels.

Type of Technique: Monitoring/Diagnostic

Description: The QUAL2E model was originally developed in the early 1970s. It represents the stream as a system of reaches of variable length, each subdivided into computational elements of the same length in all reaches. It also simulates up to 15 water quality constituents, including temperature, DO, N (organic, ammonia, nitrite, nitrate), P (organic and dissolved), algae as Chlorophyll a, BOD (ultimate or 5 day), coliform bacteria, and up to three conservative minerals.

Some general characteristics of a water quality sampling network include (1) the upstream or headwater of each stream segment to be modeled, (2) mouths of all significant tributaries (<5-10% of flow or mass loadings) not otherwise included explicitly in the model, (3) effluent samples for all point sources before they enter the stream, (4) upstream and downstream ends of segments affected by nonpoint sources, and (5) the downstream end of the study area.

Upstream extremities are needed to define boundary conditions of flows and background concentrations. The tributary and effluent data are needed to define the loading rates. Data are needed at the downstream end for calibration and validation. Additional stations may be established in biologically sensitive areas, locations where known or suspected water quality violations may be occurring, and areas where stream geometry changes are likely to cause kinetic changes. All intermediate locations add additional discriminative power and help to ensure correct results. Sampling frequency

173

for water temperature is commonly done hourly because digital recorders have become very cost effective. Measurements should be taken for other meteorological and flow conditions to improve the accuracy of the model and to improve the statistical power of validation tests. For protocols for sampling and analyzing water quality constituents, refer to the American Public Health Association (APHA)(1995), which covers the sampling, treatment, and analysis of the full range of water quality variables. The protocols specified by the APHA are standard for water quality analysis, and stakeholders will expect these methods to be followed.

Typically, the instream flow practitioner is concerned with organic decomposition and the dissolved oxygen cycle. The important constituents to measure for an oxygen-balance study include (1) dissolved oxygen concentration; (2) temperature; (3) biochemical oxygen demand; (4) discharge (river and point sources); (5) ammonia, nitrite, and nitrate concentration; (6) sediment oxygen demand; (7) chlorophyll a; (8) phosphate concentrations; and (9) light.

Appropriate Scale: The appropriate use for this model is at the reach, segment, or watershed level.

Ecosystem Component(s) Addressed: Water Quality

Assumptions:
1) Major transport mechanisms, advection and dispersion, are significant only along the main direction of flow (the longitudinal axis of the stream or canal). Water in the system is instantaneously and thoroughly mixed at all times. Thus, there is no lateral temperature distribution across the stream channel, nor is there any vertical gradient in pools.
2) Many parameters dealing with water quality kinetics (e.g., BOD rates) are difficult and expensive to measure. Thus, most applications make use of parameter values measured in other research studies, not site-specific measurements.
3) Distribution of lateral inflow between points of known flow is uniformly apportioned throughout the segment length.
4) Chlorophyll a is used as the indicator of planktonic algae biomass. This may or may not be true, and may vary through time.

5) Hydraulically, QUAL2E is limited to the simulation of time periods during which both the streamflow in river basins and input waste loads are essentially constant. The effects of dynamic forcing functions, such as headwater flows or point loads, cannot be modeled in QUAL2E.
6) Limits:
   a) Reaches—a maximum of 50
   b) Computational elements—no more than 20 per reach or a total of 500
   c) Headwater elements—a maximum of 10
   d) Junction elements—a maximum of 9
   e) Point source and withdrawal elements—a maximum of 50

Level of Effort: This model requires intensive fieldwork.

Historical Development: The National Council for Air and Stream Improvement, the Department of Civil Engineering at Tufts University, and the U.S. Environmental Protection Agency (USEPA) developed the model. The EPA's Office of Science and Technology developed a Microsoft Windows-based interface for QUAL2E that facilitates data input and output evaluation. The QUAL2E model is one of the models included in the EPA's Better Assessment Science Integrating Point and Nonpoint Sources (BASINS; 2001) www.epa.gov/ost/basins

Application: The model may be limited to ice-free conditions. If reservoir operations are an issue, other models such as the EPA's Water Quality Simulation Program (WASP) or HEC-5Q should be used. The oxygen-balance model requires a lengthy list of reaction coefficients for which values must be provided in preparation for calibration. Most of these coefficients are provided as a range of values, which means they can be legitimately adjusted upward or downward during the calibration process. Values for many of these coefficients can be obtained from the published literature.

The Enhanced Stream Water Quality model has been applied where attached algae need to be simulated by applying a benthic sink rather than a source of ammonia nitrogen (Paschal and Mueller 1991). One of the most important things to look for is whether the nonconservative constituents behave according to first-order reactions. One quick way to address this issue is to find out if the stream has an appreciable amount of algae. If so, there is a strong probability that there will be second-order kinetics that cause extreme diurnal or seasonal deviations from the mean. Also, the calibration data should be looked at to see if sampling was conducted around the clock. The fluctuation of dissolved oxygen, in particular, can provide an immediate idea about the severity of oxygen depletion due to respiration and may give clues about other potential problems, such as ammonia build-up due to algal decay.

Strengths: The QUAL2E model is extremely well documented and is thoroughly recognized as the standard by academic and industry professionals through repeated applications. The model has been polished to be user-friendly in terms of input and output options and does not take a tremendous amount of computer literacy to use. The program is in the public domain and is supported by a federal agency that provides training and technical assistance. Computer resources to use the model are reasonable. The model has been used widely for stream waste load allocations and discharge permit determinations in the United States and other countries. An advantage of QUAL2E is that it includes components that allow quick implementation of uncertainty analysis using sensitivity analysis, first-order error analysis, or Monte Carlo simulation (Bovee et al. 1998). The QUAL-2E is considered to be the standard water quality model for small streams and medium-sized rivers (Brown and Barnwell 1987).

Limitations and Constraints: The model works best for streams, rather than reservoirs or stratified lakes. It only handles steady flows and is one-dimensional. Special cases of water quality modeling, however, may require more sophisticated approaches than QUAL2E can handle. If ice conditions (sheet or frazil) are involved, this model will not work.

Calibration and Validation: Calibration and validation are typically conducted by splitting the empirical data set. The first half is used to calibrate the model and the second half is subsequently used to validate the model results. Field sampling locations must be established for use as calibration or verification nodes for the model.

Critical Opinion: The QUAL2E model is the model of choice for application in streams and rivers where water quality has been identified as a concern. It has been widely used for stream waste

load allocations and discharge permit determinations. The QUAL2E model only addresses the water quality component of a river ecosystem. Additional analyses, separate from this, must be conducted to adequately address the hydrologic variability (inter- and intraannual), geomorphology, biology, and connectivity.

STREAM NETWORK TEMPERATURE MODEL (SNTEMP) AND STREAM SEGMENT TEMPERATURE MODEL (SSTEMP)

Summary: The SNTEMP/SSTEMP models are mechanistic one-dimensional heat transport models that use a dynamic temperature-study flow equation.

Objective: The purpose of these models is to predict the daily mean and maximum water temperature as a function of discharge, stream distance, and environmental heat flux.

Type of Technique: Monitoring/Diagnostic, Incremental

Description: The SNTEMP/SSTEMP models include (1) a solar model to predict the solar radiation penetrating the water as a function of latitude and time of year; (2) a shade model that quantifies riparian and topographic shading; (3) algorithms that correct air temperature, relative humidity, and atmospheric pressure for changes in elevation within the watershed; and (4) regression algorithms that smooth and/or fill missing observed water temperature measurements.

The SNTEMP model requires that the spatial layout of the hydrologic network be divided into segments. In addition to having homogeneous streamflow characteristics, segments for SNTEMP are defined according to width, slope, roughness (Manning's n) or travel time, and shading characteristics. The meteorological influences are air temperature, relative humidity, wind speed, percent of possible sun (inverse of cloud cover) and ground-level solar radiation. Other required inputs include water flow into the segment and groundwater accretions along the segment, along with their temperatures. The SNTEMP model:

1) Applies to a stream network of any size or order.

2) Predicts the solar radiation penetrating unshaded water as a function of latitude and time of year.

3) Predicts the riparian and topographic shading of that radiation.

4) Corrects air temperature, relative humidity, and atmospheric pressure as functions of elevations within the watershed.

5) Fills and optionally smoothes missing observed water temperature measurements.

6) Provides statistical goodness-of-fit tables to help judge the model's power of estimation.

7) Uses time steps ranging from one month to one day.

8) Uses readily available data.

Because SNTEMP is relatively complex, the basic processes have been abstracted into a simplified version, the Stream Segment Temperature model, or SSTEMP. This model provides a friendlier way to learn about temperature modeling compared to SNTEMP. Data input parameters may range from "back of the envelope" calculations to detailed micro-meteorological field measurements with corresponding degrees of reliability.

Appropriate Scale: The appropriate scale for these models is a stream network of any size or order. The SSTEMP model is useful for handling one to a few stream reaches for a limited number of time periods; SNTEMP is useful when there are five or more stream segments coupled with 30 or more time periods or scenarios.

Riverine Component(s) Addressed: The models address the water temperature aspects of Water Quality.

Assumptions:
1) Water in the SNTEMP system is instantaneously and thoroughly mixed at all times. Thus, there is no lateral temperature distribution across the stream channel, or is there any vertical gradient in pools.

2) All input data (e.g., stream geometry, meteorology, hydrology) are characterized by 24-hour and longitudinal mean conditions. This implies that the output best characterizes mean daily water temperatures. Maximum daily water temperatures are estimated from the means.

3) Distribution of lateral inflow between points of known flow is uniformly apportioned throughout the segment length.

4) The model assumes that maximum temperatures may be derived from heating a parcel of water from solar noon to sunset. Depending on the travel time, that parcel may have originated above the segment being modeled, and therefore may have traveled through radically different conditions. This problem is minimized when segments are long (generally greater than 10 km) so that the downstream segment conditions dominate all heat flux.

5) The SNTEMP model assumes a strictly dendritic system with no branching in the downstream direction, with the exception of transport tunnels or canals with no effective heat flux.

6) Applications should be limited to ice-free conditions (>4 C) in the northern hemisphere.

7) Limits:
   a) Time - 366 increments
   b) Space - effectively none

Level of Effort: The SNTEMP model is a diagnostic tool that can be used as an incremental method in some situations but requires intensive field effort. For the most part, SNTEMP incorporates published meteorological and physical data and, therefore, requires minimal field effort.

Historical Development: The models were developed by the Biological Resources Division of the U.S. Geological Survey (USGS), Mid-continent Ecological Science Center, Fort Collins, Colorado (formerly the U.S. Fish and Wildlife Service, National Ecology Research Center), as one of the tools comprising the macrohabitat component of the Instream Flow Incremental Methodology (IFIM)(Theurer et al. 1984; Bartholow 1989). Software and training registration information is available from the USGS website: www.mesc.usgs.gov/pubs/online/temp-ss.html.

The SNTEMP/SSTEMP models were developed to help aquatic biologists and engineers predict the consequences of stream manipulation on water temperatures. The models are capable of generating temperature data either in the form of a time-step average or as a minimum value. Max/min temperature can be used in situations where it is essential to know if temperature criteria for the species of interest are being exceeded. Time-averaged temperature model output can be used in situations where an understanding of directive, control or growth related factors is required.

Application: The SNTEMP/SSTEMP models are used primarily for simulating temperature characteristics in steady-state conditions and use an empirical approach to predict maximum daily temperatures. Turbulence is assumed to thoroughly mix the stream vertically and transversely (i.e., no microthermal distributions).

Strengths: The SSTEMP model is very easy to use for first-order sensitivity analysis. Although very data intensive, it provides an ability to look at an entire stream network and is particularly applicable to regulated systems. It generally requires little or no calibration for mean daily temperatures, can deal with equilibrium releases, and is well documented and supported.

Limitations and Constraints: The SSTEMP model becomes tedious and error-prone as the number of stream segments or time periods increases. Neither SSTEMP nor SNTEMP predict maximum temperatures very well without calibration. For stream segments below reservoirs, the user must have water temperature outputs from the reservoir. This requires temperature output for season, flow, reservoir stage, and withdrawal depth. For older reservoirs where temperature is monitored at a gaging station downstream, the task is easy. If such data are not available, temperature data for reservoir outflows must be provided through the use of other models.

One of the most serious problems with meteorological data for water temperature modeling is that long-term weather records may not be very representative of the conditions at the study area. For example, weather station data are often collected at airports, an unlikely place to conduct an instream flow study. Similar considerations are proximity to oceans or other large bodies of water, topographic characteristics, and thermal inversions. In particular, two of the most influential meteorological variables used in the temperature model—air temperature and relative humidity—can be very different on-site compared to a weather station that is relatively far away. At a minimum, some on-site data should be collected. A particular problem is estimating nighttime cloud cover. These data are likely to either be missing or incorrect. Because percent possible sun is used in the model as a surrogate for cloud cover, measurements that are recorded may not be good estimates for nighttime conditions, especially in areas with marked diurnal weather patterns.

Calibration and Validation: Calibration is defined as a measure of the "goodness-of-fit" between the model's output and the observed system. Calibration of the SNTEMP model involves the process of determining the "proper" values for the model's rate parameters. Calibration involves the adjustment to these parameters until the predicted water temperature agrees with the measured temperature within a set of specified standards. The process is repeated for many time-steps and locations until a mix of parameter values is found that gives the best overall agreement between measured and predicted temperatures. A rule-of-thumb is to not change input data that are accurately measured. Parameters that cannot be measured accurately, or may not be very transferable, are the ones that are usually changed in the calibration step to achieve a fit between modeled and measured temperatures. A relatively complete validation study of the model with a comprehensive set of published data was conducted on the Upper Colorado River basin and the Trinity River (U.S. Fish and Wildlife Service and Hoopa Valley Tribe 1999).

Critical Opinion: The model only addresses water temperature, which is one aspect of water quality. Additional tool analysis is necessary to recommend flows for other riverine components. The SSTEMP model is useful as a reconnaissance model to identify potential water temperature issues. It is so easy to use that it should be used routinely to check recommended flow regimes for unanticipated water temperature problems. When water temperature issues are evident, SNTEMP or other water temperature models are appropriate for temperature-based flow prescriptions. These models do not provide instream flow recommendations by themselves and must be used in combination with other instream flow methods, such as Physical Habitat Simulation in the IFIM, to simulate the total usable habitat available in time and space throughout a network of stream segments.

SEVEN-DAY, TEN-YEAR LOW FLOW ($7Q_{10}$)

Summary: The $7Q_{10}$ is not an instream flow method. It is a flow statistic used for identifying the volume of water needed to meet point discharge water quality thresholds. The hydrologic statistic has often been misused as a minimum flow for keeping fish alive.

Objective: This drought flow statistic is used by sanitary engineers to set standards for dilution of wastewater. It can be used as a check for low flow prescriptions derived from other methods to ensure that water quality standards are not violated.

Type of Technique: Monitoring/Diagnostic

Description: The $7Q_{10}$ refers to the lowest average streamflow expected to occur for seven consecutive days with an average frequency of once in ten years. It can also be expressed as a drought flow equal to the lowest mean flow for seven consecutive days, adjusted to nullify any effects of artificial flow regulation, that has a 10% chance of occurring in any given year. The $7Q_{10}$ is a flow statistic used to simulate drought conditions in water quality modeling to evaluate waste load allocation.

Appropriate Scale: Stream reach

Riverine Component(s) Addressed: Water quality

Assumptions: A sewage treatment can be designed to discharge during low flow conditions such that the integrity of the receiving water body is protected. Because natural streamflow almost always exceeds the $7Q_{10}$ flow, a wastewater treatment facility designed to meet water quality standards at $7Q_{10}$ would meet them under almost all naturally occurring conditions.

Level of Effort: Low

Historical Development: The origin of the $7Q_{10}$ is not certain. At about the time the Clean Water Act was enacted, the U.S. Environmental Protection Agency (USEPA) was directed by Congress to establish water quality criteria for a very large number of chemicals. In response to this directive, sanitary engineers selected the $7Q_{10}$ as a design flow for determining waste load allocations.

Application: This method should only be used to determine wastewater discharge criteria. It has been used in some states as an instream flow standard to protect aquatic life (Reiser et al. 1989). The only data requirement is sufficient gaging records

for low flow periods to allow the statistic to be estimated.

Strengths: This method is expedient as a design standard for wastewater discharges.

Limitations and Constraints: This method does not protect aquatic life (Camp, Dresser and McKee 1986) and its use as a standard to do so is inappropriate. The $7Q_{10}$ for some streams is zero; hopefully all investigators will agree that aquatic life needs a bit more water.

Calibration and Validation: There is no direct relation between $7Q_{10}$ and aquatic life protection (Camp, Dresser and McKee 1986).

Critical Opinion: The $7Q_{10}$ should never be used to make instream flow prescriptions for riverine stewardship. Its use is appropriate only as a water quality standard and, thus, it has utility as a check against low flow recommendations from other methods to ensure that water quality standards are not violated. The $7Q_{10}$ drought flow is inadequate to conserve aquatic life or ecological integrity. For most streams, this flow is less than 10% of the average annual flow and can be expected to result in severe degradation of aquatic communities if it becomes established as the only flow protected in a stream (Tennant 1976a, 1976b). Tennant further described the conditions that are typically associated with such a low flow:

1) Short-term survival of most aquatic life.
2) Fifty percent or more of the stream bottom is likely to be dewatered.
3) Side channels (important for early life stages of many fish species) are likely to be severely or totally dewatered.
4) Riparian vegetation may suffer.
5) Stream bank cover will be severely diminished.
6) Fish will have difficulty migrating upstream over and through riffle areas.
7) Fish are crowded into pools and vulnerable to over-harvest.
8) Water temperature may become too high for some fish species.

Fish communities can generally withstand near-drought conditions that occur infrequently and for short periods. However, setting such a flow as a long-term condition will not sustain them. The influence of flow on aquatic organisms includes more than just magnitude and frequency; duration and season are also important. Making such a low flow the norm is like recommending the sickest day of your life as a satisfactory level for future well-being.

Use of the $7Q_{10}$ persists because it favors off-stream water uses. However, it does so by sacrificing the fish and wildlife resources that belong to the public and over which government has a stewardship responsibility.

CONNECTIVITY

FLOODPLAIN INUNDATION METHOD

Summary: The Floodplain Inundation method represents a conceptual overbank flow using channel and hydraulic variables in floodplain reaches of rivers.

Objective: The method is used to determine flows to protect aquatic, riparian, wetland, and floodplain resources or compare alternative flow regimes.

Type of Technique: Incremental

Description: This model consists of the following sequential steps:

1) Determine representative floodplain cross-sectional elevations through (a) the Federal Emergency Management Agency (FEMA) and/or the U.S. Army Corps of Engineers (USACOE) flood risk maps; (b) topographic maps; (c) on-site surveys, including aerial photogrammetric techniques.

2) Determine cross-section/stage-discharge relation by (a) measuring and surveying, (b) gage calibration rating table, or (c) gage records.

3) Determine wetted perimeter versus discharge relation and inflection points for floodplain cross section.

4) Tabulate phenology and inundation needs for floodplain and riparian vegetation and timing of floodplain-dependent life stages of fishes and other floodplain-dependent fauna.

5) Determine historical, unmodified hydrological timing, and magnitude of high flows.

6) Evaluate surface connectivity between main channel and off-channel habitats such as oxbow lakes through review of information obtained in steps 1 and 2, above.

7) Evaluate timing and duration needed to address biological needs tabulated in step 4 and historical hydrology, step 5.

8) Develop flow recommendation or compare alternatives based on review of information, steps 5-7.

Appropriate Scale: River reaches and segments

Riverine Component(s) Addressed: Lateral connectivity is addressed with this method.

Assumptions: Floodplain inundation hydrology is a major control of floodplain biota, and examination of the natural hydrologic record will provide the necessary information to sustain the biological processes on the floodplain.

Level of Effort: Low to high. The method requires topography, hydrology, stage-discharge relation, and knowledge of the flood-dependent biota and their inundation needs. In a poorly- known area, effort might be high if stage-discharge relation and surveying had to be done by the person applying the method. Benke et al. (2000) used aerial photography to map inundation at different flows; this reduces time but at high hourly cost.

Historical Development: This method was first published in 2000 (Benke et al. 2000).

Application: This method is suitable in floodplain stream reaches if used in conjunction with other methods to address other seasons and riverine components. If used in regulated streams, the practitioner must reestablish the natural hydrology before applying the method. Experimental tests of the method have been applied to the Ogeechee River, Georgia (Benke et al. 2000).

Strengths: This method fills a critical gap for analyzing floodplain-rivers, particularly in the southeastern United States. Sommer et al. (2001) reported on the contribution of floodplain to chinook salmon (Oncorhynchus tshawytscha) production in the Sacramento Basin and Muth et al. (2000) described the importance of overbank flows for endangered Colorado River fishes; thus, the method also has promise in regions outside the southeastern United States. It links lateral connectivity and biology.

Limitations and Constraints: Understanding of life histories and inundation needs is limited to descriptive information in most cases. This method does not address suitable flows during the remainder of the year when the floodplain is not inundated.

Calibration and Validation: See steps 1-3 above for calibration. The method has not been validated to determine whether its application achieves the stated objective of protecting instream and riparian resources. Validation will involve applying the method to many sites with known floodplain inundation and different degrees of hydrologic alteration and then comparing the biological responses (e.g., tree or vegetation growth, fish production, wildlife abundance) across different levels of alteration.

Critical Opinion: This method is an incremental method that has considerable promise for organizing a diverse array of information, but the subjective element remains large. This method should be used in conjunction with detailed hydrological methods, such as Indications of Hydrologic Alteration. The two-dimensional hydraulic models hold promise for simulation of inundation-discharge relation and should be considered for use in conjunction with this method. Other methods will also be needed to address seasons when floodplain inundation is not applicable.

MIGRATION CUE METHOD

Summary: The Migration Cue method identifies a 20% flow increment in a regulated stream as the flow needed to stimulate salmon and steelhead migration in the absence of a natural freshet (Dr. Brian Winter, personal communication, National Marine Fisheries Service, Seattle).

Objective: The method is used to determine minimum pulse flows providing migration stimulus for anadromous salmonids in regulated streams.

Type of Technique: Standard setting

Description: This method was developed to simulate a freshet in a regulated stream. It is a minimum prescription to get salmonids to move upstream for spawning or to stimulate downstream smolt migrations.

Appropriate Scale: Segment, reach

Riverine Component(s) Addressed: Biology, connectivity

Assumptions: If natural freshet has not occurred, an increase of at least 20% in the flow is expected to stimulate migration. Salmonid migration is stimulated by such an increase in flow and fish can sense a 20% increase. Without this migration cue they suffer higher mortality and lower productivity.

Level of Effort: This is an office technique that requires very low effort. The basic method requires only that the flow occurring before migration be known and that it be multiplied by a factor of 1.2 to achieve the recommended flow.

Historical Development: Review of published literature and records of fish migration and flow.

Application: This method has very narrow application to regulated streams inhabited by migratory fish where flow can be artificially augmented if natural conditions combined with regulation have not provided freshets.

Strengths: The method is easy to apply.

Limitations and Constraints: This method does not consider flow-dependent migration barriers. It addresses only specific aspects of Connectivity and Biology/Habitat for anadromous fish. The recommended pulse of 20% is subjective. Methods are needed to address the full suite of ecosystem components.

Calibration and Validation: The method is a simple rule-of-thumb supported by a limited amount of smolt out-migration monitoring in the Yakima River, Washington. Application in other regions or for other species requires determination of migration cue threshold flows (if any), and comparison of temporal patterns of abundance of migrant fish and patterns of discharge.

Critical Opinion: The main value of this method is that the only datum it requires is the flow immediately prior to flow augmentation. Although the recommended pulse of 20% is subjective, this level of flow seems reasonable until other studies establish that a different level is appropriate. If this method is used—whether for salmonids or other fish species (e.g., lake sturgeon [*Acipenser fulvescens*], resident trout, and redhorse [*Moxostoma sp*])—validation of flow prescriptions for magnitude and duration needs to be conducted. The method is to be used only on regulated streams.

POWERS AND ORSBORN SALMON BARRIER METHOD

Summary: The Salmon Barrier method is a collection of engineering tools used to evaluate what is and what is not a barrier to salmon and steelhead passage. Because the method includes hydraulic evaluation of passage barriers at different flows, it can be considered an incremental method.

Objective: The purpose of the method is to determine if waterfalls or culverts are impassable at certain discharges or passable at any time.

Type of Technique: Incremental

Description: The method, which is used for waterfalls, chutes, and cascades involves:

1) Physical equations to determine height and horizontal distance that anadromous salmonids can jump.
2) A classification of barriers based on flow patterns, site geometry, bed slope, pool depth, elevation difference (a function of discharge), water velocity, slope length, and discharge.
3) Calculation of velocity at critical depth at different flows and fish sustained swimming speed.

This method includes application to culverts involving determination of the relation between discharge and velocity and relating velocity to fish swimming speed.

Appropriate Scale: Reach, mesohabitat, microhabitat

Riverine Component(s) Addressed: The method involves biological criteria for determining connectivity.

Assumptions: Fish leaping ability fits geometric equations, which can be related to hydraulic conditions.

Level of Effort: The method requires intensive effort to survey and determine hydraulic parameters.

Historical Development: As habitat degradation and exploitation of Pacific Northwest salmon have limited these fish relative to demand, fishery agencies have sought to increase natural production through expansion and rehabilitation of anadromous salmonid fish spawning and rearing habitat. See Powers and Orsborn (1985) and Furniss et al. (2000) for more information on this method.

Application: This method can be used as a baseline to determine upstream boundaries of anadromous salmonid use in any type of stream, one site (waterfall, cascade, chute, culvert) at a time, or to prescribe flows to enable passage around potential barriers. In addition, this method is used to design culverts to provide passage. Powers and Orsborn used this method in work throughout Washington State and adjacent regions. It might be feasible to put some of the equations into spreadsheets to facilitate calculations, but analysis and surveying are a major part of the effort required. Furniss et al. (2000) presented software (Fish Xing) that helps integrate the biology, hydrology, and hydraulic components of fish passage problems into a model that enables comparison of fish swimming capabilities to culvert hydraulics across a range of streamflow.

Strengths: The analysis provided is highly quantified—with clear engineering-based rationale and thoroughly researched biological input—and makes the method relatively easy to defend.

Limitations and Constraints: The method does not address any of the other riverine components or other aspects of Connectivity. Any passage flow determination must be matched to the season when it is needed. The method requires knowledge of swimming and leaping ability of all species of interest, but considerable data on salmonids are published in standard fisheries and engineering resources. If fish other than salmonids are of interest, new criteria would need to be developed and equations modified accordingly.

Calibration and Validation: Requires on-site measurement of slopes, heights, and some hydraulic data. Validation requires measurement and computations at known barriers and known partial barriers.

Critical Opinion: Instream flow biologists and engineers in the habitat program of the Washington Department of Fish and Wildlife use this method to evaluate passability of potential migration barriers for anadromous salmonids. It is not generally used to determine instream flow needs beyond those required for fish movement past a described barrier. It is adequate for the intended purpose of assessing passage if the barrier described is the primary constraint to movement or if all barriers to movement have been considered.

TIDAL DISTRIBUTARY/ ESTUARY METHOD

Summary: The Tidal Distributary/Estuary method is an incremental technique designed to provide flows to maintain low tide in-channel refugia and adequate salt marsh inundation at high tides.

Objective: The purpose of this technique is to determine flows that will maintain estuarine processes and resources.

Type of Technique: Incremental

Description: This method uses a regression model that correlates river and estuary stage as a function of tide and discharge to establish adequate habitat for maintaining estuarine fishes and salt marsh vegetative communities.

Appropriate Scale: Estuarine segment

Riverine Component(s) Addressed: Connectivity. Uses hydraulic habitat to address the Biology component.

Assumptions: The method assumes that the existing estuarine ecology is healthy and that maintaining current conditions will ensure its continued health. It also assumes that the existing frequency of over-marsh inundation to 1ft (0.3 m) deep provides a valuable function for estuarine fishes and should not be reduced significantly. Maintenance of the frequency of inundation is also needed to maintain salt marsh plant communities. Velocity is constantly changing as tide rises and ebbs; therefore, depth is the hydraulic parameter measured. The prescribed minimum channel depths during low tide provide adequate in-channel refugia for estuarine fishes.

Level of Effort: Very high. The method requires determining the relations among flow, tide, and stage throughout different estuarine zones based on vegetation and elevation and through the complete range of flows.

Historical Development: Developed by multiple parties based on review of literature and extensive monitoring experience by Skagit System Cooperative tribal biologists, together with evaluation of potential impacts of flow changes on estuarine fish habitat.

Application: The method is useful to identify combinations of flows and tides that achieve threshold levels of inundation of salt marsh and minimum levels of low tide refuge in tidal channels (Duke Engineering 1999). The procedure for applying this method involves the following steps:

1) Stratify the tidal influence zone of the river based on elevation and vegetation and to identify the upper limit of tidal influence. The next step is to locate the closest and most suitable continuously recording (preferably internet accessible) streamflow gage and tide gage.

2) Place sensitive continuous stage recorders (pressure transducers) at selected locations in each estuarine zone. Selected locations should include main river flow channels, secondary flow channels, and blind channels that drain the marsh. A transect across the channel and extending out into the estuary should be surveyed at each stage recorder location. For each stage recorder transect, determine at what part of the tide cycle the tide influences stage by matching stream gage recording with tide gage record and station stage recorder.

3) Determine flows that ensure low tide tidal channel refuge (at least 1 ft [0.3 m] deep) and combinations of flow and tide that just overtop tidal channel banks and that overtop them by at least 1 ft (0.3 m).

4) Determine the area inundated as a function of bank over-top stage.

5) Determine frequencies of different stages at different seasons and tides.

Strengths: The method uses the depth fluctuations imposed by a tidal cycle and river discharges to identify the degree to which instream flows maintain low tide refuge, high tide foraging area, and inundation of salt marsh vegetation.

Limitations and Constraints: This method requires real time or 15-minute stage measurements in the estuary for a series of stream discharges in reasonable proximity to the estuary as well as a number of pressure transducers and frequent (1 or 2 per week) downloading. The method does not address salinity, which is an important factor influenced by flow in estuaries. In larger or steeper estuaries, layering of fresh water on top of salt water may make this an acceptable shortcoming, but if the stream is small and/or the gradient is low, then salinity must be addressed. The model

requires extensive analysis and provides information, but no answers.

Calibration and Validation: See Description above for calibration. To validate this method, correlate daily growth and survival rates of selected estuarine fish with extent of marsh inundation or degree of low tide refuge. Monitor health and distribution of salt marsh vegetation community.

Critical Opinion: This empirical method requires voluminous amounts of input data and of itself only provides information on stage in the estuary. The 1-ft deep criterion is subjective, based on professional judgment, and needs to be validated regarding its relation to the resource it is intended to maintain. This method may be useful to identify river flows critical to maintain refugia in estuaries; however, more work needs to be done to associate overbank stage with area of marsh inundation and the effects of alteration. The method is reasonable overall and a useful tool until other studies provide a basis for modifying or replacing it.

SALINITY-BASED ESTUARY INFLOW METHODS AND APPROACHES

Summary: Salinity distribution (including variation over time) relative to depth and substrate is assumed to be a primary determinant of production and distribution of estuarine flora and fauna. Hydrodynamic circulation models of estuaries are used to determine how freshwater inflows affect spatial distribution of salinity, nutrients, sediment, and turbidity in different zones of the estuary. Zones differ in historic productivity of different biological resources. Flows that provide physical conditions characteristic of historic productivity at appropriate seasons are identified. An overlay of historic productivity in relation to historic flows has been used to describe some of the consequences associated with different flow regimes. Biological collections have been taken over a relatively limited range of environmental conditions and do not include extreme low flow conditions, especially those predicted for the future. Changes were documented during naturally occurring low flows. By consulting hydrologic records we could determine the frequency of an observed discharge. Although natural extremes occur, water management can avoid increasing the frequency or duration of extreme events.

Objective: The purpose of the method is to determine beneficial freshwater inflow needs to protect estuarine productivity and processes.

Type of Technique: Standard setting through incremental

Description: Three approaches have been developed to analyze instream flow needs of estuaries: statistical regression models (Martin 1987; Flannery et al. 2002), physical oceanographic models (Matsumoto et al. 1994; Powell et al. 2002) and optimization models to examine the relations between physical conditions and indicator species (Tung et al. 1990; Longely 1994; Lewis 1997; Adams et al. 2002; Doering et al. 2002; Kimmerer 2002). Specific two-dimensional (2-D) and three- dimensional (3-D) hydrodynamic models are referenced in the cited reports. Operational rules for limiting the reduction of inflow to estuaries were developed by Adams et al. (2002); Flannery et al. (2002); and Powell et al. (2002).

Appropriate Scale: Whole estuary (equates to watershed because inflow to an estuary results from the entire watershed).

Riverine Component(s) Addressed: Water quality (salinity, sediment, nutrients); biology (based on the relations between water quality and biology).

Assumptions: This method assumes that geomorphology is fixed, adequate historical data exist to develop numerical relations, indicator species are reasonably representative of the ecosystem, biology and hydrology processes are consistent (i.e., influence of events like hurricanes or sea level rise are assumed to be nonexistent), and the amount and timing of inflows to the estuary can be controlled.

Level of Effort: Hydrodynamic models require relatively extensive bathymetric measurements, followed by measurements of salinity and velocity and direction of current at multiple locations, under different combinations of inflow and tide. Combining the results of hydrodynamic models with locations of different biotic communities requires extensive sampling of those communities at all seasons using a variety of sampling methods. Biological sampling must span a range of environmental conditions. Interpolation is more reliable than extrapolation, and biological response to changes in many of these variables is nonlinear

with threshold effects. Sample size and distribution must be sufficient to have a reasonable chance of identifying thresholds.

Historical Development: In Texas, Lambert and Fruh (1978) developed a method to demonstrate how estuarine needs can be determined if ecological goals for an estuary are identified. Lewis (1997) and Livingston et al. (1997) described and cited long-term studies that led, in part, to sufficient understanding of estuarine processes in the Apalachicola River estuary to allow development of an approach to define inflow needs. Monitoring biological consequences of drought contributed to this understanding (Livingston et al. 1997, 2000). Similarly, Flannery et al. (2002) and Powell et al. (2002) relied on long-term estuarine studies in southwest Florida and Texas. Several of these researchers incorporated concepts developed by Richter et al. (1996, 1997).

Application: Bathymetry is available from navigational charts for most of the larger estuaries of commercial significance, but development of hydrodynamic models will require 3-D physical oceanographic models, combined with maps, using geographic information systems to describe the location of different biological resources. Flannery et al. (2002) and Mattson (2002) used inflections on response curves to determine shifts in salinity zones as an indicator of effect, whereas the Apalachicola group used mapped locations of salinity zones (Lewis 1997). Powell et al. (2002) developed a performance curve to relate productivity to inflow.

Strengths: Salinity is an index of a number of inflow-related features that drive estuarine production (e.g., nutrients, turbidity; see Mortazavi et al. 2000), and it is relatively easy to measure and model. It is directly controlled according to riverine inflow, tidal fluxes, and bathymetric features. At its simplest, Flannery et al. (2002) tried to simplify the method to specifying a percent of natural flow that is the upper limit for diversion (e.g., see Tennant method), but such a rule-of-thumb has not been confirmed. When it is, it will be more generally and rapidly applicable, but with all the caveats associated with rules-of-thumb.

Limitations and Constraints: Intensive long-term study seems to be a prerequisite for the most detailed version of this method, but Flannery et al. (2002) narrowed the study requirements. Gulf coast estuaries are vulnerable to periodic reshaping by hurricanes, which also introduce large quantities of freshwater that can reset many biological and physical processes (e.g., Livingston et al. 2000). If an estuary is reshaped (e.g., barrier islands breached), circulation will be modified—requiring new hydrodynamic modeling—and distribution of biological communities will be altered.

Calibration and Validation: Biological monitoring to relate inflows to productivity serves as the basis for calibrating most estuarine methods. As with any ecological relation, the ability to measure extremes in an independent variable contributes to understanding the effects of that variable (e.g., freshwater inflow) on dependent variables (e.g., salinity, primary productivity, secondary production, distribution of biological resources). In the case of freshwater inflows, as with other environmental variables, the extremes may drive the system. This fact is critical to gaining perspective on how to manage the resource. A large sample size covering the extremes of variables is necessary to account for influences of variables other than freshwater inflow, such as tide, wind, season, and temperature. An additional step to verify the recommended solution is to compare predicted circulation and salinity with naturally observed patterns of species abundance and distribution in the estuary.

Critical Opinion: This approach embraces a continuum of tactics from standard setting through incremental techniques. Estuaries are central to marine fisheries and thus have significant economic value. Therefore, public outlay for the extensive studies required for such methods may be supported. The approaches described by the various studies referenced above address the complex estuarine relations between biological communities and physical and chemical processes. Monitoring the effects of extreme events is key to identifying limiting flows.

MULTIPLE COMPONENTS
(but do not address all)

DEMONSTRATION FLOW ASSESSMENT (DFA) METHOD

Summary: The Demonstration Flow Assessment (DFA) method provides visual observation and assessment of flows.

Objective: The purpose of the method is to assess instream flow needs using professional judgment, with few or no measurements.

Type of Technique: Standard setting

Description: A team of "experts" views and evaluates a number of specific flows. A consensus rating is developed based on collaborative discussions. Beyond this general characterization, DFA methods may differ in several ways: (1) the interdisciplinary composition of the team, (2) the selection of study reaches, (3) the definition of the observation area, (4) the use of physical measurements to either inform the rating process or contribute numerically to the final rating, and (5) the type of rating system used. Rating systems can be simple, such as a numerical ranking scale from 1(poor) to 5 (excellent), or fairly complex. Demonstration flow assessments have been used alone or to confirm the results of other methods.

Appropriate Scale: Reach or segment

Riverine Component(s) Addressed: The DFA method often focuses on fish habitat but can also be planned to address hydrology, geomorphology, aesthetics, and recreation. The aspect addressed requires corresponding expertise of practitioners on the assessment team.

Assumptions: The DFA method assumes that flows can be assessed visually by a group of experts in a way that depicts reasonably objective and repeatable results.

Level of Effort: Low to moderate. Effort in the field is relatively high because a team must assess multiple flows. However, the amount of office time required is low.

Historical Development: Many different DFA variations have been developed to fit specific applications, and some methods have incorporated quantitative aspects and systematic procedures to make them more objective and scientifically rigorous. The Tennant method (Tennant 1976a) evolved from a series of visual observations.

Application: Demonstration Flow Assessments can take many different forms and address a variety of issues, including fish habitat, fishability, geomorphology, aesthetics, and recreation. A DFA can be used for any type of stream, although many such methods tend to result in a single flow standard.

Some DFAs mimic the Physical Habitat Simulation system and combine physical measurements with visual observation. For example, a Vermont study (New England Power 1994) established binary habitat suitability criteria for various target organisms to guide assessment. The habitat rating was determined as the percentage of the observation area meeting the criteria times the wetted width.

In South Africa, the Building Block Method (King and Tharme 1994) relies on habitat and channel flow needs to develop recommendations. Information about flow needs for channel maintenance can be obtained from painting rocks and observing their relocation following a flow event. The DFA has also been used to assess the aesthetic characteristics of various flows at waterfalls and dams (Central Vermont Public Service Corporation 2000).

Boating assessments range from descriptive to relatively quantitative (Corbett 1991; Merrill and O'Laughlin 1993; Whittaker et al. 1993). For example, qualified paddlers who paddle each flow and rate its suitability across several categories sometimes assess the suitability of various flows for whitewater boating.

Strengths: The DFA method is relatively inexpensive and easy to understand. It can be used where obtaining in-channel measurements is a safety concern, or where channel characteristics make flow measurements and modeling difficult. Few if any field measurements are required. An entire area of stream can be assessed as opposed to just a few transects. Collaborative work by the assessment team may build consensus. Direct communication amongst interdisciplinary experts can result in an integrated flow recommendation that addresses multiple components. The method can be used to provide a reality check on the results of other

methods (Halliwell, unpublished report). The method considers site-specific characteristics. It can be used for low priority waters, such as areas with low habitat value. High quality professional judgments can provide high quality results.

Limitations and Constraints: This method is useful for river recreation assessment and to assemble and mobilize experts to view flow levels in the field. It represents a good first step to examine the interrelations of all river components, especially connectivity, and determine next steps, including additional studies and study focus. By itself, this method typically does not address any of the temporal aspects of hydrology, especially interannual variability. Focus on recreational flows or aesthetic flows may result in prescriptions for summer, weekends, or "daylight" hours only and is ecologically unsound.

Because the method does not involve flow modeling, multiple flows must be observed. Strict attention must be given to selection of appropriate flow levels for observation, and emphasis should be placed on representing the entire range of flows for viewing. Fieldwork is time consuming and necessitates participation by a team of experts. The DFA method is more subjective than quantitative. It is often used as a minimum flow method resulting in a single flow, without maintaining hydrologic variability. Minimums derived by ten experts are not any better than a minimum recommendation from one person.

Calibration and Validation: The repeatability of the results (whether by the same team or a different one) has not been adequately tested. Swales and Harris (1995) compared DFAs with the results of two other instream flow methods. They concluded that the results provided "some validation" of their DFA method. They also compared the independent assessments of two different teams and found that the results were often quite different. Validation is likely to apply only to the specific variation of the DFA tested. A DFA of walleye spawning and incubation habitat in the Clyde River, Vermont, produced results that were consistent with the natural, seasonal hydrograph (Citizens Utilities Company 1993).

Critical Opinion: Demonstration Flow Assessment is a logical and appropriate tool to visually observe flow releases but does not suffice as the only flow assessment tool because the approach does not address all five riverine components. However, it can improve one's understanding of the river system and aid in the interpretation of quantitative flow study results. The real value of this technique is in getting experts together. It should be a mandatory step for any flow assessment. A flow recommendation cannot be made without actually seeing that flow in the stream. This method is very important for assessing connectivity. The team used to conduct the DFA should be composed of interdisciplinary experts representing all riverine components. Typically, this is not the case when recreation specialists dominate team membership.

Complex DFAs are time consuming and may require just as much effort as a parallel quantitative method. If a DFA assesses attributes that can be measured, it is preferable to conduct the measurements and use a quantitative method instead. If reliable measurements cannot be obtained, a properly constructed DFA may be appropriate for short bypass reaches. Although based on professional opinion, this method is subjective and its repeatability has not been adequately tested. Observers should have the proper expert qualifications. Field methods and observations should be well documented and include a photographic record.

INSTREAM FLOW INCREMENTAL METHODOLOGY (IFIM)

Summary: The Instream Flow Incremental Methodology (IFIM) is a modular decision support system for assessing potential flow management schemes. This method quantifies the relative amounts of total available habitat available throughout a network of stream segments for selected aquatic species under proposed alternative flow regimes. It was designed to prescribe instream flow regimes that result in no net loss of total habitat, or to develop mitigation plans to compensate for habitat potentially lost as a result of proposed flow management.

Objective: The IFIM is designed to assist natural resource and water management agencies in comparing the relative impacts of proposed instream flow management schemes with existing conditions (as determined from recent historical hydrology).

Type of Technique: Incremental

Description: The IFIM is composed of a library of linked analytical procedures that describe the spatial and temporal features of habitat resulting from a given river regulation alternative. The unique feature of the IFIM is the simultaneous analysis of habitat variability over time and space. This methodology is composed of a suite of computer models, manuals, and data collection procedures that address hydrology, biology, sediment transport, and water quality (see Stalnaker et al. 1995 and Bovee et al. 1998). Several studies have demonstrated the relation between usable habitat and fish populations (Orth and Maughan 1982; Nehring and Miller 1987; Bovee 1988; Jowett 1993; Nehring and Anderson 1993). Other authors questioned the utility of the method (Williams 1996; EPRI 2000) but, unfortunately, equated IFIM with PHABSIM.

Appropriate Scale: River segments, stream networks, and subbasins.

Riverine Component(s) Addressed: Hydrology, biology, water quality, and connectivity. Geomorphology is empirically measured.

Assumptions: The IFIM assumes that the pattern of high and low values of total usable habitat as simulated for reference hydrological time series are correlated with strong and weak year-classes (or standing crops) of fish in the stream segment(s) modeled. Total usable habitat is defined by hydraulic habitat for the species of interest and suitable water quality calculated over the hydrologic reference period (see habitat suitability discussion under Physical Habitat Simulation [PHABSIM] system). The IFIM assumes that preference and avoidance behavior(s) are adequately captured by the habitat suitability criteria used. Whenever one or more of the ecosystem components is not explicitly described or evaluated in some manner, the user further assumes that the ignored component is not constraining the aquatic organisms in the stream segments studied and will not become limiting under any of the alternative flow regimes studied. This is especially critical for alluvial streams when practitioners ignore the sediment transport capacity of the stream and, therefore, ignore the channel dynamics leading to invalid results with any change in the flow regime or sediment inputs.

Level of Effort: High. Intensive site-specific analyses are required.

Historical Development: The Ecological Services Division of the U.S. Fish and Wildlife Service (USFWS) was responsible for consulting under the Fish and Wildlife Coordination Act on federal projects and the Endangered Species Act, including the large water development projects constructed by the U.S. Bureau of Reclamation (USBOR) and U.S. Army Corps of Engineers (USACE) in the 1950s and 1960s. The dewatering and "minimum flow" releases (often only dam leakage) below many of these projects throughout the western United States prompted the USFWS to establish the Office of Biological Service in the early 1970s to make relevant science available to instream flow practitioners. One of the first actions of the Office of Biological Services was to organize an interdisciplinary program to develop a scientifically defensible means of assessing the instream flow impacts of water development projects. As a result, the Cooperative Instream Flow Service Group was established in 1976 in Fort Collins, Colorado. The group brought together scientists and professionals from the USFWS and experts on detail from the USBOR, the USACE, the U.S. Environmental Protection Agency, the Soil Conservation Service, the U.S. Geological Survey (USGS), and Bureau of Outdoor Recreation as well as professionals from the states of Idaho, Kentucky, Montana, and Utah under the Intergovernmental Personnel Act. This interdisciplinary group of scientists synthesized state-of-the-art tools from the disciplines of hydrology, water quality, water resource engineering, geomorphology, and political science into an integrated impact analysis process for studying the instream flow needs of fish, invertebrates, and recreation. After the initial synthesis of the tools, the program shifted to training, testing, and research until the early 1990s when the research program of the USFWS became part of the National Biological Survey, and, subsequently, the USGS.

Synthesis of the literature and general consensus of practitioners indicated that the primary change impacting aquatic organisms in regulated stream environments was the hydrologic pattern. Changes in the hydrograph in most cases altered the temperature regime in a significant manner as well as the instream hydraulics, both of which are important components of the physical habitat. The more drastic streamflow alterations also impact the water quality and channel geometry. Specific models were developed to address these instream habitat attributes. Armour and Taylor (1991) reviewed the use of the IFIM and described the

component models. Early development focused on hydrologic time series (extending stream gage data to habitat sites, synthesis of hydrographs, reservoir operation, and water routing); temperature (Stream Network Temperature model [SNTEMP]; Theurer et al. 1984; Bartholow 1989); water quality (Greeney and Krazewski 1981); hydraulic habitat (see separate write-up on PHABSIM) and habitat time series (Milhous et al. 1990). Recent development has focused on linkage to water resource operations and water routing, salmonid fish population response to flow and habitat manipulations, and large river sampling emphasizing two-dimensional hydraulics.

Application: An application of the IFIM typically operates at several scales. A hierarchical classification scheme, similar to that described by Hawkins et al. (1993) is used to describe and aggregate the habitat throughout the river network studied. The stream segment is the fundamental habitat accounting unit, several of which comprise the stream network or subbasin. Each segment is further stratified into mesohabitats, and sampling (both macro- and micro- habitat attributes) is typically at the mesohabitat level with extrapolations made to the segment level. Two-dimensional descriptions of the hydraulics and channel geometry at the microhabitat level are longitudinally integrated with macrohabitat variables of water quality and temperature to develop functional relations between total usable habitat and discharge for an entire stream segment. Studies using IFIM generally incorporate PHABSIM, SNTEMP, and the water quality models in common use by water resource or public health agencies of the region (see Schneider and Nestler (1996) for an example of integrating macro- and microhabitat). In alluvial streams, channel structure may also be analyzed at the microhabitat level to evaluate changes in geomorphology. Such analysis usually consists of empirical measurements, examination of the hydrological flow records, and comparison with historical records and photos to determine if the stream is in a state of dynamic equilibrium or not (for examples see McBain and Trush 1995; Potyondy and Andrews 1999). In some cases where a change in the channel dynamics is suspected (or even desired for rehabilitation or restoration), scour and fill are evaluated using physical process models such as HEC-6 and HEC-RAS, developed by the USACE. A recent example application of the IFIM process for developing prescriptions for a stream corridor restoration program for chinook salmon (*Oncorhynchus tshawytsch*) is described by the USFWS and the Hoopa Valley Tribe (1999).

Strengths: The integration of the output from a suite of models in IFIM allows the practitioners to evaluate spatial and temporal aspects of instream habitat as a consequence of proposed water management actions. Habitat time series in conjunction with effective habitat analysis enables practitioners to determine if there are associations between weak or strong year-classes and patterns of habitat reduction (habitat bottlenecks) or abundance of available habitat in the simulated history of the stream. The SALMOD model further simulates fish population production as a consequence of alternative flow management schemes for trout or salmon (Bartholow et al. 1993, 1999).

Limitations and Constraints: This methodology has been designed for quantifying potential impacts to instream resources subject to intensive water development, and it requires an interdisciplinary team for credible application. Data collection is detailed and time consuming and can be difficult and dangerous on large turbid rivers unless appropriate boats equipped with sophisticated GPS sounding and acoustic dopler velocity profiling gear are available. Most of the biological data needed for IFIM analyses are limited to individual species of well-studied fishes and some invertebrate groups. Habitat using guilds of warm-water fishes are little studied but show promise (Leonard and Orth 1988; Bain and Knight 1996). For all the uncertainties indicated above and the general lack of data, most applications of IFIM are best focused toward helping to make judgments on which of several proposed flow management alternatives are least likely to cause significant negative impacts to the instream habitat. Because of the inherent sophistication of this methodology, the potential for misuse is very high. The IFIM demands interdisciplinary expertise to run all components; practitioners commonly abuse the methodology by selecting single components (i.e., PHABSIM) and ignoring others (e.g., water quality, sediment transport, temporal aspects). Interpretation of the analysis requires astute biologists, who are familiar with the river, management goals, the species, and their habitat requirements.

Calibration and Validation: Standard practice in applying simulation models requires collection of independent observations of depth and velocity, water quality, and temperature to establish the validity of model output. Procedures for testing the spatial distribution of fish use with PHABSIM habitat model output is described by Thomas and Bovee (1993). In addition, some fish population data must be collected on-site to calibrate effective habitat simulations.

Critical Opinion: No set of tools no matter how sophisticated will produce "the answer". Decision support systems and simulation models as described in IFIM, when properly calibrated and validated, are most appropriate for relative comparisons of habitat potential from among several alternative flow management proposals. Multidisciplinary expertise is strongly suggested when applying IFIM to regulated rivers. Practitioners of IFIM are expected to use their best judgment in organizing their logic, documenting their assumptions, and establishing the validity of model applications. This method is not intended for prescribing instream flow standards. However, it can be the method of choice when a stream is subject to significant regulation and the resource management objective is to protect the existing healthy instream resources by prescribing conditions necessary for no net loss of physical habitat. Instream flow prescriptions resulting from an IFIM analysis always incorporate seasonal (intraannual) and water year type (interannual) flow recommendations. Practitioners who prescribe single, minimum flow values by examining the flow/habitat or flow/temperature relation (e.g., output from PHABSIM or SNTEMP) and present the results as an IFIM analysis are misusing the methodology and fueling the controversy regarding the appropriate use of the tools. Likewise, IFIM can be useful for quantifying habitat loss as necessary for mitigation in those situations when no net loss of a particular resource is politically infeasible.

Our lives begin to end the day we become silent about the things that matter to us.
— Martin Luther King, Jr.

CHAPTER SEVEN

Conclusions

North American society and much of its landscape has changed significantly from the time of our forebears. Changes in the quantity and quality of natural resources have been mirrored by adjustments in public values and legal systems. The one constant, however, is the reliance of sustainable economies on high-quality air, water, and lands. Although economic development is almost always dependent on the use of natural resources, most uses diminish or alter the original or natural state of these resources in some way.

Historically, little concern was placed on the amount and type of natural resource alteration or whether it was possible to restore degraded resources. Over the last 200 years, people assumed that most natural resources needed to be extracted and modified to have or generate value. Most of us now know the shortcomings of that overly simplistic perspective. Today, natural resource development usually acknowledges the ecological and social values of minimally or unaltered systems. However, quantifying the type and level of alteration that provides sustainable use of riverine resources while accommodating the evolving needs of our society remains a significant challenge.

Although much is unknown about the intricate links among natural systems, a considerable body of knowledge exists that allows societies to make reasoned decisions about how they want the world around them to look and what qualities of air, land, and water they are willing to exchange for the products those resources can provide.

Contrary to some public perceptions, protecting sufficient quantities of water for instream flow is not a question of providing water for fish and other instream uses at the expense of people. Water in the United States and Canada is typically held in trust and managed by the state or province, which means it is the property of all citizens. Determining the amount of water to be dedicated to instream use is almost always the product of a public process that reflects public desire to use that amount of water for a specific purpose (such as maintaining fisheries). Thus, it is not the fish or wildlife that hold an instream flow water right or permit any more than it is the grass that holds a water right to irrigation for hay in Oregon, a pasture in Nebraska, or a golf course in Georgia. Rather, instream flow rights are owned and shared by all the citizens of the state or province as a public benefit, just like an individual rancher or farmer owns rights or permits for irrigation. By virtue of this public ownership, claims by individual consumptive water right or permit holders that they are being discriminated against by fish or wildlife when water rights are regulated to provide instream flows have a certain emotional appeal, but no basis in law. In fact, it is legitimate to argue that instream flow rights held or permits issued by the state have a higher value than water rights or permits held by individuals because all citizens own those rights. Some consider this right to be a public trust right spanning back 2000 years to the times of the Roman Empire.

Instream flow needs assessment has been incorrectly characterized as the science of identifying minimum flows. It is, instead, a complex, scientific water management profession based on quantifying the amount of water needed to protect riverine and lake resources. The process of determining instream flow needs necessarily integrates science and public involvement within the unique legal, institutional, and administrative framework of each state or province. The purpose of *Instream Flows for Riverine Resource Stewardship* is to guide instream flow professionals toward better management of fisheries and aquatic ecosystems by emphasizing the process-oriented nature of protecting and restoring instream flows in lotic settings. It is important to note, too, that there are other aspects of instream flow that are not addressed here, such as recreation and lakes.

The book's process orientation should help resource managers and the public better understand that good science and good law go hand-in-hand. Although good science cannot supersede the law, scientific advances can help shape or reshape legal interpretations and social values. It is the complex interaction between science and law that makes the instream flow professional's job challenging. The instream flow professional serves society by providing scientific leadership and the best possible information regarding protection of aquatic ecosystems.

The best possible information includes not only raw data but also knowledge about the important role of instream flows in maintaining economic well-being. Water managers, fishery biologists, and others who think instream flow is not important because they have what they now consider surplus water are missing this vital perspective. History provides numerous examples of the perils associated with assuming that today's values, knowledge, and standards will extend into the future. For example, in the Colorado River Compact of 1922 water managers who allocated water among seven western states incorrectly estimated the growth potential of the West. They also failed to account for changing hydrologic patterns that have since occurred and yield much less water today than originated in the basin when the document was signed (Wyoming Water Development Commission 2001).

Even in water-rich areas, changing societal values and technological developments can threaten the form and function of rivers and lakes by a combination of new and different land and water management practices and regulations. Global warming models imply that there will be significant hydrologic shifts and the effect of these changes on riverine systems must be acknowledged and addressed to the extent possible. Similarly, state and provincial governments that still have largely unaltered waterways may have a false sense of security in believing that their water resources will remain in good condition for the foreseeable future, thus failing to take direct proactive measures to protect them while the opportunity still exists. It is this same lack of vision that led to the extirpation of the passenger pigeon and near annihilation of American bison. The future of water management will bring increased uses of water, many of which we cannot imagine today. Virtually all states and provinces have opportunities to protect water in their lakes and rivers for present and future generations, opportunities that most likely will not exist 100, 50, or even 20 years from now. Today is a critically important time to act in order to maintain and effectively manage our riverine resources and habitats (Figure 7-1).

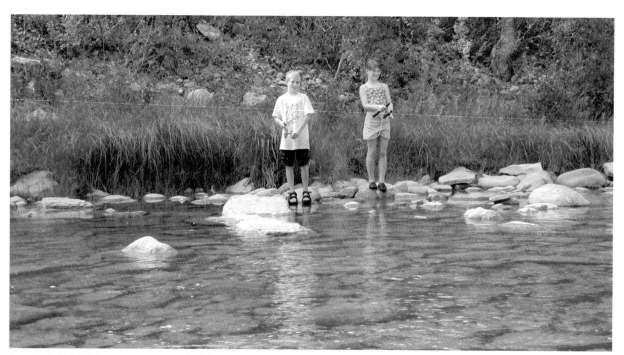

FIGURE 7-1. Water management decisions made today will impact rivers and surrounding watersheds for generations to come. The primary focus of The Instream Flow Council is to foster a better understanding of the need to protect riverine resources for present and future generations. Too often we forget that, "We did not inherit the Earth from our ancestors; we borrow it from our children" (Source: Ancient Native American Proverb).

Likewise, state and provincial governments that believe instream flow is not important because most rivers and lakes are already severely degraded by development fail to recognize their responsibility to save, rehabilitate, or restore what is left. Water management and fishery professionals must answer the challenge to identify opportunities to manage riverine resources and to improve the condition of degraded resources to replicate natural form and function to whatever degree the law and public support will allow. In many situations, fishery managers may not fully appreciate the support that exists for such actions. Effective instream flow management must address the perceptions of political leaders and the public and articulate the benefits that accrue from protecting the flowing water resource.

After 30 years of legislative development in many states and provinces to establish instream flow programs, some believe that sufficient protections are now in place. However, these programs are only a beginning (Larry MacDonnell, personal communication). In fact, a perspective that the Instream Flow Council (FC) commonly hears is that their real challenge is to focus on improving the scientific knowledge and public involvement processes. This is a great misconception. Although most states and provinces do indeed have instream flow laws of some sort, very few have laws that provide the opportunity or flexibility needed to achieve instream flow objectives. In most jurisdictions, instream flow protection does not enjoy the same institutional prerogatives that are afforded private water rights holders. Evaluation of many state and provincial laws reveals that most are so vague or limited in scope that administrators often use them as excuses to *not* provide the full range of instream flows. These institutional deficiencies clearly show the importance of making sure that the language in existing laws is as precise and enabling as possible and that a full suite of laws is on the books of each state and province. Although a good understanding of ecosystem processes is important for quantifying instream flow needs, the greatest gains will be made by expanding and improving the laws that govern the management of rivers, streams, and lakes.

There are no simple solutions to quantifying and protecting instream flows, let alone monitoring and enforcing water uses. Although simple rule-of-thumb methods exist, they, like any tool, must be used in situations for which they were designed. Otherwise, they may not provide healthy instream resources. The best approach for assessing the amount of water needed to protect the health of instream resources requires a holistic approach that integrates the five components of a riverine system: (1) hydrology, including spatial and temporal processes; (2) biology, including in-channel and riparian organisms; (3) geomorphology, including watershed and valley forming processes; (4) water quality, including temperature, sediment, and dissolved oxygen; and (5) connectivity, including disconnections caused by physical or hydrologic fragmentation, alteration of energy production, changes in water quality, and isolation of estuarine production. Because each instream flow situation is unique, the solution to each will necessarily involve a combination of tools that address all components adequately.

Uncertainty is a characteristic of almost any design—whether it is an engineering plan or instream flow recommendation. Prudent engineers always err on the conservative side of project implementation to protect the value of their investment. It is also acceptable for instream flow professionals to similarly err on the safe side and "learn by doing". Science often does not have all the answers, due, in part, to insufficient information, different interpretations of scientific findings, or conditions that are not amenable to scientific analysis. In the real world of natural resources management, accurately predicting future outcomes is uncertain. In these situations it is wise to adopt what is known as the precautionary principle—that when in doubt about outcomes or their potential harm to the protection or restoration of valuable public resources, society also should err on the conservative side when making decisions. In all natural resource management decisions, the challenge is to understand how to assess the data and possible risks. In some cases, uncertainties and risks may warrant an adaptive management approach.

Although adaptive management is an acceptable and potentially valuable tool for resolving uncertainties in some settings, it is not appropriate for every situation. In some cases, instream flow determinations can be reached in short order with little controversy and reasonable certainty of resource protection. In other situations, stakeholders, such as developers, may not be able or willing to participate in a long-term adaptive management program. Such situations, however, do not justify foregoing such a program or accepting an unsatisfactory short-term process. Despite the recent popularity of adaptive management, there are few examples of post-licensing monitoring related to instream flow. Additional case studies and guidance on such studies are needed.

Representing fishery and wildlife interests in adaptive management programs is only one of many settings in which state and provincial fishery and wildlife management agencies advocate on behalf of their citizens for the protection and wise use of fish and wildlife and their habitats. Regardless of whether they are acting in this capacity to build an instream flow program or recommend instream flow prescriptions, natural resource managers must address all components of the ecosystem, including riverine and policy components. Within this framework, legal and institutional concerns, as well as public involvement, are key elements. Providing opportunities to inform the public and solicit community input should be the responsibility of every state and provincial fishery and wildlife agency.

Whereas public involvement is recognized as an important part of recommending instream flow prescriptions, it is a time-consuming and challenging endeavor and few, if any, fishery and wildlife managers invest enough time in this effort. An agency's ability to act is driven not only by citizen demand but available resources. Budgetary constraints and lack of trained staff often hinder an agency's ability to fulfill its public involvement responsibilities. However, even in the face of these limitations agencies should make a concerted effort to involve the public as much as possible. Such an effort has the potential to afford greater benefits for fishery and wildlife resources.

Despite this recognition of the importance for a comprehensive perspective, additional research is needed to improve the understanding of the primary factors that determine the biological, physical, and chemical characteristics of riverine ecosystems. What is ultimately needed are scientific studies that document the long-term effects of instream flow prescriptions at various levels. Work that addresses the effect of streamflow level on individual components, such as fish or insect populations, is often confounded by their interrelations with other components (e.g., geomorphology, water quality, and connectivity). Through careful selection of study areas and thorough (long-term) scientific studies of each of the riverine components, watershed-wide restoration or rehabilitation can provide insight into underlying mechanisms and important temporal and spatial scales and processes. Although others have identified specific research needs (e.g., Reiser et al. 1989; Hardy 1998), the IFC encourages more fundamental and applied research that is directed toward improving the

basic understanding of interactions among the five riverine components. This book is not the first to document connectivity as critical for riverine ecosystems but methodologies necessary for quantifying this component have not been well developed. In temperate climates, additional research is necessary to better understand the relation between streamflow and ice-forming processes and the subsequent implications for aquatic organisms, habitats, and adjacent human communities.

Managing instream flows to protect public natural resources within the legal and institutional bounds of water allocation is a highly complex job. It is a daunting and potentially confusing maze that state and provincial instream flow scientists and water managers must negotiate to fulfill their responsibilities. Few, if any, fishery biologists possess the skill to integrate their own biological knowledge with knowledge of hydrologic and geomorphologic concepts, legal and administrative processes, and public involvement. Clearly, agency managers need to expand their horizons. To fulfill fishery and wildlife management responsibilities for present and future generations, state and provincial fishery and wildlife agencies must make water management a top priority, hire and retain qualified and trained staff, and participate fully in water management decisions.

It is this recommendation that serves as the central focus throughout *Instream Flows for Riverine Resource Stewardship*. Although the book is not intended as a definitive treatise on instream flow management, it does represent a concerted and comprehensive attempt to encourage natural resource managers to address *all* ecosystem components, including the actions and influences of humans, in the management of instream uses of water. This broad-based approach not only underscores the complexity and magnitude of a comprehensive riverine management program but also provides a wide range of information that will ultimately guide us all to becoming better stewards of our riverine resources.

APPENDIX A

Summary of Instream Flow Council Policies

Title	Page	Policy
Public Input	57	Effective instream flow programs should incorporate public input in the decision-making process.
Public Education	58	State and provincial instream flow programs should include specific actions to inform the public about instream flow concepts, how instream flows are admin istered, what benefits the programs provide, and what opportunities exist for public involvement.
Effective Communication	58	Information intended for public consideration in instream flow decision-making processes should be straightforward, free of jargon, and provide a basic understanding of technical and legal concepts, biological processes, and trade-offs.
Public Trust Doctrine	69	Laws, regulations, and/or policies affecting fishery and wildlife resources and the habitats upon which they depend should be based on the state or province's legal stewardship responsibilities to manage those resources for the benefit and enjoyment of present and future generations.
Federal Water Management	71	Federal agencies should integrate their water and riverine management efforts within the constructs of state and provincial laws, regulations, and policies to protect riverine resources.
State and Provincial Water Rights	71	State and provincial laws, regulation, and policies should provide the authority, opportunity, procedure, and process to enable a state or provincial fishery and wildlife agency the right to obtain and/or hold instream water rights, reservations or licenses in perpetuity for the specific purpose of protecting, rehabilitating, restoring and managing fishery and wildlife resources and habitats and other trust resources.
Private Instream Flows	72	State and provincial laws, regulations, and policies should provide the authority, opportunity, procedure, and process to enable an organization, group, or individual the right to obtain, retain, secure, and/or hold instream water rights for individual streams or rivers, or specific sections of individual streams or rivers, for the specific purpose of benefiting fisheries and wildlife and other in-channel purposes.
Priority and Legal Standing	73	Instream flow rights, reservations, and licenses to restore, manage, and/or protect the aquatic resources of streams, rivers, and lakes should have priority and legal standing to protect aquatic resources.

Appendix A *(continued)*

Title	Page	Policy
Water Rights Certainty	74	State and provincial instream water rights, reservations, and licenses should be afforded permanent status to enable them to fulfill their custodial trust obligations for riverine resources.
Public Interest	76	States and provinces should designate instream uses of water as in the public interest and/or beneficial uses to ensure that riverine resources and processes are considered on an equal basis with other traditional uses of water.
Connectivity of Surface and Ground- Water (Legal)	77	The hydrological interconnectivity between ground-water and surface flows should be recognized, and these waters should be conjunctively managed to protect the short- and long-term fundamental public value of fishery and wildlife resources and habitats.
Fishery and Wildlife Agency Role	78	State and provincial fishery and wildlife agencies should have the primary authority for determining appropriate stream and river flow quantity, quality, and other needs and requirements necessary to restore, manage, and protect fishery and aquatic wildlife resources and processes.
Water Conservation	80	State and provincial governments should develop and implement legal opportunities to enable consumptive water users to conserve water and dedicate conserved or unused water to instream purposes.
Water Quality Standards	80	State and provincial fishery and wildlife agencies should include stream and river flow quantity and other needs and requirements necessary to restore, manage, and protect aquatic and riparian fishery and wildlife resources and habitats within water quality standards and permitting processes.
Public Funding	81	Public funding for water management projects should include conditions for the protection of instream flows necessary to meet the needs and requirements of aquatic and riparian fishery and wildlife resources and habitats.
Riverine Resource Stewardship	86	All streams and rivers should have instream flows that maintain or restore, to the greatest extent possible, ecological functions and processes similar to those exhibited in their natural or unaltered state.
Public Trust Advocacy	88	Advocacy for and protection of the principles of the Public Trust Doctrine must be among the fundamental guiding principles of an effective instream flow program.
Native Species	89	Instream flow programs should acknowledge the importance of and need to manage stream communities and indigenous aquatic biota. Management of nonnative species should not threaten the long-term health or survival of native species and their habitats.
Reservoir Management	90	Instream flow programs should acknowledge the effects of new and existing dams on sediment transport and allow managers the ability to recommend strategies for water releases and sediment management that minimize negative effects to existing channel, riparian, and flood plain properties and processes below the dam.

Appendix A *(continued)*

Title	Page	Policy
Dam Removal	91	Instream flow programs should support the removal or modification of dams or in-channel barriers and restoration or rehabilitation of affected riverine resources to more natural conditions and functions when those structures' benefits no longer outweigh their societal costs.
Process Development	92	Instream flow programs should establish a process for quantifying instream flow needs that allows the state, or provincial, fishery and wildlife management agency to identify or approve study needs, study design, data analysis, and flow implementation.
Legal Authority	93	Effective instream flow programs must be based on a clear recognition of legal authorities to protect, enhance, and restore instream flow for public riverine resources.
Legal Counsel	93	Instream flow programs should have ready access to specifically trained legal counsel familiar with water law statutes and instream flow programs in order to obtain consistent representation and maximize instream flow benefits under existing laws and regulations.
Negotiation	95	Effective instream flow programs should include personnel who are trained in negotiation skills, supported by their agency administration, and engaged in appropriate negotiation from the start of projects.
Interdisciplinary Teams	95	Effective instream flow programs require a well-coordinated, interdisciplinary team with adequate staff, training, and funding to address all instream flow and related issues that fall under the agency's responsibilities.
Comprehensive Water Resource Planning	96	Comprehensive water resource planning that includes recognition of instream flows as an essential water use is an important part of an effective instream flow program.
Drought Planning	97	State and provincial instream flow programs should support and participate in development of mechanisms or plans to implement water use reductions during drought periods to protect essential instream flows.
Flow Variability	101	Instream flow prescriptions should provide inter-and intraannual variable flow patterns that mimic the natural hydrograph (magnitude, duration, timing, rate of change) to maintain or restore processes that sustain natural riverine characteristics.
Riverine Components	103	Instream flow studies must evaluate flow needs and opportunities in terms of hydrology, biology, geomorphology, water quality, and connectivity.
Stream Gaging	103	Instream flow programs must support individual gaging stations and networks of gaging stations necessary to quantify hydrographs, make and defend instream flow prescriptions, and monitor and enforce instream flow compliance.
Discharge Measurements	103	Discharge meters, stream gaging devices, and flow data collection protocols should meet accepted standards of the U.S. Geological Survey and/or Environment Canada.

Appendix A *(continued)*

Title	Page	Policy
Synthetically Derived Hydrologic Data	105	Instream flow assessments based on synthetically developed hydrologic information should acknowledge the source and quality of data. Final decisions or agreements should be based on collection and use of appropriate field data to refine the precision of the original estimates.
Land Use	105	Instream flow practitioners should recognize the effects of land use practices on instream flows and work with land managers to promote land use practices that maintain or restore the natural hydrograph and avoid or minimize those that negatively affect the natural hydrograph.
Habitat	106	Instream flow prescriptions must maintain spatially complex and diverse habitats, which are available through all seasons.
Ice Processes	107	Water management decisions for streams that are prone to ice formation should document the potential effects that the proposed action might have on the stream channel or associated aquatic organisms and, where appropriate, include measures to minimize or avoid potentially negative effects of project-related ice forming processes.
Channel Maintenance	109	Channel maintenance flow is an essential component of instream flow prescriptions for alluvial channels, and the maintenance, rehabilitation, restoration, and preservation of stream channel form and associated biological communities.
Flushing Flow	110	For many stream types, a flushing flow for removing fine sediments is a necessary component of instream flow prescriptions.
Channel Modification	111	Any proposed stream channel modification should document the hydrologic and geomorphic character and function of the watershed and floodplain and incorporate principles of applied fluvial geomorphology and natural habitat features.
Instream Mining	112	Instream mining as a source of sand, gravel, or other materials should only be considered as a last option, and the mining operation should only be allowed to remove material in excess of the normal sediment transport carrying capacity of the stream.
Water Quality	112	Instream flow prescriptions must recognize the relation between the quantity and quality of water in streams, document the effects of water quality changes on riverine resources, and implement prescriptions that maintain or improve water quality characteristics for natural riverine resources.
Riparian Connectivity	113	Instream flow prescriptions must recognize the connectivity between instream flows and riparian areas and maintain or establish riparian structure and functions.
Floodplain Connectivity	114	Instream flow prescriptions should maintain or re-establish connectivity between instream flows and floodplains.

Appendix A *(continued)*

Title	Page	Policy
Groundwater Connectivity (Management)	116	Instream flow prescriptions should recognize and describe the extent and nature of connectivity between instream flows and groundwater and manage groundwater withdrawals to avoid potentially negative impacts on instream flows and riverine resources.
Longitudinal Connectivity	117	Instream flow prescriptions should recognize and document the importance of connectivity within defined stream segments and the stream system in general. Management actions should avoid creating longitudinal disconnectivity where appropriate and restore connectivity where needed.
Monitoring	124	Monitoring riverine resource responses to instream flow prescriptions is a fundamental component of effective instream flow programs. Monitoring studies should be based on long-term ecosystem processes as opposed to short-term responses of individual species.
Adaptive Management	128	Adaptive management can be an effective tool but should be used selectively to answer critical uncertainties for instream flow-setting processes.

An Instream Flow Awareness Campaign

GENERATING PUBLIC SUPPORT FOR INSTREAM FLOWS

One of the primary roles of state and provincial fishery and wildlife agencies is to educate the public about fish and wildlife management issues. Educating the public about instream flow issues is a multifaceted task. The hope is that an educated public will support instream flow protection, in general, and develop a concern for the flow conditions in specific waterways.

To assist managers in their efforts to develop public information programs, we provide an example of an instream flow awareness campaign. An effective program should include most, if not all, of the suggestions outlined below.

Problem Assessment

Establishing instream flow levels for waterways is a complex problem throughout the United States and Canada. A necessary step in developing instream flow protection programs is to raise public concern about the local issues affecting important waterways in the community. Issues can be identified and discussed through a range of venues--public meetings, printed materials, radio and television talk shows, community organizations, stakeholders' groups, writers' associations, and even schools. To further heighten public awareness, local or state politicians may be able to provide assistance. The goal is to provide an objective problem assessment that the public can rely upon.

Media Relations

A series of news releases for local newspapers (daily and weekly) should be developed to increase public concern about local issues affecting community waterways. These releases should be provided to environmental reporters. It is also useful to organize media tours to specific waterways during times of the year that will allow reporters to see the problems associated with maintaining minimum flow. Important discussion points include:

- A definition of instream flow and an explanation of its importance to the community,
- How maintenance of instream flow affects public water supply,
- Why maintenance of instream flow is important to wildlife, and
- A history of the river(s) in the community and how the resource has affected the development and daily life of the community.

To be most effective, press releases and brochures should avoid technical jargon and be written in terms that the lay public can understand. Additional information should include such things as results from attitudinal surveys of the public and biological assessments, quotes from agency directors, and the phone number of the agency's contact person. A database of names and addresses of those who contacted the agency for more information about instream flow issues should be maintained; it can be used to advise people of future meetings and events.

Another useful step is to encourage the agency director to write editorials for local newspapers. Newspaper editors are often interested in publishing the perspectives of agency directors. Such editorials can provide a unique opportunity to articulate the agency's perspective and policy.

In addition, it is essential to develop a press kit that includes news releases, editorials, survey and biological assessment results, and other pertinent instream flow information that can be distributed to the media.

Other Communication Platforms

Whether an awareness campaign is a short- or long-term event, agency directors or instream flow managers should strive to form personal relationships with influential people or groups that have visibility in the community. Such people often have access to public forums or publication outlets and, therefore, the ability to inform the public about community concerns.

Speakers' Bureau. The agency could develop a speakers' bureau so that organizations--such as community clubs, citizen support groups, and schools--interested in environmental issues can identify potential guest speakers for their meetings. Taken a step further, the instream flow program manager could make sure that potential speakers have access to a slide show and are sufficiently well briefed on instream flow issues that they can effectively conduct a question and answer session. One advantage of developing a speakers bureau, speaker support materials, and briefing speakers before they present talks is that these steps ensure that the agency will present a consistent, well thought out message.

Radio and Television Talk Shows. Another approach is to identify an effective agency spokesperson to make the majority of public presentations and write press releases. A spokesperson could also appear on local radio or television stations with a talk show format to answer questions and provide the latest information about local issues affecting community waterways. Also, some biologists and conservation rangers have talk shows and spokespersons are often invited to be guests. If possible, such appearances should coincide during times that maintaining instream flow is an issue so that listeners can gain a better appreciation for the issues the spokesperson is discussing. The spokesperson should also develop a press kit that includes news releases, editorials, survey and biological assessment results, and other pertinent instream flow information.

Stakeholders' Groups. It is often beneficial to seek out stakeholders' groups such as anglers, canoeists, birdwatchers, homeowners' associations, and river protection organizations that have an interest in the health and welfare of the waterway and its wildlife. Many of these groups publish regular newsletters and may be willing to disseminate information through their publications. They also hold meetings, which sometimes include guest speakers who present short slide shows followed by question and answer sessions. Attempts should be made to submit news releases and provide guest speakers to as many of these groups as possible. As with any potential support group, a mailing list should be kept so that these organizations can be alerted to future public meetings and events.

These groups should be encouraged to write letters to local newspaper editors expressing their concerns about the local issues affecting community waterways. They also may be willing to write local or state politicians in support of agency policies. It is helpful if agency managers can provide draft sample letters for this purpose.

Writers' Associations. An instream flow manager might ask to be included on the agenda of the state or regional outdoor writers' association meeting (e.g., Georgia Outdoor Writer's Association). People who specialize in writing about the outdoors usually have an interest in environmental issues. Some may take the opportunity to write articles for outdoor magazines and local newspapers that explain the instream flow issue and its importance to the community.

Local and State Politicians. One of the most effective learning experiences to appreciate the ecological health of a river is through direct interaction with a stream. People understand complex environmental problems best when they can see for themselves the effects of disturbances. Therefore, local or state political leaders could be invited to participate in a field trip to a stream where instream flows are of concern. This way they can see the flow condition and visualize how changes in the periodicity of low flow affects the overall health of the stream. When in the field, they can discuss the importance of protecting the waterway to the local community and interact with stream management specialists within a learning environment. Specialists can discuss the effects of development and long-term planning on the health of the waterway. The hoped for result is that political leaders can become actively involved in understanding the benefits the waterway provides their community. One way to do this is to actually let the political leaders participate in a management activity such as population sampling or flow measurement. Because the question will inevitably be part of the discussion, it is important to have local economic information available to describe how the waterway provides income and supports the quality of life in the local community through fishing, tourism, public drinking water, agricultural irrigation, and the like.

To involve as many political leaders as possible, it is important to provide alternative field experiences. For those who cannot make a field trip, arrangements should be made to hold meetings at which those who did participate can brief others on the issues as well as what they learned from the field experience. Information packets—including any local media clippings demonstrating public interest and concern—should be distributed at these meetings.

Perhaps the ultimate result from such a round of field trips and meetings would be a draft resolution expressing support from local governing boards for the development of an instream flow policy. Passing such a resolution would also provide another opportunity for media coverage.

Meeting Promotion and Advertisement

Advanced planning is important to properly promote and advertise public meetings. Announcements should appear several weeks in advance of scheduled meetings. One way to advertise meeting dates and purposes is through local newspapers and organizational newsletters, such as stakeholders' groups. If organizations will provide a mailing list of their members, a notice of the meeting can be sent directly to the membership.

Ten days before the scheduled event a notice should be sent to all individuals whose names appear in the agency's database, which has been maintained for this purpose.

One week before, a news release announcing the date, time, and purpose of the forthcoming meeting should be sent to the local media. This should be followed up by phone calls to confirm publication of the news release. Also, 30-second public service announcements should be prepared that can be aired on local radio stations.

Two days before the meeting, a Fax should be sent to the local media reminding them about the meeting and encouraging their attendance. The day before the meeting, a follow up phone call should be made to make sure they received the fax. Press kits should be available at the meeting and sent to those who were unable to attend the event.

Summary of the Public Trust Doctrine

Much has been said and written about the Public Trust Doctrine. Because some of those comments border on one extreme interpretation or the other, it is not surprising that this topic generates uncertainty and distrust. To better understand the doctrine requires a basic knowledge of its origin, characteristics, and use.

I. Origin

    A. The Public Trust Doctrine originated in the sixth century A.D. as Roman Civil Code ("By the law of nature these things are common to mankind—the air, running water, the sea, and consequently, the shore of the sea)."

    B. The Romans imparted this legacy into English and French laws when they occupied those lands.

    C. The English Common Law was adopted in the United States by the original 13 colonies; thus, the Public Trust Doctrine is one of this country's oldest laws.

II. Basic Characteristics

    A. The doctrine is common law.

        1.. Some components are "common" to all who recognize it because the law arises from precedent and prior judicial opinions.

        2. The doctrine is not established by statute or legislation.

        3. Because the law is not codified in all states or provinces, it can gradually evolve over time to address the needs of the beneficiaries.

    B. The doctrine is state law.

        1. Within the broad constraints of the doctrine (e.g., the requirement that trust properties be managed for the benefit of the citizens including future generations), the law has developed differently in each state. Although there are commonalities in applications from state-to-state, each state must determine the limit and application of the Public Trust Doctrine depending on its own customs, founding documents, and earlier court cases.

        2. States may not give up their trustee role.

        3. Because the doctrine is rooted in state law, not federal law, there is no potential for a national or global legal framework--a fear expressed by some private interests.

        4. Some states (Hawaii and Alaska) have incorporated the Public Trust Doctrine into their constitutions; other states, such as Colorado, make no mention of it whatsoever in their constitutions. However, the doctrine may exist even if it is not formally recognized. Lack of formal recognition does not limit application of the doctrine or its potential to "emerge" in the future.

    C. The doctrine is property law.

        1. The corpus of the trust consists of such common properties as fisheries, wildlife, air, and water.

        2. It is the responsibility of the sovereign as trustee to protect and enhance the value of the trust—just like a banker is charged with preserving money in a trust for heirs of an estate. The trustee may loan "money" from the trust, but cannot give the "money" away.

        3. Public trust is not the same as public interest. Public interest relates primarily to matters of economics, welfare, and security of the public. The sovereign is charged with acting in the public interest while maintaining the value of the public trust. Nevertheless, it is possible and common for the state to act in the public interest yet harm the trust. It is important for state and provincial governments to acknowledge their trusteeship over trust resources so they can adjust their actions to resolve any possible conflicts.

        4. The property under the Public Trust Doctrine consists of two components: the jus publicum (public ownership of the property), and jus privatum (ability of private parties to use trust properties for commerce and personal gain). Thus, the state can allow private parties to use trust resources (such as water permits) but cannot, and does not, give away ownership of the property (water).

III. Use

A. Because it is not statutory law, the doctrine is never used as a sole authority or basis for action. It is primarily used in combination with statutory laws to remind governing entities of their trustee responsibilities.

B. Individual states have applied the doctrine on a case-by-case basis in deciding matters pertaining to perceived harm to trust properties.

1. The famous Mono Lake case in California dealt with water rights specific to one situation and was not used or intended to be used to overturn the entire water rights system in the state. In that case, the California Supreme Court ruled that these particular consumptive water rights are subject to the Public Trust Doctrine, but the ruling did not apply broadly to all consumptive water rights in the state.

2. Another California case provides an example of the courts applying the Public Trust Doctrine to streamflow—in this case, allocating water in the American River. The judge also found that the Public Trust Doctrine must be integrated with the state's Reasonable Use Doctrine. That doctrine states, in part, that water resources in California must be put to beneficial use to the fullest extent possible. Therefore, the judge mandated a plan by which water could be diverted and instream values protected.

C. There are no examples in which the Public Trust Doctrine has been used to supplant a state's system for administering water, such as the prior appropriation doctrine.

1. In fact, it seems clear that the system of prior appropriation is consistent with the Public Trust Doctrine in most situations because the state retains ownership of the trust property while giving up only the right to use that property to private citizens and business.

2. In some situations where it can be shown that the extent of water allocation is causing significant harm to trust resources (such as navigation in navigable rivers), the Public Trust Doctrine can be called upon—in combination with other state laws—to protect, rehabilitate, or restore the public's interests.

D. Legal actions under the Public Trust Doctrine may be brought by a wide range of public interest groups, not just environmentalists. For example, navigation interests may reference the doctrine when they believe flow changes have affected the public's ability to travel or conduct commerce on navigable rivers. Likewise, others who contend that degradation of clean water and air is a source of harm to the general public may also find cause to employ the doctrine.

Alberta Water Act

CHAPTER W-3.5

Provincial Planning Framework

7   (1) The Minister must establish a framework for water management planning for the Province within 3 years after the coming into force of this Act.

(2) The framework for water management planning must include a strategy for the protection of the aquatic environment, as described in section 8, and may include

(a) water management principles,
(b) the geographical limits or boundaries within which water management planning is to be carried out in the Province, including limits or boundaries for the development of strategic and operational plans,
(c) criteria for establishing the order in which water management plans are to be developed,
(d) an outline of the processes for developing, implementing, reviewing and revising water management plans, including opportunities for local and regional involvement,
(e) matters relating to integration of water management planning with land and other resources, and
(f) matters relating to the development of water conservation objectives.

(3) The Minister must, in a form and manner that the Minister considers appropriate, consult with the

(4) public during the development of the framework for water management planning.

Aquatic Environment Protection Strategy

8   (1) In this section, "biological diversity" means the variability among living organisms and the ecological complexes of which they are a part, and includes diversity within and between species and ecosystems.

(2) The Minister must establish a strategy for the protection of the aquatic environment as part of the framework for water management planning for the Province.

(3) The strategy referred to in subsection (2) may include
(a) identification of criteria to determine the order in which water bodies or classes of water bodies are to be dealt with,
(b) guidelines for establishing water conservation objectives,
(c) matters relating to the protection of biological diversity, and
(d) guidelines and mechanisms for implementing the strategy.

(4) The Minister must, in a form and manner that the Minister considers appropriate, consult with the public during the development of the strategy.

Water Management Plans

9   (1) The Minister may require a water management plan to be developed by the Director or another person.

(2) The Director or other person developing a water management plan
(a) may adopt an integrated approach to planning with respect to water, land and other resources;
(b) may co-operate with
(i) any persons,
(ii) local authorities,
(iii) Government agencies and other Government departments, and
(iv) the governments and government agencies of other jurisdictions;
(c) may, with the consent of the Minister, carry out any studies that the Director or other person considers appropriate;
(d) may consider any information, documents or other water and land management plans;

(e) must follow the framework for water management planning established under this Division;

(f) must engage in public consultation that the Minister considers appropriate during the development of the water management plan.

Water Management Planning Areas

10   The Minister may establish water management planning areas for the purpose of developing or implementing a water management plan or approved water management plan.

Water Conservation Objectives

15   (1) The Director may establish water conservation objectives.

(2) The Director must engage in public consultation that the Director considers appropriate during the establishment of a water conservation objective.

(3) Information on a water conservation objective established by the Director must be made available to the public in a form and manner satisfactory to the Director.

Example of How to Conduct an Instream Flow Study

Not all instream flow studies involve the same level of detail in data collection, analysis, or implementation. Each situation typically involves its own unique issues and opportunities. Although practitioners may approach solutions to each problem differently, they should usually begin by asking a series of questions—derived from the ecosystem components—noting that answers will not necessarily warrant a direct or equal level of treatment for each problem. The questions below could be addressed in an instream flow assessment.

I. **Riverine Components**
   A. Hydrology
      1. Is the source of water in the river an important element (e.g., snowmelt, rainfall, springs)? If so, why?
      2. Is the current versus natural pattern of flow between years an issue? If so, why?
      3. Is the current versus natural pattern of flow within a single year an issue? If so, why?
      4. What factors in the watershed affect the pattern (quantity) of streamflow (e.g., dams, watershed hardening, dewatering, vegetation management)? Are these important issues? If so, why?
      5. What features of the hydrology contribute to riparian vegetation recruitment and loss (e.g., natural snowmelt floods, rainfall floods, ice jam related floods)? Are these features important to maintain or restore? If so, why?
      6. What features of hydrologic processes contribute to recruitment and transport of large woody debris? Are these features important to maintain or restore? If so, why?
      7. Do ice formation processes (ice-up, ice cover, ice-out) affect hydrology at different times of the winter and/or between different years? What opportunities (short- and long-term) exist to affect those processes? Are these features important to maintain or restore? If so, why?
      8. Do opportunities (short- and long-term) exist to restore hydrologic patterns to those necessary to achieve desired streamflow? Describe the opportunities that exist and identify perceived limitations.

   B. Geomorphology
      1. Is the stream channel significantly altered from its natural state in terms of width/depth, sinuosity, slope, water conveyance capacity, or stream bank stability? If so, how will proposed water management change it?
      2. Is the upstream watershed sediment yield in equilibrium with the capacity of the present stream channel to transport sediment through the segment on a long-term basis? If not, is the channel aggrading, degrading, or laterally active? Is this condition supported by data or observation?
      3. Is the stream form controlled by bedrock or is it cutting through previously deposited alluvium (e.g., considered an alluvial or colluvial stream)?
      4. Is the relative composition of bed materials such as boulders, cobble, gravel, or fine sediment a biologically important habitat component of the channel? If so, is the composition likely to be modified? Will any change be a significant issue?
      5. What land management activities are influencing sediment yield and what opportunities (short- and long-term) exist to affect those processes?
      6. If appropriate, how do ice formation processes affect bed load transport, bank stability, and channel shape? Is this an important issue? Why? What opportunities (short- and long-term) exist to affect those processes?

   C. Biology
      1. What species of fish, birds, mammals, invertebrates, aquatic plants, or riparian vegetation are of greatest concern?
      2. Will proposed management actions and flows protect habitat for the most flow-sensitive species or life-stage of fish?
      3. Is the flow prescription intended to address assemblages of organisms (e.g., fish communities, riparian vegetation)?
      4. If the prescription is primarily related to individual or multiple species of nonnative sport fish, will the prescription affect hydraulic habitat for native species? If so, how?

5. What time(s) of year are most critical for each organism, suite of organisms, or life stage targeted by the management team or individual species? What data support this belief?

6. What habitats are most limiting and what is the importance of drought, flooding, and intermediate flow conditions for developing and maintaining these habitats and habitat processes? What data support this belief?

7. Are ice processes (ice-up, ice cover, ice-out) an issue and, if so, how do they affect hydraulic habitat for in-channel and riparian organisms throughout the winter? Is more information needed?

8. Is riverine habitat important for maintaining fish populations in hydrologically connected lakes or reservoirs? What data support this statement?

9. Are flows sequenced to support sequential life stages? For example, are incubation flows and spawning flows matched to probable controlled and uncontrolled conditions such as extreme high and low flows? Prescriptions that maximize habitat for one life stage may of limited value if the organism will be subjected to adverse conditions, such as scouring or dewatering in another life stage.)

10. Does the existing or proposed temporal pattern for both the quantity and quality of usable hydraulic habitat vary significantly from natural, unaltered conditions? Strategies to consider include:

    (a) Arranging time series (discharge and hydraulic habitat) into at least three water supply year types (wet, average, dry).

    (b) Adjusting post-project discharge time series until the magnitude, timing, and duration of habitat patterns for wet, average, and dry years are similar to preproject conditions (as described with baseline habitat time series)

11. If reservoir releases are needed to provide the recommended flow, what will be the effect on the reservoir fishery?

12. Does sufficient preproject monitoring exist of the organism or organisms of interest?

13. Is adequate postproject monitoring planned and funding provided? Who will do this work?

14. Are there laws, policies, or regulations that enable adjustment of water management based on monitoring results? Are objectives identified and criteria for decision making well defined? If not, is a process in place to identify these?

D. Water Quality

1. What water quality components are of greatest concern to the target organisms, life stages, or riverine processes (i.e., dissolved oxygen, suspended sediment, temperature, chemical elements, nutrients)? Why?

2. In what way(s) and to what extent are target organisms affected by water quality (favorably or unfavorably)?

3. How are water quality components affected by flow characteristics during the year and between different years? Are these patterns important? Why?

4. Do water quality characteristics change in the river, it's tributaries, lakes, and estuaries (if any) throughout the watershed? If so, how do they change? Are these changes important?

5. Do land management activities affect water quality? If so, how do they affect riverine processes and organisms?

6. Do ice formation processes affect water quality (e.g., temperature [frazil ice formation], suspended sediment, dissolved oxygen, chemical)? If so, how do these occur? Are these effects important?

7. Do opportunities (short- and long-term) exist to manage water quality-related factors in the watershed? Describe the opportunities that exist and identify perceived limitations.

E. Connectivity
(hydrological, biological, energetic)

1. Is lateral connectivity to the floodplain an important issue (e.g., to maintain or restore wetlands and riparian communities, provide spawning habitat, attenuate floods, maintain water quality)? If so, why?

2. Is longitudinal connectivity an important issue (e.g., including connectivity to headwaters, tributaries, lakes, reservoirs, and estuaries). If so, why?

3. Is vertical connectivity an important issue (e.g., groundwater recharge, flow depletion from pumping, biological habitat). What data support this belief?

4. Are lateral, longitudinal, and vertical connectivity concerns different at different times of year? If so, how and why is that important?

5. Is it necessary for flow to be adequate and continuous at all times to achieve the desired riverine condition? If so, why?

6. Is disconnectivity of flow in some years or times of year, such as periods associated with drought, a necessary component of maintaining target organisms and habitat processes? If so, how or why?

7. Is upstream migration or out-migration facilitated or hindered by certain flows? If so, what flows, which stream segments, and what time(s) of year? What data support this belief?

8. Are there structures (artificial or natural) that modify hydrology, sediment movement to or

within the channel, or fish movement throughout the stream system?

9. Are ice or ice formation processes (ice-up, ice cover, or ice-out) an important factor that can affect hydrological or biological connectivity? Are these processes destructive or ecologically necessary? Why?

10. Do opportunities (short- and long-term) exist to maintain, rehabilitate, or restore perceived connectivity processes? Describe the opportunities that exist and identify perceived limitations.

II. **Public Involvement**

A. Educational opportunities

1. Have efforts been made to identify potentially affected parties, gauge their level of interest, and assess their desire for involvement in the project (e.g., have parties been involved from the earliest stages of the project)?

2. What information has been made available to the public and how was it distributed? Are there more effective ways to distribute information?

3. Has information been reviewed by focus groups or others prior to its formal release to make sure it is understandable by nonscientists?

B. Public input

1. What opportunities exist for public involvement in the project?

2. What means have been established to receive input from the public (e.g., public comment periods, public meetings or hearings, interactive web sites)? Are there other ways to gather public input more effectively?

3. Has an interdisciplinary team been formed to address the five riverine components? Who from outside the agency should be on these teams?

4. Is there a plan or protocol for how public input will be used? Has this information been clearly explained to the public so that their expectations are realistic in terms of state or provincial resource management responsibilities?

C. Activism

1. Are activist groups likely to support or oppose the goals of the project by working outside of traditional venues? Can their concerns be reasonably addressed?

2. How likely is it that activist groups can significantly affect the outcome of the project? Have serious efforts been made to directly contact potential activist groups or individuals to address their concerns?

3. What strategies or other steps are appropriate for dealing with opposition groups?

III. **Legal/Institutional**

A. How do federal, state, or provincial laws limit or affect the ability to achieve an acceptable, enforceable, long-term solution?

B. Do federal, state, or provincial laws limit the kind of scientific studies that can or should be conducted to quantify streamflow needs in terms of the five riverine components? What other strategies, if any, can be used within existing law to achieve prescriptive flows that address the ecological needs defined by the five riverine components?

C. What actions are required to comply with state or provincial laws (e.g., addressing broader public interest issues, soliciting public involvement, coordinating with other agencies and entities)? Are these within the ability of the agency's personnel?

D. How do institutional policies affect the administration of federal, state, or provincial laws? (e.g., Is the interpretation of existing law a factor that limits the ability to achieve a suitable instream flow condition?)

E. Are there opportunities for other agencies, or the public, to affect institutional policies in the short- or long-term?

F) Are new laws needed to allow better protection of riverine resources as determined using the five riverine components? What are they and what is the likelihood that such laws might be developed in the short- or long-term?

G. Is the Public Trust Doctrine—in combination with other resource stewardship laws and regulations—a viable tool for helping secure favorable instream flows? If so, what efforts have been taken to use the doctrine? With what existing laws can the doctrine be used?

H. If the Public Trust Doctrine is not a viable tool for helping secure favorable flows, what steps are needed to enhance its application? Are these steps within the ability of agency personnel to achieve or is assistance needed from other individuals or groups?

I. Are there individuals or groups interested and able to work with legislators to develop or improve state or provincial laws or achieve more favorable interpretations of existing laws?

Glossary

Abiotic - The nonliving material components of the environment such as water, sediment, and temperature.

Accretion – 1. Addition of flows to the total discharge of the stream channel, which may come from tributaries, springs, or seeps. 2. Increase of material such as silt, sand, gravel, water.

Adaptive management - A process whereby management decisions can be changed or adjusted based on additional biological, physical or socioeconomic information.

Aggradation - 1. Geologic process in which inorganic materials carried downstream are deposited in streambeds, floodplains, and other water bodies resulting in a rise in elevation in the bottom of the water body. 2. A state of channel disequilibrium, whereby the supply of sediment exceeds the transport capacity of the stream, resulting in deposition and storage of sediment in the active channel.

Allocation - See water allocation.

Alluvial stream - A stream with a bed and banks of unconsolidated sedimentary material subject to erosion, transportation, and deposition by the river.

Anadromous - Fish that mature in seawater but migrate to fresh water to spawn.

Annual flow - The total volume of water passing a given point in one year. Usually expressed as a volume (such as acre-feet) but may be expressed as an equivalent constant discharge over the year, such as cubic feet per second.

Appropriation - A specified amount of water set aside by Congress, other legislative body or state or provincial water regulatory authority to be used for a specified purpose at a specified place, if available.

Aquatic habitat - A specific type of area and its associated environmental (i.e., biological,

chemical, or physical) characteristics used by an aquatic organism, population, or community.

Aquatic life - All organisms living in or on the water. This includes plants from the smallest phyroplankton through algae, pheriton, and emergent vegetation as well as animal life from zooplankton through benthic invertebrates, fishes, and amphibians, reptiles, birds, and mammals.

Aquifer - An underground formation that contains sufficient saturated permeable material to yield significant quantities of water to wells and springs.

Armoring - 1. The formation of an erosion-resistant layer of relatively large particles on the surface of a streambed or stream bank that results from removal of finer particles by erosion, and which resists degradation by water currents. 2. The application of materials to reduce erosion. 3. The process of continually winnowing away smaller substrate materials and leaving a veneer of larger ones.

Average daily flow – The long-term average annual flow divided by the number of days in the year usually expressed as an equivalent constant discharge such as cubic feet per second. In some settings, the value can be used to represent only the portion of the daily flow values in a defined period such as those that occur within a calendar month.

Average velocity – In a channel, it is equal to the discharge divided by the cross-sectional area of the cross section. For any point along the cross section, a measurement of 60% of the depth, measured from the surface, closely approximates the average velocity for the water column. In water greater than 76 cm (2.5 ft) deep, the average of measurements made at 20% and 80% of the depth approximates the mean column velocity.

213

Backwater - 1. A pool surface created in an upstream direction that results from damming a vertical or horizontal channel that impedes the free flow of water. 2. In general, an off-shoot from the main channel with little flow and where the water surface elevation is maintained by conditions in the main channel acting on the downstream end of the backwater.

Bankfull discharge - The discharge corresponding to the stage at which the floodplain begins to be inundated, usually provided by natural peak flow every 1-2 years. The maximum discharge that the channel can convey without overflowing onto the floodplain. Calculating the bankfull discharge is one deterministic method of calculating the channel forming discharge.

Base flow - Streamflow contributed solely from shallow groundwater in the absence of significant precipitation, runoff events or supplemental release from storage above the natural flow.

Baseline - The conditions occurring during the reference timeframe, usually referring to water supply habitat values, or population status. Baseline is often some actual recent historical period but may also represent the same climatological-meteorological conditions but with present water development activities on line; the same climatological-meteorological conditions but with both current and proposed future development on line; or virgin or pre-development conditions. The definition of baseline is dependent on the objectives of the study. Quite often, two or more baseline conditions may be necessary to evaluate a specific project.

Bedload - Material moving on or near the streambed and frequently in contact with it.

Bedload discharge - The quantity of bedload passing a transect in a unit of time.

Bed material - Mixture of substances composing the stream's bed.

Beneficial use - A cardinal principle of the prior appropriation doctrine. It has two components: the nature or purpose of the use and the efficient or non-wasteful use of water. State constitutions, statutes, or case law may define uses of water that are beneficial. Those uses may be different in each state, and the definition of what uses are beneficial may change over time.

Benthic - Associated with the bottom of a body of water.

Biological diversity - The variety and variability among living organisms and the ecological complexes in which they occur. Diversity can be defined as the number of different items and their relative frequency. For biological diversity, these items are organized at many levels, ranging from complete ecosystems to the chemical structures that are the molecular basis of heredity. Thus, the term encompasses different ecosystems, species, genes, and their relative abundance.

Biotic - Of or pertaining to the living components of an ecosystem.

Braided - Pattern of two or more interconnected channels typical of alluvial streams.

Bypass - 1. A channel or conduit in or near a dam that provides a route for fish to move through or around the dam without going into the turbines.

2. That stream reach below a dam that is essentially skirted by the flow used to generate electricity.

CFS - Cubic feet per second (measure of streamflow or discharge).

Channel - That cross section containing the stream that is distinct from the surrounding area due to breaks in the general slope of the land, lack of terrestrial vegetation, and changes in the composition of the substrate materials.

Channel-forming flow - A theoretical discharge that, if maintained indefinitely, would produce the same channel geometry as the natural long-term hydrograph. Generally applicable only to stable, alluvial streams that have the ability to change their shape and are neither aggrading nor degrading. Often referred to as the bankfull flow, dominant flow, effective flow, or a flow of a specified recurrence interval, typically between the mean annual and 5-year peak flow.

Channelization - The mechanical alteration of a natural stream by dredging, straightening, lining, or other means of accelerating the flow of water.

Channel-maintenance flow – 1. A range of flows making up a portion of the rising and falling limbs of the annual hydrograph that is capable of keeping the stream in a condition of sediment equilibrium over time (years) by moving all sizes and amounts of bedload sediment, scouring vegetation, and maintaining riparian vegetation. The range of flows required begins at a flow that mobilizes hydraulically limited gravels and extends up to the instantaneous 25-year flow. 2. A range of flows that transports bedload sediment through the channel network, prevents constriction of the channel by sediment and vegetation, and sustains channel bank and floodplain vegetation.

CMS - Cubic meters per second (measure of streamflow or discharge). Also, expressed as m^3/s.

Colluvial - Pertaining to material or processes associated with transportation and/or deposition by mass movement (direct gravitational action) and local, unconcentrated runoff on side slopes and/or at the base of slopes.

Conjunctive management - The coordinated use of surface water and groundwater, which derives from the recognized interconnection between both resources.

Connectivity - Maintenance of lateral, longitudinal, and vertical pathways for biological, hydrological, and physical processes.

Consumptive use - Represents the difference between the amount of water diverted and the amount of the return flow to the system (e.g., surface stream or underground basin). It is that amount by which the total resource is depleted.

Cover - Structural features (e.g., boulders, log jams) or hydraulic characteristics (e.g., turbulence, depth) that provide shelter from currents, energetically efficient feeding stations, and/or visual isolation from competitors or predators.

Cross section - A plane across a stream channel perpendicular to the direction of water flow.

Cross-sectional area - The area of the stream's vertical cross section, perpendicular to flow.

Degradation - 1. A decline in the viability of ecosystem functions and processes.
2. Geologic process by which streambeds and floodplains are lowered in elevation by the removal of material (also see Down cutting).

Density - Number of individuals per unit area.

Deposition - The settlement or accumulation of material out of the water column and onto the streambed.

Detritus - Nondissolved organic debris such as leaves and twigs.

Dewatered - A length of stream without water (due to human removal).

Diadromous - Fishes that move between marine and fresh waters for purposes of spawning (i.e., anadromous and catadromous).

Discharge -The rate of streamflow or the volume of water flowing at a location within a specified time interval. Usually expressed as cubic meters per second (cms) or cubic feet per second (cfs).

Diversion - A withdrawal from a body of water by means of a ditch, dam, pump or other manmade contrivance.

Diversity - That attribute of a biotic (or abiotic) system describing the richness of plant or animal species or complexity of habitat.

Domestic use - Water used for normal household purposes, such as drinking, food preparation, bathing, washing clothes and dishes, flushing toilets, and watering lawns and gardens. Also called residential water use or domestic water use. The water may be obtained from a public supply or may be self-supplied.

Dominant discharge – See channel forming discharge

Down cutting (degradation) - Geologic process by which streambeds and floodplains are lowered in elevation by the removal of bed material.

Drainage area -The total land area draining to any point in a stream. Also called catchment area, watershed, and basin.

Drought - A prolonged period of less-than-average water availability.

Dry year - A time period with a given probability of representing dry conditions; for example, a given year may be as dry or drier than 80% of all other similar periods.

Dynamic equilibrium - A quasi steady-state condition attained in an alluvial channel, whereby sediment supplies are just balanced by sediment transport capacity, resulting in no net change in average streambed elevation over time.

Ecological integrity -The ability to support and maintain a balanced, integrated, adaptive community of organisms having a species composition, diversity, and functional organization comparable to that of the natural habitat of the region.

Ecosystem - Any complex of living organisms interacting with nonliving chemical and physical components that form and function as a natural environmental unit.

Effective discharge - The flow that transports the largest fraction of the average annual bed material load. Calculating the effective discharge is one deterministic method of calculating the channel forming discharge.

Effective habitat - 1. That portion of available physical habitat occupied by a life stage due to mortality (or other constraint) of previous life stages. Effective habitat analysis implies following cohorts of habitat use through time, as a population-limiting habitat event may not manifest itself until some later date. 2. Habitat effectively available due to hydropeaking or other flow fluctuations reducing the habitat for a single life stage.

Electivity - A mathematical index intended to demonstrate the disproportionate use of a resource with respect to its availability.

Embeddedness - The degree that larger particles (boulders, rubble, or gravel) are surrounded or covered by fine sediment. Usually measured in classes according to percent of coverage.

Energy slope - The difference in total energy (potential plus kinetic) of a fluid between two points divided by the linear distance between the two points.

Estuary - The zone between the fresh water of a coastal stream and the seawater of an ocean influenced by the tide.

Evapotranspiration - The combined loss of water from open-surface evaporation and the transpiration of water from leaf and stem tissues of growing vegetation.

Exceedence - That probability of an event exceeding others in a similar class. Note that this may be "equal or exceed" or "exceed only." Probabilities may also be expressed as nonexceedence; that is, the probability of being "less than or equal" or just "less than."

Existing fishery – A dynamic process in which fish population levels and community structure fluctuate on an intra-and interannual basis within limits constrained by habitat, climate, human use, and other factors. The fishery that exists today is formed and maintained by the present habitat, climate, land use conditions, and human behavior patterns.

Exotic - Introduced species not native to a given area.

Feeding station - 1. A microhabitat type that provides conditions for obtaining large amounts of food with minimal expenditure of energy. 2. Microhabitat that simultaneously maximizes feeding efficiency and minimizes predation risk.

Fiduciary - To act in relation to a matter in the interests of another, in a manner that is defined or understood by both parties, and is entrusted with a power to affect such interests. The other person relies on or is otherwise dependent on this undertaking, and, as a result, is vulnerable to the exercise of such power; the first person knows, or should know, of such reliance and vulnerability. The nature and circumstances giving rise to the undertaking are such that loyalty and good faith are intrinsic elements of the consequent duty.

Fill - The localized deposition of material that is eroded and transported from other areas, resulting in a change in bed elevation. This is the opposite of scour.

Fishery - 1. The interaction of aquatic organisms and aquatic environments and their human users to produce sustained benefits for people; (2) a dynamic product of physical, biological, and chemical processes. Each component (process) is important, affects the other, and presents opportunities for impacting or enhancing the nature or character of fisheries resources. Fish populations are merely one attribute of a fishery.

Flood - Any flow that exceeds the bankfull capacity of a stream or channel and flows out on the floodplain.

Floodplain - 1. The area along waterways that is subject to periodic inundation by out-of-bank flows. 2. The area adjoining a water body that becomes inundated during periods of over-bank flooding and that is given rigorous legal definition in regulatory programs. 3. Land beyond a stream channel that forms the perimeter for the maximum probability flood. 4. A relatively flat strip of land bordering a stream that is formed by sediment deposition. 5. A deposit of alluvium that covers a valley flat from lateral erosion of meandering streams and rivers.

Flow - 1. The movement of a stream of water or other mobile substance from place to place. 2. Discharge. 3. Total quantity carried by a stream.

Flow regime - The distribution of annual surface runoff from a watershed over time such as hours, days, or months (see also Hydrologic regime).

Flushing flow - A stream discharge with sufficient power to remove silt and sand from a gravel/cobble substrate but not enough power to remove gravels.

Fluvial - Pertaining to streams or produced by river action.

Frazil ice - Fine spicules of ice formed in water (i.e., slush) that are the first stage of ice formation. They may accumulate to form cap ice or anchor ice in settings that have high turbulence.

Free-flowing - A stream or stream reach that flows unconfined and naturally without impoundment, diversion, straightening, rip-rapping, or other modification of the waterway.

Gradient -The rate of change of any characteristic, expressed per unit of length. (see Slope.) May also apply to longitudinal succession of biological communities.

Groundwater - In general, all subsurface water that is distinct from surface water; specifically, that part which is in the saturated zone of a defined aquifer. Sometimes called underflow.

Habitat -The physical, chemical, and biological surroundings in which an organism or population (living and nonliving) lives; includes life requirements such as food and shelter (see Physical habitat).

Habitat bottleneck - The cumulative constraint on species abundance caused solely by repeated reductions in habitat capacity through time due to microhabitat or macrohabitat limitations.

Habitat guild - Groups of species that share common characteristics of microhabitat use and selection at various stages in their life histories.

Habitat suitability curves - Collectively refers to category one to four suitability index (SI) curves.

Head cutting - Upstream migration or deepening of a stream channel that results from erosion of the stream channel due to high water velocities.

Headwater - The source for a stream in the upper tributaries of a drainage basin.

Hydraulic control - A horizontal or vertical constriction in the channel, such as the crest of a riffle, which creates a backwater effect.

Hydrograph - A graph showing the variation in discharge over time.

Hydrologic regime -The distribution over time of water in a watershed, among precipitation, evaporation, soil moisture, groundwater storage, surface storage, and runoff.

Hydropeaking - The practice of abruptly alternating between a low base and a high peak flow, for electrical power generation during periods of high demand. Compare with hydropulsing in which flows may also range from low to high, but are gradually varied over a longer period.

Hyporheic zone - 1. The layer of stream channel substrate that extends as deep and wide as interstitial flow. 2. The interface between the stream bed and shallow groundwater.

IFIM - The Instream Flow Incremental Methodology.

Impervious - A term applied to a material through which water cannot pass or passes with great difficulty; impermeable.

Incremental method - The process of developing an instream flow policy that incorporates multiple or variable rules to establish-- through negotiation-- flow-window requirements or guidelines to meet the needs of an aquatic ecosystem, given water supply or other constraints. It usually implies the determination of a habitat-discharge relation for comparing streamflow alternatives through time (see Standard setting).

Index of biotic integrity - A numerical gauge of the biological health of stream fish communities based on various attributes of species richness, species composition, trophic relations, and fish abundance and condition.

Indigenous - A fish or other aquatic organism native to a particular water body, basin, or region.

Instantaneous flow - 1. Discharge that is measured at any instance in time. 2. Flow that is measured instantaneously and not averaged over longer time such as day or month. (Instream flow references are generally related in cubic feet per second (cfs) but regardless of unit of measure are not accomplished through averaging discharge volume over time.)

Instream cover - Any material located within the water column of a stream that provides protection from predators or competitors, or mitigates the imports of other stream conditions for fish wildlife and aquatic animals.

Instream flow – Any quantity of water flowing in a natural stream channel at any time of year. The quantity may or may not be adequate to sustain natural ecological processes and may or may not be protected or administered under a permit, water right, or other legally recognized means.

Instream flow requirement - 1. That amount of water flowing through a natural stream course that is needed to sustain, rehabilitate, or restore the ecological functions of a stream in terms of hydrology, geomorphology, biology, water quality, and connectivity at a particular level.

2. That amount of water flowing through a natural stream course needed to sustain instream values at an acceptable level based on appropriate study. Instream values and uses include protection of fish and wildlife habitat, migration, and propagation; outdoor recreation activities; navigation; hydropower generation; waste assimilation (water quality); and ecosystem maintenance, which includes recruitment of fresh water to the estuaries, riparian vegetation, floodplain wetlands, and maintenance of channel geomorphology. Water requirements sufficient to maintain all of these uses at an acceptable level are the instream flow requirements.

Instream flow reservation - A specified streamflow or water level below which further diversion is not allowed. Instream flow reservations are typically recognized and administered under the authority of some type of legal means such as a water right, permit, or operating agreement.

Instream flow rights - A legal property right to maintain or protect a designated streamflow for in-channel purposes. Such rights are limited to a specified amount of water within its natural course.

Instream use - Any use of water that does not require diversion or withdrawal from the natural watercourse, including in-place uses such as navigation and recreation.

Invertebrate - All animals without a vertebral column; for example, aquatic insects.

Large woody debris - Any large piece of woody material that intrudes into the stream channel; often defined as having a diameter greater than 10cm and a length greater than 1 m. Synonyms: Large organic debris, woody debris, log.

Larva - An immature form that must pass through one or more metamorphic changes before becoming an adult.

Lentic - Standing water such as lakes, reservoirs, ponds, and marshes.

Life stage - An arbitrary age classification of an organism into categories related to body morphology and reproductive potential, such as spawning, egg incubation, larva or fry, juvenile, and adult.

Longitudinal succession - Gradation in the composition of communities along a spatial gradient.

Macrohabitat - Abiotic habitat conditions in a segment of river controlling longitudinal distribution of aquatic organisms, usually describing channel morphology, flow, or chemical properties or characteristics with respect to suitability for use by organisms.

Macroinvertebrate - An invertebrate animal without a backbone that can be seen without magnification.

Main stem - The main channel of a river, as opposed to tributary streams and smaller rivers that feed into it.

Mean column velocity - The average velocity of the water measured on an imaginary vertical line at any point in a stream. A measurement of 60% of the depth, measured from the surface, closely approximates the average velocity for the water column. In water greater than 76 cm (2.5 ft) in depth, the average of measurements made at 20% and 80% of the depth approximates the mean column velocity.

Meander -The winding of a stream channel.

Mean monthly flow – The average flow for one month that is computed from several years' worth of data for that month, which is usually expressed as cfs or cms.

Mesohabitat - A discrete area of stream exhibiting relatively similar characteristics of depth, velocity, slope, substrate, and cover, and variances thereof (e.g., pools with maximum depth <5 ft, high gradient riffles, side channel backwaters).

Microhabitat - Small localized areas within a broader habitat type used by organisms for specific purposes or events, typically described by a combination of depth, velocity, substrate, or cover.

Minimum flow – 1. Traditionally thought of as the lowest streamflow required to protect some specified aquatic function as established by agreement, rule, or permit. In the absence of higher flows at other times of year, aquatic habitat may change, which leads to significant changes in aquatic community structure, which can lead to a subsequent conclusion that a lower minimum flow will maintain aquatic function. 2. The lowest discharge recorded over a specified period of time.

Mitigation - An action taken to avoid, alleviate, or compensate for potentially adverse effects to aquatic habitat that have been modified through human actions.

Natural flow - The flow regime of a stream as it would occur under completely unregulated conditions; that is, not subjected to regulation by reservoirs, diversions, or other human works. Also referred to as the virgin flow.

Natural hydrograph - A graph showing the variation in discharge (or river stage) that would exist in the absence of any human alteration, over a specific time period.

Naturalized flow - Measured flows that are adjusted for upstream water licenses or uses to approximate the flows that would occur in the absence of regulation and extraction.

Nose velocity - The velocity at the approximate point vertically in the channel where a fish is located.

One-dimensional (1-d) model - Models for rivers that solve mass continuity and total energy loss between cross sections. They do not explicitly deal with velocity distribution across cross sections. Both velocity and mass flux are calculated as a single value for each cross section. Velocity distribution is handled empirically and conditions between cross sections are assumed to be linearly interpolated. Models exist that can handle either steady state or dynamic channel characteristics.

Open channel hydraulics - The analysis of water flow and associated materials in an open channel with a free water surface, as opposed to a tunnel or pipeline.

Operating rule - Criteria by which managers of water projects decide when and how much water to store, release, or divert.

Overhead cover - Material (organic or inorganic, including surface ice) that provides protection to fish, wildlife, or other aquatic animals from above.

Period of record - The length of time for which data for an environmental variable have been collected on a regular and continuous basis.

PHABSIM - (pronounced P-HAB-SIM) The Physical HABitat SIMulation system; a set of software and methods that allows the computation of a relation between streamflow and physical habitat for various life stages of an aquatic organism or a recreational activity.

Phenology - The periodic natural patterns of maturation, timing, or distribution in the life history of an organism.

Physical habitat -Those abiotic factors such as depth, velocity, substrate, cover, tempera-ture, water quality that make up some of an organism's living space.

Pool - Part of a stream with reduced velocity, often with water deeper than the surrounding areas, which is usable by fish for resting and cover.

Preference curves - See suitability curves.

Prior Appropriation Doctrine - The system of water law dominant in the western United States under which (a) the right to water was acquired by diverting water and applying it to a beneficial use; (b) a right to water acquired earlier in time is superior to a similar right acquired later in time; (c) the right is limited to the amount that is beneficially used; and (d) the water must be used or the right is lost.

Priority - Under appropriative water law systems, priority of use refers to the date a water right is acquired, with senior rights prevailing over junior rights. Priority is only important when the quantity of available water is insufficient to meet the needs of all those having a right to use water. Under the prior appropriation system, shortages are not shared. Some western state statutes contain priority or preference categories of water use under which higher priority uses (such as domestic) have first right to water in times of shortage, regardless of priority date.

Public interest - An interest or benefit accruing to society, in general, rather than to individuals or groups of individuals within the society. Generally an economic concept; for example, actions that generate a net economic gain are in the public interest.

Public Trust Doctrine - A common law doctrine under which the state holds its navigable waters and underlying beds in trust for the public and is required or authorized to protect the public interest in such waters. All water rights issued by the state are subject to the overriding interest of the public and the exercise of the public trust by state administrative agencies.

Public trust resources - Natural resources, including but not limited to fish and wildlife and aquatic habitats, which are managed by the states and provinces as a trust for the common benefit of its citizens.

Q7$_{10}$ - The lowest continuous 7-day flow with a 10-year recurrence interval. Sometimes called 7Q$_{10}$.

Ramping rate -The rate of change in discharge from base flow to generation flow below a peaking hydroelectric facility.

Rapids - A part of a stream with considerable turbulence where the current is moving with much greater velocity than usual and where the water surface is broken by obstructions, but without a sufficient break in slope to form a cascade.

Reach - A comparatively short length of a stream, channel, or shore. One or more reaches compose a segment. The actual length is defined by the purpose of the study but is usually no greater than 5-7 times the channel width.

Reasonable use - A rule with regard to percolating or riparian water restricting the landowner to a reasonable use of his own rights and property in view of and qualified by the similar rights of others, and the condition that such use not injure others in the enjoyment of their rights.

Recharge - Process by which water is added to the zone of saturation, as recharge of an aquifer.

Recurrence interval - The average time interval between events equaling or exceeding a given magnitude in a time series.

Regime - The general pattern (magnitude and frequency) of flow or temperature events through time at a particular location (such as snowmelt regime, rainfall regime).

Regulated flow – Artificial modification of the natural flow of a stream by reservoirs, diversions, or other works of humans to achieve a specified purpose or objective.

Rehabilitate - To bring about changes in management that allow the physical and biological processes of a stream, river, or lake to function in a more natural way in order to achieve or more closely approximate a condition of dynamic equilibrium or balance. Rehabilitation does not necessarily mean restoring a riverine resource to predevelopment conditions.

Reserved water rights - This class of water rights is a judicial creation derived from Winters v. United States (207 U.S. 564, 1907) and affirmed by several subsequent federal case laws, which collectively hold that when the federal government withdraws land from general use and reserves it for a specific purpose, the federal government by implication reserves the minimum amount of water unappropriated at the time the land was withdrawn or reserved to accomplish the primary purpose of the reservation. Federal reserved water rights may be claimed when Congress has by statute withdrawn lands from the public domain for a particular federal purpose or the President has withdrawn lands from the public domain for a particular federal purpose pursuant to congressional authorization.

Restoration – To return a stream, river, or lake to its natural, predevelopment form and function. Restoration typically eliminates the human influences that degraded or destroyed riverine processes and characteristics.

Riffle - A relatively shallow reach of stream in which the water flows swiftly and the water surface is broken into waves by obstructions that are completely or partially submerged.

Riparian - Pertaining to anything connected with or adjacent to the bank of a stream or other body of water.

Riparian Doctrine -The system of law dominant in Great Britain and the eastern United States (also in some Midwestern and southern states, and the state of California, which also uses the appropriation doctrine), in which owners of lands along the banks of a stream or water body have the right to reasonable use of the waters and a correlative right protecting against unreasonable use by others that substantially diminishes the quantity or quality of water. The right is appurtenant to the land and does not depend on prior use. It applies to all bodies of water (streams, lakes, ponds, and marshes). In almost all jurisdictions, the doctrine has been modified to fit local conditions. The courts generally resolve disputes over what constitutes reasonable use. Fundamental principles of the doctrine state that (a) Ownership of land along a body of water (riparian ownership) is essential to the existence of a right to that water; and (b) Each riparian owner has an equal right to make use of the water in its natural state (no storage), no matter when use of the water was initiated; thus, shortages are shared.

Riparian right - The right—as to fishing or the use of water—of one who owns land situated along the bank of a stream or other body of water.

Riparian vegetation - Vegetation that is dependent upon an excess of moisture during a portion of the growing season on a site that is perceptively more moist than the surrounding area.

Riparian zone - The transitional zone or area between a body of water and the adjacent upland identified by soil characteristics and distinctive vegetation that requires an excess of water. It includes wetlands and those portions of floodplains that support riparian vegetation.

River - A large stream that serves as the natural drainage channel for a relatively large catchment or drainage basin.

River continuum concept - A framework for integrating predictable and observable biological features of lotic systems based on consideration of the gradient of physical factors formed by the drainage network.

Run - A portion of a stream with low surface turbulence that approximates uniform flow, and in which the slope of the water surface is roughly parallel to the overall gradient of a stream reach.

Scour - The localized removal of material from the streambed by flowing water. This is the opposite of fill.

Sediment - Solid material, both mineral and organic, that is in suspension in the current or deposited on the streambed.

Sediment load - A general term that refers to material in suspension and/or in transport. It is not synonymous with either discharge or concentration. (see Bedload).

Segment - Terminology from IFIM meaning: 1. A relatively long (e.g., hundreds of channel widths) section of a river, exhibiting relatively homogeneous conditions of hydrology, channel geomorphology, and pattern. 2.The fundamental accounting unit for total habitat.

Side channel - Lateral channel with an axis of flow roughly parallel to the main stem, which is fed by water from the main stem; a braid of a river with flow appreciably lower than the main channel. Side channel habitat may exist either in well-defined secondary (overflow) channels, or in poorly-defined watercourses flowing through partially submerged gravel bars and islands along the margins of the main stem.

Sinuosity - The ratio of channel length between two points on a channel to the straight-line distance between the same two points.

Slope - The inclination or gradient from the horizontal of a line or surface. The degree of inclination can be expressed as a ratio, such as 1:25, indicating one unit rise in 25 units of horizontal distance or as 0.04 height per length. Often expressed as a percentage and sometimes also expressed as feet (or inches) per mile.

Spatial variability - Pertaining to or involving a species positioning in space, occurrence in space, and variability in occurrence in space (vertically, horizontally, and laterally).

Stage - The distance of the water surface in a river above a known datum.

Standard setting - 1. A streamflow policy or technique that uses a single, fixed rule to establish minimum flow requirements. 2. The process of determining minimum flow requirements for a water project or water right. The recommended flow may, to varying degrees, consider generic ecosystem needs.

Standing crop - Quantity of living organisms present in the environment at a given time.

Stewardship - Responsible management of something entrusted to one's care. In this document, it pertains specifically to the states' and provinces' responsibility to wisely manage natural resources, including instream flow, fish and wildlife populations, riparian corridors, and the like, to ensure that the societal benefits of these natural resources are sustained and protected for future generations.

Stochastic - Allowing for randomness or variability in processes. Literally, making a best guess.

Storage - Water artificially impounded in surface or underground reservoirs for future use. Water naturally detained in a drainage basin, such as ground- water, channel storage, and depression storage.

Stream - A natural watercourse of any size containing flowing water, at least part of the year, supporting a community of plants and animals within the stream channel and the riparian vegetative zone.

Streambed - The bottom of the stream channel; may be wet or dry.

Stream classification - Various systems of grouping or identifying streams possessing similar features according to hydrogeomorphic structure (e.g., gradient), water source (e.g., spring creek), associated biota (e.g., fish species), or other characteristics.

Stream competency -The maximum size particle that a stream can carry, dependent upon water velocity and gradient.

Stream corridor - A perennial, intermittent, or ephemeral stream and adjacent vegetative fringe. The corridor is the area occupied during high water and the land immediately adjacent, including riparian vegetation that shades the stream, provides input of organic debris, and protects banks from excessive erosion.

Substrate - The material on the bottom of the stream channel, such as rocks or vegetation.

Suitability - A generic term used in IFIM to indicate the relative quality of a range of environmental conditions for a target species.

Suspended sediment - Particles having such a density or grain size as to permit suspension in the moving water column for long distances downstream. Much of this material settles out when water movement slows or ceases.

Sustainability - A state in which all humans, present and future, can live at a prescribed level within the limits of what nature can provide to our species and withstand from it in continuity and at no undue harm to other forms of life.

Temporal variability - Pertaining to, or involving the nature of time, occurrence in time, and variability in occurrence over some increment in time (e.g., diurnally, daily, monthly, annually).

Terrace - An alluvial feature of streams that is formed by down-cutting and subsequent abandonment of a former floodplain, with the development of a new floodplain within the walls of the escarpment.

Thalweg - A longitudinal profile of the lowest elevations of a sequential series of cross sections.

Three-dimensional model (3-d) - Models for rivers that solve mass continuity and momentum flux between elements defined by mesh nodes. The entire area of river is represented by the mesh so the length of interpolation is smaller. Hydrodynamic conditions are calculated at the nodes and interpolated along mesh edges. Solution of the momentum equations allows explicit description of velocity vectors at each node. As the mesh has nodes arranged vertically as well as horizontally, simulated velocities vary with depth so secondary currents can be described. Model formulations are typically fully dynamic, but are often solved to steady state equilibrium.

Time-series analysis - Analysis of the pattern (frequency, duration, magnitude, and time) of time-varying events. These events may be discharge, habitat areas, stream temperature, population factors, economic indicators, power generation, and so forth.

Time step - The interval over which elements in a time series are averaged.

Transferability - 1. Applicability of a model (e.g., habitat suitability criteria) to settings or conditions that differ from the setting or conditions under which the model was developed. 2. Applicability of data obtained from a remote source (e.g., a meteorological station) for use at a location having different environmental attributes.

Tributary - A stream feeding, joining, or flowing into a larger stream (at any point along its course or into a lake). Synonyms: feeder stream, side stream.

Turbidity - A measure of the extent to which light passing through water is reduced due to suspended materials.

Turbulent flow - Type of flow in which any particle of water may move in any direction with respect to any other particle. Flow in which the velocity at any point varies erratically.

Two-dimensional model (2-d) - Models for rivers that solve mass continuity and momentum flux between elements defined by mesh nodes. The entire area of river is represented by the mesh so the length of interpolation is smaller. Hydrodynamic conditions are calculated at the nodes and interpolated along mesh edges. Solution of the momentum equations allows explicit description of velocity vectors at each node. Simulated velocities are depth-averaged. Model formulations are typically fully dynamic, but are often solved to steady state equilibrium.

Velocity - The distance traveled by water in a stream channel divided by the time required to travel that distance.

Vertical - A location along a transect across a river where microhabitat-related data are collected.

Water allocation - Determining the quantity of water from a given source that can or should be ascribed to various instream or out-of-stream uses. May be referred to as water reservation in some settings.

Water body - Any natural or artificial pond, lake, stream, river, estuary, or ocean that contains permanent, semi-permanent, or intermittent standing or flowing water.

Water budget - 1.The balance of all water moving in and out of a specified area in a specified period. 2. An administratively segregated volume of water reserved for a specific use.

Water management - Application of practices to obtain added benefits from precipitation, water, or water flow in any of a number of areas, such as irrigation, drainage, wildlife and recreation, water supply, watershed management, and water storage in soil for crop production. Includes irrigation water management and watershed management.

Water quality standard - 1. A plan for water quality management specifying the use of the water (e.g., recreation, fish and wildlife, propagation, drinking water, industrial, or agriculture). 2. Criteria to measure and protect these uses; implementation and enforcement plans. 3. Antidegration statement to protect existing water quality.

Water resources -The supply of groundwater and surface water in a given area.

Water right - A legally protected right to use surface or groundwater for a specified purpose (such as crop irrigation or water supply), in a given manner (such as diversion or storage), and usually within limits of a given period of time (such as June through August). While such rights may include the use of a body of water for navigation, fishing, hunting, and other recreational purposes, the term is usually applied to the right to divert or store water for some out-of-stream purpose or use.

Watershed - See drainage area.

Weighted usable area (WUA) -The wetted area of a stream weighted by its suitability for use by aquatic organisms or recreational activity. Units: square feet or square meters, usually per specified length of stream.

Wetted perimeter - The length of the wetted contact between a stream of flowing water and the stream bottom in a plane at right angles to the direction of flow.

Wet year - A water year characterized by above average discharge. Exact measure of deviation from some average, or median value depends on the decision setting.

Withdrawal - Water taken from a surface or groundwater source for off-stream use.

References

Aadland, L. P. 1993. Stream habitat types: Their fish assemblages and relationship to flow. North American Journal of Fisheries Management 13:790-806.

Aadland, L. P., C. M. Cook, M. T. Negus, H. G. Drewes, and C. S. Anderson. 1991. Microhabitat preferences of selected stream fishes and a community-oriented approach to instream flow assessments. Investigational Report No. 406. St. Paul: Department of Natural Resources, Fisheries Section.

Adams, J. B., G. C. Bate, T. D. Harrison, P. Huizinga, and others. 2002. A method to assess the freshwater inflow requirements of estuaries and application to the Mtata Estuary, South Africa. Estuaries 25 (6B):1382-1393

Adams, J. G., and M. W. Street. 1969. Notes on the spawning and embryological development of blue-back herring (Alosa aestivalis Mitchell) in the Altamaha River, Georgia. Contribution Series No. 16. Brunswick: Georgia Department of Natural Resources, Marine Development, Coastal Fisheries Division, and Game and Fish Commission.

Aiken, J. D. 1990. First Nebraska instream appropriation granted. Rivers 1(3):231-235.

Alaska Power Authority. 1988a. Susitna hydroelectric project document index: Alphabetical listing by author. APA Document No. 3572. Anchorage: Alaska Power Authority. 257 pp.

Alaska Power Authority. 1988b. Susitna hydroelectric project document index: Listing sorted by number. APA Document No. 3573. Anchorage: Alaska Power Authority. 257 pp.

American Public Health Association (APHA). 1995. Standard Methods for the Examination of Water and Wastewater. 19th edition. Washington, DC: American Public Health Association, American Water Works Association, and Water Environment Federation. 1100 pp.

American Society of Civil Engineers (ASCE). 1997. Guidelines for retirement of dams and hydroelectric facilities. Task Committee on Guidelines for Retirement of Dams and Hydroelectric Facilities of the Hydropower Committee of the Energy Division of the ASCE. New York.

Amoros, C., A. L. Roux, J. L. Reygrobellet, J. P. Bravard, and G. Pautou. 1987. A method for applied ecological studies of fluvial hydrosystems. Regulated Rivers: Research and Management 1:17-38.

Anderson, R. J., and D. K. MacKay. 1973. Preliminary study of the seasonal distribution of flow in the Mackenzie Delta, Northwest Territories. Pages 71-110 in Hydrologic Aspects of Northern Pipeline Development. Task Force on Northern Oil Development. Quebec: Department of the Environment, Water Resources Branch, Environmental Social Program (Report No. 73-3).

Anderson, R. M., and R. B. Nehring. 1985. Impacts of stream discharge on trout rearing and recruitment in the South Platte River, Colorado. Pages 59-64 in F. W. Olson, R. G. White, and R. H. Hamre, editors. Proceedings of the Symposium on Small Hydropower and Fisheries. Bethesda, MD: American Fisheries Society.

Andrews, E. D. 1980. Effective and bankfull discharges of streams in the Yampa River basin, Colorado and Wyoming. Journal of Hydrology 46:311-330.

Angermeier, P. L., and J. R. Karr. 1983. Fish communities along environmental gradients in a system of tropical streams. Environmental Biology of Fishes (9):117-135.

Annear, T. C., and A. L. Condor. 1984. Relative bias of several fisheries instream flow methods. North American Journal of Fisheries Management 4:531-539.

Annear, T. C., W. Hubert, D. Simpkins, and L. Hebdon. 2002. Behavioural and physiological response of trout to winter habitat in tailwaters in Wyoming, USA. Hydrologic Processes 16:915-922.

Annear, T. C., and J. M. Neuhold. 1983. Characterization of Yampa and Green River ecosystems: a systems approach to aquatic resource management. Pages 181-192 in V. D. Adams, and V. A. Lamarra, editors. Aquatic Resources Management of the Colorado River Ecosystem. Ann Arbor, MI: Ann Arbor Science.

Anonymous. 1974. R2-Cross Program: A sag-tape method of channel cross-section measurements for use with minimum instream flow determination. Denver: U.S. Forest Service, Region 2.

Arctic Environmental Information and Data Center. 1981. An assessment of environmental effects of construction and operation of the proposed Terror Lake hydroelectric facility, Kodiak Island, Alaska. Final report to Kodiak Electric Association. Prepared by Arctic Environmental Information and Data Center, University of Alaska.

Arden, R. S., and T. E. Wigle. 1972. Dynamics of ice formation in the upper Niagara River. Pages 1296-1313 in Proceedings of the International Symposium on the Role of Snow and Ice in Hydrology. Volume 2. WMO-4. Symposium on Measurement and forecasting specific to river and lake ice, UNESCO/WMO/IAHS, Banff, Canada.

Arend, K. K. 1999. Classification of streams and reaches. Pages 57-74 in M. B. Bain, and N. J. Stevenson, editors. Aquatic Habitat Assessment: Common Methods. Bethesda, MD: American Fisheries Society.

Armour, C. L. 1991. Guidance for evaluating and recommending temperature regimes to protect fish. Instream Flow Information Paper No. 28. Fort Collins, CO: U.S. Fish and Wildlife Service, National Ecology Research Center (Biological Report 90 [22]).

Armour, C. L., and J. G. Taylor. 1991. Evaluation of the Instream Flow Incremental Methodology by the U. S. Fish and Wildlife Service field users. Fisheries 16(5):36-43.

Aspen Institute. 2002. Dam Removal: A New Option for a New Century. Queenstown, MD: The Aspen Institute.

Auble, G. T., J. M. Friedman, and M. L. Scott. 1994. Relating riparian vegetation to present and future streamflows. Ecological Applications 4(3):544-554.

Ausness, R. 1983. Water rights legislation in the east: A program for reform. William and Mary Law Review 24: 547-590.

Australian Water Association. 2001. Performance monitoring report 1999-2000. Sydney: Australian non-major Urban Water Utilities, Australian Water Association (ISSN 1444-0172).

Bachman, R. A. 1984. Foraging behavior of free-ranging wild and hatchery brown trout in a stream. Transactions of American Fisheries Society 113:1-32.

Bain, M. B., J. T. Finn, and H. E. Booke. 1988. Streamflow regulation and fish community structure. Ecology 69:382-392.

Bain, M. B., and J. G. Knight. 1996. Classifying stream habitat using fish community analyses. Pages B107-B117 in M. Leclerc, H. Capra, S. Valentin, A. Boudreault, and Y. Cote, editors. Ecohydraulics 2000. Proceedings of the Second International Symposium on Habitat Hydraulics, Quebec. INRS-Eau, copublished with EQSA, IAHR/AIRH.

Bain, M. B., and M. S. Meixler. 2000. Defining a target fish community for planning and evaluating enhancement of the Quinebaug River in Massachusetts and Connecticut. , Ithaca: New York Cooperative Fish and Wildlife Research Unit, Cornell University.

Baker, C. O., and F. E. Votapka. 1990. Fish passage through culverts. San Dimas, CA: U.S. Forest Service, Technology and Development Center (Report No. FHWA-FL-90-006).

Balon, E. K. 1975. Reproductive guilds of fishes: A proposal and definition. Journal of the Fisheries Research Board of Canada 32:821-864.

Barber, L. B., G. K. Brown, and S. D. Zaugg. 2000. Potential endocrine disrupting organic chemicals in treated municipal wastewater and river water. Pages 97-123 in L. H. Keith, T. L. Jones-Lepp, and L. L. Needham, editors. Analysis of Environmental Endocrine Disruptors. Reprinted from American Chemical Society, Symposium Series 747. Denver: American Chemical Society.

Barinaga, M. 1996. A recipe for river recovery? Science 273:1648-1650.

Barrineau, C. E. 2003. Evaluation of the design of instream habitat structures relative to winter trout habitat in a Wyoming foothills stream. Master's thesis. Laramie: University of Wyoming, Department of Zoology and Physiology.

Bartholow, J. M. 1989. Stream temperature investigations: Field and analytic methods. Instream Flow Information Paper No.13. Washington, DC: U.S. Fish and Wildlife Service (Biological Report 89 [17]). 139 pp.

Bartholow, J. M., J. L. Laake, C. B. Stalnaker, and S. C. Williamson. 1993. A salmonid population model with emphasis on habitat limitations. Rivers 4(4):265-279.

Bartholow, J. M., J. Sandelin, B.A.K. Coughlin, J. Laake, and A. Moos. 1999. SALMOD: A population model for salmonids. User's manual. Fort Collins, CO: U. S. Geological Survey, Midcontinent Ecological Science Center. 92 pp.

Bartholow, J. M. and T. J. Waddle. 1986. Introduction to stream network habitat analysis. Instream Flow Information Paper No. 22. Washington, DC: U.S. Fish and Wildlife Service (Biological Report 86[8]). 242 pp.

Bauersfeld, K. 1978a. Stranding of juvenile salmon by flow reductions at Mayfield Dam on the Cowlitz River, 1976. Technical Report 36. Olympia: Washington Department of Fisheries.

Bauersfeld, K. 1978b. The effect of daily flow fluctuations on spawning fall chinook in the Columbia River. Technical Report 38. Olympia: Washington Department of Fisheries.

Baxter, R. M. 1977. Environmental effects of dams and impoundments. Annual Review of Ecological Systems 8:255-283.

Bayha, K. 1978. Instream flow methodologies for regional and national assessments. Instream Flow Information Paper No. 7. Fort Collins, CO: U.S. Fish and Wildlife Service (FWS/OBS-78/61). 97pp.

Bayha, K., and C. Koski, editors. 1974. Anatomy of a River. Vancouver, WA: Pacific Northwest River Basins Commission.

Bechera, J. A., M. Leclerc, L. Belzile, and P. Boudreau. 1994. A numerical model for modeling the dynamics of the spawning habitat of landlocked salmon. Pages 170-184 in Proceedings of the First International Symposium on Habitat Hydraulics. Trondheim: The Norwegian Institute of Technology.

Becker, C. D., D. H. Fickeisen, and J. C. Montgomery. 1981. Assessment of impacts from water level fluctuations on fish in the Hanford Reach, Columbia River. Richland, WA: Pacific Northwest Laboratory (PNL-3813).

Becker, G. C. 1983. Fishes of Wisconsin. Madison: University of Wisconsin Press.

Beecher, H. A. 1987. Simulating trout feeding stations in instream flow models. Pages 71-82 in J. F. Craig and J. B. Kemper, editors. Regulated Streams: Advances in Ecology. New York: Plenum Press.

Beecher, H. A.. 1990. Standards for instream flows. Rivers 1(2):97-109.

Beecher, H. A., J. P. Carleton, and T. H. Johnson. 1995. Utility of depth and velocity preferences for predicting steelhead parr distribution at different flows. Transactions of the American Fisheries Society 124:935-938.

Beecher, H. A., W. C. Hixson, and T. S. Hopkins. 1973. Fishes of a Florida oxbow lake and its parent river. Florida Scientist 40 (2):140-148.

Beecher, H. A., T. H. Johnson, and J. P. Carleton. 1993. Predicting microdistributions of steelhead parr from depth and velocity criteria: Test of an assumption of the instream flow incremental methodology. Canadian Journal of Fisheries and Aquatic Sciences 50(11):2380-2387.

Beltaos, S. 1995. River Ice Jams. Highlands Ranch, CO: Water Resources Publications, LLC. 372 pp.

Benke, A. C., I. Chaubey, G. M. Ward, and E. L. Dunn. 2000. Flood pulse dynamics of an unregulated river floodplain in the southeastern U.S. coastal plain. Ecology 81(10): 2730-2741.

Benson, N. G. 1981. The freshwater inflow to estuaries issue. Fisheries 6 (5): 8-10.

Betschta, R. L., and W. J. Jackson. 1979. The intrusion of fine sediments into a stable gravel bed. Journal of Fisheries Research Board of Canada 36:204-210.

Bingham, J. L., and G. A. Gould. 1992. Opportunities to protect instream flows and wetland uses of water in Nevada. Resource Publication 189. Washington, DC: U.S. Fish and Wildlife Service.

Binns, N. A., and F. M. Eiserman. 1979. Quantification of fluvial trout habitat in Wyoming. Transactions of the American Fisheries Society 108(3): 215-228.

Bisson, P. A., and D. R. Montgomery. 1996. Valley segments, stream reaches, and channel units. Pages 23-42 in R. F. Hauer and G. A. Lambert, editors. Methods in Stream Ecology. San Diego, CA: Academic Press. 674 pp.

Bisson, P. A., K. Sullivan, and J. L. Nielsen. 1988. Channel hydraulics, habitat use, and body form of juvenile coho salmon, steelhead, and cutthroat trout in streams. Transactions of the American Fisheries Society 117 (3): 262-273

Bjornn, T. C. 1969. Embryo Survival and Emergence Studies-Job 5. Salmon Steelhead Investigation. Annual Completion Report. Boise: Department of Fish and Game (Project No. F-49-R-7).

Black, P. E. 1972. Hydrograph responses to geomorphic model watershed characteristics and precipitation variables. Journal of Hydrology 17:309.

Blease, C. A. 1999. What water does the public trust doctrine carry? Pages 19-22 in G. E. Smith and A. R. Hoar, editors. The Public Trust Doctrine and its Application to Protecting Instream Flows. Proceedings of a Workshop. Sponsored by the National Instream Flow Program Assessment (NIFPA-08). Anchorage: Alaska Department of Fish and Game and U.S. Fish and Wildlife Service, Region 7.

Bohn, C. C., and J. G. King. 2001. Stream channel responses to streamflow diversion on small streams in Idaho. Stream Notes. Fort Collins, CO: U.S. Forest Service, Stream Systems Technology Center.

Booth, D. B., D. Hartley, and R. Jackson. 2003. Forest cover, impervious surface area and the mitigation of stormwater impacts. Journal of the American Water Resources Association 38(4):835-845.

BOSS International. Internet accessed 4/26/2000. www.bossintl.com/html/hec-ras.

Bounds, R. L., and B. Lyons. 1979. Existing reservoir and stream management recommendations: Statewide minimum streamflow recommendations. Austin: Texas Department of Parks and Wildlife (Federal Aid Project F-30-R-4).

Bouwer, H., and T. Maddock, III. 1997. Making sense of the interactions between groundwater and streamflow: Lessons for water masters and adjudicators. Rivers 6:19-31.

Bovee, K. D. 1974. The determination, assessment, and design of instream value studies for the northern Great Plains region. Master's thesis. Columbia: University of Missouri.

Bovee, K. D. 1982. A guide to stream habitat analysis using the Instream Flow Incremental Methodology. Instream Flow Information Paper No. 12. Washington, DC: U.S. Fish and Wildlife Service (FWS/OBS-82/26).

Bovee, K. D. 1986. Development and evaluation of habitat suitability criteria for use in the instream flow incremental methodology. Washington, DC: U. S. Fish and Wildlife Service (Biological Report 86[7]). 235 pp.

Bovee, K. D. 1988. Use of the instream flow incremental methodology to evaluate influences of microhabitat variability on trout populations in four Colorado streams. Proceedings of the Annual Conference Western Association of Fish and Wildlife Agencies 68:227-257.

Bovee, K. D. 1996. Perspectives on two-dimensional river habitat models: The PHABSIM experience. Pages

B149-162. In M. Leclerc , H. Capra, S. Valentine, A. Boudreault, and Y. Cote, editors. Ecohydraulics 2000. Proceedings of the Second International Symposium on Habitat Hydraulics. Quebec: INRS-Eau, Copublished with FQSA, IAHR/AIRI I.

Bovee, K. D., B. L. Lamb, J. M. Bartholow, C. D. Stalnaker, J. Taylor, and J. Henriksen. 1998. Stream habitat analysis using the Instream Flow Incremental Methodology. Fort Collins, CO: U.S. Geological Survey, Biological Resources Division (Information and Technical Report USGS/BRD-1998-0004). 131 pp.

Bovee, K. D., and R. T. Milhous. 1978. Hydraulic simulation in instream flow studies: Theory and technique. Instream Flow Information Paper No. 5. Washington, DC: U.S. Fish and Wildlife Service (FWS/OBS-78/33).

Bovee, K. D., T. J. Newcomb, and T. G. Coon. 1994. Relations between habitat variability and population dynamics of bass in the Huron River, Michigan. Biological Report No. 21. Fort Collins, CO: National Biological Survey. 63 pp.

Bovee, K. D., and M. L. Scott. 2002. Implications of flood pulse restoration for populus regeneration on the upper Missouri River. River Research and Applications 18:287-298

Brinson, N. M., B. L. Swift, R. C. Plantico, and J. S. Barclay. 1981. Riparian ecosystems: Their ecology and status. Kearneysville, WV: U.S. Fish and Wildlife Service (FWS/OBS-81/17).

Brock, T. D. 1967. Relationship between standing crop and primary productivity along a hot spring thermal gradient. Ecology 48: 566-571.

Brookes, A. 1998. Channelized Rivers: Perspectives for Environmental Management. Chichester, England: John Wiley & Sons. 342 pp.

Brooks, K. N., P. F. Folliott, H. M. Gregersen, and J. L. Thames. 1991. Hydrology and Management of Watersheds. Ames: Iowa State University Press. 516 pp.

Brown, D. E., C. J. Lowe, and F. Hausler. 1977. Southwestern riparian communities: Their biotic importance and management in Arizona. Pages 201-211 in R. R. Johnson and D. A. Jones, technical coordinators. Importance, Preservation and Management of Riparian Habitat: Proceedings of a Symposium, July 9, 1977, Tucson, AZ. Fort Collins, CO: U.S. Department of Agriculture, Rocky Mountain Forest and Range Experiment Station (General Technical Report RM-43).

Brown, L. C., and T. O. Barnwell, Jr. 1987. The enhanced stream water quality models QUAL-2E and QUAL-2E-UNCAS: Documentation and user's manual. Athens, GA: U.S. Environmental Protection Agency. Environmental Research Laboratory (EPA/600/3-87/007). 189 pp.

Brown, R. S, and W. C. Mackay. 1995. Fall and winter movements and habitat use by cutthroat trout in the Ram River, Alberta. Transactions of the American Fisheries Society 124:873-885.

Brown, R. S., S. S. Stanislawski, and W. C. Mackay. 1994. Effects of frazil ice on fish. Pages 261-278 in T. D. Prowse, editor. Proceedings of the Workshop on the Environmental Aspects of River Ice, Saskatoon, Sask., 18-20 August 1993. NHRI Symposium Series No.12. Saskatoon, Sask: National Hydrology Research Institute.

Bryan, C. F., and D. S. Sabins. 1979. Management implications in water quality and fish standing stock information in the Atchafalaya River Basin, Louisiana. Pages 193-316 in J. W. Day, Jr., D. D. Culley, Jr., R. E. Turner, and A. J. Humphrey, Jr., editors. Proceedings of the Third Coastal Marsh and Estuary Symposium. Baton Rouge: Louisiana State University, Division of Continuing Education.

Bunte, K., and S. R. Abt. 2001. Sampling surface and subsurface particle-size distributions in wadable gravel- and cobble-bed streams for analyses in sediment transport, hydraulics, and streambed monitoring. Fort Collins, CO: U.S. Forest Service (General Technical Report RMRS-GTR-74).

Butler, R. L. 1979. Anchor ice, its formation, and effects on aquatic life. Science in Agriculture 26 (2):12-19.

Calow, P., and G. E. Petts. 1992. The Rivers Handbook: Hydrological and Ecological Principles. Volume 1. Boston: Blackwell Scientific Publications. 526 pp.

Calow, P., and G. E. Petts. 1994. The Rivers Handbook: Hydrological and Ecological Principles. Volume 2. Boston: Blackwell Scientific Publications. 523 pp.

Camp, Dresser and McKee. 1986. Minimum instream flow study. Final report to the Commonwealth of Virginia State Water Control Board, Annandale, Virginia.

Campbell, K. L., S. Kumar, and H. P. Johnson. 1872. Stream straightening effects on flood-runoff characteristics. Transactions of the American Society of Agricultural Engineers 15:94-98.

Carling, P. 1995. Implications of sediment transport for instream flow modeling of aquatic habitat. Pages 17-32 in D. Harper and A. Ferguson, editors. The Ecological Basis for River Management. Chichester, England: John Wiley & Sons.

Castleberry, D. T., J. J. Cech, Jr., D. C. Erman, D. Hankin, and others. 1996. Uncertainty and Instream Flow Standards. Fisheries 2(8):20-21.

Castro, N. M., and G. M. Hornberger. 1991. Surface-subsurface water interactions in an alleviated mountain stream channel. Water Resources Research 27:1613-1621.

Cavendish, M. G., and M. I. Duncan. 1986. Use of in streamflow incremental methodology: A tool for negotiations. Environmental Impact Assessment Review 6:347-363.

Central Vermont Public Service Corp. 2000. Aesthetics flow report. Lamoille River Hydroelectric Project,

FERC No. 2205. Rutland, VT: Central Vermont Public Service Corp.

Chapin, D. M., R. L. Beschta, and H. W. Shen. 2002. Relationship between flood frequencies and riparian plant communities in the upper Klamath Basin, Oregon. Journal of the American Water Resources Association. 38:603-617.

Chapman, R. J., T. M. Hinckley, L. C. Lee, and R. O. Teskey. 1982. Impact of water level changes on woody riparian and wetland communities. Volume 10. Kearneysville, WV: U.S. Fish and Wildlife Service (OBS-82/83).

Chase, L. C., W. F. Siemer, and D. J. Decker. 2002. Designing stakeholder involvement strategies to resolve wildlife management controversies. Wildlife Society Bulletin. 30(3):937-950.

Chauvet, E., and H. Décamps. 1989. Lateral interactions in a fluvial landscape: The River Garonne, France. Journal of the North American Benthological Society 8(1):9-17.

Citizens Utilities Company. 1993. Clyde River instream flow aquatic needs assessment. Schedule B information appending application before the Federal Energy Regulatory Commission for license, Clyde River Hydroelectric Project, AIR No. 6.

Clipperton, G. K., C. W. Koning, A. G. H. Locke, J. M. Mahoney, and B. Quazi. 2003. Instream flow needs determinations for the South Saskatchewan River Basin, Alberta, Canada. Calgary: Alberta Environment and Sustainable Resource Development. (Pub No. T/719). 271 pp + appendices.

Colborn, T., and C. Clement, editors. 1992. Chemically-induced Alterations in Sexual and Functional Development: The Wild/Human Connection. Princeton, NJ: Princeton Scientific, Princeton.

Colborn, T., and K. Thayer. 2000. Aquatic ecosystems: harbingers of endocrine disruption. Ecological Applications 10(4):949-957.

Colborn, T., F. S., Vom Saal, and A. M. Soto. 1993. Developmental effects of endocrine disrupting chemicals in wildlife and humans. Environmental Health Perspectives 101:378-384.

Collier, M. P., R. H. Webb, and E. D. Andrews. 1997. Experimental flooding in the Grand Canyon. Scientific American 276:82-89.

Collier, M. P., R. H. Webb, and J. C. Schmidt. 1996. Dams and rivers: A primer on the downstream effects of dams. Denver: U.S. Geological Survey Circular 1126.

Collings, M. R. 1974. Generalization of spawning and rearing discharges for several Pacific salmon species in western Washington. USGS Open File Report. Tacoma, WA: U.S. Geological Survey. 39 pp.

Collings, R. M., R. W. Smith, and G. T. Higgins. 1972. The hydrology of four streams in western Washington as related to several Pacific salmon species. U.S. Geological Survey Water Supply Paper 1968. Washington, DC: U.S. Geological Survey. 109 pp.

Collinson, J. D. 1971. Some effects of ice on a riverbed. Journal of Sedimentary Petrology 41(2):557-564.

Committee on River Ice Processes and The Environment. 1995. Winter environments of regulated rivers. In D. D. Andres, editor. Proceedings of the Eighth Workshop on the Hydraulics of Ice Covered Rivers. Kamloops, BC. Canadian Geophysical Union, Hydrology Section.

Conder, A. L., and T. C. Annear. 1987. Test of weighted usable area estimates derived from a PHABSIM model for instream flow studies on trout streams. North American Journal of Fisheries Management 7:339-350.

Connecticut River Atlantic Salmon Commission. 1998. Strategic plan for the restoration of Atlantic salmon to the Connecticut River. Sunderland, MA. 106 pp.

Conner, W. H., and J. W. Day. 1976. Productivity and composition of a bald cypress-water tupelo site and a bottomland hardwood site in a Louisiana swamp. American Journal of Botany 63:1354-1364.

Cook, G. 1993. The Public Trust Doctrine in Alaska. 8 Environmental Law and Litigation Reporter 1.

Copeland, B. J. 1966. Effects of decreased river flow on estuarine ecology. Journal of Water Pollution Control Federation 38(11):1831-1839.

Corbett, R. 1991. Minimum instream flow requirements for recreational boating. Science Applications International Corp. McLean, Virginia (Report No. 01-0239-0920-01).

Cornell Instream Habitat Program. Website accessed 2003. www.dnr.cornell.edu/research/IHP/.

Corning, R. V. 1970. Water fluctuation: A detrimental influence on trout streams. Proceedings of the Twenty-Third Annual Conference of the Southeastern Association of Game and Fish Commissioners 23:431-454

Covich, A. P., W. D. Shepard, E. A. Bergey, and C. S. Carpenter. 1978. Effects of fluctuating flow rates and water levels on chironomids: Direct and indirect alterations of habitat stability. Pages 141-155 in J. H. Thorp and J. W.Gibbons, editors. Energy and Environmental Stress in Aquatic Systems. Oak Ridge, TN: U.S. Department of Energy, Technical Information Center.

Crance J. H. 1988. Relationships between palustrine wetlands of forested riparian floodplains and fishery resources: a review. Washington DC: U.S. Fish Wildlife Service (Biol. Rep. 88[32]) 27 pp.

Creuze des Chatelliers, M. C., and J. L. Reygrobellet. 1990. Interactions between geomorphical processes, benthic and hyporheic communities: First results on a by-passed canal of the French Upper Rhone River. Regulated Rivers: Research and Management (11):139-158.

Crisp, D. T. 1987. Thermal "resetting" of streams by reservoir releases with special reference to effects on salmonid fishes. Pages 163-182 in J. F. Craig, and J. B. Kemper, editors. Regulated Streams: Advances in Ecology. New York: Plenum Press.

Cross, R. D., and D. L. Williams, editors. 1981. Proceedings of the National Symposium on Freshwater Inflow to Estuaries. Volume 2. Washington, DC: U.S. Fish and Wildlife Service (FWS/OBS-81-04).

Cummins, K. W. 1980. The natural stream ecosystem. Pages 7-24 in J. V. Ward and J. A. Stanford, editors. The Ecology of Regulated Streams. New York: Plenum Press.

Cunjak, R. A., and D. Caissie. 1994. Frazil ice accumulation in a large salmon pool in the Miramichi River, New Brunswick: Ecological implications for overwintering fishes. Pages 261-278 in T. D. Prowse, editor. Proceedings of the Workshop on the Environmental Aspects of River Ice, 18-20 August 1993, Saskatoon, Sask: NHRI Symposium Series No.12. Saskatoon: National Hydrology Research Institute.

Cunjak, R. A., and G. Powers. 1986. Winter habitat utilization by stream resident brook trout (Salvelinus fontinalis) and brown trout (Salmo trutta). Canadian Journal of Fisheries and Aquatic Sciences 43:1970-1981.

Cushman, R. M. 1985. Review of ecological effects of rapidly varying flows downstream from hydroelectric facilities. North American Journal of Fisheries Management 5:330-339.

Dasman, R.C. 1973. A rationale for preserving natural areas. Journal of Soil and Water Conservation 28(3):114-117.

Davis, J. C. 1975. Minimal dissolved oxygen requirement of aquatic life with emphasis on Canadian species: A review. Journal of the Fisheries Research Board of Canada 32(12):2295-2332.

Dawson, K. J. 1984. Planting design inventory techniques for modeling the restoration of native riparian landscapes. Pages 465-470 in R. E. Warner and K. M. Hendrix, editors. California riparian systems: Ecology, conservation, and productive management. California Water Resources Report No. 55. Berkeley: University of California Press.

Dawson, T. J. 1999. The Public Trust Doctrine and limits on private water rights. Pages 27-30 in G. E. Smith and A. R. Hoar, editors. The Public Trust Doctrine and its Application to Protecting Instream Flows. Proceedings of a Workshop. Sponsored by the National Instream Flow Program Assessment (NIFPA-08). Anchorage: Alaska Department of Fish and Game and U.S. Fish and Wildlife Service, Region 7.

Day, J. W., Jr., T. J. Butler, and U. H. Conner. 1977. Production and nutrient export studies in a cypress swamp and lake system in Louisiana. Pages 255-269 in M. Wiley, editor. Estuarine Processes. Volume 2. New York: Academic Press.

Decamps, H., J. Capblanq, H. Casanova, and J. M. Tourrenq. 1979. Hydrobiology of some regulated rivers in the southwest of France. Pages 273-288 in J. V. Ward, and J. A. Stanford, editors. The Ecology

of Regulated Streams. New York: Plenum Press.

Dellapenna, J. W. 1998. Issues arising under riparian rights: Replacing common law riparian rights with regulated riparianism. In K. R. Wright editor. Water rights of the eastern United States,. Available from American Water Works Association www.normas.com/AWWA/pages/20427.html.

Denslinger, T. L., W. A. Gast, J. J. Hauenstein, D. W. Heicher, and others. 1998. Instream Flow Studies, Pennsylvania and Maryland. Publication 191. Harrisburg, PA: Susquehanna River Basin Commission. 293 pp.

Dillon, R. T., Jr. 2000. The Ecology of Freshwater Molluscs. Cambridge, UK: Cambridge University Press.

Dishlip, H. 1993. Instream flow water rights: Arizona's approach. Pages 10.1-14 in L. J. MacDonnell, and T. A. Rice, editors. Instream Flow Protection in the West. Revised edition. Boulder: University of Colorado Natural Resources Law Center.

Dixon, W. D. and W. E. Cox. 1985. Minimum flow protection in riperian states. Journal of Water Resources Planning and Management 111(2):149-156.

Dodson and Associates, Inc. Accessed April 27, 2000. www.dodson-hydro.com.

Doering, P. H., R. H. Chamberlain, and D. E. Haunert. 2002. Using submerged aquatic vegetation to establish minimum and maximum freshwater inflows to the Caloosahatchie estuary, Florida. Estuaries 25(6B):1343-1354.

Doyle, M. W., K. F. Boyd, and P. B. Skidmore. 1999. River restoration channel design: Back to the basics of dominant discharge. Second International Conference on Natural Channel Systems. March 1-4, 1999. Manotick, Ontario. Rideau Valley Conservation Authority, Niagara Falls, Canada. Paper available on CD ROM.

Duke Engineering. 1999. Final report to Skagit Public Utility District, Mt. Vernon, Washington. Duke Engineering, Bellingham, WA.

Dunbar, M. J., A. Gustard, M. C. Acreman, and C.R.N. Elliott. 1998. Overseas approaches to setting river flow objectives. Environment Agency, Bristol, U.K. (R&D Technical Report W6B [96]4).

Dunne, T., and L. B. Leopold. 1978. Water in Environmental Planning. New York: W. H. Freeman and Company. 818 pp.

Dynesius, M., and C. Nilsson. 1994. Fragmentation and flow regulation of river systems in the northern third of the world. Science 266(4):753-762.

Edwards, R. J. 1978. The effects of hypolimnion reservoir releases on fish distribution and species diversity. Transactions of the American Fisheries Society 107:71-77.

Edwards, R. L. 1988. History and contributions of the Woods Hole Fisheries Laboratory. Marine Fisheries Review 50(4):13-17.

Einstein, H. A. 1950. The bed-load function for sediment

transportation in open channel flows. Soil Conservation Servive. Technical Bulletin No. 1026. Electric Power Research Institute (EPRI). 2000. Instream flow assessment methods: Guidance for evaluating instream flow needs in hydropower licensing. Palo Alto, CA (Report No. 1000554).

Elwood, J. W., J. D. Newbold, R. V. O'Neill, and W. Van Winkle. 1983. Resource spiralling: An operational paradigm for analyzing lotic systems. Pages 3-27 in T. D. Fontaine, and S. M. Bartell, editors. Dynamics of Lotic Ecosystems. Ann Arbor, MI: Ann Arbor Science Publishers.

Emmett, W. W. 1980. A field calibration of the sediment-trapping characteristics of the Helley-Smith bed-load sampler. Professional Paper No. 1139. Washington, DC: U.S. Geological Survey. 44 pp.

Emmett, W. W. 1981. Measurement of bedload in rivers. Pages 3-15 in Proceedings of the International Symposium on the Measurement of Erosion and Sediment Transport, Florence, Italy, June 22-25. Publication No. 133. International Association Hydrological Sciences.

Emmett, W. W. 1999. Quantification of channel-maintenance flows for gravel-bed rivers. Pages 77-83 in D. S. Olsen, and J. P. Potynondy, editors. Wildland Hydrology. Herndon, VA: American Water Resources Association (TS-99-3). 536 pp.

Environmental Management Associates. 1994. Instream flow needs investigation of the Bow River: Part I - Fisheries. Report to Alberta Environmental Protection, Edmonton, AB. 130 pp + appendixes.

Espegren, G. D., and D. C. Merriman. 1995. Development of instream flow recommendations in Colorado using R2-Cross. Denver: Colorado Water Conservation Board.

Estes, C. C. 1984. Evaluation of methods for recommending instream flows to support spawning by salmon. Master's thesis. Pullman: Washington State University.

Estes, C. C. 1998. Annual summary of instream flow reservations and protection in Alaska. Fishery Data Series No. 98-40. Anchorage: Alaska Department of Fish and Game.

Estes, C. C., and J. F. Orsborn. 1986. Review and analysis of methods for quantifying instream flow requirements. Water Resources Bulletin 22(3): 389-398.

Evans, D. H. 1997. The Physiology of Fishes. Boca Raton, FL: CRC Press.

Evans, J. W., and H. England. 1995. A recommended method to protect instream flows in Georgia. Social Circle: Georgia Department of Natural Resources, Wildlife Resources Division.

Everest, F. H., R. L. Beschta, J. C. Scrivener, K. V. Koski, and others. 1987. Fine sediment and salmonid production: A paradox. Pages 98-142 in E. O. Salo, and T. W. Cundy, editors. Streamside Management: Forestry and Fishery Interactions.

Contribution No. 57. Seattle: University of Washington, Institute of Forest Resources.

Ewing, K. L. 1978. Riparian ecosystems: Conservation of their unique characteristics. In R. R. Johnson and J. F. McCormack, editors. Strategies for protection and management of floodplain wetlands and other riparian ecosystems. Washington, DC: U.S. Forest Service (General Technical Report WO-12).

Extence, C. A. 1981. The effect of drought on benthic invertebrate communities in a lowland river. Hydrobiologia 83:217-224.

Fausch, K. D. 1984. Profitable stream positions for salmonids: Relating specific growth rate to net energy gain. Canadian Journal of Zoology 62: 441-451.

Fausch, K. D., C. L. Hawkes, and M. G. Parsons. 1988. Models that predict standing crop of stream fish from habitat variables: 1950-85. Portland, OR: U.S. Forest Service (General Technical Report, PNW-GTR-213). Pacific Northwest Research Station. 52 pp.

Fausch K. D, J. R. Karr, and P. R. Yant. 1984. Regional application of an Index of Biotic Integrity based on stream fish communities. Transaction of the American Fisheries Society 113:39-55.

Federal Energy Regulatory Commission (FERC). 1985. Bradley Lake Hydroelectric Project, No. 8221. Final supplemental environmental impact statement. Washington, DC: Federal Energy Regulatory Commission, Office of Hydropower Licensing. Available from Division of Public Information.

Federal Energy Regulatory Commission (FERC). 1995. Relicensing the Ayers Island hydroelectric project in the Pemigewasset/Merrimack River basin. Washington, DC: FERC Final Environmental Impact Statement (Project No. 2456-009).

Federal Interagency Stream Restoration Working Group (FISRWG). 1998. Stream corridor restoration: Principles, processes, and practices. Washington DC: FISRWG (GPO Item No. 0120-A; SuDocs No. A 57.6/2:EN 3/PT.653).

Fernet, D. A., R. F. Courtney, and C. P. Bjornson. 1990. Instream flow requirements for fishes downstream of the Oldman River Dam. Report to Alberta Public Works, Supply and Services, Edmonton, AB. Prepared by Environmental Management Associates, Calgary. 133 pp + appendixes.

Fernet, D. A., R. L. Vadas, Jr., C. P. Bjornson, and C. Briggs. 1999. Red Deer River instream flow needs study. Report to Alberta Environmental Protection, Cochrane, AB. Prepared by Golder Associates, Calgary. 42 pp + appendixes.

Filipek, S., W. E. Keith, and J. Geise. 1987. The status of the instream flow issue in Arkansas. Proceedings of the Arkansas Academy of Science 41(1):43-48.

Findlay, S. 1995. Importance of surface-subsurface exchange in stream ecosystems: The hyporheic zone. Limnology and Oceanography 40:159-164.

Finger, T. R. 1982. Fish community-habitat relations in a

central New York stream. Journal of Freshwater Ecology 1:343-352.

Finger, T. R., and E. M. Stewart. 1987. Response of fishes to flooding regime in lowland hardwood wetlands. Pages 86-92 in W. J. Matthews and D. C. Heins, editors. Community and Evolutionary Ecology of North American Stream Fishes. Norman: University of Oklahoma Press.

Fisher, S. G., and A. Lavoy. 1972. Differences in littoral fauna due to fluctuating water levels below a hydroelectric dam. Journal of the Fisheries Research Board of Canada. 29:1472-1476.

Fisheries and Recreation Enhancement Working Group (FREWG). 2001. Kananaskis River system assessment: Lower Kananaskis Lake and the Kananaskis River from Lower Kananaskis Lake to Barrier Lake. Calgary, Alberta: Fisheries and Recreation Enhancement Working Group. 43pp + appendixes.

Flannery, M. S., E. B. Peebles, and R. T. Montgomery. 2002. A percent-of-flow approach for managing reductions of freshwater inflows from unimpounded rivers to southwest Florida estuaries. Estuaries 25 (6B): 1318-1332.

Folmar, L. C., N. D. Denslow, V. Rao, M. Chow, and others. 1996. Vitellogenin induction and reduced serum testosterone concentrations in feral male carp (Cyprinus carpio) captured near a major metropolitan sewage treatment plant. Environmental Health Perspectives 104(10):1096-1101.

Food and Agriculture Organization (FAO). 1995. Precautionary approach to fisheries. Part 1: Guidelines on the precautionary approach to capture fisheries and species introductions. Rome: Food and Agriculture Organization of the United Nations (Fisheries Technical Paper No. 350).

Franklin, J. F., K. Cromack, and W. Dension. 1981. Ecological characteristics of old-growth Douglas-fir forests. Portland, OR: U.S. Forest Service Pacific Northwest Forest and Range Experiment Station (General Technical Report PNW-118).

Fraser, J. C. 1972. Regulated discharge and the stream environment. Pages 263-285 in R. T. Oglesby, C. A. Carlson, and J. A. McCann, editors. River Ecology and Man. New York: Academic Press.

Freeman, M. C., Z. H. Bowen, and K. D. Bovee. 1999. Transferability of habitat suitability criteria. North American Journal of Fisheries Management 19:626-628.

Frenette, M., M. Caron, and P. Julien. 1984. Interaction entre le debit et les populations de tacons (Salmo salar) de la riviere Matamec. Canadian Journal of Fisheries and Aquatic Sciences 41:954-963.

Friedman, J. M., W. R. Osterkamp, M. L. Scott, and G. T. Auble. 1998. Downstream effects of dams on channel geometry and bottomland vegetation: regional patterns in the Great Plains. Wetlands 18(4):619-633.

Frissell, C. A. and D. Bayles. 1996. Ecosystem management and the conservation of aquatic biodiversity and ecological integrity. Water Resources Bulletin 32(2):229-240.

Frissell, C. A., W. J. Liss, C. E. Warren, and M. D. Hurley. 1986. A hierarchical framework for stream habitat classification: viewing streams in a watershed context. Environmental Management 10:199-214.

Fry, F.E.J. 1947. Effects of the environment on animal activity. Biological Series No. 55. Toronto: University of Toronto, Ontario Fisheries Research Laboratory. 62 pp.

Furniss, M. J., S. Firor, and M. Love. 2000. Fish Xing 2.0 software and learning system for analysis of fish migration through culverts. Stream Notes. Fort Collins, CO: U.S. Forest Service, Stream Systems Technology Center.

Galay, V. J., R. Kellerhals, and D. I. Bray. 1973. Diversity of river types in Canada. Pages 217-250 in Fluvial Processes and Sedimentation. Proceedings of the Symposium on Hydrology, Ottawa. National Research Council of Canada.

Gallagher, R. P. 1979. Local distribution of ichthyoplankton in the lower Mississippi River, Louisiana. Master's thesis. Baton Rouge: Louisiana State University.

Gallagher, S. P., and M. F. Gard. 1999. Relationship between chinook salmon (Oncorhynchus tshawytscha) redd densities and PHABSIM-predicted habitat in the Merced and Lower American rivers, California. Canadian Journal of Fisheries and Aquatic Sciences 56(4): 570-577.

Galli, J. 1990. Thermal impacts associated with urbanization and stormwater management best management practices. Metropolitan Washington Council of Governments. Maryland Deparmtent of Environment. Washington, D.C. 188 pp.

Garcia, S. M. 1994. The precautionary principle: Its implications in capture fisheries management. Ocean and Coastal Management 22:99-125.

Gerking, S. D. 1950. Stability of a stream fish population. Journal of Wildlife Management 14:193-202.

Gerking, S. D. 1959. The restricted movement of fish populations. Biological Reviews of the Cambridge Philosophical Society 34:221-242.

Ghanem, A., P. Steffler, F. Hicks, and C. Katopodis. 1994. Two-dimensional modeling of hydraulic habitat in rivers with large bed roughness. Pages 84-98 in Proceedings of the First International Symposium on Habitat Hydraulics. The Norwegian Institute of Technology, Trondheim, Norway.

Giger, R. D. 1973. Streamflow requirements of salmonids. Final report to Oregon Wildlife Commission, Portland, Oregon. Project AFS-62-1.

Gillilan, D. M., and T. C. Brown. 1997. Instream Flow Protection: Seeking a Balance in Western Water Use. Washington DC: Island Press. 417 pp.

Gilvear, D. J. 1987. Suspended solids transport within regulated rivers experiencing periodic reservoir releases. Pages 245-255 in J. F. Craig and J. B. Kemper, editors. Regulated Streams: Advances in Ecology. New York: Plenum Press.

Gippel, C. G., and M. Stewardson. 1996. Use of wetted perimeter in defining minimum environmental flows. Pages A571-A582 in M. Leclerc, H. Capra, S. Valentin, A. Boudreault, and Y, Cote, editors. Echohydraulics 2000. Proceedings of the Second International Symposium on Habitat Hydraulics, Quebec: INRS-Eau, copublished with FQSA, IAHR.AIRH.

Gislason, J. C. 1985. Aquatic insect abundance in a regulated stream under fluctuating and stable diel flow patterns. North American Journal of Fisheries Management 5:39-46.

Glennon, R. J. 1995. The threat to river flows from groundwater pumping. Rivers 5(2):133-139.

Goldfarb, W. 1988. Water Law. 2d edition. Chelsea, MI: Lewis Publishers. 284 pp.

Goldman, C. R., and A. J. Horne. 1983. Limnology. New York: McGraw-Hill. 464 pp.

Goldstein, P. Z. 1999. Functional ecosystems and biodiversity buzzwords. Conservation Biology 13(2):247-255.

Goodbred, S. L., R. J. Gilliom, T. S. Gross, N. P. Denslow, and others. 1997. Reconnaisance of 17-Estradiol, 11-Ketotestosterone, vitellogenin, and gonad histopathology in common carp of United States streams: Potential for contaminant-induced endocrine disruption. Open-File Report 96-627. Denver: U.S. Geological Survey, Information Services, Federal Center.

Goodstein, E. 1999. The Trade-Off Myth: Fact and Fiction About Jobs and the Environment. Washington, DC: Island Press. 195 pp.

Goodwin, C. N. 1999. Fluvial classification: Neanderthal necessity or needless normalcy? Pages 229-236 in D.S. Olson and J.P. Potyondy, editors. Wildland Hydrology. Herndon, VA: American Water Resources Association (TPS-99-3).

Gordon, N. 1995. Summary of technical testimony in the Colorado Water Division 1 Trial. Denver: U.S. Forest Service (General Technical Report RM-GTR-270). 140 pp.

Gordon, N. D., T. A. McMahon, and B. L. Finlayson. 1992. Stream Hydrology. Chichester, England: John Wiley & Sons.

Gore, J. A., J. B. Layzer, and J. Mead. 2001. Macroinvertebrate instream flow studies after 20 years: A role in stream management and restoration. Regulated Rivers: Research and Management 17: 527-542.

Gorman, O.T., and J. R. Karr. 1978. Habitat structure and stream fish communities. Ecology 59:507-515.

Gosselink, J. G., S. E. Bayley, W. H. Conner, and R. E. Turner. 1981. Ecological factors in the determination of riparian wetland boundaries. Pages 199-219 in J. R. Clark and R. Benforado, editors. Wetlands of Bottomland Hardwood Forests. Proceedings of a Workshop on Bottomland Hardwood Forests of the Southeastern United States. Lake Lanier, Georgia, June 1-5, 1980. Volume 11. New York: Elsevier Science Publishing Co.

Gowan, C., M. K. Young, K. D. Fausch, and S. C. Riley. 1994. The restricted movement of stream-resident salmonids: A paradigm lost? Canadian Journal of Fisheries and Aquatic Sciences 51:2626-2637.

Grant, D. L. 1987. Public interest review of water rights allocation and transfer in the West: Recognition of public values. Arizona State Law Journal 19(4): 681-718.

Grant, G. E., J. E. Duval, G. J. Koerpe, and J. L. Fogg. 1992. XSPRO: A channel cross-section analyzer. Technical Note 287. Denver: U.S. Forest Service and Bureau of Land Management Service Center.

Grasse, J. E., and E. F. Putnam. 1950. Beaver management and ecology in Wyoming. Federal Aid Wildlife Restoration Project, WY 31-D and 30-R. Bulletin No. 6. Cheyenne: Wyoming Game and Fish Commission. 52 pp.

Gray, B. E. 1993. A reconsideration of instream appropriative water rights in California. Pages 11.1-57 in L. J. MacDonnell, and T. A. Rice, editors. Instream Flow Protection in the West. Revised edition. Boulder: University of Colorado Natural Resources Law Center.

Greenberg, I., P. Svendsen, and A. Harby. 1996. Availability of microhabitats and their use by brown trout (Salmo trutta) and grayling (Thymallus thymallus) in the River Vojman, Sweden. Regulated Rivers: Research and Management 12: 287-303.

Greeney, W. J., and A. K. Kraszewski. 1981. Description and application of the stream simulation and assessment model: Version IV (SSAM IV). Washington, DC: U.S. Fish and Wildlife Service (FWS/OBS-81/46).

Green Mountain Power Corporation. 1999. Application for New License. Major power project for the Waterbury Hydroelectric Project, FERC No. 2090. Before the Federal Energy Regulatory Commission, Washington, D.C. Federal Register 64 (250).

Gregory, K. J., and D. E. Walling. 1973. Drainage Basin Form and Process. London: Edward Arnold.

Gregory, S. V., F. J. Swanson, W. A. McKee, and K. W. Cummins. 1991. An ecosystem perspective of riparian zones. BioScience 41:540-551.

Gresswell, R. E. 1999. Fire and aquatic ecosystems in forested biomes of North America. Transactions of the American Fisheries Society 128 (2): 193-221.

Grossman, G. D., P. B. Moyle, and J. O. Whitaker, Jr. 1982. Stochasticity in structural and functional characteristics of an Indiana stream fish assemblage: A test of community theory. American Naturalist (120): 423-454.

Gumerman, G. J., editor. 1988. The Anasazi in a Changing Environment. Cambridge, UK: Cambridge University Press.

Hall, D. H., and N. J. Knight. 1981. Natural variation in abundance of salmonid populations and its implications for design of impact studies. Technical

Report 5608. Corvallis: Oregon Agricultural Experimentation Station.

Hall, H. D. 1979. The spatial and temporal distribution of ichthyoplankton of the upper Atchafalaya Basin. Master's thesis. Baton Rouge: Louisiana State University.

Halyk, L. C. and E. K. Balon. 1983. Structure and ecological production of the fish taxocene of a small floodplain system. Canadian Journal of Zoology 61(11): 2446-2464.

Hardy, T. B. 1998. The future of habitat modeling and instream flow assessment techniques. Regulated Rivers: Research and Management 14:405-420.

Hardy, T. B., and C. Addley. 2001. Evaluation of interim instream flow needs in the Klamath River, phase II. Logan: Utah State University, Institute for Natural Systems Engineering, Utah Water Research Laboratory.

Harle, M. L., and C. C. Estes. 1993. An assessment of instream flow protection in Alaska. Pages 9.1–19 in L. J. MacDonnell, and T. A. Rice. Instream Flow Protection in the West. Revised edition. Boulder: University of Colorado Natural Resources Law Center.

Harpman, D. A., M. P. Welsh, and R. C. Bishop. 1993. Nonuse Economic Value: Emerging Policy Analysis Tool. Rivers 4(4): 280-291.

Harries, J. E., D. A. Sheahan, S. Jobling, P. Matthiessen, and others. 1996. A survey of estrogenic activity in United Kingdom inland waters. Environmental Technology and Chemistry 15(11):1993-2002.

Harvey, B. C. 1987. Susceptibility of young-of-year fishes to downstream displacement by flooding. Transactions of the American Fisheries Society 116:851-855.

Hatfield, T. and J. Bruce. 2000. Predicting salmonid habitat-flow relationship for streams from western North America. North American Journal of Fisheries Management 20 (4):1005-1015.

Haugen, G. N. 1985. Strategies for riparian area management. Fisheries Bulletin 10(4):20-21.

Hawkins, C. P., J. L. Kershner, P. A. Bisson, M. D. Bryant, and others. 1993. A hierarchical approach to classifying habitat features. Fisheries 18 (6):3-12.

Hawkins, J. A., E. J. Wick, and D. E. Jennings. 1997. Icthyofauna of the Little Snake River, Colorado, 1994. Final Report. Contribution 91 of the Larval Fish Laboratory. Fort Collins: Colorado State University. 44 pp.

Hayeur, G. 2001. Summary of knowledge acquired in northern environments from 1970 to 2000. Montreal: Hydro-Quebec. Available at www.hydro-quebec.com/environment.

Heede, B. H. 1992. Stream dynamics: An overview for land managers. Fort Collins: U.S. Forest Service, Rocky Mountain Forest and Range Experiment Station (General Technical Report RM-72).

Helley, E. J., and W. Smith. 1971. Development and calibration of a pressure-difference bedload sampler.

Open File Report. Washington, DC: U.S. Geological Survey.

Hilborn, R., and C. J. Walters. 1992. Quantitative Fisheries Stock Assessment: Choice, Dynamics and Uncertainty. New York: Chapman and Hall. 570 pp.

Hildebrand, R. H., A. D. Lemly, and C. A. Dolloff. 1999. Habitat sequencing and the importance of discharge in inferences. North American Journal of Fisheries Management 19:198-202.

Hill, E. P. 1982. Beaver. Pages 256–282 in J. A. Chapman and G. A. Feldhamer, editors. Wild Mammals of North America. Baltimore, MD: Johns Hopkins University Press.

Hill, M. T., and W. S. Platts. 1998. Ecosystem restoration: A case study in the Owens River Gorge, California. Fisheries 23(11):18-27.

Hill, M. T., W. S. Platts, and R. L. Beschta. 1991. Ecological and geomorphological concepts for instream and out-of-channel flow requirements. Rivers 2(3):198-210.

Hillman, T. W., J. S. Griffith, and W. S. Platts. 1987. Summer and winter habitat selection by juvenile chinook salmon in a highly sedimented Idaho stream. Transactions of the American Fisheries Society 116 (2):185-195.

Hocutt, C. H. 1981. Fish as indicators of biological integrity. Fisheries 6(6): 28-31.

Holden, P. B., editor. 1999. Flow recommendations for the San Juan River. San Juan River Basin Recovery Implementation Program. Albuquerque, NM: U.S. Fish and Wildlife Service.

Hooper, D. R. 1973. Evaluation of the effect of flows on trout stream ecology. Emeryville: California Department of Engineering Research.

Horowitz, R. J. 1978. Temporal variability patterns and the distributional patterns of stream fishes. Ecological Monographs 48:307-321.

Hughes, R. M., and R. F. Noss. 1992. Biological diversity and biological integrity: Current concerns for lakes and streams. Fisheries 17(3):11-19.

Hupp, C. R., and W. R. Osterkamp. 1985. Bottomland vegetation distribution along Passage Creek, Virginia, in relation to fluvial landforms. Ecology 66:670-681.

Hvidsten, N. A. 1993. High winter discharge after regulation increases production of Atlantic salmon (Salmo salar) smolts in the River Orkla, Norway. Pages 175-177 in R.J. Gibson and R. E. Cutting, editors. Production of Juvenile Atlantic Salmon (Salmo salar) in Natural Waters. Special Publication of the Canadian Journal of Fisheries and Aquatic Sciences 118.

Hynes, H. B. 1970. The Ecology of Running Waters. Toronto: University of Toronto Press.

Hynes, H. B. 1975. The stream and its valley. Verhandlungen der internationalen vereinigung für theoretische und angewandte. Limnologie 19:1-15.

Inglis, C. C. 1949. The behavior and control of rivers and

canals. Vicksburg, MS: U.S. Army Corps of Engineers, Waterways Experiment Station.

Inskip, P. D. 1982. Habitat suitability index models: Northern pike. Washington, DC: U.S. Fish and Wildlife Service (FWS/OBS-83/10.55).

Jager, H. I., W. Van Winkle, and B. D. Holcomb. 1999. Would hydrologic climate change in Sierra Nevada streams influence trout persistence? Transactions of the American Fisheries Society 128 (2): 222-240.

Jakober, M. E., T. E. McMahon, R. F. Thurow, and C. G. Clancy. 1998. Role of stream ice on fall and winter movements and habitat use by bull trout and cutthroat trout in Montana headwater streams. Transactions of the American Fisheries Society 127:223-235.

Jobling, S., M. Nolan, C. R. Tyler, G. Brighty, and J. P. Sumpter. 1998. Widespread sexual disruption in wild fish. Environmental Science and Technology 32(17):2498-2506.

Johnson, A. W. and D. M. Ryba. 1992. A literature review of recommended buffer widths to maintain various functions of stream riparian areas. Final report to King County Surface Water Management Division. Aquatic Resource Consultants, Seattle.

Johnson, K. N., J. F. Franklin, J. W. Thomas, and J. Gordon. 1991. Alternatives for Management of Late-Successional Forests of the Pacific Northwest. Report to the U. S. House of Representatives by the Scientific Panel on Late Successional Forest Ecosystems. Available at www.pnwin.nbii.gov/nwfp/alternatives.pdf.

Johnson, P. A., and T. M. Heil. 1996. Uncertainty in estimating bankfull conditions. Water Resources Bulletin 32(6):1283-1291.

Jones and Stokes Associates. 1994. Environmental impact report for the review of Mono Basin water rights for the City of Los Angeles. JSA 90-171. Prepared for California State Water Resources Control Board, Division of Water Rights, Sacramento, CA.

Jones, G., J. Whittington, J. McKay, A. Arthington, and others. 2001. Independent assessment of jurisdictional reports on the environmental achievements of the COAG Water Reforms. Technical report of the Cooperative Research Centre for Freshwater Ecology, commissioned by Environment Australia, National Competition Council, Natural Heritage Trust.

Jowett, I. G. 1993. Models of the abundance of large brown trout in New Zealand rivers. North American Journal of Fisheries Management 12:417-432.

Jowett, I. G., and J. Richardson. 1990. Microhabitat preferences of benthic invertebrates in a New Zealand river and the development of in-stream flow-habitat models for Deleatidium spp. New Zealand Journal of Marine and Freshwater Research 24(1):19-30.

Judy, R. D., Jr., P. N. Seeley, T. M. Murray, S. C. Svirsky, and others. 1984. 1982 National Fisheries Survey, Volume 1. Technical report: initial findings. Washington, DC: U.S. Fish and Wildlife Service (FWS-OBS-84/06).

Junk, W.J., P. B. Bayley, and R. E. Sparks. 1989. The flood pulse concept in river-floodplain systems. Pages 110-127 in D. P. Dodge, editor. Proceedings of the International Large River Symposium. Special Publication of the Canadian Journal of Fisheries and Aquatic Sciences 106.

Just, R. 1990. Recreational instream flows in Idaho: Instream flows-they're not just for fish anymore. Rivers 1(4): 307-312.

Karr, J. R. 1981. Assessment of biotic integrity using fish communities. Fisheries 6(6):21-27.

Karr, J. R. 1991. Biological integrity: A long-neglected aspect of water resource management. Ecological Applications 1:66-84.

Karr, J. R., and E. W. Chu. 1997. Biological monitoring and assessment: using multimetric indexes effectively. Seattle: University of Washington (EPA 235-R97-001). 149 pp.

Karr, J. R., and D. R. Dudley. 1981. Ecological perspective on water quality goals. Environmental Management 5:55-68.

Karr, J. R., K. D. Fausch, P. L. Angermeier, P. R. Yant, and I. J. Schlosser. 1986. Assessing biological integrity in running waters: A method and its rationale. Special Publication 5. Champaign: Illinois Natural History Survey. 28 pp.

Karr, J. R., and I. J. Schlosser. 1978. Water Resources and the land-water interface. Science 201:229-234.

Karr, J. R., L. A. Toth, and D. R. Dudley. 1985. Fish communities of midwestern rivers: A history of degradation. BioScience 35:90-95.

Kay, J. J., and E. Schneider. 1994. Embracing complexity, the challenge of the ecosystem approach. Alternatives 20(3):32-39.

Keller, E. A., and F. J. Swanson. 1979. Effects of large organic material on channel form and fluvial processes. Earth Surface Processes and Landforms 4:351-380.

Kershner, J. L., and W. M. Snider. 1992. Importance of a habitat-level classification system to design instream flow studies. Pages 179-193 in P. J. Boon, P. Calow and G. E. Petts, editors. River Conservation and Management. New York: John Wiley & Sons.

Kimmerer, W. J. 2002. Physical, biological, and management responses to variable freshwater flow into the San Francisco estuary. Estuaries 25: 1275-1290.

King, J. M., and R. E. Tharme. 1994. Assessment of the instream flow incremental methodology and initial development of alternative instream flow methodologies for South Africa. Report to Water Research Commission, Cape Town, South Africa (WRC Report No. 295/1/94).

King, J. M., R. E. Tharme, and M. S. deVilliers. 2001.

Environmental flow assessments for rivers: Manual for the building block methodology. Cape Town, South Africa: University of Cape Town, Freshwater Institute.

Klotz, J. R., and S. Swanson. 1997. Managed instream flows for woody vegetation recruitment: A case study. Pages 483-489 in J. Warwick, editor. Water Resources Education, Training, and Practice: Opportunities for the Next Century. Proceedings of the Universities Council Symposium on Water Resources. June 29- July 3, Keystone, Colorado. American Water Resources Association, Washington, DC.

Komadina-Douthwright, S. M., D. Caissie and R. A. Cunjak. 1997. Winter movement of radio-tagged Atlantic salmon (Salmo salar) kelts in relation to frazil ice pools of the Miramichi River. Canadian Technical Report of Fisheries and Aquatic Science 2161. Ottawa: National Research Council of Canada.

Komura, S., and D. B. Simmons. 1967. River bed degradation below dams. American Society of Civil Engineers Journal of the Hydraulics Division 93:1-14.

Kondolf, G. M. 1998. Development of flushing flows for channel restoration on Rush Creek, California. Rivers 6 (3):183-193.

Koontz, T. M. 1999. Measuring agency officials' efforts to foster and use public input in forest policy. Journal of Public Administration Research and Theory 9:251-280.

Kroger, R. L. 1973. Biological effects of fluctuation water levels in the Snake River, Grand Teton National Park, Wyoming. American Midland Naturalist 89:478-481.

Kuhnle, R. A., A. Simon, and R. L. Bingner. 1999. Dominant discharge of the incised channels of Goodwin Creek. Water Resources Conference, American Society of Civil Engineers, Seattle, WA. Paper available online at www.nal.usda.gov/ttic/tektran/data/000010/42/0000104267.html.

Kuikka, S., M. Hilden, H. Gislason, S. Hansson, and others. 1999. Modeling environmentally driven uncertainties in Baltic cod (Gadus morhua) management by Bayesian influence diagrams. Canadian Journal of Fisheries and Aquatic Sciences 56(4):629-641.

Kulik, B. 1990. A method to refine the New England aquatic base flow policy. Rivers 1(1):8-22.

Lackey, R. T. 1998. Seven pillars of ecosystem management. Landscape and Urban Planning 40:21-30.

Lamb, B. L., and E. Lord. 1992. Legal mechanisms for protecting riparian resource values. Water Resources Research 28(4):965-977.

Lamb, B. L., and H. Meshorer. 1983. Comparing instream flow programs: A report on current status. Pages 435-443 in Proceedings of Advances in Irrigation and Drainage: Surviving External pressures. American Society of Engineers, Irrigation and Drainage Division, Jackson, WY.

Lamb, B. L., and P. D. Ponds. 1999. Report to respondents on knowledge-holding studies: Descriptive statistics for knowledge-holding studies of S.E. Utah, S.W. Colorado, N.W. New Mexico, and Colorado Plateau Opinion Leaders. Fort Collins: U.S. Geological Survey, Midcontinent Ecological Science Center, Biological Resources Division.

Lamb, B. L., J. G. Taylor, N. Burkhart, and P. O. Ponds. 1998. A policy made to initiate environmental negotiations. Three hydropower workshops. Human Dimensions of Wildlife 3(4):1-17.

Lambert, W. P., and E. G. Fruh. 1978. A methodology for investigating freshwater inflow requirements for a Texas estuary. Pages 403-413 in M. L. Wiley, editor. Estuarine Interactions. London: Academic Press. 618 pp.

Lambou, V. W. 1959. Fish populations of backwater lakes in Louisiana. Transactions of the American Fisheries Society 88 (1):7-15.

Landres, P. B. 1983. Use of the guild concept in environmental impact assessment. Environmental Management 7:393-398.

Lane, E. W. 1955. The importance of fluvial morphology in hydraulic engineering. Proceedings of the American Society of Civil Engineers 81(745): 1-17.

Lang, V. 1999. Questions and answers on the New England Flow Policy. Concord, NH: U.S. Fish and Wildlife Service.

Lanka, R. P., W. A. Hubert, and T. A. Wesche. 1987. Relations of geomorphology to stream habitat and trout standing stock in small Rocky Mountain streams. Transactions of the American Fisheries Society 116 (1): 21-28.

Larsen, H. N. 1981. Interim regional policy for New England streamflow recommendations. Newton Corner, MA: U.S. Fish and Wildlife Service, Region 5.

Larsen, P. 1973. Hydraulic roughness of ice covers. Journal of the Hydraulics Division ASCE 99 (1):111-119.

Larsen, P. and L. Billfalk. 1978. Ice problems in Swedish hydropower operation. Pages 235-243 in Proceedings of the International Association for Hydraulic Research Symposium on Ice Problems. Part 2. Delft, The Netherlands: International Association for Hydraulic Research.

Lau, Y. L. 1982. Velocity distributions under floating covers. Canadian Journal of Civil Engineering 9(1):76-83.

Lawrence, R. L., S. E. Daniels, and G. H. Stankey. 1997. Procedural justice and public involvement in natural resource decision making. Society and Natural Resources 10(6): 577-589.

Leclerc, M., A. Boudreault, J. A. Bechara, and G. Corfa. 1995. Two-dimensional hydrodynamic modeling: A neglected tool in the instream flow incremental methodology. Transactions of the American Fisheries Society 124 (5):645-662.

Lee, K. N., and J. Lawrence. 1986. Adaptive management: learning from the Columbia River Basin fish and wildlife program. Environmental Law 16:431-460.

Leonard, P. M., and D. J. Orth. 1988. Use of habitat guilds of fishes to determine instream flow requirements. North American Journal of Fisheries Management 8:399-409.

Leopold, L. B. 1968. Hydrology for urban land planning. Circular 554. Washington, DC: U.S. Geological Survey.

Leopold, L. B. 1994. A View of the River. Cambridge, MA: Harvard University Press. 298 pp.

Leopold, L. B., and W. W. Emmett. 1983. Bedload movement and its relation to scour. Pages 640-649 in C.M. Elliot, editor. River Meandering. Proceedings from the Conference on Rivers. New Orleans, Louisiana. American Society of Civil Engineers Waterways, Port, Coastal and Ocean Section.

Leopold, L. B., M. G. Wolman, and J. P. Miller. 1964. Fluvial Processes in Geomorphology. San Francisco: W. H. Freeman.

Lewis, F. G, III. 1997. Apalachicola River and Bay water demand element: Summary and integration of Apalachicola Bay studies. Draft final report to the ACF/ACT Comprehensive Study. Northwest Florida Water Management District, Havana, Florida.

Ligon, F. K., W. E. Dietrich, and W. J. Thrush. 1995. Downstream ecological effects of dams. BioScience 45(3):183-192.

Likens, G. E., F. H. Bormann, R. S. Pierce, J. S. Eaton, and N. M. Johnson. 1977. Biogeochemistry of a Forested Ecosystem. New York: Springer-Verlag. 146pp.

Lindstrom, J. W. 2003. Habitat selection and movements of adult cutthroat trout and brook trout from fall through winter in a meandering alluvial-valley stream. Master's thesis. Laramie: University of Wyoming, Department of Zoology and Physiology.

Livingston, R. J., F. G. Lewis, G. C. Woodsum, X.-F. Niu, and others. 2000. Modeling oyster population response to variation in freshwater input. Estuarine, Coastal and Shelf Science 50: 655-672.

Livingston, R. J., X. Niu, F. G. Lewis, III, and G. Woodsum. 1997. Freshwater input to a gulf estuary: Long-term control of trophic organization. Ecological Applications 7(1):277-299.

Lobb, M. D., III. 1986. Habitat use by fishes of the New River. Master's thesis. Blackburg, VA: Virginia Polytechnic Institute and State University.

Lobb, M. D., III., and D. J. Orth. 1991. Habitat use by an Assemblage of fish in a large warmwater stream. Transactions of the American Fisheries Society 120:65-78.

Locke, A.G.H. 1989. Instream flow requirements for fish in the Highwood River. Final report to the Fish and Wildlife Division, Edmonton. 43pp + appendixes.

Longley, W. L., editor. 1994. Freshwater inflows to Texas bays and estuaries: Ecological relationships and methods for determination of needs. Austin: Texas Water Development Board and Texas Parks and Wildlife Department.

Los Angeles Department of Water and Power. 1995. Draft Mono Basin stream and channel restoration plan. Los Angeles: Department of Water and Power.

Lotspeich, F. B. 1980. Watersheds as the basic ecosystem: this conceptual framework provides a basis for a natural classification system. Water Resources Bulletin 16(4):581-586.

Lowe-McConnel, R. H. 1987. Ecological Studies in Tropical Fish Communities. New York: Cambridge University Press.

Lowham, H. W. 1988. Streamflows in Wyoming. USGS Water Resources Report 88-4045. Washington, DC: U. S. Geological Survey.

Mac, M. J., P. A. Opler, C. E. Puckett-Haecker, and P. D. Doran. 1998. Status and trends of the nation's biological resources. Reston, VA: U.S. Geological Survey.

Maciolek, J., and P. Needham. 1952. Ecological effects of winter conditions on trout and trout foods in Convict Creek, California, 1951. Transactions of the American Fisheries Society 81:202-217.

MacKay, D. K., D. A. Sherstone, and K. S. Arnold. 1974. Channel ice effects and surface water velocities from aerial photography of Mackenzie River break-up. In Hydrologic Aspects of Northern Pipeline Development. Northern Pipelines Task Force on Northern Oil Development. Quebec: Department of the Environment, Water Resources Branch, Environmental-Social Program (Report No. 74-12).

Maddock, I. P., G. E. Petts, M. Greenwood, and C. Evans. 1995. Assessing river-aquifer interactions within the hyporheic zone. Pages 53-74 in A. G. Brown, editor. Geomorphology and Groundwater. London: John Wiley & sons.

Maguire, J. C. 1996. Fashioning an equitable vision for public resource protection and development in Canada: The public trust doctrine revisited and reconceptualized. Journal of Environmental Law and Practice 7(1):1-42.

Mahoney, J. M., and S. B. Rood. 1998. Streamflow requirements for cottonwood seedling recruitment: An integrative model. Wetlands 18(4):634-645.

Maki-Petays, A, T. Muotka, and A. Huusko. 1999. Densities of juvenile brown trout in two subarctic rivers: Assessing the predictive capability of habitat preference indices. Canadian Journal of Fisheries and Aquatic Sciences 56:1420-1427.

Martin, C. R., and T. B. Hess. 1986. Impacts of sand and gravel dredging on trout habitat in the Chattahoochee River, Georgia. Final Report (Project F-26) to Georgia Department of Natural Resources,

Game and Fish Division, Social Circle, GA.

Martin, Q. 1987. Estimating freshwater inflow needs for Texas estuaries by mathematical programming. Water Resources Research 23: 230-238.

Mathews, S. B., and F. W. Olson. 1980. Factors affecting Puget Sound coho salmon (Oncorhynchus kisutch) runs. Canadian Journal of Fisheries and Aquatic Sciences 37(9):1373-1378.

Matsumoto, J., G. Powell, and D. Brock. 1994. Freshwater-inflow need of estuary computed by Texas estuarine MP model. Journal of Water Resources Planning and Management 120: 693-714.

Matthews, R. C., and Y. Bao. 1991. The Texas method for preliminary instream flow determination. Rivers 2(4):295-310.

Matthews, W. J., and D. C. Heins, editors. 1987. Community and Evolutionary Ecology of North American Stream Fishes. Norman: University of Oklahoma Press.

Mattson, R. 2002. A resource-based framework for establishing freshwater inflow requirements for the Suwanne River estuary. Estuaries 25 (6B): 1333-1342.

McBain, S. M., and W. J. Trush. 1997. Trinity River Channel Maintenance Flow Study. Final Report to the Hoopa Valley Tribe, Trinity Task Force. Available from McBain and Trush, Arcata, California.

McCann, D. 1998. World's first hydroelectric central station lighted up Appleton with excitement. Milwaukee Journal Sentinel. Sept. 8; Sect. B: 2 (col. 1).

McCool, S. F., and K. Guthrie. 2001. Mapping the dimensions of successful public participation in messy natural resources management situations. Society and Natural Resources 14(4): 309-323.

McKay, J. M. 1994. Water planning in South Australia. The Australian Journal of Natural Resources Law and Policy 1(2):181-192.

McKernan, D. L., D. R. Johnson, and J. I. Hodges. 1950. Some factors influencing the trends of salmon populations in Oregon. Transactions of the North American Wildlife Conference 15:427-449.

McKinney, M.J. 1990. Instream flow policy in Montana: A history and blueprint for the future. Public Land Law Review 11:81-133.

McKinney, M. J. 1991 Leasing water for instream flows: The Montana experience. Rivers 2(3).247-254.

Meeter, D. A., R. J. Livingston, and G. C. Woodsum. 1979. Long-term climatological cycles and population changes in a river-dominated estuarine system. Pages 315-338 in R. J.Livingston, editor. Ecological Processes in Coastal and Marine Systems. New York: Plenum Press.

Meng, L., and S. A. Matern. 2001. Native and introduced larval fishes of Suisun Marsh, California: The effects of freshwater flow. Transactions of the American Fisheries Society 130:750-765.

Merrill, T., and J. O'Laughlin. 1993. Analysis of methods for determining minimum instream flows for recreation. Report No. 9. Moscow: University of Idaho, Idaho Forest, Wildlife and Range Policy Analysis Group. 46 pp.

Meyer, C. H. 1993. Instream flows: Integrating new uses and new players into the prior appropriation system. Pages 2.1-20 in L. J. MacDonnell and T. A. Rice, editors. Instream Flow Protection in the West. Revised edition. Boulder: University of Colorado Natural Resources Law Center.

Meyer-Peter, E., and Mueller, R. 1948. Formula for bed-load transport. Proceedings of the International Association for Hydraulic Research, 2d Meeting. Stockholm.

Meyers, L. S., T . F. Thuemler, and G. W. Kornley. 1992. Seasonal movements of brown trout in Northeast Wisconsin. North American Journal of Fisheries Management 12:433-441.

Milburn, D.,and T. D. Prowse. 1996. Open water versus under-ice rating curves for suspended sediment: An example from a large northern river. Pages 873-880 in Proceedings of the International Association for Hydraulic Research Ice Symposium. Delft, The Netherlands: International Association for Hydraulic Research.

Milhous, R. T., J. M. Bartholow, M. A. Updike, and A. R. Moos. 1990. Reference manual for the generation and analysis of habitat time series-version II. Washington, DC: U.S. Fish and Wildlife Service (Biological Report 90 [16]). 249pp.

Milhous, R. T., M. A. Updike, and D. M. Schneider. 1989. Physical habitat simulation reference manual-version II. Washington, DC: U.S. Fish and Wildlife Service (Biological Service Report 89 [16]).

Milhous, R. T., D. L. Wegner, and T. Waddle. 1984. Users guide to the physical habitat simulation system (PHABSIM). Instream Flow Information Paper No. 11. Washington, DC: U.S. Fish and Wildlife Service (FWS/OBS-81/43). Revised.

Miller, J. E., and D. L. Frink. 1984. Changes in flood response of the Red River of the North Basin, North Dakota-Minnesota. U.S. Geological Survey Water-Supply Paper 2243. Washington, DC: U.S. Geological Survey.

Miller, J. R., and J. B. Ritter. 1996. An examination of the Rosgen classification of natural rivers. Catena 27:295-299.

Minshall, G. W., K. W. Cummins, R. C. Petersen, C. E. Cushing, and others. 1985. Developments in stream ecosystem theory. Canadian Journal of Fisheries and Aquatic Science 42:1045-1055.

Mitchell, R. C., and R. T. Carson. 1989. Using Surveys to Value Public Goods: The Contingent Valuation Method. Washington, DC: Resources for the Future/Johns Hopkins University Press.

Molles, M. C., C. S. Crawford, and L. M. Ellis. 1995. Effect of an experimental flood on litter dynamics in middle Rio Grande riparian ecosystem. Regulated Rivers: Research and Management 11:275-281.

Montana Department of Fish, Wildlife and Parks. 1984. Handbook for the assessment of small hydroelectric developments. Billings: Montana Department of Fish, Wildlife and Parks.

Montgomery, D. R., and J. M. Buffington. 1983. Channel classification, prediction of channel response, and assessment of channel condition. Seattle: University of Washington, Department of Geological Sciences and Quaternary Research Center (Report FW-SH10-93-002).

Moore, I. D., and C. L. Larson. 1979. Effects of drainage projects on surface runoff from small depressional watersheds in the North Central region. Bulletin 99. St. Paul: University of Minnesota, Water Resources Research Center.

Moore, K.M.S., and S. V. Gregory. 1988. Summer habitat utilization and ecology of cutthroat trout fry (Salmo clarki) in Cascade Mountain streams. Canadian Journal of Fisheries and Aquatic Sciences 45 (11):1921-1930.

Moore, S. A. 1996. Defining "successful" environmental dispute resolution: Case studies from public land planning in the United States and Australia. Environmental Impact Assessment Review 16:151-169.

Morhardt, J. E. 1986. Instream flow methodologies. Report of research project 2194-2. Electric Power Research Institute, Palo Alto, California (EPRI EA-4819).

Morhardt, J. E., D. F. Hanson, and P. J. Coulston. 1983. Instream flow analysis: Increased accuracy using habitat mapping. Pages 1294-1304 in Waterpower 83: Proceedings of the International Conference on Hydropower. Norris, TN: Tennessee Valley Authority.

Morisawa, M. 1968. Streams: Their Dynamics and Morphology. New York: McGraw-Hill.

Morris, J. A. 1976. Instream flow evaluation for outdoor recreation. Pages 352-358 in J. F. Orsborn and C. H. Allman, editors. Instream Flow Needs. Bethesda MD: Special publication of the American Fisheries Society.

Mortazavi, B., R. L. Iverson, W. M. Landing, F.G. Lewis, and W. Huang. 2002. Control of phytoplankton production and biomass in a river-dominated estuary: Apalachicola Bay, Florida, USA. Marine Ecological Progress Series 198:19-31.

Mosley, M. P. 1981. Semi-determinate hydraulic geometry of river channels, South Island, New Zealand. Earth Surface Process and Landforms 6:127-137.

Moyle, P. B., and D. M. Baltz. 1985. Microhabitat use by an assemblage of California stream fishes: Developing criteria for instream flow determinations. Transactions of the American Fisheries Society 114 (5): 695-704.

Moyle, P. B., M. P. Marchetti, J. Baldridge, and T. L. Taylor. 1998. Fish health and diversity: Justifying flows for a California stream. Fisheries 23(7):6-15.

Moyle, P. B., and B. Vondracek. 1985. Structure and per-sistence of the fish assemblage in a small California stream. Ecology 66:1-13.

Murray Darling Basin Commission. 2000a. Murray Darling Basin agreement schedule E: Interstate transfer of water allocations schedule incorporated in Commonwealth and State acts. Canberra: Murray Darling Basin Commission.

Murray Darling Basin Commission. 2000b. Exchange rates report. Exchange rates for the interstate transfer of water entitlements in the Mallee Region. Canberra: Murray Darling Basin Commission.

Muth, R. T., L. Crist, K. LaGory, J. Hayse, and others. 2000. Flow and temperature recommendations for endangered fishes in the Green River downstream of Flaming Gorge Dam. Final report to Upper Colorado River Endangered Fish Recovery Program Project FG-53, Denver, Colorado.

Nabhan, G. P. 1995. The dangers of reductionism in biodiversity conservation. Conservation Biology 9(3): 479-481.

Naeem, S., J. Thompson, S. P. Lawler, J. H. Lawton, and R. M. Woodfin. 1994. Declining biodiversity can alter the performance of ecosystems. Nature 368:734-737.

Naiman, R. J., D. G. Lonzarich, T. J. Beechie, and S. C. Ralph. 1992. General principles of classification and the assessment of conservation potential in rivers. Pages 93-123 in P. J. Boon, P. Calow, and G. E. Petts, editors. River Conservation and Management. New York: John Wiley & Sons.

Naiman, R. J., and K. H. Rogers. 1997. Large animal and system-level characteristics in river corridors: Implications for river management. BioScience 47(8):521-529.

National Research Council. 1992. Water Transfers in the West: Efficiency, Equity, and the Environment. Washington, DC: National Academy Press. 300 pp.

National Research Council. 2002. Riparian Areas: Functions and Strategies for Management. Committee on Riparian Zone Functioning and Strategies for Management. Washington, DC: National Academy Press.

Neave, F. 1949. Game fish populations of the Cowichan River. Fisheries Research Board of Canada. Bulletin 84.

Needham, P. R., J. W. Moffett, and D. Slater. 1945. Fluctuations in wild brown trout populations in Convict Creek, California. Journal of Wildlife Management 9(1):9-25.

Neel, J. K. 1963. Impact of reservoirs. Pages 575-593 in D. G. Frey, editor. Limnology in North America. Madison: University of Wisconsin Press.

Nehring, R. B. 1979. Evaluation of instream flow methods and determination of water quantity needs for streams in the state of Colorado. Fort Collins: Colorado Division of Wildlife.

Nehring, R. B. 1988. Fish flow investigations. Final report to Colorado Division of Wildlife, Fort Collins, Colorado (No. F-51-R).

Nehring, R. B., and R. M. Anderson. 1993. Determination of population-limiting critical salmonid habitats in Colorado streams using the Physical Habitat Simulation system. Rivers 4(1):1-19.

Nehring, R. B., and D. D. Miller. 1987. The influence of spring discharge levels on rainbow trout and brown trout recruitment and survival in Black Canyon of the Gunnison River, Colorado, as determined by IFIM/PHABSIM models. Pages 388-397 in Proceedings of the Annual Conference of the Western Association of Fish and Wildlife Agencies. Salt Lake City, Utah.

Nelson, F. A. 1980. Evaluation of four instream flow methods applied to four trout rivers in southwest Montana. Final report to U.S. Fish and Wildlife Service and Montana Department of Fish, Wildlife and Parks, Boseman, Montana.

Nelson, H., and others. 1988. Operation plan evaluation and environmental assessment: Lake Traverse, Bois de Sioux River, and Orwell Reservoir. Grand Forks, ND: U.S. Army Corps of Engineers.

Nestler, J. M., L. T. Schneider, and D. Latka. 1993. Physical habitat analysis of Missouri River main stem reservoir tailwaters using the riverine community habitat assessment and restoration concept (RCHARC). Vicksburg, MS: U.S. Army Corps of Engineers, Waterways Experiment Station (Technical Report EL-93-22). 39 pp. and appendixes.

Nestler, J. M., L. T. Schneider, D. Latka, and P. Johnson. 1996. Impact analysis and restoration planning using the riverine community habitat assessment and restoration concept (RCHARC). Pages A871-A876 in M. Leclerc, H. Capra, S. Valentin, A. Boudreault, and Y. Cote, editors. Ecohydraulics 2000. Proceedings of the Second International Symposium on Habitat Hydraulics, Quebec City, Canada.

Neves, R. J., and J. C. Widlak. 1987. Habitat ecology of juvenile freshwater mussels (Bivalvia: Unionidae) in a headwater stream in Virginia. American Malacological Bulletin 5:1-7.

Newbold, J. D. 1987. Phosphorus spiraling in rivers and rivers-reservoir systems: Implications of a model. Pages 303-327 in J. F. Craig and J. B. Kemper, editors. Regulated Streams: Advances in Ecology. New York: Plenum Press.

New England Power. 1994. Harriman qualitative fisheries assessment. Federal Energy Regulatory Commission Additional Information Request No. 4, Deerfield River Project, Responses to Additional Information Request, Volume X.

Nilsson, C., and M. Dynesius. 1994. Ecological effects of river regulation on mammals and birds: A review. Regulated Rivers: Research and Management 9:45-53.

Nilsson, C., G. Grelsson, M. Johansson, and U. Sperens. 1989. Patterns of plant species richness along riverbanks. Ecology 70:77-84.

Nixon, S. W. 1981. Freshwater inputs and estuarine productivity. Pages 31-57 in R. D. Cross and D. L. Williams, editors. Proceedings of the National Symposium on Freshwater Inflow to Estuaries. Volume 1. Washington, DC: U.S. Fish and Wildlife Service, Office of Biological Services (FWS/OBS-81-04).

Normandeau Associates, Inc. 1992. An instream flow study of the mainstem and west branch of the Farmington River. Final report to the Department of Environmental Protection, Hartford, Connecticut.

Normandeau Associates, Inc. 1999. Relationships between instream flow and fisheries habitat in the Housatonic River, Connecticut. Appendix F in Connecticut Power and Light Company. Application for new license for the Housatonic River Project, August 1999 (Project No. 2597-CT). Federal Energy Regulatory Commission, Washington, DC.

Noss, R. F. 1990. Indicators for monitoring biodiversity: A hierarchical approach. Conservation Biology 4:355-364.

Noss, R. F., and A. Y. Cooperrider. 1994. Saving Nature's Legacy. Washington DC: Island Press.

Noss, R. F., E. T. LaRoe, and J. M. Scott. 1995. Endangered ecosystems of the United States: A preliminary assessment of loss and degradation. Washington, DC: National Biological Service (Biological Report No. 28).

Novak, M. A. 1972. The beaver in Ontario. Ontario: Ministry of Natural Resources. 21 pp.

Novak, M. A., and R. W. Bode. 1992. Percent model affinity: A new measure of macroinvertebrate community composition. Journal of the North American Benthological Society 11(1):80-85.

O'Brien, J. S. 1984. Hydraulic and sediment transport investigations. Report 83-8. Dinosaur National Monument, Water Resources Field Support Laboratory, Colorado State University, Fort Collins, CO.

Odum, E. P. 1969. The strategy of ecosystem development. Science 164:262-270.

Odum, E. P. 1978. The value of wetlands: A hierarchical approach. Pages 16-25 in P. E. Greeson, J. R. Clark, and J. E. Clark, editors. Wetland Functions and Values: The state of our understanding. Minneapolis, MN. American Water Resources Association.

Ohmart, R. D., and B. W. Anderson. 1986. Riparian habitat. Pages 164-199 in B. S. Cooperider, editor. Inventorying and Monitoring of Wildlife Habitat. Denver, CO: Bureau of Land Management.

Olsen, N.R.B., and K. T. Alfredson. 1994. A three-dimensional numerical model for calculation of hydraulic conditions for fish habitat. Pages 113-123 In Proceedings of the First International Symposium on Habitat Hydraulics. The Norwegian Institute of Technology, Trondheim, Norway.

Organization of Wildlife Planners. 1995. Developing Comprehensive Management Systems for Wildlife Agencies. Manual from the seminar held October 23-27, 1995, Stowe, Vermont. For more information, contact OWP at http://www.owpweb.org.

Orsborn, J. F., and C. H. Allman, editors. 1976. Proceedings of the Symposium and Specialty Conference on Instream Flow Needs. Volumes I and II. Bethesda, MD: American Fisheries Society.

Orth, D. J. 1987. Ecological Considerations in the development and application of instream flow-habitat models. Regulated Rivers: Research and Management 1:171-181.

Orth, D. J., and O. E. Maughan. 1982. Evaluation of the incremental methodology for recommending instream flows for fishes. Transactions of the American Fisheries Society 111:413-445.

Orth, D. J., and P. M. Leonard. 1990. Comparison of discharge methods and habitat optimization for recommending instream flows to protect fish habitat. Regulated Rivers: Research and Management 5:129-138.

Osborne, L. L., and D. A. Kovacic. 1993. Riparian vegetated buffer strips in water quality restoration and stream management. Freshwater Biology 29:243-258.

Osmundson, D. B., R. J. Ryel, V. L. Lamarra, and J. Pitlick. 2002. Flow-sediment-biota relations: implications for river regulation effects on native fish abundance. Ecological Applications 12 (6): 1719-1739.

Paragamian, V. L. 1978. Population dynamics of smallmouth bass in the Maquoketa River and other Iowa streams: Physical and chemical characteristics of the Maquoketa River. Annual Progress Report. Des Moines: Iowa Conservation Commission (Federal Aid Project Number F-89-2).

Parasiewicz, P. 2001. MesoHABSIM—A concept for application of instream flow models in river restoration planning. Fisheries 26(9): 6-13.

Parasiewicz, P., and A. Gallagher 2002. Ecohydrology study of Quinebaug River—Interim Report. NY Cooperative Fish and Wildlife Research Unit and Department of Natural Resources, Cornell University. Project Report to New England Interstate Water Pollution Control Commission, Ithaca, NY.

Paschal, J. E., Jr., and D. E. Mueller. 1991. Simulation of water quality and the effects of wastewater effluent on the South Platte River from Chatfield Reservoir through Denver, Colorado. Water Resources Investigations Report 91-016. Denver: U.S. Geological Survey.

Pearson, W. D., and D. R. Franklin. 1968. Some factors affecting drift rates of Baetis and Simuliidae in a large river. Ecology 49:75-81.

Peters, E. J., R. S. Holland, M. A. Callam, and D. L. Bunnell. 1989. Platte River suitability criteria. Technical Series 17. Lincoln: Nebraska Game and Parks Commission.

Peters, J. C. 1982. Effects of river and streamflow alteration on fishery resources. Fisheries 7(2):20-22.

Petts, G. E. 1984. Impounded Rivers. Chichester, England: John Wiley & Sons.

Petts, G. E. 1987. Time-scales for ecological change in regulated rivers. Pages 257-266 in J. F. Craig, and J. B. Kemper, editors. Regulated Streams: Advances in Ecology. New York: Plenum Press.

Petts, G. E. 1989. Perspectives for the ecological management of rivers. Pages 3-26 in J. A. Gore and G. E. Petts, editors. Alternatives in Regulated River Management. Boca Raton, FL: CRC Press.

Petts, G. E., and I. Foster. 1985. Rivers and Landscape. London: Edward Arnold.

Petts, G. E., and I. Maddock. 1996. Flow allocation for in-river needs. Pages 60-79 in G. Petts, and P. Calow, editors. River Restoration. London: Blackwell Science.

Phillips, R. W., R. T. Lantz, W. W. Claire, and J. R. Moring. 1975. Some effects of gravel mixtures on emergence of coho salmon and steelhead trout fry. Transactions of American Fisheries Society 104(3): 461-466.

Pimm, S. L.. 1984. The complexity and stability of ecosystems. Nature 307:321–326.

Platts, W. S. 1979. Relationships among stream order, fish populations, and aquatic geomorphology in an Idaho river drainage. Fisheries 4:5-9.

Platts, W. S., and R. L. Nelson. 1988. Fluctuations in trout populations and their implications for land-use evaluation. North American Journal of Fisheries Management 8:333-345.

Ploskey, G. R. 1986. Effects of water-level changes on reservoir ecosystems with implications for fisheries management. Pages 86-97 in G. E. Hall and M. J. Van Den Avyle, editors. Reservoir Fisheries Management: Strategies for the 80's. Bethesda, MD: Southern Division of the American Fisheries Society, Reservoir Committee.

Poff, N. L., J. D. Allan, M. B. Bain, J. R. Karr, and others. 1997. The natural flow regime: A paradigm for river conservation and restoration. Bioscience 47(11):769-784.

Poff, N. L., and J. V. Ward. 1989. Implications of streamflow variability and predictability for lotic community structure: A regional analysis of streamflow patterns. Canadian Journal of Fisheries and Aquatic Sciences 46:1805-1818.

Polzin, M. L., and S. B. Rood. 2000. Effects of damming and flow stabilization on riparian processes and black cottonwoods along the Kootenay River. Rivers 7(3):221-232.

Post, J. R., and E. A. Parkinson. 2001. Energy allocation strategy in young fish: Allometry and survival. Ecology 82:1040-1051.

Postel, S. 1992. Last Oasis: Facing the Limits. Washington, DC: Worldwatch Institute.

Potter, L. 1988. The public's role in the acquisition and enforcement of instream flows. Land and Water Law Review 28:421-441.

Potyondy J. P., and E. D. Andrews. 1999. Channel maintenance considerations in hydropower relicensing. Stream Notes. Fort Collins: U.S. Forest Service, Rocky Mountain Research Station, Stream Systems Technology Center.

Powell, G. C. 1958. Evaluation of the effect of a power dam water release pattern upon the downstream fishery. Master's thesis. Fort Collins: Colorado State University.

Powell, G. L., J. Matsumoto, and D. A. Brock. 2002. Methods for determining minimum freshwater inflows needs of Texas bays and estuaries. Estuaries 25 (6B): 1262-1274.

Power, M. E., A. Sun, G. Parker, E. Dietrich, and J. T. Wootton. 1995. Hydraulic food-chain models: An approach to the study of food-web dynamics in large rivers. BioScience 45(3):159-167.

Powers, P. D., and J. F. Orsborn. 1985. Analysis of barriers to upstream fish migration: An investigation of the physical conditions affecting fish passage success at culverts and waterfalls. Final Report 1984 (Project No. 82-14). Portland, OR: U.S. Department of Energy, Bonneville Power Administration, Division of Fish and Wildlife. xiii + 120 pp.

Prowse, T. D. 1993. Suspended sediment concentration during river ice breakup. Canadian Journal of Civil Engineering 20:872-875.

Prowse, T. D. 1994. Environmental significance of ice to streamflow in cold regions. Freshwater Biology 32: 241-259.

Prowse, T. D. 2001a. River-ice ecology. I: Hydrologic, geomorphic, and water quality aspects. Journal of Cold Regions Engineering 15(1): 1-16.

Prowse, T. D. 2001b. River-ice ecology. II: Biological aspects. Journal of Cold Regions Engineering 15(1):17-33.

Prowse, T. D., and M. Conly. 1996. Impacts of flow regulation on the aquatic ecosystem of the Peace and Slave Rivers. NRBS Synthesis Report No. 1, Northern River Basins Study, Edmonton, Canada.

Purdom, C. E., P. A. Hardiman, V. J. Bye, N. C. Eno, and others. 1994. Estrogenic effects of effluents from sewage-treatment works. Chemistry and Ecology 8:275-285.

Quigley, T. M., R. W. Haynes, and R. T. Graham, editors. 1996. Integrated scientific assessment for ecosystem management in the interior Columbia Basin and portions of the Klamath and Great basins. Portland, OR: U. S. Forest Service, Pacific Northwest Research Station (PNW-GTR-382).]

Quinn, J. W., and T. J. Kwak. 2003. Fish assemblage changes in an Ozark river after impoundment: A long-term perspective. Transactions of the American Fisheries Society 132:110-119.

Railsback, S. 1999. Reducing uncertainties in instream flow studies. Fisheries 24(4):24-26.

Rains, M. C. 2003. Hydrogeological principles useful in predicting the effects of streamflow alterations on shallow groundwater and associated riparian vegetation. Stream Notes. Fort Collins,CO: U.S. Forest Service, Stream Systems Technology Center.

Rains, M. C., and J. F. Mount. 2002. Origin of shallow groundwater in an alluvial aquifer as determined by isotopic and chemical procedures. Groundwater 40: 552-563.

Rantz, S. E., and others. 1982a. Measurement and computation of streamflow: Volume 1.Measurement of Stage and Discharge. U.S. Geological Survey Water-Supply Paper 2175. Washington, DC: U.S. Government Printing Office. 284 pp.

Rantz, S. E., and others. 1982b. Measurement and computation of streamflow: Volume 2. Computation of Discharge. U.S. Geological Survey Water Supply Paper 2175. Washington, DC: U.S. Government Printing Office. 346 pp.

Rasmussen, J. L. 1996. Floodplain Management: AFS Position Statement. Fisheries 21(4):6-10.

Raymond, H. L. 1979. Effects of dams and impoundments on migration of juvenile chinook salmon and steelhead trout from the Snake River, 1966-1975. Transactions of the American Fisheries Society 108:509-529.

Reed, M. S. 1989. A comparison of aquatic communities in regulated and natural reaches of the Upper Tallapoosa River. Final Report for Contract 14-16-0009-1550/13. Auburn University, Alabama.

Reed, S. W. 1986. The public trust doctrine: Is it amphibious? Journal of Environmental Law and Literature 1:107-109.

Reed, S. W. 1990. Conserved water in Oregon. Rivers 1(2):148-149.

Reeves, G. H., L. E. Benda, K. M. Burnett, P. A. Bisson, and J. R. Sedell. 1996. A disturbance-based ecosystem approach to maintaining and restoring freshwater habitats of evolutionarily significant units of anadromous salmonids in the Pacific Northwest. Bethesda: American Fisheries Society Symposium 17:334-349.

Reiser, D. W., M. P. Ramey, and T. R. Lambert. 1988. Review of flushing flow requirements in regulated streams. In W. R. Nelson, J. R. Dwyer, and W. E. Greenberg, editors. Flushing and Scouring Flows for Habitat Maintenance in Regulated Streams. Washington, DC: U.S. Environmental Protection Agency.

Reiser, D. W., T. A. Wesche, and C. Estes. 1989. Status of instream flow litigation and practices in North America. Fisheries 14(2) 22-29.

Reiser, D. W., and R. G. White. 1988. Effects of two sediment-size classes on steelhead trout and chinook salmon egg incubation and juvenile quality. North American Journal of Fisheries Management 8(4):432-437.

Richards, K. 1982. Rivers: Form and Process in Alluvial Channels. London: Methuen & Company.

Richardson, E. V., D. B. Simons, S. Karaki, K. Mahmood, and M. A. Stevens. 1975. Highways in the river environment, hydraulic and environmental design consideration: Training and design manual. Washington, DC: U.S. Dept. of Transportation Federal Highway Administration.

Richmond, M. C., and E. G. Zimmerman. 1978. Effect of temperature on activity of allozymic forms of supernatant malate dehydrgenase in the red shiner, Notropis lutrensis. Comparative Biochemistry and Physiology 61B:415-419.

Richter, B. D., J. V. Baumgartner, D. P. Braun, and J. Powell. 1998. A spatial assessment of hydrologic alteration within a river network. Regulated Rivers: Research and Management 14(4): 329-340.

Richter, B. D., J. V. Baumgartner, J. Powell, and D. P. Braun. 1996. A method for assessing hydrologic alteration within ecosystems. Conservation Biology 10:1163-1174.

Richter, B. D., J. V. Baumgartner, R. Wigington, and D. P. Braun. 1997. How much water does a river need? Freshwater Biology 37:231-249.

Robinson, A. T., R. W. Clarkson, and R. E. Forrest. 1998. Dispersal of larval fishes in a regulated river tributary. Transactions of the American Fisheries Society 127: 772-786.

Robinson, E. H. 1969. A procedure for determining desirable stream flows for fisheries. Concord, NH: U.S. Fish and Wildlife Service (Mimeo Report). 12 pp.

Rodriguez, C. A., K. W. Flessa, and D. L. Dettman. 2001. Effects of upstream diversion of Colorado River water on the estuarine bivalve mollusc Mulinaria coloradoensis. Conservation Biology 15(1):249-258.

Rood, S. B. and S. Heinze-Milne 1989. Abrupt downstream forest decline following river damming in southern Alberta. Canadian Journal of Botany 67:1744-1749.

Rood S. B., A. R. Kalischuk, and J.M. Mahoney 1998. Initial cottonwood seedling recruitment following the flood of the century of the Oldman River, Alberta, Canada. Wetlands 18(4): 557-570.

Rood, S. B. and J. M. Mahoney. 1990. Collapse of riparian poplar forests downstream from dams in western prairies: Probable causes and prospects for mitigation. Environmental Management 14:451-464.

Rood, S. B., and J. M. Mahoney. 2000. Revised instream flow regulation enables cottonwood recruitment along the St. Mary River, Alberta, Canada. Rivers 7(2):109-125.

Rood, S. B., J. M. Mahoney, D. E. Reid, and L. Zilm. 1995. Instream flows and the decline of riparian cottonwoods along the St. Mary River, Alberta. Canadian Journal of Botany 73:1250-1260.

Rood, S. B., S. Patino, K. Coombs, and M. T. Tyree. 2000. Branch sacrifice: Cavitation associated drought adaptation of riparian cottonwoods. Trees 14: 248-257.

Rood, S. B., K. Taboulchanas, C. E. Bradley, and A. R. Kalischuk. 1999. Influence of flow regulation on channel dynamics and riparian cottonwood recruitment along the Middle Bow River, Alberta. Rivers 7:33-48.

Root, R. B. 1967. The niche exploitation pattern of the blue-gray gnatcatcher. Ecology 37:317-350.

Rose, K., and C. Johnson. 1976. The relative merits of the modified sag-tape method for determining instream flow requirements. Salt Lake City: U.S. Fish and Wildlife Service.

Rosgen, D. L. 1985. A stream classification system. Pages 91-95 in Riparian Ecosystems and their Management. Proceedings of the First North American Riparian Conference. Fort Collins, CO: U.S. Forest Service, Rocky Mountain Forest and Range Experiment Station (General Technical Report RM-120).

Rosgen, D. L. 1994. A classification of natural rivers. Catena 22:169-199.

Rosgen, D. L. 1996. Applied River Morphology. Pagosa Springs, CO: Wildland Hydrology Books.

Ross, S. T. 1986. Resource partitioning in fish assemblages: A review of field studies. Copeia 1986:352-388.

Ross, S. T., and J. A. Baker. 1983. The response of fishes to periodic spring floods in a southeastern stream. American Midland Naturalist 109(1):1-14.

Ross, S. T., W. J . Matthews, and A. A. Echelle. 1985. Persistence of stream fish assemblages: Effects of environmental change. American Naturalist 126:24-40.

Rowntree, K. M., and R. A. Wadeson. 1998. A geomorphological framework for the assessment of instream flow requirements. Aquatic Ecosystem Health and Management 1:125-141.

Rulifson, R. A., and C. S. Manooch, III, editors. 1993. Roanoke River water flow committee report for 1991-1993. Albemarle-Pamlico estuarine study. Raleigh, NC: U.S. Environmental Protection Agency (Project No. APES 93-18).

Salo, E. O., and T. W. Cundy, editors. 1987. Streamside management: Forestry and fishery interactions. Contribution No. 57. Seattle: University of Washington, Institute of Forest Resources.

Sax, J. L. 1999. Evolution of the public trust doctrine. Pages 5-12 in G. E. Smith and A. R. Hoar, editors. The public trust doctrine and its application to protecting instream flows. Proceedings of a Workshop. Sponsored by the National Instream Flow Program Assessment (NIFPA-08). Anchorage: Alaska Department of Fish and Game and U.S. Fish and Wildlife Service, Region 7.

Sax, J. L., R. H. Abrams, and B. H. Thompson, Jr. 1991. Legal Control of Water Resources: Cases and Materials. 2d edition. St. Paul, MN: West Publishing.

Schelesinger, W. H. 1991. Biogeochemistry – An Analysis of Global Change. San Diego, CA: Academic Press.

Schlosser, I. J. 1982a. Fish community structure and function along two habitat gradients in a headwater stream. Ecological Monographs 52:395-414.

Schlosser, I. J. 1982b. Trophic structure, reproductive success, and growth rate of fishes in a natural and modified headwater stream. Canadian Journal of Fisheries and Aquatic Sciences 39:968-978.

Schlosser, I. J. 1985. Flow regime, juvenile abundance, and the assemblage structure of stream fishes. Ecology 66:1484-1490.

Schlosser, I. J. 1989. Effects of flow regime and cyprinid predation on a headwater stream. Ecological Monographs 59:41-57.

Schlosser, I. J. 1990. Environmental variation, life history attributes, and community structure in stream fishes: Implications for environmental management and assessment. Environmental Management 14:621-628.

Schlosser, I. J. 1991. Stream fish ecology: A landscape perspective. BioScience 41:704-712.

Schlosser, I. J., and P. L. Angermeier. 1990. The influence of environmental variability, resource abundance, and predation on juvenile cyprinid and centrarchid fishes. Polskie Archiwum Hydrobiologii 37:265-284.

Schneider, L. T., and J. M. Nestler. 1996. Using hydraulic and water quality modeling output for instream flow studies. Volume B. Pages B275-B281 in M. Leclerc, H. Capra, S. Valentin, A. Boudreault, and Y. Cote, editors. Ecohydraulics 2000. Proceedings of the Second International Symposium on Habitat Hydraulics, Quebec, INRS-Eau. Copublished with EQSA. IAHR/AIRH.

Schueler, T., and J. Galli. 1992. Environmental impacts of stormwater ponds. In Watershed Restoration Source Book. Washington, DC: Anacostia Restoration Team, Metropolitan Washington Council of Governments.

Schumm, S. A. 1969. River metamorphosis. American Society of Civil Engineers, Journal of Hydraulics Division, HY1:255-273.

Scott, M. L., G. T. Auble, and J. M. Friedman. 1996. Fluvial processes and the establishment of bottomland trees. Geomorphology 14: 327-339.

Shen, H. T., and T. O. Harden. 1978. The effect of ice cover on vertical transfer in stream channels. Water Resources Bulletin 14(6):1429-1439.

Sheridan, P. F., and R. J. Livingston. 1979. Cyclic trophic relationships of fishes in an unpolluted, river-dominated estuary in north Florida. Pages 143-161 in R. J. Livingston, editor. Ecological Processes in Coastal and Marine Systems. New York: Plenum Press.

Sherk, G. W. 1986. Eastern water law. Natural Resources and Environment (4):7-11-52-57.

Shuler, S. W., and R. B. Nehring. 1993. Using the physical habitat simulation model to evaluate a stream habitat enhancement project. Rivers 4:175-193.

Shuler, S. W., R. B. Nehring, and K. D. Fausch. 1994. Diel habitat selection by brown trout in the Rio Grande River, Colorado, after placement of boulder structures. North American Journal of Fisheries Management 14:99-111.

Shupe, S. J., and L. J. 1993. Recognizing the value of in-place uses of water in the West: An introduction to the laws, strategies, and issues. Pages 1.1-22 in L. J. MacDonnell and T. A. Rice, editors. Instream

Flow Protection in the West. Revised edition. Boulder: University of Colorado Natural Resources Law Center.

Shurts, J. 2000. The Winters Doctrine in its Social and Legal Context, 1800s-1930s. Norman: University of Oklahoma Press.

Simonson, T. D., and W. A. Swenson. 1990. Critical stream velocities for young-of-year smallmouth bass in relation to habitat use. Transactions of the American Fisheries Society 119:902-909.

Simpkins D. A., W. A. Hubert, and T. A. Wesche. 2000. Effects of fall to winter changes in habitat and frazil ice on the movements and habitat use by juvenile rainbow trout in a Wyoming tailwater. Transactions of the American Fisheries Society 129:101-118.

Slade, D. C., R. K. Kehoe, and J. K. Stahl. 1997. Putting the Public Trust Doctrine To Work. 2d edition. Washington, DC: Coastal States Organization, Inc. 376 pp.

Smith, A. K. 1973. Development and application of spawning velocity and depth criteria for Oregon salmonids. Transactions of the American Fisheries Society 102(2): 312-316.

Smith, D. G. 1980. River ice processes: Thresholds and geomorphologic effects in northern and mountain rivers. Pages 323-343 in D. R. Coates and J. D. Vitek, editors. Thresholds in Geomorphology. London: George, Allen, and Unwin.

Smith, I. M., and M. J. Sale. 1993. Standardizing instream flow requirements at hydropower projects in the Cascade Mountains, Washington. Pages 286-295 in W. D. Hall, editor. Waterpower '93: Proceedings of the International Conference on Hydropower. New York: American Society of Civil Engineers.

Smoker, W. A. 1953. Streamflow and silver salmon production in western Washington. Fisheries research papers. Olympia: Washington Department of Fish and Wildlife.

Smoker, W. A. 1955. Effects of streamflow on silver salmon production in western Washington. Doctoral dissertation. Seattle: University of Washington, Department of Fisheries.

Somach, S. L. 1990. The American Rivers decision: Balancing instream flow protection with other competing beneficial uses. Rivers. 1(4):251-263.

Sommer, T. R., M. L. Nobrigua, W. C. Harrell, W. Batham, and W. J. Kimmerer. 2001. Floodplain rearing of juvenile chinook salmon: Evidence of enhanced growth and survival. Canadian Journal of Fisheries and Aquatic Sciences 58(2):325-333.

Sparks, R. E. 1995. Need for ecosystem management of large rivers and their floodplains. BioScience 45:168-182.

Stalnaker, C. B. 1990. Minimum flow is a myth. Pages 31-33 in M. B. Bain, editor. Ecology and assessment of warmwater streams: Workshop synopsis. Washington, DC: U.S. Fish and Wildlife Service (Biological Report 90[5]).

Stalnaker, C. B. 1993. Fish habitat evaluation models in environmental assessments. Pages 140-162 in S. G. Hildebrand, and J. B. Cannon, editors. Environmental Analysis: The NEPA Experience. Boca Raton, FL: CRC Press.

Stalnaker, C. B. 1994. Evolution of instream flow modeling. Pages 276-286 in P. Calow and G. E. Petts, editors. River Handbook. Volume II. Oxford: Blackwell Scientific Publications.

Stalnaker, C. B., and J. L. Arnette. 1976. Methodologies for the determination of stream resource flow requirements: An assessment. Report prepared for U.S. Fish and Wildlife Service, Office of Biological Services, by Utah State University, Logan.

Stalnaker, C., B. L. Lamb, J. Henriksen, K. Bovee, and J. Bartholow. 1995. The instream flow incremental methodology: A primer for IFIM. Fort Collins: National Biological Service (Biological Report 29). 45 pp.

Stalnaker, C. B., and E. J. Wick. 2000. Planning for flow requirements to sustain stream biota. Pages 411-448 in E. E. Wohl, editor. Inland Flood Hazards. Cambridge, UK: University Press.

Stanford, J. A., and T. Gonser, editors. 1998. Rivers in the landscape: Special issue on riparian and groundwater ecology. Freshwater Biology 40(3):402-585.

Stanford, J. A., and J. V. Ward. 1988. The hyporheic habitat of river ecosystems. Nature 335:64-66.

Stanford, J. A., J. V. Ward, W. J. Liss, C. A. Frisnell, and others. 1996. A general protocol for restoration of regulated rivers. Regulated Rivers: Management and Research 12:391-413.

Stankovic, V. S., and D. Jankovic. 1971. Mechanismus der fisch-produktion im gebiet des mittleren Donaulaufes. Archiv für Hydrobiologie Supplement 36:299-305.

Stankowski, S. J. 1972. Population density as an indirect indicator of urban and suburban land-surface modifications. U.S. Geological Survey Professional Paper 800-B:B219-B224. Reston, VA: U.S. Geological Survey.

Steelman, T. A., and W. Ascher. 1997. Public involvement methods in natural resource policy making: Advantages, disadvantages, and trade-offs. Policy Sciences 30:71-90.

Sterba, O., V. Uvira, P. Mathur, and M. Rulik. 1992. Variations of the hyporheic zone through a riffle in the R. Morava, Czechoslovakia. Regulated Rivers: Management and Research (7):31-44.

Stock, J. D., and I. J. Schlosser. 1991. Short-term effects of a catastrophic beaver dam collapse on a stream fish community. Environmental Biology of Fishes 31:123-129.

Stone, A. W. 1990. Salvage: temporary changes and privatization of the water resource. Rivers 3(3): 208-210.

Streng, D. R., J. S. Glitzenstein, and P. A. Harcombe. 1989. Woody seedling dynamics in an east Texas floodplain forest. Ecological Monographs 59:177-204.

Stromberg, J. C. 1997. Growth and survivorship of Fremont cottonwood, Gooding willow, and salt cedar after large floods in central Arizona. Great Basin Naturalist 57:198-208.

Stromberg, J. C., and D. C. Patten. 1990. Riparian vegetation instream flow requirements: A case study from a diverted stream in the eastern Sierra Nevada, California, USA. Environmental Management 14(2):185-194.

Stromberg, J. C., and D. C. Patten. 1996. Instream flow and cottonwood growth in the eastern Sierra Nevada of California, USA. Regulated Rivers: Research & Management 12:1-12.

Swales, S., and J. H. Harris. 1995. The expert panel assessment method (EPAM): A new tool for determining environmental flows in regulated rivers. Pages 125-134 in D. M. Harper, and A.J.D. Ferguson, editors. The Ecological Basis for River Management. New York: John Wiley & Sons.

Swales, S., R. B. Lauzier, and C. D. Levings. 1986. Winter habitat preferences of juvenile salmonids in two interior rivers in British Columbia. Canadian Journal of Zoology 64:1506-1514.

Swift, B. L. 1984. Status of riparian ecosystems in the United States. Water Resources Bulletin 20(2):223-228.

Swift, C. H., III. 1976. Estimation of stream discharges preferred by steelhead trout for spawning and rearing in western Washington. U.S. Geological Survey Open-File Report 75-155. Tacoma: U.S. Geological Survey.

Szaro, R. C. 1986. Guild management: an evaluation of avian guilds as a predictive tool. Environmental Management 10:681-688.

Tappel, P. D., and T. C. Bjornn. 1983. A new method of relating size of spawning gravel to salmonid embryo survival. North American Journal of Fisheries Management 3(1):123-135.

Tarrant, M. A., C. Overdevest, A. D. Bright, H. K. Cordell, and D.B.K. English. 1997. The effect of persuasive communication strategies of rural resident attitudes toward ecosystem management. Society and Natural Resources 10(6):537-550.

Taylor, C. M., and R. J. Miller. 1990. Reproductive ecology and population structure of the plains minnow, Hybognathus placitus (Pisces:Cyprinidae), in Central Oklahoma. American Midland Naturalist 123:32-39.

Templet, P. H. 1995. The positive relationship between jobs, environment and the economy: An emperical analysis and review. Spectrum (Spring): 37-49.

Tennant, D. L. 1975. Instream flow regimes for fish, wildlife, recreation, and related environmental resources. Completion Report. Billings, MT: U.S. Fish and Wildlife Service.

Tennant, D. L. 1976a. Instream flow regimes for fish, wildlife, recreation, and related environmental resources. Fisheries 1(4):6-10.

Tennant, D. L. 1976b. Instream flow regimes for fish, wildlife, recreation and related environmental resources. Pages 359-373 in J. F. Osborn and C. H.

Allman, editors. Instream Flow Needs. Bethesda, MD: Special publication of the American Fisheries Society.

Terzi, R. A. 1981. Hydrometric Field Manual--Measurement of Streamflow. Inland Waters Directorate. Ottawa, Canada: Water Resources Branch.

Tessmann, S. A. 1980. Environmental assessment, technical appendix E in environmental use sector reconnaissance elements of the western Dakotas region of South Dakota study. Brookings, SD: South Dakota State University, Water Resources Research Institute.

Theurer, F. D., K. A. Voos, and W. J. Miller. 1984. Instream water temperature model. Instream Flow Information Paper No. 16. Washington, DC: U.S. Fish and Wildlife Service (FWS/OBS-84/15). 200 pp.

Thomas, J. A., and K. D. Bovee. 1993. Application and testing of a procedure to evaluate transferability of habitat suitability criteria. Regulated Rivers: Research and Management 8:285-294.

Thomas, J. C. 1993. Public involvement and governmental effectiveness: A decision-making model for public managers. Administration and Society 24(4) 444-469.

Thornthwaite, C. W., and J. R. Mather. 1955. The water balance. Laboratory of Climatology. Publication No. 8. Centerton, NJ: Drexel Institute of Technology.

Toth, L. A. 1995. Principles and guidelines for restoration of river/floodplain ecosystems - Kissimmee River, Florida. Pages 49-73 in J. Cairns, editor. Rehabilitating Damaged Ecosystems. 2d edition. Boca Raton, FL: Lewis Publishers/CRC Press.

Trihey, E. W., and C. B. Stalnaker. 1985. Evolution and application of instream flow methodologies to small hydropower development. Pages 176-183 in F. W. Olsen, R. H. White, and R. H. Hamre, editors. Proceedings of the Symposium on Small Hydropower and Fisheries. Bethesda, MD: American Fisheries Society.

Trotzky, H. M., and R. W. Gregory. 1974. The effects of water flow manipulation below a hydro-electric power dam on the bottom fauna of the upper Kennebec River, Maine. Transactions of the American Fisheries Society 103:318-324.

Trush W.,J., and S. M. McBain. 2000. Alluvial river ecosystem attributes. Stream Notes. Fort Collins: U.S. Forest Service, Stream Systems Technology Center.

Trush, W. J., S. M. McBain, and L. B. Leopold. 2000. Attributes of an alluvial river and their relation to water policy and management. In Proceedings of National Academy of Science 97(22):11858-11863.

Tung, Y. K., Y. Bao, L. W. Mays, and G. H. Ward. 1990. Optimization of freshwater inflow to estuaries. Journal of Water Resources Planning and Management 116:567-584.

Tyus, H. M. 1990. Effects of altered streamflows on fishery resources. Fisheries 15(3):18-20.

Tyus, H. M. 1992. An instream flow policy for recovering endangered Colorado fishes. Rivers 3(1):27-36.

Tyus, H. M., C. W. Brown, and J. F. Saunders, III. 2000. Movements of young Colorado pikeminnow and razorback sucker in response to water flow and light level. Journal of Freshwater Ecology 15(4): 525-535.

Tyus, H. M. and G. B. Haines. 1991. Distribution, habitat use, and growth of age-0 Colorado squawfish, Ptychocheilus lucius, in the Green, White, and Yampa rivers, Colorado and Utah. Transactions of the American Fisheries Society 120:79-89.

U.S. Army Corps of Engineers (USACE) 1962. HEC-2. Tulsa, OK: U.S. Army Corps of Engineers, Tulsa District.

U.S. Army Corps of Engineers, Hydraulic Engineering Center (USACE) 1991. HEC-6, Scour and deposition in rivers and reservoirs. User's manual. Accessed Internet May 2000. www.wrc-hec.usace.army.mil.

U.S. Army Corps of Engineers (USACE). 1996. National inventory of dams 1995-1996. CD-ROM. Also available at www.crunch.tec.army.mil/nid/web-pages/nid.cfm.

U.S. Army Corps of Engineers, Hydraulic Engineering Center (USACE). 1997. Accessed Internet May 2000. Computer program catalog. www.wrc-hec.usace.army.mil.

U.S. Army Corps of Engineers, Hydraulic Engineering Center (USACE). 2000a. Accessed Internet May 2000. Guidelines for the calibration and application of HEC-6. www.wrc-hec.usace.army.mil.

U.S. Army Corps of Engineers, Hydraulic Engineering Center (USACE) 2000b. Accessed Internet May 2000. HEC-6 on a PC. Training document 13. www.wrc-hec.usace.army.mil.

U.S. Army Corps Engineers, Hydrologic Engineering Center (USACE). Accessed Internet November 2001. The Hydrologic Engineering Center's River Analysis System, Version 3.0.1. www.waterengr.com/hecras.htm.

U.S. Environmental Protection Agency (USEPA). 1990. The quality of our nation's water: A summary of the 1988 National water Quality Inventory. Washington, DC: U.S. Environmental Protection Agency (EPA Report 840-B-92-002).

U.S. Environmental Protection Agency (USEPA). 2001. Better assessment science integrating point and nonpoint sources (BASINS) V3.0. Washington, DC: U.S. Environmental Protection Agency, Standards and Health Protection Division (4305), Office of Science and Technology, Office of Water. Available at www.epa.gov/ost/basins.

U.S. Fish and Wildlife Service (USFWS) and Hoopa Valley Tribe. 1999. Trinity River flow evaluation. Final report to Arcata Fish and Wildlife Office, Arcata, California. Available at www.ccfwo.rl.fws.gov/trflow.

U.S. Forest Service (USFS). 1988. Methods for Collection

and Analysis of Fluvial-Sediment Data. Washington, DC: U.S. Forest Service (WSDG-TP-00012). 85 pp.

U.S. Forest Service (USFS). 1995. A guide to field identification of bankfull stage in the western United States. Fort Collins, CO: U.S. Forest Service, Stream Systems Technology Center. 31 minute video.

U.S. Forest Service (USFS). 1997. An approach for quantifying channel maintenance instream flows in gravel-bed streams. Boise Adjudication Team. Boise: U.S. Forest Service.

U.S. Forest Service (USFS). 2003. Identifying bankfull stage in forested streams in the eastern United States. Fort Collins, CO: U.S. Forest Service, Stream Systems Technology Center. 46 minute video.

U.S. Geological Survey (USGS). 1991. Water Resources Data Minnesota Water Year 1990. Water-Data Report MN-90-1. St. Paul, MN: U.S. Geological Survey.

U.S. Geological Survey (USGS). 1992. Water Resources Data Minnesota Water Year 1991. Water-Data Report MN-90-1. St. Paul, MN: U.S. Geological Survey.

Vadas, R. L. 1992. Seasonal habitat use, species associations, and assemblage structure of forage fishes in Goose Creek, Northern Virginia, II. Mesohabitat patterns. Journal of Freshwater Ecology 7:149-163.

Vadas, R. L., and D. J. Orth. 1998. Use of physical variables to discriminate visually determined mesohabitat types in North American streams. Rivers 6 (3):43-159.

Vannote, R. L., G. W. Minshall, K. W. Cummins, J. R. Sedell, and C. E. Cushing. 1980. The river continuum concept. Canadian Journal of Fisheries and Aquatic Sciences 37:130-137.

Vaughan, D. M. 2002. Potential impact of road stream crossings (culverts) on the upstream passage of aquatic macroinvertebrates. Report submitted to the U.S. Forest Service, Technology and Development Center, San Dimas, CA.

Veiluva, M. 1981. The Fish and Wildlife Coordination Act in environmental litigation. Ecology Law Quarterly 9:489-517

Verner, J. 1984. The guild concept applied to management of bird populations. Environmental Management 8:1-14.

Waddle, T., P. Steffler, A. Ghanem, C. Katapodis, and A. Locke. 2000. Comparison of one- and two-dimensional open channel flow models for a small habitat stream. Rivers 7(3): 205-220.

Wadeson, R. A. and K. M. Rowntree. 1998. Application of the hydraulic biotope concept to the classification of instream habitats. Aquatic Ecosystem Health and Management 1:143-157.

Walker, H. J. 1969. Some aspects of erosion and sedimentation in an arctic delta during breakup. Pages 209-219 in Proceedings of the Symposium on the Hydrology of Deltas, 6-14 May 1969, Bucharest, Romania. International Association of Scientific Hydrology.

Walker, M. 1980. Utilization by fishes of a Blackwater Creek floodplain in North Carolina. Master's thesis. Greenville, NC: East Carolina University.

Wallace, J. B., and A. C. Benke. 1984. Quantification of wood habitat in subtropical coastal plains streams. Canadian Journal of Fisheries and Aquatic Sciences 41:1643-1652.

Wallace, J. B., J. R. Webster, and W. R. Woodall. 1977. The role of filter feeders in flowing waters. Archiv fur Hydrobiologie 79:506-532.

Walters, C. J. 1986. Adaptive Management of Renewable Resources. New York: McMillan.

Walters, C. J. 1997. Challenges in adaptive management of riparian and coastal ecosystems. Conservation Ecology 1(2):1. Available at www.consecol.org/vol1/iss2/art1.

Walters, C. J., and C. S. Holling. 1990. Large-scale management experiments and learning by doing. Ecology 71(6):2060-2068.

Walters, C. J., J. Korman, L.. E. Stevens, and B. Gold. 2000. Ecosystem modeling for evaluation of adaptive management policies in the Grand Canyon. Conservation Ecology 4(2):1. Available at www.consecol.org/vol4/iss2/art1.

Ward, J. V. 1989. The four-dimensional nature of lotic ecosystems. Journal of the North American Benthological Society 8(1):2-8.

Ward, J. V. 1998. Riverine Landscapes: Biodiversity Patterns, Disturbance Regimes, and Aquatic Conservation. Biological Conservation 83(3):269-278.

Ward, J. V., and J. A. Stanford. 1979. Ecological factors controlling stream zoobenthos with emphasis on thermal modification of regulated streams. Page 35-55 in J. V. Ward and J. A. Stanford, editors. The Ecology of Regulated Streams. New York: Plenum Press.

Ward, J. V., and J. A. Stanford. 1983. The serial discontinuity concept of lotic ecosystems. Pages 29-42 in T. D. Fontaine and S. M. Bartell, editors. Dynamics of Lotic Ecosystems. Ann Arbor, MI: Ann Arbor Science Publishers.

Ward, J. V., K. Tockner, and F. Schiemer. 1999. Biodiversity of Floodplain River Ecosystems: Ecotones and Connectivity. Regulated Rivers: Research and Management 15:125-139.

Washington Department of Fish and Wildlife and Department of Ecology. 1996 (or subsequent versions). Instream flow study guidelines. Available at www.ecy.wa.gov.

Washington State Pollution Control Hearings Board. 2000. Findings of Fact, Conclusions of Law and Order (and transcripts), Pollution Control Hearings Board, State of Washington July 21, 2000, Olympia, WA; in Public Utility District No. 1 of Pendoreille, Co. v. State of Washington Department of Ecology and Center for Environmental Law and Policy.

Water and Environment Consultants (WEC). 1980. Flushing flow discharge evaluation for 18 streams in the Medicine Bow National Forest. Completion report for Environmental Research and Technology, Fort Collins, Colorado. 15 pp.

Waters, B. F. 1976. A methodology for evaluating the effect of different streamflows on salmonid habitat. Pages 254-266 in J. F. Osborn and C. H. Allman, editors. Instream Flow Needs. Bethesda: Special Publication of the American Fisheries Society.

Waters, T. F. 1995. Sediment in streams: Sources, biological effects, and control. American Fisheries Society Monograph 7. Bethesda: American Fisheries Society.

Welcomme, R. L. 1979. Fisheries Ecology of Floodplain Rivers. London: Longmans. 317 pp.

Welcomme, R. L. 1995. Relationships between fisheries and the integrity of river systems. Regulated Rivers: Research and Management 11:121-126.

Wenzel, C. R. 1993. Flushing flow requirements of a large, regulated Wyoming river to maintain trout spawning habitat quality. Masters thesis. Laramie: University of Wyoming. 162 pp.

Wesche, T. A. 1976. Development and application of a trout cover rating system for instream flow need determinations. Pages 224-234 in J. F. Orsborn and C. H. Allman, editors. Instream Flow Needs. Bethesda: Special Publication of the American Fisheries Society.

Wesche, T. A., V. R. Hasfurther, W. A. Hubert, and Q. D Skinner. 1987. Assessment of flushing flow needs in a steep, rough, regulated tributary. Pages 59-70 in J. F. Craig and J. B. Kemper, editors. Regulated Streams: Advances in Ecology. New York: Plenum Press.

Wesche, T. A., and P. A. Rechard. 1980. A summary of instream flow methods for fisheries and related research needs. Eisenhower Consortium Bulletin 9. Laramie: University of Wyoming, Water Resources Research Institute. 122 pp.

Whalen, K. G., D. L Parrish, and M. E. Mather. 1999. Effect of ice formation on selection of habitats and winter distribution of post-young-of-the-year Atlantic salmon parr. Canadian Journal of Fisheries and Aquatic Science 56:87-96.

Wharton, C. H., and M. M. Brinson. 1979. Characteristics of southeastern river systems. Pages 32-40 in R. R. Johnson, and J. F. McCormick, technical coordinators. Strategies for protection and management of floodplain wetlands and other riparian ecosystems. Washington, DC: U.S. Forest Service (General Technical Report WO-12).

Wharton, C. H., W. M. Kitchens, E. C. Pendleton, and T. W. Sipe. 1982. The ecology of bottomland hardwood swamps of the Southeast: A community profile. Washington, DC: U.S. Fish and Wildlife Service, Biological Services Program (FWS/OBS-81/37). 133 pp.

Wharton, C. H., V. W. Lambou, J. Newsome, P. V. Winger, and others. 1981. The fauna of bottomland hardwoods in the southeastern United States. Pages 87-160 in J. R. Clark and J. Benforado, editors. Wetlands of Bottomland Hardwood Forests. New York: Elsevier Scientific Publishing Company.

White, D. C., R. J. Livingston, R. J. Bobbie, and J. S. Nickels. 1979. Effects of surface composition, water column chemistry, and time of exposure on the composition of the microflora and associated macrofauna in Apalachicola Bay, Florida. Pages 83-116 in R. J. Livingston, editor. Ecological Processes in Coastal and Marine Systems. New York: Plenum Press.

White, R. J. 1991. Objectives should dictate methods in managing stream habitat for fish. Pages 44-52 in J. Colt and R. J. White, editors. Proceedings of the Symposium on Fisheries Bioengineering. Bethesda: American Fisheries Society (Symposium 10).

Whitelaw, E., editor. 2003. A Letter from Economists to President Bush and the Governors of Eleven Western States Regarding the Economic Importance of the West's Natural Environment. December 3. Available at salmonand economy.org/pdf/120303letter.pdf..

Whiting, P. J. 1998. Floodplain maintenance flows. Rivers 6(3):160-170.

Whittaker, D., B. Shelby, W. Jackson, and R. Beschta. 1993. Instream flows for recreation: A handbook on concepts and research methods. Corvallis: Oregon State University and the National Park Service. 103 pp.

Williams, G. P., and M. G. Wolman. 1984. Downstream effects of dams on alluvial rivers. Professional Paper 1286. Washington, DC: U.S. Geological Survey.

Williams, J.G. 1996. Lost in space: minimum confidence intervals for idealized PHABSIM studies. Transactions of the American Fisheries Society 125:458-465.

Williams, J. G., T. P. Speed, and W. F. Forest. 1999. Comment: transferability of habitat suitability criteria. North American Journal of Fisheries Management 19:623-625.

Winters, T. C., J. W. Harvey, O. L. Franke, and W. M. Alley. 1998. Groundwater and surface water: A single resource. U.S. Geological Survey Circular 1139. Denver: U.S. Geological Survey, Branch of Information Services. 79 pp.

Wolman, M. G. 1954. A method of sampling coarse riverbed material. Transactions of the American Geophysical Union 35(6): 951-956.

Wondolleck, J. M., and S. L. Yaffee. 2000. Making Collaboration Work: Lessons from Innovation in Natural Resource Management. Washington, DC: Island Press.

Wuerthner, G., and M. Matteson, editors. 2002. Welfare Ranching: The Subsidized Destruction of the American West. Washington, DC: Island Press. 368 pp.

Wurbs, R. A., and E. D. Sisson. 1999. Comparative evaluation of methods for distributing naturalized streamflows from gaged to ungaged sites. Technical Report No. 179. College Station: Texas A&M University, Water Resources Institute.

Wydoski, R. S., and E. D. Wick. 1998. Ecological value of floodplain habitats to razorback suckers in the upper Colorado River basin. Final Report of U.S. Fish and Wildlife Service and U.S. National Park Service to Upper Colorado River Endangered Fish Recovery Program, Denver, Colorado.

Wyoming Water Development Commission. 2001. Green River basin 2001 water plan. www.waterplan.state.wy.us/basins/green/green.html.

Yin, K., P. J. Harrison, and R. J. Beamish. 1997. Effects of a fluctuation in Fraser River discharge on primary production in the central Strait of Georgia, British Columbia, Canada. Canadian Journal of Fisheries and Aquatic Sciences 54 (5):1015-1024.

Zafft, D. J., P. Braaten, K. Johnson, and T. Annear. 1995. Comprehensive study of the Green River fishery between the New Fork River Confluence and Flaming Gorge Reservoir, 1991-1994. Completion Report. Wyoming Game and Fish Department, Cheyenne.

About the Authors

Tom Annear is the instream flow supervisor for the Wyoming Game and Fish Department in Cheyenne. He has been involved with instream flow management since 1981 and helped establish the Game and Fish Department's instream flow program. He cochaired the IFC steering committee from 1995 to 1998 and served as the first president of the IFC from 1998 to 2000.

Ian Chisholm is the stream habitat program supervisor in the Ecological Services Division of the Minnesota Department of Natural Resources. He has worked with instream flow and related river management issues since 1983. Ian served on the IFC Steering Committee from 1995 to 1998, is the Minnesota Governing Council representative of the Instream Flow Council, and chaired one of the two subcommittees that produced *Instream Flows for Riverine Resource Stewardship*.

Hal Beecher has been the instream flow specialist for the Washington Department of Fish and Wildlife since 1979. His research has focused on stream fish ecology in Florida and Washington State, evaluation of instream flow models, and habitat suitability of salmonid fishes. He currently serves as the IFC Director of Region 1 (western states).

Allan Locke is the provincial instream flow needs specialist for the Alberta Department of Sustainable Resource Development. He has worked with various aspects of instream flow management since 1981. From 1998 to 2000 he served on the IFC Executive Committee as the first IFC Director of Region 5 (Canadian Provinces). He is currently the IFC president-elect.

Peter Aarrestad is the supervising fisheries biologist for the Habitat Conservation and Enhancement Program of the Connecticut Department of Environmental Protection's Inland Fisheries Division. Since 1989 he has been involved primarily with studies of fisheries habitat issues and has conducted environmental assessments of various proposed activities that may affect inland, diadromous, and estuarine fisheries resources, including diversion of groundwater and surface water.

Chuck Coomer is currently the chief of fisheries for the Georgia Department of Natural Resources, Wildlife Resources Division. He has been involved with instream flow issues since 1982 and served as the representative for the southeastern states on the National Instream Flow Program Assessment (NIFPA) project. In 2001 he was part of a successful effort to change the instream flow policy in Georgia from one based on the $7Q_{10}$ flow to an interim policy designed to better protect aquatic life in streams. He is now part of an ongoing effort to conduct studies in Georgia to develop a final instream policy to protect Georgia's aquatic resources.

Christopher Estes is chief of the Statewide Aquatic Resources Coordination Unit for the Alaska Department of Fish and Game. He has been involved with various aspects of instream flow and aquatic habitat research and management since 1975 and initiated the department's program to obtain reservations of water in 1986. He founded and cochaired the National Instream Flow Assessment (NIFPA) project and is director at large on the IFC Executive Committee.

Joel Hunt is the Manager of the Aquatic Ecosystem Section for Manitoba Water Stewardship and has worked on fisheries management projects since 1986. Since 1995 he has been working on instream flow-related issues throughout the province. He is currently the IFC Director of Region 5 (Canadian provinces).

251

Rick Jacobson is a certified fisheries biologist and Assistant Director of the Connecticut Inland Fisheries Division. In his 20 years of fisheries management work, he has led many instream flow studies, established the Connecticut Department of Environmental Protection's current instream flow policy, and been the catalyst for the formation of the state's Instream Flow Task Force. He served as secretary-treasurer for the IFC from 1998 to 2000.

Gerrit Jobsis worked for the South Carolina Department of Natural Resources for 13 years where he focused on hydroelectric dams and their effects on instream flow. He presently works for the South Carolina Coastal Conservation League as leader of their rivers project.

John Kauffman is a regional fisheries manager with the Virginia Department of Game and Inland Fisheries and has worked in the fisheries management field for over 30 years. He has published articles in various scientific journals and coauthored chapters in several books on riverine management. John is chair of the American Fisheries Society Southern Division Instream Flow Committee and was the IFC Director of Region 3 (southeastern states) from 2000 to 2002.

John Marshall recently retired as the environmental administrator for the Ohio Division of Wildlife where he worked for 23 years in habitat protection. He has served as Ohio's representative to the IFC governing council since its inception and chaired one of the two subcommittees that produced this book. At the time of his retirement in spring 2001, John was the IFC Director of Region 2 (midwestern states).

Kevin Mayes is the river assessment team leader in the River Studies Program at the Texas Parks and Wildlife Department. Since 1989 he has worked on diverse instream flow issues in Texas--from prairie streams to rich spring-fed ecosystems.

Gary Smith is leader of California Department of Fish and Game's Stream Requirements Program and has been the department's statewide instream flow coordinator since 1980. He was instrumental in establishing the department's instream program and led the department's efforts in addressing Mono Lake issues. Currently, he serves as an advisor on Klamath River assessments and water allocation issues. In the early 1980s Gary represented western states on the National Instream Flow Program Assessment (NIFPA) project. He was co-chair of the IFC steering committee from 1995-1998 and served as the IFC Director of Region 1 (western states) from 1998-2000.

Clair Stalnaker has been a key player in the instream flow arena for over 30 years—in research, method development and implementation, and policy. He organized and served as leader of the Cooperative Instream Flow Service Group under the U.S. Fish and Wildlife Service. This program brought together an interagency group of multidisciplinary scientists for the purpose of advancing state-of-the-art science and elevating the field of instream flow to national prominence. He recently retired as a senior scientist with the U.S. Geological Survey.

Rod Wentworth is an impact assessment specialist with the Vermont Department of Fish and Wildlife. Since 1986 he has devoted much of his time to instream flow issues and is recognized as a state expert on instream flow science. He served as the IFC Director of Region 4 (northeastern states) from 1998 to 2000 and is currently President of the IFC.

Seated left to right: Joel Hunt, Gary Smith, Rick Jacobson
Standing left to right: John Marshall, Clair Stalnaker, Tom Annear, Hal Beecher, Allan Locke, John Kauffman, Rod Wentworth, Peter Aarrestad, Christopher Estes, Kevin Mayes, Chuck Coomer, Nina Burkardt.
Missing: Ian Chisholm, Gerrit Jöbsis

Index